A
REPUBLIC
NO MORE

A
REPUBLIC
NO MORE

Big Government and the Rise
of American Political Corruption

JAY COST

Encounter Books
New York | London

© 2015 by Jay Cost

First American edition published in 2015 by Encounter Books,
an activity of Encounter for Culture and Education, Inc.,
a nonprofit, tax exempt corporation.
Encounter Books website address: www.encounterbooks.com

Manufactured in the United States and printed on
acid-free paper. The paper used in this publication meets
the minimum requirements of ANSI/NISO Z39.48–1992
(R 1997) (*Permanence of Paper*).

FIRST AMERICAN EDITION

LIBRARY OF CONGRESS CATALOGING-IN-PUBLICATION DATA

Cost, Jay.
A republic no more : big government and the rise of
American political corruption by Jay Cost.
pages cm
Includes bibliographical references and index.
ISBN 978-1-59403-727-6 (hardcover : alk. paper) — ISBN 978-1-59403-728-3 (ebook)
1. Political corruption—United States. 2. Republicanism—United States. I. Title.
JK2249.C69 2015
364.1'3230973—dc23
2014032671

This book is dedicated to the memory
of Daniel R. McKenzie

"The stock-jobbers will become the pretorian band of the Government, at once its tool & its tyrant; bribed by its largesses, & overawing it by clamours & combinations."
—JAMES MADISON,
LETTER TO THOMAS JEFFERSON, AUGUST 8, 1791

"I decided to get far enough along to be able to control legislation that meant something to men with real money and let them foot the bills. Never commit yourself but always be in a position where you can if you choose. The men with money will look you up then and you don't have to worry about campaign expenses."
—SENATOR BOIES PENROSE
(REPUBLICAN, PENNSYLVANIA)

"We manage our political risk with the same intensity that we manage our credit and interest rate risks."
—FRANKLIN REINES,
FORMER CEO OF FANNIE MAE,
IN A 1999 MEETING WITH INVESTORS

Contents

Preface

To BEGIN, a warning to the reader: this book is about political corruption, but it is not about Watergate. It is not about Abscam. It has little to say about Teapot Domes, and you will not find a word between these covers about Monica Lewinsky or Paula Jones. There are books out there that chronicle, in lurid detail, these events. This book is not one of them.

All of those stories have a few items in common. Somebody breaks the law and (more or less) gets punished for it. There is a perp walk of some sort to reassure us that—in the end—good triumphed because indecency was exposed for what it was. Even if the bad guys go to the grave escaping the long arm of the law, the arm of the historian reaches farther still, and the audience can rejoice in the culprits' reputations duly suffering for their civic transgressions.

This book, rather, has much more to do with the guys who got away with it, in particular the guys who flaunted it while getting away with it. In the 1890s, as Congress was writing tariff laws governing sugar, Pennsylvania's political boss, Senator Matthew Quay, admitted that, yes indeed, he was speculating in the sugar markets, that he would go right on doing so even as he voted on the sugar tariff, and there wasn't a damned thing anybody could do about it, thank you very much. He was right. A decade later, William Randolph Hearst exposed his successor, Boies Penrose, as being on the take from Standard Oil. Nothing came of it, and Penrose was reelected several times thereafter. He died in office.

Why did nothing happen to those men? Simple: *they were not breaking the laws of their day.* That is the fascinating feature about corruption—often, it has absolutely nothing to do with illegal activity. There are plenty of ways, as we shall see, to be corrupt without being criminal. More often than not, the criminals merely lack self-control or self-awareness. That makes them easy targets for rebuke, and thus reasons to feel good about ourselves and our government.

But as Quay and Penrose prove, the law often has trouble keeping up with corruption, in no small part because the people who write the laws like it that way. Perhaps George Washington Plunkitt, a sachem (or boss) of New York City's Tammany Hall about a century ago, puts it best:

> Everybody is talkin' these days about Tammany men growin' rich on graft, but nobody thinks of drawin' the distinction between honest graft and dishonest graft. There's all the difference in the world between the two. . . . I've not gone in for dishonest graft—blackmailin' gamblers, saloonkeepers, disorderly people, etc.—and neither has any of the men who have made big fortunes in politics.
>
> There's an honest graft, and I'm an example of how it works. I might sum up the whole thing by sayin': "I seen my opportunities and I took 'em."
>
> Just let me explain by examples. My party's in power in the city, and it's goin' to undertake a lot of public improvements. Well, I'm tipped off, say, that they're going to lay out a new park at a certain place.
>
> I see my opportunity and I take it. I go to that place and I buy up all the land I can in the neighborhood. Then the board of this or that makes its plan public, and there is a rush to get my land, which nobody cared particular for before.

There was nothing honest about Plunkitt's fraud, but he was onto something in drawing the distinction he did. "Dishonest" graft is criminal activity that harms people directly, whereas "honest" graft is technically legal, and the victim is the common good, not a particular individual. What Plunkitt was doing in his day would be outlawed today, but honest graft nevertheless survives, in different forms, always changing to stay one step ahead of the law.

Why is this the case? The answer to that question is the subject of this book.

So, what follows is not a tale of heroes and villains. Herein, you will not find clear-cut victories, glorious moments of truth being spoken to power, or exhilarating climaxes when the hard-charging civic hero triumphs and the citizen's faith in government is restored. If you're looking for that, go read *All the President's Men*. Similarly, the story here does not have the satisfaction that Calvinism supplies: government in this account is not a hopeless, immoral cesspool where everybody is out for themselves and nobody does what is right, and the only thing to do is await the cleansing hellfire unleashed by the Almighty. If you're looking for something like that, *House of Cards* is for you.

Instead, this book is about corruption as a permanent, institutionalized feature of our government. Less sexy, perhaps, but it makes for an interesting puzzle. After all, our Founding Fathers were frankly concerned about corruption, so much so they designed a system to prevent it from occurring. Yet it has occurred anyway. Understanding this irony is the purpose of the book in your hands. While this may not offer much by way of emotional gratification, it is—on closer inspection—much more fascinating. And it can teach us some very important lessons about how our government actually works.

"The Violence of Faction"

Understanding Political Corruption

POLITICAL CORRUPTION is incompatible with a republican form of government. A republic strives above all else to govern for the public interest; corruption, on the other hand, occurs when government agents sacrifice the interests of everybody for the sake of a few. Corruption can take many forms, as we shall see. It can be patronage. It can be intentionally lax regulatory oversight. It can be tax laws written to favor special interests. Corruption can benefit just one person, a small group, a large minority, or maybe even a majority, just as long as those interests are incompatible with those of the public at large. Sometimes it is illegal; more often it is not. The particulars may vary, but the result is always the same: the government puts private interests before public interests.

In this book, we shall look at corruption primarily as *the maldistribution of federal resources*. There are other ways to look at corruption (e.g., in the administration of justice or corruption at the state level), but that shall not be our focus here. Instead, we shall examine how agents of the government—in particular the president and the Congress—distribute scarce resources in ways that run contrary to the public interest. In focusing on this, we shall be getting to the heart of the republican political philosophy articulated by James Madison.

We Americans take our government to be a republic, but in point of fact we have never been able to check corruption effectively. On the contrary, it has spread over time. Why has our republican rhetoric not matched civic reality? Answering this question is our purpose in the pages that follow.

We shall show that political corruption is a consequence of the growth of that government, specifically growth beyond the original boundaries established by the Framers of the Constitution. As the government expanded beyond its initial purpose, the system of checks and balances meant to keep corruption in line began to break down, in some cases even making a bad situation worse.

Here, we shall examine corruption from an institutional perspective, rather than an ethical one. In other words, we will not explain corruption as a consequence of too many bad guys and not enough good guys, but rather of structural defects in the constitutional regime itself.

While making our argument, we embrace a Madisonian treatment of the subject. To be clear, this is not to imply that Madison's take on the Constitution was the only one, or that it was the correct one. Almost as soon as the Constitution was ratified, there grew a wide divide among those who were crucial in its construction and ratification. Madison, for instance, squared off against George Washington and Alexander Hamilton on questions regarding public finance; and this was just a few short years after he had been closely allied with them. All three men were integral in the design of the new government, and for them to disagree as they did suggests that legalistic assertions about the Constitution's "correct" meaning are often facile. It meant different things to different people—then and now. Therefore, we are not privileging Madison's view as an empirical matter; we are not saying that Madison understood what the Constitution *really* said while Hamilton and Washington did not. We are rather asserting that his larger theory about republican government, and how he applied it to the Constitution, was insightful, and that we would be wise to heed his counsel.

Heavily influenced by Calvinist theology, Madison broke with classical political theorists to argue that civic virtue could not explain why republican governments flourish or perish. Indeed, his lack of faith in public morality is one reason he dedicated so much time to developing sturdy governmental structures; he believed that they were the only sure guards against corruption that a true republic could ever enjoy.

According to Madison, corruption is intimately connected to *factionalism*. He begins his famed *Federalist #10* by worrying about the "violence of faction," a very evocative phrase, and claiming that the principal job of a "well constructed union" is to "break and control" this danger. He explains:

> By a faction, I understand a number of citizens, whether amounting to
> a majority or a minority of the whole, who are united and actuated by

some common impulse of passion, or of interest, adversed to the rights of other citizens, or to the permanent and aggregate interests of the community.

This gives us a very useful definition of corruption: it occurs when the government does *violence* to the public interest or individual rights by allowing factions to dominate public policy for their own ends. It is incompatible with a republican form of government, and so its suppression is at the very heart of the Madisonian project.

Importantly, in the Madisonian schema, corruption is not limited to venality, although it certainly includes it. This might come as a bit of a surprise. After all, Madison opens *Federalist* #10 by talking about violence, so it is easy to figure that corruption is caused by bad people who hurt others for their own ends. Yet later on Madison implicates the whole human race in factionalism, arguing that the potential for corruption is, in fact, "sown into the very nature of man." He goes on:

> A zeal for different opinions concerning religion, concerning government, and many other points, as well of speculation as of practice; an attachment to different leaders ambitiously contending for pre-eminence and power; or to persons of other descriptions whose fortunes have been interesting to the human passions, have, in turn, divided mankind into parties, inflamed them with mutual animosity, and rendered them much more disposed to vex and oppress each other than to co-operate for their common good. So strong is this propensity of mankind to fall into mutual animosities, that where no substantial occasion presents itself, the most frivolous and fanciful distinctions have been sufficient to kindle their unfriendly passions and excite their most violent conflicts.

So, everybody is capable of factionalism. Indeed, people are wont to war against one another even when there are no real issues to divide them. In those cases, they will just make something up!

Factionalism is unavoidable, particularly in a form of government that relies upon what Madison calls the "republican principle," or the idea that rulers should be chosen by the citizenry. If people can be riven by factionalism, then so too can their representatives in government. In that case, per Madison, "the most numerous party, or, in other words, the most powerful faction must be expected to prevail." This helps explain why so many republics had failed up to that point in the world's history; the very idea upon which they were premised sowed the seeds of their own destruction. A few years prior to the *Federalist* essays, Madison wrote a short treatise called *Vices of the Political System of the United States*, where he poses this paradox:

In republican Government the majority however composed, ultimately give the law. Whenever therefore an apparent interest or common passion unites a majority what is to restrain them from unjust violations of the rights and interests of the minority, or of individuals?

Typically, Americans today take majority rule as a normative standard, as if it necessarily signals the true public interest. Yet Madison clearly rejects this principle, though he admits that majority rule remains essential to republican government.

Worse, Madison sees another path by which corruption in a republic can occur: legislators are too often subject to forces other than the interests of their own constituents. In the *Vices*, Madison claims:

Representative appointments are sought from 3 motives. 1. ambition 2. personal interest. 3. public good. Unhappily the two first are proved by experience to be most prevalent. Hence the candidates who feel them, particularly, the second, are most industrious, and most successful in pursuing their object: and forming often a majority in the legislative Councils, with interested views, contrary to the interest, and views, of their Constituents, join in a perfidious sacrifice of the latter to the former.

This is a prototypical explanation of what rational choice theorists have since labeled the "principal-agent problem." In other words, how can voters get their representatives to do their bidding in government? That is easier said than done; as Madison notes, concern for the public interest is often a weak factor in the considerations of legislators. And the people as a whole are not always a reliable guardian against legislative malfeasance:

A succeeding election it might be supposed, would displace the offenders, and repair the mischief. But how easily are base and selfish measures, masked by pretexts of public good and apparent expediency? How frequently will a repetition of the same arts and industry which succeeded in the first instance, again prevail on the unwary to misplace their confidence?

So, republican government is prone to factionalism and corruption. First, we have the potential for the majority to demand policy deleterious to the public good. Second, we have legislators who are prone to put their own interests ahead of the common interest. Little wonder that, up to that point in world history, a true republic was more a myth than reality.

Yet Madison was committed to turning the theoretical into the actual. He believed that majority rule was indeed essential to a true republic, but it had to be channeled through well-designed institutions that carefully distributed governing power to protect the public interest. The Framers adopted many such institutions; some they borrowed from previous thinkers, some they developed themselves. These include:

- *A written constitution ratified by the representatives of the people.* The Framers believed that the king had violated the rights they enjoyed as Englishmen under the British Constitution, which was unwritten. A formal document, explicitly endorsed by the people at large, would check the capacity of the government to abuse the public trust.
- *Separation of powers between the three branches.* The utility of separating powers was a key insight of French philosopher Montesquieu, and the Framers made it integral to their system. According to Madison, separated powers would make "ambition . . . counteract ambition." Separate branches would give politicians competing, and often contradictory, incentives, so a corrupt initiative in one branch could be stopped by another.
- *A bicameral legislature.* The Framers were quite concerned about the legislature's capacity to encroach upon the spheres of the rival branches. A second branch, argues Madison, would require "the concurrence of two distinct bodies in schemes of usurpation or perfidy, where the ambition or corruption of one would otherwise be sufficient."
- *An independent judiciary.* The experience during the colonial period, when the king controlled colonial judges, convinced the Framers that the judiciary had to be separated from the rest of the government, or else it could not be a fair arbiter.
- *A government encompassing a large sphere.* This was an innovation unique to Madison. Previously, republican philosophers advocated a small polity so that the people could be reasonably homogenous. But Madison had seen too many small republics behave incorrigibly. A larger sphere, he asserts, would "make it less probable that a majority of the whole will have a common motive to invade the rights of other citizens."
- *A Senate with equal representation for all states.* A device to win over the small states during the Constitutional Convention, this guaranteed that larger states could never form a dominant faction within the government.
- *A government of discrete powers.* Madison and the Virginia delegation to the Constitutional Convention originally wanted a government that could legislate wherever the states were deemed incompetent. Skeptics of this plan were fearful of a government acquiring too many powers to

harass the citizenry, and a compromise was made to grant the government specific (and limited) powers.

- *A bill of rights.* Like the specification of powers, this was meant to restrict what the government could do. Thus, even if a faction did acquire control of the government, there would be limits to what it could do.

Woodrow Wilson once called the constitutional regime a Newtonian system, with forces carefully calibrated against one another. In other words, the rules of the constitutional game are structured so that the vast array of forces within the public sphere will combine to produce something that is in the common interest, regardless of how self-interested the initial impulses may have been. The idea is that a faction may have representatives who will do its bidding in the government, but those agents will only possess limited power and will often be stymied by agents aligned with other factions. Per Madison's theory of government, it is irrelevant if those who check these selfish ambitions are themselves driven by private motives. All that matters is the result: the only proposals that should make it through the constitutional gauntlet and be enacted into law will be those that benefit the people generally. Everything else will fall by the wayside, thus offering a decisive check on corruption and preserving the republican integrity of the government.

Considering how regularly this country has fought over morals, it is interesting that morality does not enter into the Madisonian system in any direct way. Classical republican theorists had emphasized the necessity of virtue, but our system—reflecting in part Madison's Calvinist background—eschews that. Far from building a sturdy republican government by outlawing avarice, he seeks to do the opposite: let those who enter the Madisonian fray be as self-interested as they want; his system will pit them against one another, confident that the public good will win out in the end.

———————

That's the theory, at any rate. What about in practice? Given the extensive efforts of the founding generation, and Madison in particular, to curtail corruption, why has it persisted? The answer: because we have not heeded Madison's prescriptions on how to "break and control the violence of faction."

Different sides of the political spectrum have different attitudes toward the Constitution these days. The left sees a living Constitution that is supposed to adapt and evolve beyond the historical contingencies of any era. On the other hand, the right views the Constitution more as laying down time-less principles and practices that the country would be foolhardy to ignore.

In a sense, both sides have some purchase on the truth. As suggested in the previous section, there is a timeless aspect to the Constitution. It is a document trying to build structures to supplement the principle of majority rule in ways to ensure the survival of the new republic. Similarly, the *Federalist Papers* are grappling with enduring issues that defy historical contingency.

On the other hand, the Constitution *also* represents a compromise be-tween various factions within society in the year 1787. The nationalist faction—led by Hamilton, Washington, and, for a time, Madison—wanted a government of expansive powers wielded by nationalistic institutions. Meanwhile, a faction composed of men like George Clinton and Patrick Henry were suspicious of centralized power and wanted to retain a local preeminence in the government's institutions. The Constitution occupied a middle ground between these sides, although many Anti-Federalists op-posed its ratification until the very end.

A comparison between the dueling plans at the Constitutional Conven-tion—the Virginia Plan, largely the brainchild of Madison, and the New Jersey Plan, offered by William Paterson of New Jersey—is illustrative. The Virginia Plan would have given the government the right to legislate, "in all cases to which the separate States are incompetent: or in which the harmony of the United States may be interrupted by the exercise of individual legislation." It also would have made it much less dependent upon local interests. For instance, the Senate would have been apportioned by population, with no guaranteed representation for states; further, the national legislature would have veto authority over state legislatures, and a Council of Revision would have review power over national laws. Mean-while, Paterson would have retained the same Congress as existed under the Articles of Confederation. There was to be no single president, but rather an executive council selected by Congress. Further, Congress would have the power to tax and regulate interstate commerce, but state courts would hear initial disputes over these powers.

Thus, the fight between the two sides was not simply about the power of the government, but also its design. And the final Constitution represents a compromise along both dimensions—the nature of federal power and the nature of federal institutions. Power was expanded and institutions were nationalized relative to the Articles of Confederation, yet by less on both counts than what the Virginia Plan called for. But there is more to it than this. The only way a system of checks and balances could ever possibly work is by ensuring that each institution possesses the right amount of power to guard against encroachments from the others. Thus, the Framers could not merely split the difference between the two sides of the debate; instead, they had to find an intellectually coherent middle ground. The debate over the Constitution was not like a fight over appropriations or taxes in contemporary politics, where both sides pick a number in the middle regardless of whether it makes sense. The Framers had to satisfy all sides while also building institutions that could wield their powers responsibly.

Think of it this way. It would have been grossly irresponsible of the Framers simply to have granted the parochial Congress under the Articles of Confederation all the powers in the new Constitution. The old Congress would have failed miserably because it was not designed to handle such important responsibilities. By the same token, it would have been a waste of effort to create a new, more nationalistic set of institutions without expanding the powers granted under the Articles of Confederation. Instead, the powers the new government was to wield had to fit logically with the institutions that were to wield them. The Constitution is not just a compromise between various factions on one question about powers and another question about institutional design. Rather, it is a sensible blend of the views on *both* questions.

So how does corruption enter the picture? In this way: since virtually the start of the federal government, politicians have been intent on expanding its powers without revising the institutions that manage those powers. In this, they have dutifully followed public opinion. The country has increasingly demanded nationalistic authority for the government, but has refused to abandon the parochialism inherent to the original design. Indeed, Americans are wont to celebrate the contradiction: we unabashedly demand that our government exercise sweeping powers to solve big, national problems while also remaining excessively sensitive to local concerns. This inconsistency has disrupted the carefully constructed balance set forth in the Constitution. The institutions the Framers created were competent to handle responsibly the powers they assigned them; Americans since then have added extra powers under the false assumption that the same institutions could handle the extra load responsibly. But they cannot, and so the government now behaves irresponsibly. This produces corruption.

Return to Wilson's metaphor of the Constitution as a Newtonian system. Each provision is like a force that has a unique vector, and the Framers carefully constructed each one so that the totality of these forces would not only promote true republican government but also satisfy the political demands of the day. Over time, political demands evolved, and politicians have responded by expanding the powers that Washington possesses. In doing so, they have altered the vectors of many of the constitutional forces. But they have never taken care to ensure that the necessary republican balance is retained, by updating the institutions supposed to implement the new powers. Thus, the sum of all the forces produced by the constitutional regime no longer generates public-spirited policy.

To be clear, the problem is not with expansive governmental powers per se. Rather, it has to do with the institutions of government that exercise those powers. Specifically, we use eighteenth century institutions, originally meant to do much less, to exercise virtually limitless power in the twenty-first century. We could, in theory, redesign the government to make it handle these powers responsibly; we could rebuild the system from the bottom-up following the general principles set forth by Madison. But of course, we have never done that. We have never even really thought seriously about that prospect. Instead, we have chosen to have our cake and eat it too—a government of vast nationalistic powers with parochial institutions. The cost of our ambivalence is corruption.

There are three major nationalistic powers the government has acquired that the Constitution, as produced in Philadelphia in 1787, never really anticipated. The first is the power to forge a national economic marketplace, the battle over which produced the first great political upheaval in the 1790s. As we shall see in Chapter One, the cornerstone of Hamilton's program was a nationally chartered bank, which the Constitutional Convention in Philadelphia had explicitly rejected as a federal power. Yet this was deemed an implied power through the Necessary and Proper Clause of the Constitution, and thus began a precedent of interpreting the powers within the Constitution as broadly as politically possible. Since Hamilton's day, both sides of the partisan divide have embraced the idea that the federal government should promote the national economy, and both sides seek to do it in ways that are not really reconcilable with the Constitution as understood at ratification. This is a power that expanded slowly throughout the ages. In the nineteenth century, it began with the Bank, then proceeded to internal improvements, then tariff protections for business, then direct subsidies for the railroads. Today, there is a vast system of federal supports for businesses, from the tax code to corporate welfare to selective tariff preferences. Putting aside whether these items were constitutional in a legal sense, the fact remains that the Framers envisioned very little of this regime.

A second power is the restriction of the marketplace to secure non-economic goals. The first major innovation of this type was the Interstate Commerce Act, which regulated the railroads. The nation has expanded on this regulatory power again and again. Often, these regulations are justified via the Commerce Clause, in Article I, Section 8 of the Constitution, yet the most prominent interstate commerce controversy of which the Framers were aware was a dispute over waterways between Virginia and Maryland. They had no idea that it would one day justify penalties against wheat farmers who grew their crop for private use, as happened in *Wickard v. Filburn*. The Commerce Clause has become the means by which the federal government can regulate virtually any aspect of American life. Again, whether this is strictly constitutional is not nearly as relevant as the fact that the Framers never saw this development coming.

The third power is the direct promotion of social welfare, akin to Franklin Delano Roosevelt's freedom from want in his Four Freedoms speech of 1941. The first major promotion of social welfare on the federal level came with Civil War veterans' pensions, but those were targeted and temporary. Since then, we have added Social Security, Medicare, food stamps, farm subsidies, and a vast array of other benefits. Again, none of this was imagined in the 1780s. For starters, the nation simply was not wealthy enough to have national support programs for the needy. On top of that, the kind of bureaucratic principles necessary to implement such programs had not been invented yet. So, once more, regardless of whether our modern welfare regime comports with the ideal of securing a more perfect union, the fact is that the men who signed the Constitution, and the states that ratified it, never anticipated such a state of affairs—and of course did not build institutions meant to handle it effectively.

Taken together, these powers represent a level of nationalism that was unanticipated in 1787. They have grown over time—sometimes slowly, sometimes in great bursts—as leaders have grappled with public problems. Importantly, the government acquired those powers without substantially altering the constitutional structure. As we shall see in Chapter Six, about the only politician of any national prominence who has contemplated revisiting the institutional design to handle these powers was Wilson, at least in his early academic work. There, he bemoaned the irresponsibility of the government, pointing the finger at Madison's separation of powers and calling for formal integration between the executive and legislative branches. But when a political career beckoned, Wilson decided that vigorous presidential leadership could substitute. As we shall see in Chapter Six, however, the hope of strong presidential leadership was a false one; outside foreign relations, the chief executive's real power is too unreliable to give our governing institutions a more nationalistic bent.

How have these expansive new powers unbalanced the Madisonian system? There are four principal ways. First, and most important, Congress cannot handle the powers it has been given. The Framers never would have handed the Congress of the Articles of Confederation the powers in the Constitution, and we should never have given the Congress of the Constitution such expansive authority. As we move through our story, we shall find that congressional incompetence is usually the main driver of corruption. The reason is that Congress, as designed, is simply too parochial. It is actually a fallacy of composition to suggest that Congress is a national branch at all; it is, rather, the meeting place of the representatives from discrete regions all across the country. This was not a problem for the powers handed to the Congress by the original grant, but it became a problem as power after power was added. We shall discover there is a wide variety of ways Congress behaves irresponsibly, but it usually gets back to a single concept: members use the vast national powers they have since acquired to please the parochial factions that are so critical to their electoral efforts. This is the unifying link between problems as seemingly varied as the nineteenth century spoils system and the failure to regulate properly the financial services industry in the twenty-first century.

Second, they denude the force of the republican principle. Madison depended upon majority rule to thwart minorities that had seized control of the government, though as we saw, he had his doubts because it would be difficult for voters to identify who exactly is to blame. Growing the power of this government has exacerbated that problem to extreme proportions. From the very beginning, the complicated nature of our system made it difficult to assign blame for bad policies. The addition of power after power to the government has resulted in an enormous amount of additional complexity, and no citizen can practically keep an eye on the government to ensure that it behaves. Presidents, senators, representatives, and bureaucrats too often retain plausible deniability for their role in corrupt outcomes, undermining the power of the people to advance the public good through elections.

The third way becomes apparent when we consider the two greatest institutional alterations of the original design: the democratization of the Electoral College and the rise of political parties. These concepts are not originally in the Constitution, nor were they formally amended into it, but they are nevertheless part of the landscape now. Opening up the presidency to public voting, more than anything else, facilitated the national political parties, forging cross-state political alliances to reap the benefits the top office provides. The problem with this is that parties are formal, enduring factions, but the presidency itself was supposed to be insulated from factionalism. Democratizing the presidency, and thrusting the office into the partisan battle, inevitably changed the calculus of the occupant. He must build and maintain a coalition that almost invariably amounts to a subset of the nation at large, which means it is often in his interests to affix his gaze on something quite less than the public good. This in turn means that the president is much less able to control the localism of the Congress by the veto, especially when he is bound to its members via a political party. Thus, what should have been in theory an office that tamps down on corruption is, in practice, just as often an office that facilitates it. The more power that is granted to the executive branch, the greater capacity the president has to use that power for corrupt purposes.

Fourth, we have built new institutions within government whose role in the system is difficult to reconcile with the Constitution. For instance, the First Bank of the United States was a private corporation that nevertheless derived a great deal of support from the feds. Ditto more recent institutions like Fannie Mae and Freddie Mac. How are such institutions to be understood vis-à-vis checks and balances, especially considering the Constitutional Convention's opposition to such publicly chartered corporations? The public-private nature of these institutions can be a breeding ground for corruption, as was particularly evident during the early years of the Second Bank of the United States, and with the accounting scandals that plagued Fannie and Freddie in the early 2000s.

The modern bureaucracy may be classified similarly. Of course, there was an executive bureaucracy from the very beginning of the country, but its size and scope have increased so enormously that it becomes difficult—if not impossible—for Congress to supervise it properly. Indeed, one of the most important insights of political science literature in recent decades is that Congress is more likely to monitor the bureaucracy when the transaction costs of such an inquiry are paid for by interest groups, via information or campaign contributions. This, in turn, often induces bureaucrats to yield to the interests of the most connected pressure groups.

In sum, we have a Congress that is too parochial to wield the nationalistic powers that it has been granted. We have a public that is necessarily too ill-informed to protect the republican principle. We have a politicized presidency that often lacks the capacity to check Congress for the national interest. We have these strange extraconstitutional organizations that do not fit cleanly into the schema. What does that mean? Again, consider Wilson's metaphor for the Constitution, a Newtonian system. Various selfish interests enter the arena, are checked by and balanced with other such forces, and the final product that emerges on the other end is supposed to be in the public interest. But these new governmental powers altered the original structure in these four ways, and thus have broken the Newtonian system. Nowadays, too much of what Washington produces is not in the public interest.

To be clear, this argument does not lead inevitably to advocacy for a night-watchman state, nor will this book call (explicitly or implicitly) for a return to the Constitution as it was understood upon ratification. Based on the premises established here, one could just as easily argue the converse position. In such a conception, the problem was that the Federalists ceded too much ground to the Anti-Federalists, and thus accepted a structure not built to operate necessary powers. The argument here cannot be situated on today's left-right divide; it is, rather, that the powers the government now wields are poorly suited to the structures it employs to wield them, with corruption being the attending result.

The rest of this book is dedicated to demonstrating the theory developed above. To do that, it is part history and part contemporary policy analysis.

Chapter One looks at the battle between Madison and Hamilton over the First Bank of the United States, which established a tension that has existed ever since: leaders like Hamilton have sought to expand the powers of the government beyond the original scope of the charter to solve pressing problems. Yet those expansions come with a major downside in that they undermine the balance Madison thought the Constitution created.

Chapter Two examines the behavior of the Jeffersonian Republican Party once it acquired control of the government in 1800. It shows that expansions of federal power are more or less permanent, for the Jeffersonians, who opposed Hamilton in the 1790s, came to accept almost all of his innovations, and even added a few themselves. The result was rampant political corruption through much of the 1820s, culminating in the Bank War of the early 1830s, a sobering time in the nation's history when the rule of law was sacrificed for the sake of political leverage.

Chapter Three brings the political parties into the analysis. As we shall see, they are integral in any understanding of American political corruption, for they politicized the presidency, forcing the occupant to use federal resources to maintain his electoral coalition. The first way that presidents did this was through patronage, or the provision of government jobs and contracts to their supporters. That will be the focus there.

Chapter Four will be the first to demonstrate a central theme of political corruption: when it is not being actively opposed, it tends to spread. Like cancer or wood rot, it will work its way through an entire body politic, destroying every last vestige of the republican principles that once existed. Something like this happened with the patronage regime. First developed during Andrew Jackson's administration, it was expanded and "perfected" by the early 1870s, so that the entirety of federal politics was reducible, more or less, to the maintenance of massive, statewide patronage machines.

Chapter Five will continue this theme about how corruption spreads by looking at the continued federal efforts to promote the national economy. As Chapters One and Two will have shown, this was an early breeding ground for corruption in the nineteenth century, and by the end of that century the corruption had gone from rudimentary to exceedingly complicated and virtually insuperable. After federal patronage dried up with the Pendleton Civil Service Act of 1883, politicians—particularly the leaders of the Republican Party and its bosses in machine-dominated states—turned to big business for funds. In so doing, they perverted the bold nationalism of Hamilton's original agenda into a corrupt logroll that benefited midwestern manufacturers and northeastern financiers at the expense of poor farmers, particularly in the South and West.

Chapter Six will introduce the progressive movement to the story. The progressives successfully curtailed many of the corrupt practices of the late nineteenth century, but they failed to end them once and for all. Indeed, they made matters worse. While a handful of progressives like Wilson identified the root cause of corruption as having to do with the incapacity of the government to exercise its powers responsibly, they failed to fix this problem. Moreover, the progressives were responsible for popularizing the second nationalistic power mentioned above, that of regulating the economy for noneconomic goals. Absent structural reforms to the government, this would become another potential source for corruption.

Chapter Seven will look at the New Deal period. A massive expansion in government, this period also (and not coincidentally) produced a startling reinvigoration of corruption, along all three dimensions we will have discussed by that point. First, efforts to revive the domestic economy were captured by congressional logrolls that distributed money based on political considerations. Second, federal jobs were used to create state and even national political machines, as early progress on civil service reform was basically wiped away. Third, the new regulatory powers of the federal government were captured by the most powerful elements in society to secure their economic status, at the expense of smaller businesses, consumers, unions, poor farmers, and the public interest at large.

Chapter Eight will look at the rise of the interest group society, which accelerated after the Great Depression. It will serve as a fulcrum for the final half of this book. The New Deal/World War II period saw the government do more than ever to promote the economy, regulate the economy, and provide groups with direct subsidies. All of this provided further incentives for factions to organize or, in the case of businesses, to improve their extant organizations. The result of this rapid process was the rise of what has since become known as the interest group society. Today, public policy is often the product of the push and pull of organized pressure groups. Contrary to the optimistic assessment of some pluralist theories of governance, this has had a profoundly negative effect on the body politic, ultimately producing the rampant corruption of the current period. The shady bosses of the Gilded Age may be long gone, but corruption is now as problematic as ever thanks to this new way of doing government business.

The remainder of the book will expand on the argument of Chapter Eight to evaluate various contemporary policy domains to see the ways in which factions dominate the government, manipulating legislation and regulations toward their own ends. Chapter Nine will explore farm subsidies to show how noble federal intentions to support disaffected groups devolved into naked payouts to well-connected industries. Chapter Ten will look at the modern "pork barrel," or the ways that members of Congress raid the federal treasury to reward local voters, donors, and themselves. Chapter Eleven discusses Medicare, detailing the ways that pressure groups representing senior citizens, doctors, hospitals, and others ensure that an unsustainable status quo is nevertheless retained. Chapter Twelve reviews how crony capitalism has become a durable, regrettable feature of the body politic, as politicians misuse their power to support the national economy. It will give special attention to the tax code; originally a progressive innovation designed to undermine the crooked regime of protective tariffs, the income tax is now rife with rewards for well-heeled interests. Chapter Thirteen will look at regulations, particularly those governing Fannie Mae and Freddie Mac, to show how adept interest groups can be at capturing congressional committees and executive regulators to ensure that their bottom lines are protected.

While no single chapter will be dedicated to the effect of governmental growth on the constitutional structure, those four themes (an incompetent Congress, a denuded republican principle, a partisanized presidency, and novel, ad hoc institutions) will be apparent. We will see Congress mishandle and abuse the nationalist powers it has been granted. For instance, in Chapter Eleven we will see how the legislature, at the behest of powerful interest groups, has been totally incapable of reforming the welfare state, despite clear knowledge that reforms are urgently needed. We will see the public struggle to comprehend the policies that legislators in Washington are promoting, and how in turn that enabled them to get away with corrupt practices they otherwise never would have. For instance, in Chapter Five we will see how Nelson Aldrich, senator from Rhode Island and chief Republican defender of the tariff, used the arcana of the law to pay off scores of interest groups, most notably the sugar trust, without any public rebuke. We will see the politicization of the presidency due to electoral pressure, and the attending problems that creates. For instance, in Chapter Seven we shall document FDR's efforts to misuse federal resources to secure his reelection in 1936 against recalcitrant urban party bosses, and later to purge conservative Democrats from the Senate. We shall see how quasi-independent institutions often create corrupt practices because they fail to fit properly into the Madisonian schema. For instance, in Chapter Two the debauched story of the Second Bank of the United States will clearly illuminate the dangers of chartering an institution whose role in the system is ambiguous. Chapter Thirteen, by looking at Fannie and Freddie, will make a similar point.

After the Constitutional Convention was finished with its work, delegate James McHenry reported that, as Benjamin Franklin left Independence Hall, a woman asked him, "Well, Doctor, what have we got? A republic or a monarchy?" Franklin replied, "A republic, if you can keep it." The argument in the pages to follow essentially boils down to: we couldn't keep it.

We couldn't keep it because we failed to remember something that Madison had so well understood, which is that the design of a government is essential to its success, and that when one goes about redesigning a government—as he and the Framers did in 1787—one must be careful to do it properly. Indeed, never in world history had a people dedicated so much of its efforts to debating a *structure* of government, rather than the policies the government would produce.

Today, we have forgotten that almost entirely, and we hardly give a second of critical thought to our government's design. Generation after generation has altered that design in subtle but important ways without considering the effect on the broader schema. That makes the Madisonian concept of checks and balances almost like a meaningless catechism nowadays. We dutifully and solemnly repeat it, but we forget about what inspired it in the first place. Implicitly, we assume that Madison solved the problems of factionalism and corruption once and for all. As this work will show, he did not. Even so, he delineated a method for us to solve it. We have to think carefully about how the various institutions within the government exercise the power they have been granted, and we have to adjust those institutions accordingly, so that they do not fall prey to corruption. We have not made a real effort to do so since 1787, which means that, even as we acclaim the singular genius of Madison, we are in actuality anything but Madisonian.

1

"The Great Desideratum"

Madison, Hamilton, and the
First Bank of the United States

AMERICANS NOWADAYS are wont to speak about the Founders, the men who led the way against the British to forge a new nation at the end of the eighteenth century, as a unified group. In many senses of the phrase, they were. They shared disgust with the heavy-handed treatment the colonies received from the English; they believed that the colonies would be better off independent; and they pledged their lives, fortunes, and sacred honor to see that through to the end.

But there were wide disagreements between them on many matters, some peripheral but others quite vital. Nowhere was this divide more evident than in the views of James Madison of Virginia and Alexander Hamilton of New York during the early days of the new republic. While the two were in agreement on the superiority of the Constitution over the Articles of Confederation, they had deep disagreements about the nature of the new government that was to be implemented. Though not at issue during the period of ratification, their philosophical clash dominated the American political scene for the first decade under the Constitution, and remained an important dividing line for forty years thereafter.

The flashpoint for the controversy was Hamilton's proposal to charter a Bank of the United States. Hamilton saw the Bank as a vital economic institution that could secure the prosperity of the nation in the face of foreign competition. Madison, on the other hand, made his strongest arguments against the Bank on the philosophical front. He and Thomas Jefferson saw it as an unconstitutional expansion of federal power that placed the legislature in hock to the executive branch and favored wealthy, northeastern merchants over the rest of the country.

It is important to note that the Bank was actually never as bad as Madison feared it might become. This is not so much because Madison was wrong, but because of the singular genius of Hamilton, who expertly navigated the nation through a financial panic in 1792. Later on, the able stewardship of Albert Gallatin, who served as secretary of the treasury during the early 1800s, ensured that the Bank did not threaten the national interest.

Even so, the Bank *was* problematic in the ways Madison argued, and it does serve as a microcosm of the argument in this book: the Bank was an institutional innovation that altered and disrupted the power relations within the government, tended to favor some factions over others, and, were it not for Hamilton's capable management, the speculative frenzy it generated might have had a severely negative effect on the nation's well-being.

The Constitution, as understood by Madison, intends to "break and control the violence of faction" by carefully balancing the structures of government against its powers. But this design implies that the two must be in sync—adjusting one without toggling the other can lead to corruption. Though supported by many eminent members of the Founding generation, the Bank nevertheless was a challenge to Madison's view of the Constitution because it disturbed this synchronicity. While his worst fears were never realized, the Bank still serves as an apt metaphor for our story.

We shall begin our story by examining the problem of republican government that Madison and the Framers faced in the 1780s. Put simply, it did not seem to work very well. We shall then look at Madison's proposed solution to the problems he saw, and how his ideas influenced the constitutional design. Then, we shall turn our attention to Hamilton, who had other views and priorities. The dispute between them remained latent during the ratification phase, but it became active when Hamilton proposed his Bank. In the final analysis, Hamilton certainly had the better arguments about the economic necessity of the Bank, but Madison's warnings about its threat to the republic turned out to be prescient.

Prior to the Revolution, republican government had typically depended on the balancing of different estates. Government derived its authority not merely from the people at large, but rather a mixture of the common folk, a nobility, the clergy, and in the case of Great Britain a monarchy as well. The point of this arrangement was to balance the interests of the various classes of society, so that ultimately the public good would be promoted. Each must maintain its appropriate station so as to retain the proper equilibrium, as the English had attested when they responded to the excesses of James II with the Glorious Revolution of 1688. No less a republican eminence as Montesquieu endorsed England as the only country whose laws offered political liberty.[1]

Revolutionary Americans were deeply familiar with republican philosophy, as well as with the discontents in the British system who denied the perfection of Albion's constitution.[2] The Country party ideology of Cato's *Letters* and Bolingbroke pointed backward in time, toward an idyllic (and largely fictional) period before the Norman Invasion, when the hearty Anglo-Saxon race did not have to swear fealty to an overbearing monarch. In that view, the once-virtuous English system had been corrupted by the leadership of Sir Robert Walpole, the first British prime minister who was accused of bribing members of Parliament. When Americans looked at the interference of the Crown in their affairs following the Seven Years War, they saw a similar pattern, and resolved to do something about it— something quite radical.

Their solution was to inaugurate a government heretofore unseen by modern eyes: there would be no special status for landed, moneyed, or otherwise elite interests; there would be no king; there would only be the people. This radicalism rings forth in the most famous passage of the Declaration of Independence:

> We hold these truths to be self-evident, that all men are created equal, that they are endowed by their Creator with certain unalienable Rights, that among these are Life, Liberty and the pursuit of Happiness.—That to secure these rights, Governments are instituted among Men, deriving their just powers from the consent of the governed,—That whenever any Form of Government becomes destructive of these ends, it is the Right of the People to alter or to abolish it, and to institute new Government, laying its foundation on such principles and organizing its powers in such form, as to them shall seem most likely to effect their Safety and Happiness.[3]

There is no mixed estate here. Governmental authority begins and ends with the people. Today, we take this as a given—and indeed are wont to criticize the Founders for not following through on this premise by promoting, for instance, universal suffrage, abolition, or women's rights—but in the summer of 1776 the Declaration of Independence was the boldest statement on behalf of popular government yet written.

Yet the experience of the Revolution, and especially of the decade that followed, seemed to prove the Americans wrong and the advocates of a mixed estate right. America had done away with established privilege, replacing its toehold in government with democratic institutions, and had met with economic and social misery. The people seemed incapable of ruling.

For starters, the national government created to replace the king—organized under the measly Articles of Confederation—was chronically strapped for cash. Lacking the ability to raise taxes, it was dependent upon requisitions from the states, which they regularly did not provide. This ultimately led to the Newburgh Conspiracy in the spring of 1783, in which senior army officers as well as members of Congress plotted to force Congress to fund their pensions. It was only through the influence of George Washington—who resolved to be a true republican general in the mold of Cincinnatus—that the coup went nowhere.[4]

Unfortunately, that was not the end of governmental incompetence following the war. The impotence of the central government meant that the rights of British loyalists, as granted under the Treaty of Paris, often went ignored by state governments. Meanwhile, the British regularly violated their own commitments, particularly in the West, with little fear of reprisal from the American government. What's more, foreign governments gleefully played states off one another, utilizing the lack of central management to maximize their trading profits. The states themselves had difficulty even coordinating over shared waterways like the Potomac River.

The most dangerous want of central authority had to do with a fast-spreading dispute between debtors and creditors, which occurred in part because of the economic downturn of the decade, and threatened an outbreak of widespread civil unrest. In the state of Rhode Island, a coalition of debtors won control of the government and enacted very liberal laws on the repayment of debts, basically forcing creditors—even those from other states—to take massive haircuts. Meanwhile, in neighboring Massachusetts, eastern creditors held the balance of power and refused to offer debt relief to the farmers of the west. Their inattention to the yeomanry's grievances eventually led to the civil unrest known as Shays' Rebellion.[5]

Madison, then in his mid-thirties and serving in the Virginia House of Delegates after a stint in the Continental Congress, had, like many of his contemporaries, surmised that the core problem was the Articles of Confederation itself. According to Madison, it was a "treaty of amity and commerce and alliance, between independent and sovereign states."[6] But Madison took his analysis much farther than any other politician of the era. He had, thanks to books supplied from France by his good friend Jefferson, taken a careful study of previous confederations between independent states, and found similar defects to what plagued the American nation in that decade.[7] That spring, he wrote a systematic treatise entitled the *Vices of the Political System of the United States*, detailing his complaints.

The problems, Madison argues, were many. Without a strong central authority, the state governments had failed to follow through on requisitions, regularly encroached the national government's authority, violated the laws of nations, trespassed on the rights of other states, failed to act in concert when mutual interests suggested they should, behaved illiberally to political minorities, and generally failed to pass sensible and forward-looking laws. The reason for all of these troubles, Madison suggests, was that the states had been ruined by factionalism, or battles between "a number of citizens, whether amounting to a majority or minority of the whole, who are united and actuated by some common impulse of passion, or of interest, adverse to the rights of other citizens, or to the permanent and aggregate interests of the community."[8]

Influenced by his Calvinist education at Princeton, Madison believed that self-interested behavior was an inevitable aspect of social and political life, and thus governmental success depended not on the virtue of the people, but rather on how well the state managed the selfishness. America in 1787 was an abject failure on that front, with a federal government powerless to do anything and state governments gripped by the very factional gamesmanship that needed management.[9]

Toward the end of the *Vices*, Madison lays down a vital marker:

The great desideratum in Government is such a modification of the Sovereignty as will render it sufficiently neutral between the different interests and factions, to controul one part of the Society from invading the rights of another, and at the same time sufficiently controuled itself, from setting up an interest adverse to that of the whole Society.[10]

This is arguably the most succinct statement of the republican problem ever delivered up to that point in history. Madison's ability to perceive and articulate this fundamental question of government is one reason he has been remembered as one of the most acute political thinkers this nation has ever produced. Unfortunately, this desideratum (or need) is easier described than fulfilled, and nearly five years after the Americans defeated the British, they only knew of solutions that had not worked.

Unsurprisingly, the delegates who arrived at the Constitutional Convention in the spring of 1787 had very different views on how to solve the problems that plagued America. The most extreme alternative to the Confederation was supplied by thirty-one-year-old Colonel Hamilton, a former chief of staff to General Washington, whose prodigious intellectual talents combined with a natural sociability and cosmopolitan worldview to make him stand out in an era chock full of formidable men.[11] As even his soon-to-be adversary Jefferson would admit years later, Hamilton was "a singular character. Of acute understanding, disinterested, honest, and honorable in all private transactions, amiable in society, and duly valuing virtue in private life."[12] The energetic young colonel possessed a very sour view of the capacity of the people to manage their affairs directly, and his alternative was reminiscent of the British Constitution. In Hamilton's proposal, a lower chamber of Congress would be elected by the people, but both the Senate and the presidential office would be filled by appointment, with those positions being life-tenured. So far out of the mainstream of thinking at the Constitutional Convention was Hamilton that his fellow delegates never took up his proposal for a vote—yet, as we shall see, Hamilton's views of government would become much more relevant during Washington's administration.[13]

On the other end of the spectrum were delegates like Elbridge Gerry of Massachusetts, George Mason of Virginia, and William Paterson of New Jersey, whose plan allowed Congress to collect taxes and created a new executive committee, but offered little else in terms of centralization. This proposal attracted the support of small state delegates, as well as some who would ultimately oppose the final draft produced by the Constitutional Convention.

Madison's solution was embodied in the Virginia Plan, proposed by Governor Edmund Randolph but really the junior statesman's brainchild. This plan effectively occupied a middle ground between Hamilton and Paterson. It differed substantially from the final version of the Constitution in many respects (e.g., by imagining a much more nationalized array of institutions that wielded much greater powers), but it nevertheless dominated the agenda of the Constitutional Convention and, in the end, served as the framework for the eventual Constitution. As a consequence, both exhibit key features of Madison's thinking at the time, and represent his attempts to solve the republican puzzle he had succinctly described in his *Vices*.

Both the Virginia Plan and the Constitution retained the radical innovation of the Declaration; there would be no established, mixed estates within the new nation. How then did the young Virginian address the problems of factionalism that this had presented? Madison would discard another dominant theme of previous republican philosophy: that of a small, reasonably homogenous polity. It was Aristotle who had originally argued that a true polity had to be of limited territory, population, and diversity, so that citizens could communicate with one another, share knowledge of their circumstances, and know who could be trusted to run the government.[14] The Anti-Federalists would come to argue fervently for this principle, believing that in anything but a small republic (as embodied by the states), the people's voice would be lost to the desires of the elites.[15] Madison had developed an opposite view. The experience of the state governments had disproved for him the idea that small states could embody the republican ideal.[16] Diversity was inevitable due to the natural divisions between men; even a state as small as Rhode Island was rent in two by the dispute over debts. What was key, in Madison's opinion, was how the government managed those factions, and the larger the sphere the more manageable the factions would become.[17] In *Vices*, Madison asserts:

> Place three individuals in a situation wherein the interest of each depends on the voice of the others, and give to two of them an interest opposed to the rights of the third? Will the latter be secure? The prudence of every man would shun the danger. . . . Will two thousand in a like situation be less likely to encroach on the rights of one thousand? The contrary is witnessed by the notorious factions & oppressions which take place in corporate towns limited as the opportunities are, and in little republics when uncontrouled by apprehensions of external danger. If an enlargement of the sphere is found to lessen the insecurity of private rights, it is not because the impulse of a common interest or passion is less predominant in this case with the majority; but because a common

interest or passion is less apt to be felt and the requisite combinations less easy to be formed by a great than by a small number.[18]

Having abandoned this core principle of classical republicanism, Madison went on to modify another. An institution like the House of Lords had served the purpose of guaranteeing the rights of some sort of aristocratic estate, and indeed the general view of theorists was that a bicameral legislature should protect the "better" class of people. Madison turned that notion on its head: the purpose of a Senate would not be to carve out protections for the wealthy minority, but rather to create purely artificial distinctions within the government among the whole populace, so as to facilitate the combat of interests. This is not to say that Madison had no expectations for the role of a natural aristocracy; instead, he hoped that a better sort of leader would emerge in the national government, in particular the Senate.[19] The point, however, is that all power would flow from the people, and only the people, but it would flow in different ways in different intervals to different points of concentration, thus facilitating what Madison anticipated would be a grand clash of interests and factions. As he argues in *Federalist #51*:

> Whilst all authority in (the government) will be derived from, and dependent on the society, the society itself will be broken into so many parts, interests and classes of citizens, that the rights of individuals or of the minority, will be in little danger from interested combinations of the majority.[20]

Thus, Madison believes that a "well-constructed union" covering a large geographical sphere could "break and control the violence of faction."[21] In fact, the two pieces fit together: as long as the government is designed appropriately, a proliferation of factions would actually be beneficial. The structure of government would channel their fights properly, and a multiplicity of groups would ensure that nobody gains the upper hand for long.

The implications of these innovations are profound, for Madison premises republican government not on virtue—a common theme dating back more than a millennium—but on a decided lack thereof.[22] That is not to say that Madison expects men to be the villainous brigands that Thomas Hobbes envisions in the state of nature, but rather that civic virtue—generally defined by theorists as the capacity to put the good of the community ahead of one's selfish interests—is an unreliable safeguard. Writing at the end of the 1780s—a decade when state after state, faction after faction, and person after person put their own interests ahead of the common good—this was less an assumption than a sad acknowledgement of reality.[23] But Madison brushes this aside: let there be a congeries of competing, parochial interests; the more the merrier, in fact. Madison's separation of powers—or, rather, the separation of powers that emerged in the Constitution after all the compromises had been made—would balance these interests, ensuring that the final product would advance the public good and respect private rights.[24]

———————

Madison was not completely satisfied with the final draft of the Constitution, but considered it a major improvement over the Articles of Confederation, and he committed himself to its defense. Largely absent during the Constitutional Convention, Hamilton joined the fray with characteristic vigor. He and Madison joined with John Jay, the architect of the Treaty of Paris, to pen the *Federalist Papers*, anonymous essays published in New York to promote adoption of the Constitution.

It has often been remarked that the subsequent break between Hamilton and Madison was peculiar, given their collaboration on the essays. Indeed, before historians were taking up this puzzle, contemporary observers—and even the principals themselves—pondered the nature of the divide. Often, the blame is placed upon Madison, in no small part because he became a critic of many Hamiltonian provisions that he had previously supported. Some have claimed that Madison's change of heart was due to the spell that Jefferson had over him; when the former returned from his diplomatic duties in Paris, the latter (so the claim goes) shifted from a staunch nationalist to a skeptic of central power. Others have speculated that it was due to Madison's Anglophobia; similarly, Hamilton once remarked that his former ally had a "womanly attachment" to France.[25] Still others have suggested that regional concerns were in play; Hamilton's economic program favored the Northeast and Madison, a member of the House during the first three Congresses, was sensitive to the worries of his Virginia constituents.

Madison, however, had a very different answer. Late in his life, in conversation with Nicholas Trist, he said:

> As to (whether) I deserted Colonel Hamilton, or rather Colonel H. deserted me; in a word, the divergence between us took place—from his wishing . . . to administer the government . . . into what he thought it ought to be; while, on my part, I endeavored to make it conform to the

Constitution as understood by the Convention that produced and recommended it, and particularly by the State conventions that *adopted* it.[26]

This view has gained less purchase among popular and academic writers, but it does much to squash the idea that Madison changed his mind. From his perspective, it is irrelevant that he supported certain policies before the government came into being; as long as he believed those policies violated the new governing charter, he was obliged to oppose them.

So, perhaps neither deserted the other. Perhaps instead the two were allied with one another on the first question (is the Constitution preferable to the Articles of Confederation?) but diverged on the next (what shape should federal policy take in light of this new Constitution?). This conclusion runs contrary to the conventional wisdom, which holds that Madison had flip-flopped on his attitude about the government between the time of the *Federalist Papers* and the inauguration of the new government. Even so, a careful reading of those famous documents supports the idea that, deep down, the two agreed less than they may once have thought.[27] We have already looked closely at Madison's thinking, so it is time to turn to Hamilton's.

Hamilton's contributions to the *Federalist Papers* are likely greater in number than Madison's, but none is remembered in the same way as Madison's efforts in #10 and #51. These are broad-based, largely philosophical arguments for the utility of the proposed union. Hamilton, on the other hand, was at his best in the early part of the series, with powerful jeremiads about the inevitable troubles that would befall the nation if it rejected the Constitution. Then, in the final third of the essays, he offered persuasive entries defending the new executive and judiciary. Even so, *Federalist* #11 comes as close as anything to outlining Hamilton's core convictions about the potentials of the new American government, à la Madison's ideas in #10 and #51. Read at the time of its publication, *Federalist* #11 may not have been as illuminating, but considered in the context of his economic program, it is perhaps his most foundational work.

In that essay, Hamilton opens with a point that reflects his cosmopolitan worldview: "The importance of the Union, in a commercial light, is one of those points about which there is least room to entertain a difference of opinion. . . . This applies as well to our intercourse with foreign countries as well as each other." He goes on to assert that the "adventurous spirit" of America has "already excited uneasy sensations . . . in the maritime powers of Europe." He believes that a united America could "oblige foreign countries to bid against each other, for the privileges of our markets."[28] In other words, Hamilton sees the possibility of a great commercial empire, one that could even force the fearsome Great Britain to deal with the United States on terms dictated by the latter.

But, as Hamilton had demonstrated in the preceding essays, disunion among the several states kept the United States from making the most of its potential. A lack of a central authority had enabled the European powers to play each state off the others, and ultimately get for themselves a better deal than they would have if Americans were bound together in a tighter union. Hamilton sees worse things to come should the states fail to unite:

> It would be in the power of the maritime nations, availing themselves of our universal impotence, to prescribe the conditions of our political existence . . . and confine us to a *passive commerce*. . . . The unequalled spirit of enterprise, which signalizes the genius of the American merchants and navigators, and which is in itself an inexhaustible mine of national wealth, would be stifled and lost, and poverty and disgrace would overspread a country which, with wisdom, might make herself the admiration and envy of the world.[29]

On the other hand, a "vigorous national government . . . directed to a common interest, would baffle all the combinations of European jealousy to restrain our growth." But even more than this, the sort of economic coordination that could come only from a central government would bind the country together in a shared quest for ever-increasing prosperity:

> An unrestrained intercourse between the States themselves will advance the trade of each by an interchange of their respective productions, not only for the supply of reciprocal wants at home, but for exportation to foreign markets. The veins of commerce in every part will be replenished, and will acquire additional motion and vigor from a free circulation of the commodities of every part.[30]

Taken as a whole, *Federalist* #11 is a magnificently prescient statement, and a testament to the brilliance of Hamilton. Somehow, he saw beyond the America of 1787—an undeveloped, disconnected, fractious collection of states dominated by subsistence farmers—and perceived the vast economic powerhouse that the United States is today. Thanks to her commerce, America today dominates the world without having to hold a single foreign people prisoner, and Hamilton saw this potential before anybody else in the country or the world. He is the originator of the concept of American exceptionalism.

At the same time, however, the potential for conflict with Madison should be obvious. Madisonian balance and Hamiltonian prosperity are goals that are not necessarily in conflict, but they are not necessarily in harmony, either. A Hamiltonian government that promotes national development may not retain a balance between all factions; quite the contrary, it may systematically favor those deemed most helpful to the leadership's long-term goals. In fact, as we shall see, one of Hamilton's goals was to yoke the prosperity of the wealthy merchant class to the fate of the Union through policies that favored both. Madison was thoroughly appalled by this.

The potential for tension is especially apparent when we consider *Federalist* #11 in light of Hamilton's view of the English Constitution. As mentioned above, Hamilton envisioned an executive branch almost entirely independent of swings in the mood of the public. He had a similar desire to see the Senate so inoculated. Only the House would be directly tied to the people, and here Hamilton once explained to Jefferson that he was comfortable with the executive wielding extralegal influence within that chamber, much as the king of Great Britain used patronage to acquire the votes of recalcitrant members of Parliament. In his notes, Jefferson recorded a dinner conversation he once had with John Adams and Hamilton:

> Conversation began on other matters and, by some circumstance, was led to the British constitution, on which Mr. Adams observed "purge that constitution of its corruption, and give to its popular branch equality of representation, & it would be the most perfect constitution ever devised by the wit of man." Hamilton paused and said, "purge it of its corruption, and give to its popular branch equality of representation, & it would become an impracticable government: as it stands at present, with all its supposed defects, it is the most perfect government which ever existed."[31]

What is Hamilton on about here? Return to his broader theory of republican government: the people's representatives were not to be trusted to perceive the public interest, let alone sacrifice their own parochial desires for the sake of the common good. What was needed was a strong executive, largely free from public meddling, that had the capacity to, in effect, bribe small-minded members of the legislature to do the things that they should otherwise be doing. For Hamilton—a man who never took a dishonest dollar—this is not about venality for its own sake. This is about compelling venal men to do what they really ought to do, anyway.[32]

Intentions aside, one can see why Madison would not truck with any of this. In his vision of the new American republic, there were simply to be no special favors whatsoever to be dispensed by the government—no patronage, no sinecures, no insider information leading to vast fortunes. The whole point of his system was to enable factions to rise up to prevent other factions from doing precisely these things, so that the only product of public policy was well and truly public spirited. Corruption was not a tool to be used ultimately for the public good by a natural elite; instead, it was a form of cancer that could pervert otherwise good men into destroying the republic itself. Ironically, the main focal point of the disagreement was none other than their old colonial master: Great Britain. In the old mother country, Hamilton saw an example of republican empire to be emulated while Jefferson and Madison saw a cautionary tale of how a true republic may be destroyed.[33]

Thus, what united them in defense of the Constitution was not so much a shared vision of what the new government should be, but rather what it should not be. Both judged the Constitution to be a supreme improvement over the Articles of Confederation, but once the fight to replace it was won, it is not terribly surprising—in historical retrospect, at any rate—that the two would part ways, and indeed become leaders of the political factions that would dominate American politics for the next decade.[34]

In the final analysis, it was not so much that the two held views that necessarily contradicted one another; rather, they possessed different priorities that could, and did, come into conflict. For Madison, the ultimate goal of the new government was to balance different factions and produce public policy that was only in the public interest; for Hamilton, the goal was a vigorous government to spur the country on to national greatness. Insofar as these views suggested divergent policy demands, Madison and Hamilton could be expected to turn from allies into opponents. That is precisely what happened, as the public debate turned from ratification to the Bank—a controversial institution that may have been necessary from Hamilton's perspective, but was anathema to Madison.

Washington was chosen unanimously to be the nation's first president, and while his cabinet did not sample from Anti-Federalist sentiment, it drew from a broad spectrum of nationalist political opinion.[35] Jefferson—a skeptic of expansive federal power—became secretary of state. Randolph—who refused to sign the Constitution but eventually supported it for ratification—became attorney general. Washington chose for secretary of the treasury his former chief of staff Hamilton, who had grand plans for the office. In *Federalist* #11, he hopes to make "one great American system, superior to the controul of all trans-atlantic force or influence."[36] The first step in this process was to get a handle on America's disastrous public finances.

That would be no little feat, as there were centuries' worth of precedent demonstrating America's reckless approach to its debt. Some of this was due to Great Britain refusing to allow the colonies to coin their own money, but the balance of the blame lay with the colonial governments, the first in the world to print fiat paper money. The result was rampant inflation and eventually an insistence by Britain that the colonies cease and desist. The Continental Congress was little better either, printing fiat "Continentals" that quickly became debased; by 1781, a single dollar of specie (or hard currency) was worth a whopping 168 Continental dollars. Farmers and merchants refused such worthless paper, and so the Continental Army was forced to impress supplies, with loan certificates promising future repayment.[37] But the impotent national government counted on just $500,000 per year in requisitions from the states during the 1780s, so there was no repayment, meaning the certificates were basically worthless, often snatched up by speculators for pennies on the dollar.[38]

All told, the creditworthiness of the United States was very low indeed by the time Hamilton was sworn in as the first secretary of the treasury. This was Hamilton's top concern because, as he writes in the *Report on Public Credit*, the nation was "possessed of little active wealth, or in other words, little monied capital" and needed the capacity to borrow on "good terms."[39] Accordingly, he suggests guaranteeing the repayment of existing federal debt, for the federal government to assume the states' debt loads, and a new tax on alcohol, tea, and coffee.[40] This, he asserts, would help the flow of currency, extend trade, promote agriculture and manufacturing, and lower interest rates.[41]

In the *Report on a National Bank* Hamilton proposes the chartering of a national bank, which he argues would have several beneficial effects. First, it would help the nation's economy, as gold and silver deposited in a bank with good credit can generate much greater capital flows than just their sum in hard coin. Second, it would give the government a reliable resource for borrowing money at favorable rates of interest. Third, it would facilitate the payment of taxes. The Bank, Hamilton proposes, would be largely held by private interests, though the government would supply

$2 million of its $10 million capitalization limit via a loan from the Bank itself. The rest would come from private purchases of bank stock, with 25 percent up front in gold or silver and the rest to be paid over time at an interest rate of 6 percent.[42]

Finally, Hamilton proffers a vast system of public support for manufacturing, which at this point in the country's history badly trailed the advances being made in Great Britain. In his *Report on Manufactures*, he offers a series of justifications to diversify the economic basis of the American economy, from a virtual agricultural hegemony to one where industry had a prominent role to play. This would diversify, sharpen, and streamline existing labor; it would promote the application of time- and expense-saving machinery; it would improve employment opportunities; it would promote immigration; it would provide more opportunities for expression of the people's creative talents; and it would create new domestic markets for the consumption of foodstuffs. Thus, Hamilton advances tariffs on manufactured items, regulations on exports of vital materials, bounties, premiums, tariffs and tax breaks on raw materials, and more. All of this, Hamilton asserts, would stimulate the people to dedicate time and capital toward manufacturing.[43]

Hamilton had submitted all these proposals by December 1791. Considering that this work followed right on the heels of his defense of the Constitution, both as an anonymous author of an estimated fifty-one *Federalist* essays and as a delegate to the New York State ratifying convention, and that he had done all of this before he turned thirty-five years of age, we can appreciate clearly why Jefferson once commented that Hamilton was "a host unto himself."[44] It was Hamilton above all else who gave the young government energy and purpose during Washington's first term.[45]

Considered in light of *Federalist* #11, it is pretty clear what Hamilton intended to do. His goal was to harness the natural bounty of the United States, as well as the energetic, intrepid character of its people, to transform the young nation into a world power. To do that, the debt problem had to be solved, interest rates had to be brought under control, the veins of credit had to be opened, and a forward-looking industrial policy had to be implemented. And, in a subtext that runs through all four proposals, he intended to tie the interests of the well-to-do to the success of the government itself. Their private prosperity would hinge on it thriving, and Hamilton adopted the logic of Madison's large geographical sphere to prop up the republic; he would use the private interests that past philosophers had argued was its greatest threat. But while Madison was concerned about keeping a proper balance between factions, Hamilton was particularly worried about capturing the moneyed class and bending it toward the public good.

In general, Hamilton believed Americans had to follow the example of their former British masters, whose economy and military had benefited greatly by a sensible system of public finance such as what Hamilton was offering.[46] That these ideas, in the main, constituted the economic thinking of the later Whig and Lincolnian Republican parties for the whole of the nineteenth century is a testament to his far-sightedness.

It also signals his culpability in the rise of partisan politics, for these policies provoked heated backlash, at least in due course. According to historian Ron Chernow, by the summer of 1791 Hamilton had become the *"enfant terrible* of the early republic, and a substantial minority of the country was mobilized against him."[47] There were a host of reasons for this opposition; Hamilton's proposals tended to favor the Northeast over the West and South, indebted states like Massachusetts over fiscally responsible ones like Virginia, commercial interests over poor farmers, and so on. Even so, these issues, while certainly salient, do not really capture the essence of the critique against Hamilton, which was universal in scope, rather than merely dependent on one's geographic or socioeconomic status, and was symbolized by the name his opponents chose for themselves—that of the *Republicans.*

Today, this party is often called the "Democratic-Republican" Party, to distinguish it from the modern Republican Party and to signal that it eventually became the modern Democratic Party. Here, we are going to avoid this term and stick with "Republicans" or "Jeffersonian Republicans." "Democratic-Republican" is not generally what they called themselves, and anyway the modern Democratic Party was just one off-shoot from a later split within the Jeffersonian Republicans. The other off-shoot became the National Republican Party for a time, then finally the Whig Party. The Whigs *did* form the basis for the modern Republican Party.[48]

The cluster of views that historian Lance Banning calls the "Republican persuasion" did not develop immediately; opposition to the early elements of Hamilton's plan was present, but usually followed regional lines.[49] In fact Jefferson—Hamilton's eventual archrival—helped broker a deal to bring about the federal assumption of state debts. It was only after Hamilton proposed the Bank that the Republicans began to put together a systematic critique.

Some of their arguments were antiquated; for instance, their commonplace fears of banks as institutions belied a lack of knowledge of public finance and leaned heavily on the simple prejudices of the age. Some were paranoid; for instance, many were convinced that Hamilton and his friends were looking to establish an American monarchy.[50] Some were too influenced by the hyperbole of Britain's Country Party; the most radical Republicans were ready, willing, and able to interpret any trifling insult as a portent of the republic's impending doom.[51] But amidst these unpersuasive claims, the Republicans leveled some extremely cogent assertions that ring true even today. Three interrelated complaints stand out in particular.

First, in Madison's view, Hamilton was going against the plain meaning of the Constitution as understood at the time of ratification. Though Madison himself had proposed at the Constitutional Convention a power for Congress to grant charters, such as the Bank's, the Convention had voted it down.[52] Moreover, the clauses in the Constitution that Hamilton was using to justify the Bank's legality (the General Welfare and Necessary and Proper Clauses) were ones that the advocates of the Constitution had assured its opponents during the ratification debate would not lead to unlimited legislative power.[53] Many observers at the time, and indeed historians ever since, have strained to reconcile Madison's constitutional interpretation of the 1790s to his advocacy for vast federal powers in 1787. But that misses the point. Madison had long been worried about the capacity for government—especially the legislative branch—to overstep its legal boundaries, which is exactly what he thought was happening here. Regardless of what he wanted in 1787, he believed that what the government was doing was contrary to the guarantees about the Constitution that its advocates made during the ratification debates, and therefore what the people thought it meant when their representatives assented to it.[54] From this perspective, it is easy to appreciate why Madison would fear this power grab, even if it was a power he thought the government should have, as a sign that the Constitution's republican balance, which was his paramount concern, was being disrupted.

Second, the Republicans worried that Hamilton's program was showering benefits upon a select few, notably friends of Hamilton as well as the commercial interests in the Northeast. In point of fact, the Republicans were absolutely correct. Though Hamilton himself did not become wealthy due to his economic policy, many people with connections to him most certainly did. For instance, rumors of Hamilton's funding plan were so widely known in certain circles before he released its details that a speculator as far away as Amsterdam had advance warning. Ultimately, this facilitated a transfer of wealth from the South and West to the Northeast, as speculators who were in the know sent their agents to the back areas of the country to snatch up as much government paper as they could.[55]

Nobody was more culpable in this corruption than William Duer, Hamilton's friend and first assistant secretary of the treasury. Previously a business partner of Hamilton's wealthy father-in-law, William Schuyler, Duer was well positioned to collect information about Hamilton's intentions, and when he left the Treasury Department he put his knowledge to good use. In late 1791 and early 1792, Duer and members of a speculative company tried to corner the market on U.S. debt securities, and in so doing overextended their credit lines. When they couldn't pay their creditors, a panic began and a run on Bank deposits threatened to bring the whole American financial system down. It was only through the acumen of Hamilton, who directed some $100,000 in Bank open-market purchases of securities, that the credit crisis was quelled.[56]

Ultimately, the core driver of the Republican complaint on this front was essentially the provision of a government rent to those who had the means to take advantage. With the new government backing the Bank, it was a sure-fire winner. Writing to Jefferson from New York City in the summer of 1791, Madison was appalled by the speculative frenzy that had been launched:

> It seems admitted on all hands now that the plan of the institution gives a moral certainty of gain to the Subscribers with scarce a physical possibility of loss. The subscriptions are consequently a mere scramble for so much public plunder which will be engrossed by those already loaded with the spoils of individuals. . . . It pretty clearly appears also in what proportions the public debt lies in the Country. What sort of hands hold it, and by whom the people of the U.S. are to be governed. [57]

A month later, Madison wrote his friend once again:

> It is said that packet boats & expresses are again sent from this place to the Southern States, to buy up the paper of all sorts which has risen in the market here. These & other abuses make it a problem whether the system of the old paper under a bad Government, or of the new under a good one, be chargeable with the greater substantial injustice. The true difference seems to be that by the former the few were the victims to the many; by the latter the many to the few.[58]

In the view of the Republicans, this was precisely the sort of occurrence that a good government was supposed to prevent. How can one region of the nation, one class of society, or one clique with insider information profit at the expense of the rest of the citizenry? The answer, they believed, was that the republic had been corrupted, in much the same way they believed that Rome and England had been transformed from republics into something much worse.[59] Per Madison, this result was just as bad as that which had occurred under the Articles of Confederation. In the 1780s, fractious majorities in the states legislated against the rights of the minority and the good of all; now, however a northeastern minority was violating private rights and public good.

How could a minority possibly get away with plundering a majority like this? The answer lies in the Republicans' third cogent attack on the Hamiltonian system: it had employed the Bank to buy off a faction within the legislature, much as the Republicans believed King George III had done with the Parliament. To buttress these claims, the Republicans relied heavily on the accounts of John Beckley, the first clerk of the House of Representatives and a staunch ally of Jefferson and Madison. In late winter of 1793, Beckley had reported to Jefferson that some nineteen members of the House, plus an additional seven in the Senate, were "paper men" (i.e., had invested heavily in Bank shares). Beckley also reported to Jefferson rumors of Hamilton bending the rules to benefit well-positioned investors.[60] In a private letter to Washington dated September 9, 1792, Jefferson argued:

> [Hamilton's system is] calculated to undermine and demolish the republic, by creating an influence of his department over the members of the legislature. I saw this influence actually produced, & its first fruits to be the establishment of the great outlines of his project by the votes of the very persons who, having swallowed his bait were laying themselves out to profit by his plans: & that had these persons withdrawn, as those interested in a question ever should, the vote of the disinterested majority was clearly the reverse of what they made it. These were no longer the votes then of the representatives of the people, but of deserters from the rights & interests of the people: & it was impossible to consider their decisions, which had nothing in view but to enrich themselves, as the measures of the fair majority.[61]

Taking these concerns about private gains and public corruption together, Madison worried to Jefferson that the holders of Bank shares "will become the pretorian band of the Government, at once its tool & its tyrant; bribed by its largesses & overawing it by clamours & combinations."[62] In other words, the Hamiltonian finance system threatened the balance that he sought to construct in the Constitution and that he defended in the *Federalist Papers*. Who, in the original schema, was supposed to check an executive branch that was too partial to one faction? The answer: the legislative branch. But Madison and Jefferson believed that the new institution, one not envisioned by the Constitutional Convention (and indeed voted down by it), had stymied this vital check by bribing them. This, in turn, freed the Bank to pursue a fractious agenda, and gave Duer an opening to make his run, almost bringing the economy down with him.

Fortunately, the sound and sure management of the Treasury by the exemplary Hamilton meant that the worst fears of the Republicans were not to be realized—at least not in the 1790s. Still, their critique of the Bank identifies the basic trajectory that corruption will take over the next 225 years. Some new government power may be a necessary tonic to a national ailment, but absent corresponding revisions to the institutions that exercise that power, it has the potential to distort the vital process of checks and balances, which in turn can breed corruption. In the case of the Bank, it granted new powers to an extraconstitutional institution that, per the Republicans, were used in part to bribe legislators. The result may have been benevolent in the grand scheme of things, but that had more to do with the singularity of Hamilton. Bank policies were indeed factional and could indeed have been catastrophic, if the secretary had not acted so effectively to stop the panic induced by Duer's failed scheme.

What can we make of this now, almost 225 years after this feud burned so hot? For starters, Hamilton's program was an ingenious plan to modernize the U.S. financial system, stabilize government debt, and diversify the economy. Even a cursory survey of the American economy in the late 1780s demonstrates that such a program was sensible, if not absolutely vital, for the nation's long-term prosperity. That moderate Republicans (including, above all Madison himself!) some twenty years later would finally adopt much of his program, which in turn formed the basis of Whig and Lincolnian Republican economic policy for the next century, demonstrates just how perspicacious it was.

Meanwhile, the Jeffersonian Republicans were much less pragmatic. The gentry farmers of Virginia may have dreamed of a true republic in the sense that the Country Party imagined it, but what of Napoleon? What of George III? What of Charles IV? The great powers of Europe were not finished with the American continent, not by a long shot, and were intent—as

Hamilton argues persuasively—on forcing America into a "passive commerce." Hamilton doubted that the structure of the Constitution, at least as Madison envisioned it, was sufficient to ensure America's security in the international world.

This has been the general consensus of historians for generations, and it is by and large fair. But there is another way to look at the matter, one that is more sympathetic to Jefferson and especially Madison, who clearly and rightly saw civic dangers lurking in the shadows cast by Hamilton's Bank. Return to those three criticisms that they leveled so effectively, for they are causally linked: Hamilton had extended the power of the government beyond its original scope, his argument about the Necessary and Proper Clause notwithstanding; this extension undermined the balance between powers and structures that the Framers had implemented, as patronage from the executive-run Bank came to influence members of Congress; and the final result produced factionalism, corruption, and almost—were it not for Hamilton's vigorous intervention—economic catastrophe.

This gets to the heart of the Madisonian perspective on the Constitution. His system was designed to survive venality and self-interestedness; indeed, as noted above, it assumed a baseline presence of such vices. As Madison writes in *Federalist* #51, "ambition must be made to counteract ambition," which implies a soundly designed structure remains in place to make it so. Unbalancing the system, as the Bank did, prevented it from counteracting ambition against ambition properly, giving an undue advantage to the financial elites in the Northeast, especially Duer. We can see that most clearly in how the Bank ensnared members of Congress, according to Beckley. As Jefferson asserted to Washington, a fair vote on the Bank might have produced a very different result, had it not been for the profit members were taking from the Bank. Little wonder that Madison flipped from being a proponent of federally chartered institutions to one of its fiercest critics. This sort of behavior is exactly what had appalled him in the states in the 1780s.

Historians, political pundits, and the civic minded have long viewed the fight over the Bank as the opening salvo in the battle between partisans in the debate over more or less government, a conflict that continues to this very day. It also serves as an epitome for the argument of this book. For the style of corruption bred by the Bank will recur time and again: ambitious national leaders see some problem that the existing powers granted under the plain meaning of the Constitution do not allow; they expand those powers successfully; this may or may not solve the problem, but it disrupts the balance the Constitution hopes to achieve; and it lends itself to corruption as one faction or another can take advantage of the new weaknesses within the system.

And, as we shall see in the next chapter, such innovations in governmental power—once successfully claimed—are virtually irrevocable. The Republicans rode to power on a wave of popular discontent in 1800, but once installed in office, they accepted many Hamiltonian innovations and added several new powers to the federal menu. Corruption, unsurprisingly, followed soon thereafter, in no small part because the managers of these powers could not hold a candle to Hamilton.

As Madison argues in *Federalist* #10:

> It is in vain to say that enlightened statesmen will be able to adjust these clashing interests, and render them all subservient to the public good. Enlightened statesmen will not always be at the helm. Nor, in many cases, can such an adjustment be made at all without taking into view indirect and remote considerations, which will rarely prevail over the immediate interest which one party may find in disregarding the rights of another or the good of the whole.[63]

Fortunately, there was an enlightened statesmen to manage the nation's financial affairs in the early 1790s. As we shall see, Gallatin—himself possessed of extraordinary capacities—would manage ably the Bank after the Republicans took control. But, per Madison, it is in vain to say that men like Hamilton and Gallatin will be there when they are most needed. The Bank may not have exhibited the worst potentialities that Madison feared, *but its successor would.* As hack politicians replaced exemplary souls at its helm, a corrupt Second Bank would bring the country unneeded economic misery in 1819. And worse would soon follow.

2

"The Spirit of the Nation Forbids It"

Nationalism and Corruption from Jefferson to Jackson

FOR HOW FIERCE the battle between Republicans and Federalists raged during the 1790s, it is amazing that the latter's vision of America would so thoroughly triumph in a relatively short order. It is more amazing still that the Republicans would be key players in the Federalist policy victory. Yet that is precisely what happened. If the James Madison of 1789 can be reconciled to the Madison of 1791, as argued in the prior chapter, it is harder to reconcile him to the Madison of 1816, whose attitude toward the national government was often indistinguishable from many of the Federalists he had once so vehemently opposed.

After the Republican victory in 1800, the Federalists were to limp slowly off the political scene, with Alexander Hamilton suffering a brutal end, slain in a duel with Vice President Aaron Burr in 1803. The Republicans were then faced with the very problems that plagued Hamilton. For all their philosophical scruples, they had no novel answers on how to grow and manage the new nation, and they ultimately relied upon the insights he had laid out more than a decade before: a powerful national government based on a generous interpretation of the Constitution could yield a more perfect union by guiding national policy—foreign and domestic—toward a series of sensible goals like economic growth and sovereign independence.

Indeed, both the Federalists and Republicans—in their ways—committed to a kind of American empire. Hamilton, as we saw in *Federalist* #10, proposed an economically powerful America that could rival the

41

European powers, and his policies were designed to bring that about. The Republicans hated the Hamiltonian program, which they saw as expanding the powers of government too far. Even so, once in power they were similarly drawn to what Thomas Jefferson had once called an "Empire of Liberty." The Republicans envisioned a nation that filled in the vast expanses of the North American continent, and to bring that about they too advanced a program that stretched the powers of the Constitution well beyond their original limits. They called for protective tariffs, territorial acquisition, federal internal improvements, and even a Second Bank of the United States.

But the original insights of the old Republican opposition were no less valid, even if they were impractical for managing an empire: growing the powers of the government without modifying its structures ran the risk of corruption. It undermined the principle of checks and balances, and limited the capacity of the government to self-correct, to make sure that only the public interest was being served, rather than private and parochial interests.

Thus, it should come as no surprise that the upsides of Hamiltonianism —sensible economic policy; vigorous foreign policy—also brought the downsides—corruption. Governmental perfidy became rampant during the James Monroe administration of 1817 to 1825, but it was during the tenure of Andrew Jackson that it transformed into outright lawlessness. Jackson believed that he was a defender of the old Republican faith, but in reality he supported a big government when and as it suited his political agenda, and worse he was more than happy to enforce or not enforce the law according to similar dictates. In Nicholas Biddle, the president of the Second Bank of the United States, he met a foe every bit as crafty and deluded as he, and the lawless battle between the two dragged the American economy into a needless recession.

———————

The political battles of the 1790s were some of the most polarizing and divisive that the country has ever seen. Hamilton's economic agenda of the early part of the decade set the stage, but the outbreak of war between Britain and France—the country's two largest trading partners—meant that foreign affairs would dominate much of George Washington's second term. The Federalists narrowly carried the day in 1796, with Vice President John Adams barely edging former Secretary of State Jefferson in the Electoral College. Political intrigue by the French gave the pro-British Federalists the advantage in the 1798 midterm elections, after which they controlled nearly 60 percent of all House seats and better than two-thirds of the Senate.

But the Federalists overplayed their hand, expanding the military and passing the grossly un-republican Alien and Sedition Acts, politicized laws that trampled on the Bill of Rights to target their Republican opposition. That, plus the abatement of war fever, led to a Republican resurgence in 1800, with Jefferson narrowly winning the presidency and the Republicans taking control of the entire Congress.

This would mark the beginning of the end for the Federalist Party. Ironically enough, it was strong trade with Britain that facilitated economic prosperity and thus the Republicans' political victories during the first term of Jefferson. The breakdown of relations with Britain in Jefferson's second term and Madison's first term helped bring about a Federalist mini-revival in the Northeast, but none of this was enough to give them control of either chamber of Congress, let alone the presidency. During the War of 1812, economic tumult hit the Northeast particularly hard, and radical Federalists in New England floated the idea of secession during the Hartford Convention in 1814, which further delegitimized Hamilton's old party.[1] With the conclusion of the war in 1816, the country rejoiced and the Federalists were finished, not even running a presidential candidate in 1820.[2]

With the decline of the Federalists, New England was essentially left on the outside looking in. Control of the country shifted to a coalition of the South and West, helmed for twenty-four years by the "Virginia Dynasty." Jefferson served two terms as president, to be followed by his friend Madison for another two, then for another two by Monroe, a sometimes friend, sometimes foe of Madison but always a close confidant of Jefferson. To this day, the Republican dominance of government for the first quarter of the nineteenth century is unmatched in American history in terms of length and breadth.[3]

This dominance of the government meant that the Republicans alone had to face the very problems that had bedeviled the Federalists during the 1790s. And of course, these were tribulations that Republicans did not have to endure at that point, seeing as how they were a minority coalition. Jefferson and Madison could cite chapter and verse of republican philosophy to decry the Bank of the United States, but that is not to say they had an alternative to stabilize the currency, promote credit, or facilitate tax payments. They did not.

This goes a long way to explaining why, after acquiring control of the government, they slowly but surely adopted much of the Federalist program, and even expanded the scope of government beyond what the Hamiltonians had proposed. And as for the republican ideals of the 1790s? Implicitly, the Republicans adopted a vaguely aristocratic attitude: as long as the government was controlled by sensible Republicans (such as they), the country need not fear the kind of corruption that was supposed to have been ruining the body politic in the decade prior.

The Republican comfort with governmental power began to grow in Jefferson's first term. His first annual message to Congress called for the reduction of taxes, a cut in the military, and a plan to retire the national debt, all consistent with the Republican policy of the 1790s. However, Jefferson ultimately made no moves against the Bank. Over the course of his term, he made noises within his cabinet about ending the Bank's monopoly on federal deposits, but his secretary of the treasury, Albert Gallatin, consistently stayed his hand. An enormously influential Republican who had served as Republican House leader after Madison departed the lower chamber, the Swiss-born Gallatin was a close confidant of Jefferson and probably the only major party leader with a firm grasp of how public credit actually functioned. He saw the utility of the Bank and consistently sidestepped the issue whenever Jefferson pressed him to take action on it.[4]

Interestingly, the Jefferson administration also spent *more* on internal improvements than either of its Federalist predecessors, despite the Republican insistence on economy in government. The Republicans could have their cake and eat it too: economic prosperity meant they could cut taxes while also spending more than Washington or Adams had on domestic projects. Yet Jefferson's most extraordinary expansion of government power, especially the authority of the president, came in the realm of foreign affairs.

The Louisiana Purchase is the most striking example. After the successful coup by former slaves in Haiti, Napoleon Bonaparte effectively gave up his pretensions to a French empire in North America, and looked to divest his nation of its expansive holdings on the continent. The Republicans, naturally, were more than happy to cut a deal, but Jefferson worried about the constitutional implications. There was nothing in the founding document to empower the government not only to acquire new territory, but also integrate foreign peoples such as those living in New Orleans. The president floated the idea of an amendment so empowering the government, but concerns about whether the fickle Napoleon would have second thoughts made that inadvisable.

In the end, Jefferson cast aside his constitutional scruples, implicitly adopting the very same sort of rationale that Hamilton had argued in his defense of the Bank to Washington some twelve years prior: that this power, while not explicitly enumerated, was nonetheless implicit in the very nature of sovereignty itself.[5] According to John Quincy Adams, Jefferson's action was "an assumption of implied powers greater in itself and more comprehensive in its consequences than the assumptions of implied powers in the twelve years of the Washington and Adams administrations put together."[6]

The prosperity the nation enjoyed during Jefferson's first term turned out to be fleeting, premised largely upon Great Britain indulging American traders with unique access to its markets. But as the Napoleonic Wars once again heated up, Britain cracked down, and soon so also did Napoleon. How would America handle this two-sided squeeze? Madison, who by this point was serving as Jefferson's secretary of state, suggested an embargo: America would not trade with either country as long as they violated her rights as a sovereign and independent nation.

Madison believed that this would inflict more pain on the European powers than the Americans, but he was sorely mistaken. American commerce suffered and, worse, the federal government instituted what historian Forrest McDonald calls a "15 month reign of oppression and repression that was unprecedented in American history."[7] In response to the embargo, many merchants simply ignored the law, prompting Jefferson to come down on state governors with a vehemence that was uncharacteristic of the eighteenth-century champion of states' rights. What's more, Jefferson proposed that the government be empowered to seize cargo without a warrant or promise of a trial, even on the barest suspicion of violation; he also suggested that the army and navy be empowered to enforce the Embargo Act. Such a failure of public policy was this initiative, and so contrary to the republican principles that led to Jefferson's triumph in 1800, that the Republicans replaced it with the less onerous Non-Intercourse Act early in Madison's tenure, and historians have since judged it a black mark on Jefferson's record.[8]

It is easy to castigate Jefferson for his hypocrisy in both instances, but that would overlook the tension at the heart of the early nineteenth century, between American aspirations to greatness and her republican ideals. This was hardly resolved by the defeat of the Federalists in 1800; instead, the burden, and priorities, of the empire shifted to the Republicans. Hamilton primarily envisioned an Atlantic-focused empire, or at least his policies were primarily concerned with carving out America's role in the world vis-à-vis the European powers. Meanwhile, the Republicans were much more focused on expanding into and developing the interior of the continent, an Empire of Liberty already mentioned above.[9] Regardless of emphasis, the word "greatness" is an apt description of both policy agendas, and their quests for greatness invariably came into conflict with the republican limits implied by the Constitution.

It was the Republican quest that precipitated the most ill-conceived war the United States would find itself in during the whole of the nineteenth century, the War of 1812. By the end of Madison's first term, diplomacy had failed to induce England or France to respect America's trading rights, and a new generation of Republican politicians—men like Henry Clay of Kentucky and John C. Calhoun of South Carolina—had entered the government with a hunger for glory. For them, nothing could be better than the acquisition of Canada from the British.[10] Thus, the United States declared war on Great Britain on June 18, 1812.

Unfortunately, the county lacked the institutions necessary to carry on an effective war effort. The Bank's charter expired in 1811, and while Gallatin—whom Madison retained as secretary of the treasury—urged a renewal, the president was largely silent on the matter and Congress narrowly rejected it. As the conflict with Great Britain approached, Republicans assumed that acquiring loans to run the government during wartime would be an easy matter, but they were wrong.[11] So hard up during the war was Gallatin that he actually proposed an executive charter of a new bank without the assent of Congress.[12] Worse, the destruction of the Bank brought into being a large number of local banks chartered to fill the void. These institutions lent with gross irresponsibility, and the proliferation of bank notes during the early years of the war led to the eventual suspension of specie payments and devastating levels of price inflation.[13]

The military was also woefully underprepared for war with Britain. An integral aspect of the Republican ideology was the virtue of the volunteer militia. Standing armies were a Jeffersonian bugaboo, and the Republicans believed that citizen soldiers could do the work just as well without threatening the republican quality of the nation.[14] They were wrong, and as a consequence the American invasion of Canada was a complete failure. Worse, after Napoleon abdicated in the spring of 1814, the British were free to counterattack. Washington was burned to the ground, and it was only for improbable victories at Plattsburgh and Baltimore that America did not have to cede any territory when the peace was finally signed.[15]

Jackson's victory in the Battle of New Orleans—coming a few weeks after the Treaty of Ghent was negotiated—salvaged American pride, but the reality was that the country accomplished none of its initial goals. Fortunately, the final conclusion of Britain's long conflict with Napoleon meant that the pressure on American commerce was removed.[16] Historians have since judged this conflict to be largely fruitless, but Americans of that day and age did not see things that way. They felt that it was a vindication of their sovereign rights as an independent nation, and a laudable demonstration of the American will. Amidst all this enthusiasm, Monroe was elected to succeed Madison in 1816, winning every state except Connecticut, Delaware, and Massachusetts.

Yet the "victory" in the War of 1812 ultimately brought discord within the Republican coalition. A growing nationalist faction within the party began pushing for an expansion of federal authority, beyond that which Jefferson had sanctioned. Leaders like Clay, Calhoun, and Quincy Adams— with the backing of Monroe (and, for the most part, Madison)—began to recognize the limits of strict Republicanism, and promoted a decidedly Hamiltonian program of protective tariffs to encourage American industry, a Second Bank to stabilize the nation's finances, internal improvements to bind the country together, and an expanded military.[17] Perhaps Monroe summarizes this Republican change of heart better than anybody:

> By the war we have acquired a character and rank among other nations which we did not enjoy before. We stand pledged to support this rank and character by the adoption of such measures as may evince on the part of the United States a firm resolution. We cannot go back. The spirit of the nation forbids it.[18]

This is more than a little reminiscent of Hamilton's call to national greatness in *Federalist* #11. Indeed, if the former secretary of the treasury had not been killed by Burr some twelve years earlier, he might have responded, "I told you so!"

In that famous dinner conversation between Adams, Jefferson, and Hamilton, the last expressed not only a level of comfort with corruption in government, but thought it integral to its proper function. As we noted in Chapter One, he declared of the British Constitution, "Purge it of its corruption, and give to its popular branch equality of representation, & it would become an impracticable government."

The Republicans of the 1810s and '20s thought they could have a Hamiltonian-sized government without the corruption, but they were wrong. Though many historians have remembered the twenty or so years after the War of 1812 as the dawning of American nationalism, it also marked the rise of rampant political corruption, which reached such a level by Jackson's second term that it challenged the very concept of the rule of law.[19] This was the price that America had to pay for accepting a more expansive notion of government without insisting on institutional reforms.

The most infamous example during this period came during the election of 1824. The story of the "corrupt bargain" between Clay and Quincy Adams has been told again and again. Clay, then the speaker of the House, had it in his power to decide who would be the next president, and after a private meeting chose Quincy Adams, who in turn named him secretary of state. While there is no direct evidence of a quid pro quo, the sequence of events rightly prompted nationwide outrage. Historian Harry Watson makes the point that an explicit bargain was not necessary for the outcome to be offensive: "to preserve their consciences in the expected proprieties of the day, the two men probably failed to state the bargain explicitly, but their gentlemen's agreement had violated the standards of strict Republican morality."[20] But that breach of the public trust had less to do with the growth of government than the decay of the first party system, about which we will have more to say in Chapter Three.

Government growth nevertheless bred many innovative forms of perfidy, which unfortunately would become models for future generations of politicians on the make. Congress, unsurprisingly, had its fair share of scoundrels. The Republican embrace of internal improvements led to congressional logrolling (where legislators agree to support each other's pet projects), such as with the omnibus rivers and harbors legislation of 1826.[21] This meant in practice that Clay's "American System"—a harmonization of sectional interests into a unified whole—achieved much less coherence than promised.[22]

Protective tariffs had a similar effect, facilitating regional payoffs and political corruption beyond what was previously possible. The most egregious example involved the aptly named "Tariff of Abominations" in 1828. Recognizing a growing national demand for a new protective tariff, Jackson's allies in Congress sought to have it both ways. Jackson's political base in the South did not want a new tariff, but the Mid-Atlantic swing states, especially Pennsylvania, desperately desired new protection; so Martin Van Buren and Silas Wright of New York and James Buchanan of Pennsylvania conspired to draft a tariff so extreme that (they thought) it would inevitably fail. Their tariff proposal layered gift upon gift for this industry and that sector of the economy, especially those situated in the Keystone State. Southern members of the House allowed the bill to pass through the lower chamber, believing that it would be struck down in the Senate, as it contained duties deemed too onerous for New England. But the Southerners miscalculated; after some amendments to make the tariff palatable to the Northeast, it passed through the Congress and was signed into law by President Quincy Adams. The Jacksonians reaped a huge political windfall and the Mid-Atlantic won an enormous economic payoff, but the southern economy suffered.[23]

Members of Congress not only played fast and loose with the legislature's taxing and spending powers, they also gladly collected kickbacks from powerful men in society. Perhaps the most notorious, but certainly not the only, legislator on the take was Daniel Webster, the famous orator who for half a century defended American nationalism with an unmatched eloquence. Webster, nevertheless, was an avid speculator with a taste for the finer things in life. He was persistently hard-pressed for money and was more than happy to use his influence for personal gain, as well as tip his friends and family off about public policy that could prove profitable.[24] He was not alone. Clay was on the payroll of the Second Bank and Missouri senator Thomas Hart Benton was a legal representative for John Jacob Astor.[25] Even presidents were on the hook: Monroe borrowed a tidy sum from Astor during the War of 1812 and was persistently unable to pay back his wealthy benefactor. No matter! Astor eventually leaned on President Monroe to rescind an order prohibiting foreigners from engaging in the fur trade, something that greatly aided his American Fur Company.[26]

Corruption was rampant in the executive departments as well, especially the Department of War and the all-important Treasury Department, which had oversight over the Second Bank and its state satellites.[27] The Second Bank in particular was a cesspool of corruption in its early years. Modeled after its predecessor, most of its directors were picked by private shareholders while the government named a minority.[28] The Madison administration chose five solid Republicans for the board and worked behind the scenes to have a Republican crony selected as president.[29] That duty fell to William Jones, former secretary of the navy and interim secretary of the treasury. In the latter position, he had proven himself wholly incapable of his duties, but in the former had demonstrated a keen understanding of how the political game worked, doling out patronage to friends, family, and political allies with great skill.[30] That, plus his Republican bona fides as well as his residence in Philadelphia (where the Second Bank was head-quartered) made him a natural choice. His ignorance of public finance was not a concern.

The administration of Jones, a "corrupt and venal man" as historian Robert Remini describes him, stands in stark contrast to that of Hamilton during his tenure at the Treasury Department.[31] In the 1790s, Republicans cried bloody murder about the potentially devastating corruption that could emanate from the Bank, but while venality did spring forth from it, the capable management of Hamilton meant that its broader effects were generally limited. This went a long way to proving the viability of Hamilton's assumption that a natural aristocracy could handle a large governmental operation, managing and controlling corruption with an eye toward the public good. But what happens when a party functionary is at the helm, rather than a natural aristocrat? The public found out in the first few years of the Second Bank's operation, as Jones was totally out of his depth, and on the take.

For starters, he and the Second Bank's directors allowed a clique of stockjobbers to take control of the Baltimore branch, which was robbed of more than $1 million before the truth came out.[32] The president of the branch, one of the directors, and the cashier formed a company intent on cornering the market on bank stock with an eye to inflating its price.[33] They purchased something on the order of $4.5 million worth of bank stock, financed in part by loans from the Second Bank itself: $1.7 million from the Baltimore branch and $2 million from the Philadelphia headquarters. They also farmed out nominal ownership of the shares to thousands of dummy investors to get around rules limiting how many votes any single investor could have. Ultimately, as few as fifteen people in Baltimore owned three-fourths of the stock there.[34] Jones noticed none of this, nor any of the stockjobbing going on all across the country; indeed, he even accepted an $18,000 gift from officers at the Second Bank, which had been made on rampant speculation.[35]

Worse than this was Jones's gross mismanagement of the nation's economy. In theory, the Second Bank's monopoly over federal deposits gave it control over the state banks, and therefore capacity to regulate credit and even the broader business cycle. In practice, nominating a political hack whose tenure at the Treasury Department was a model of incompetence meant that the Second Bank was part of the problem in the postwar economy.

Following the War of 1812, American exports boomed to meet a growing demand for staples in Europe. Banks all across the country lent generously, and thus a credit-fueled bubble quickly followed. It finally burst in late 1818 when the price of cotton plummeted on the Liverpool exchange, and the forthcoming Panic of 1819 plunged the country into a nasty recession.[36] The Second Bank was not the primary culprit for the panic, but it did shoulder some of the burden. If Jones had been an able and sensible manager of the national credit, he could have foreseen what was coming and acted in advance to tighten credit and gain control over the irresponsible practices of the state banks. Instead, he did precisely the opposite, fueling the credit bubble. In August 1817, he waived the requirement that the second installment of payments for Second Bank stock be remitted in specie, or hard coin, enabling investors to retain their shares with very little money down.[37] He also did not mandate that the branch banks have fixed capital, meaning that there was no rational credit plan emanating from Philadelphia. Bank branches in the South and West, managed by men whose ignorance of finance matched Jones's, happily authorized loans that could never practically be paid back.[38] By July 1818, the Second Bank's demand liabilities were $22.4 million compared to just $2.4 million worth of specie in its vaults, double the legal limit.[39]

At that point, the game was up and the Second Bank initiated a painful contraction of credit that contributed to a depression in prices. Exports, valued at $83 million in 1818, fell to $54.5 million in 1821; import prices fell from $120 million to $54.5 million.[40] As historian George Dangerfield notes, "Trade stagnated; the price of staples swooned downwards; real property depreciated and its rents or profits vanished; merchants, even the most reputable, were ruined; and in the larger cities, unemployment spread like a plague."[41]

Under enormous political pressure, Jones resigned in 1819, and his successor—Langdon Cheves of South Carolina—continued the contraction. By 1820, the Second Bank notes in circulation amounted to $3.5 million, down from $8 million in 1818. Cheves restored the Second Bank's financial soundness, but the damage to the broader economy was great. According to contemporary economist (and hard money advocate) William Gouge, "The bank was saved, and the people were ruined."[42] Modern economic research has confirmed this analysis, concluding that Cheves's contraction was more severe than necessary. By April 1819, the Bank was fundamentally sound, but the contraction continued until Cheves was pushed out in 1823, to be replaced by Biddle of Pennsylvania.

Biddle comes across the pages of history much as Hamilton does: cosmopolitan, intelligent, broad-minded, ahead of his time, and exceedingly arrogant. Both men believed in a natural aristocracy and felt as though they were rightful members of it, and both were, more or less, correct. Unlike his predecessors, Biddle understood the beneficial role the Second Bank could play in the national economy, and he set about realizing that goal. To his everlasting credit, he was quite successful, taking the concept of a central bank farther than had been accepted even in England by that point.[43] From the time Biddle took control of the Second Bank in 1823 until Jackson's reelection in 1832, it expanded its loans many times over, especially in the South and West.[44] Even still, it managed successfully to restrain the state banks and even get in front of an economic panic that was brewing in England by 1825.[45] Little wonder that, by the time of the Second Bank's request for recharter in 1832, it had achieved broad popularity. Gallatin, by that point the *éminence grise* of Republican finance, gave it his blessing.[46]

Yet Biddle was not above the political fray, even though he personally claimed no interest in partisan gamesmanship. The fact is that Biddle had a lot of friends in high places, in no small part because he purchased them. The case of Webster has been noted above, as were Calhoun and Clay, all of whom Biddle courted assiduously. Various other members of Congress were also lubricated with generous loan terms as well as the privilege of receiving advances on their salaries.[47] Newspapermen were also eligible for loans that were not strictly above board.[48] Additionally, the primary responsibility of Biddle was to the Second Bank itself, despite his pretensions to being a magnanimous agent of national prosperity. Recent economic scholarship notes that the Second Bank made a tidy sum in the domestic exchange market, and it questions whether it really facilitated it or just profited off this emerging form of commerce.[49]

Nevertheless, contemporary sentiment regarding the Second Bank was generally positive by the end of the 1820s, and has more or less been vindicated by modern scholarship. Unfortunately for the Second Bank—and, as it turned out, the country at large—there was one implacable foe standing in its path. Jackson—"Old Hickory," the "Hero of New Orleans," the "Sharp Knife" as the Native Americans called him—wanted nothing more than to destroy the Second Bank, and as with so much else, he ended up getting his way.

In his three-volume biography of Jackson, Remini sets up his entrance into national politics as a tonic for the "Age of Corruption" we have been discussing. He argues that Old Hickory saw himself fundamentally as a reformer, in the mold of Jefferson and the old guard Republicans (who by that point fancied themselves as the "Quids," or a third force aligned against the remaining Federalists and the National Republicans), carving out the rot that had grown within the institutions of government. Indeed, examining Jackson's two most noteworthy policy messages—his vetoes of the Maysville Road spending bill and of the recharter for the Second Bank—it is clear that he saw himself as a Republican committed to limited, constitutional government as a bulwark against corruption.

Yet a fair examination of the historical record demonstrates that, while Jackson may have been reacting to the venality of his age, he approached the office of president with a level of capriciousness that had not been seen before his day, and perhaps not after, either. As we shall see, Jackson's sins against the republican virtues he presumed to defend were certainly greater than those that got Andrew Johnson and Bill Clinton impeached, and his crimes against the Native Americans were far worse than anything Richard Nixon ever did.

Jackson often comes across as a kind of American caesar. Deeply committed to the rule of law and the empowerment of the common folk, he nevertheless conflated, time and again, those virtues with his own interests. Indeed, as historian Daniel Walker Howe ably demonstrates, "It was his personal authority, rather than that of the federal government or even the presidential office, which Jackson zealously maintained."[50]

His character was fully evident well before he ever assumed the presidency. His past deeds included holding the city of New Orleans under martial law until well after news of the Treaty of Ghent was made known; extorting fraudulent treaties from the Native Americans, in which the latter were forced to give up tens of thousands of acres; disobeying orders by attacking Spanish positions in Florida, then declaring martial law; and even profiting from his military adventures (his family and friends received advance notice of his Florida conquest, with an advisory that land prices in Florida would soon be going upward).[51] As chief executive of the United

States from 1829 to 1837, Jackson's record does not so much justify his self-perception as a Republican reformer combating corrupt practices, but rather portrays a fundamentally lawless ruler using corruption to combat (equally corrupt) politicians whose interests diverged from his own.

At the core of the republican ideology is the idea that similarly situated people should be treated similarly; deviation from this norm suggests the existence of corruption, be it technically legal or not. And on that measure Jackson was enormously deficient, in small ways and large. On the small end of the scale was his hypocrisy on internal improvements. In the statement accompanying his veto of the Maysville Road—a favored project of his political rival Clay—Jackson worries that the Constitution did not permit such an expenditure, which "concedes to the government an unlimited power."[52] Instead, he claims to favor only internal improvements based on the principle that they benefit the nation as a whole. Otherwise, the country ran the risk of

> promot(ing) a mischievous and corrupting influence upon elections by holding out to the people the fallacious hope that the success of a certain candidate will make navigable their neighboring creek or river, bring commerce to their doors, and increase the value of their property. It thus favors combinations to squander the treasure of the country upon a multitude of local objects, as fatal to just legislation as to the purity of public men.[53]

If ever there was a fair articulation of the Republican concern about internal improvements, this was it, but Jackson failed to live up to his own rhetoric. The fact of the matter is that government spending on internal improvements skyrocketed during Jackson's tenure, reaching an average cost of nearly $0.13 per person, more than any other president in the antebellum period.[54] And this spending did not follow pure Republican principle; rather, federal appropriations during this period had the distinct flavor of pork barrel politics to it. Jackson and his party loyalists in Congress often distributed funds for internal improvements based on the political salience of the appropriation.[55]

Jackson was also an inconsistent advocate of national authority, with the only clear dividing line being what was and was not his political priority. The story of Jackson staring down the South Carolina nullifiers is well known. The Palmetto State's Ordinance of Nullification of 1832 declared the tariff laws recently passed into law null and void in South Carolina. Jackson—whose political coalition had been responsible for the abusive Tariff of Abomination—reacted with righteous indignation. He warned

South Carolina that it had no authority to do that, and promised "that if a single drop of blood shall be shed there in opposition to the laws of the United States, I will hang the first man I can lay my hand on engaged in such treasonable conduct, upon the first tree I can reach."[56]

Jackson, of course, was right to be outraged by South Carolina's blatantly illegal actions. What is less known, however, is how happily he excused the equally lawless maneuvers by the states of Georgia and Mississippi in their efforts to oust the Native Americans from their legal property. Sharp Knife had stronger opinions on Native American affairs than any of his recent predecessors in the White House; while the latter acknowledged that removal of the native tribes to an area west of the Mississippi was advisable, Jackson made this a priority of his administration.[57] The trouble for Jackson was that the tribes of the region had treaties with the federal government that protected their lands from state encroachment. It was such a treaty with the Creek nation that prompted Quincy Adams to send the federal attorney to Georgia to warn that, if the state's agents entered Creek territory to conduct an illegal survey, they would be arrested. While not as celebrated as Jackson's victory over the South Carolina nullifiers, Adams's justification rested on the same basis: the supremacy of federal laws over the states.[58] But Jackson had no time for any of this. Clearing the Native Americans out was a priority for him, and he used the states as the bad cop to his good cop. Taking on the pretensions of a benevolent father, Jackson warned the Native American tribes that he could not stop the states from abusing the treaties, and urged them to remove to the West.[59] Never mind, of course, that he simultaneously was threatening to hang South Carolinians who violated the tariff laws.

In Jacksonian America, "princeps legibus solutus est": the sovereign is not bound by the law.[60] Biddle would learn this the hard way.

If the experience of the War of 1812 taught the Republicans that their nationalistic pretensions were incompatible with their Republican scruples, then the Bank War between Biddle and Jackson served to dramatize the point. By 1832, America had chartered a national bank to promote the economy and empowered a kinglike president to pursue (his vision of) the national good. Neither of these institutions was entirely in keeping with the principles of the past generation; certainly, both ran more than a modest risk of the corruption that the Republicans of the 1790s found intolerable. When they were arrayed against one another, as in the Bank

War, the result was economic hardship and rampant lawlessness. If Hamilton would have had cause to gloat in 1816, certainly Jefferson would have been due a similar indulgence in 1834.

As noted above, the Second Bank was popular by the time Jackson entered the White House in 1829, and not just in New England and Philadelphia, where one presumes the economy favored such an institution. Biddle's efforts to expand credit to the South and West created a broad base of support in those regions as well. When the recharter came up for a congressional vote in 1832, it received support from all sectors of the country, and testimonials in favor of the Second Bank streamed in from the South and West.[61]

Indeed, it was the popularity of the Second Bank that Biddle thought he could leverage against Jackson, who had expressed his disregard for the institution as early as his first annual presidential message. Jackson's own financial difficulties had led him to distrust banks in general, and prefer only specie as the circulating medium.[62] He further believed that the Second Bank represented everything that was wrong with the "Era of Good Feelings"; it concentrated power within the hands of a few, unelected moneymen who had the authority to make or break millions of ordinary Americans. On this matter, as with so many others, it is clear how the lines between Jackson's own prejudices and his sense of the national interest were so easily blurred.

Biddle knew that Jackson was indisposed to his institution, but he also knew that Old Hickory was looking to roll up an enormous reelection victory in 1832, which required the support of pro-Second Bank Pennsylvania. Thus, he contemplated submitting a bill for recharter in 1832, four years before the existing charter expired, in the hopes that political pressure on Jackson would force it through. On this matter Clay, who was running for president on the National Republican ticket and looking for an issue to campaign on, encouraged him. On the other hand, the administration's friends of the Second Bank, above all Secretary of the Treasury Louis McClane, warned him that the request would provoke Jackson's anger. In the end, the most persuasive advice came from House Ways and Means Committee Chairman George McDuffie, an ally of Calhoun, who predicted Old Hickory would never assent to a recharter, and the time to strike was now, when members of Congress would be feeling the heat in advance of the election.[63]

It is difficult to square Biddle's political gamesmanship on the recharter with the principles of republican virtue. It certainly was not to be found in the Second Bank's charter that its president had the authority to pressure politicians the way Biddle so clearly did. And from Old Hickory's perspective, it was downright outrageous. Though the historical record suggests that Biddle was not in fact in cahoots with Clay, he nevertheless submitted a petition for recharter shortly after the National Republicans formally declared themselves in favor of the Second Bank.[64] This raised Jackson's dander, and he would not rest until this enemy was destroyed.

The Congress overwhelmingly voted to recharter the Second Bank, but Jackson sent back a veto message that has served as clarion call for class warriors ever since:

> It is to be regretted that the rich and powerful too often bend the acts of government to their selfish purposes. Distinctions in society will always exist under every just government. Equality of talents, of education, or of wealth can not be produced by human institutions. In the full enjoyment of the gifts of Heaven and the fruits of superior industry, economy, and virtue, every man is equally entitled to protection by law; but when the laws undertake to add to these natural and just advantages artificial distinctions, to grant titles, gratuities, and exclusive privileges, to make the rich richer and the potent more powerful, the humble members of society-the farmers, mechanics, and laborers-who have neither the time nor the means of securing like favors to themselves, have a right to complain of the injustice of their Government. There are no necessary evils in government. Its evils exist only in its abuses. If it would confine itself to equal protection, and, as Heaven does its rains, shower its favors alike on the high and the low, the rich and the poor, it would be an unqualified blessing. In the act before me there seems to be a wide and unnecessary departure from these just principles.[65]

This message has been quoted widely over the years, even making an appearance in Ted Kennedy's famous Dream Will Never Die speech at the 1980 Democratic convention. Regardless, its constitutional claims had essentially been rendered moot by the Supreme Court; its economic reasoning was rubbish (an "unctuous mixture of agrarianism and laissez faire" is how historian Bray Hammond puts it); and its provenance was pure hypocrisy, coming as it did from the president who had done more than any predecessor to pervert the rule of law to his own ends. For better or worse, it set a new precedent that presidents could veto bills simply because they did not like them; prior to the Second Bank veto, the operative rule was that the president was obliged to sign into law all constitutionally valid measures of Congress.

It also marked the start of a truly lawless period of American government, as Jackson and Biddle both violated their legal and moral responsibilities in a vain quest to destroy each other. Biddle launched the first salvo by committing the Second Bank thoroughly to the defeat of Jackson in the upcoming presidential campaign. He poured thousands upon thousands of dollars of the Second Bank's money into the battle, prompting New York senator and Jackson ally William Marcy to fret, "The U.S. Bank is in the field and I cannot but fear the effect of $50,000 or $100,000 expected in conducting the election in such a city as New York."[66] Biddle even went so far as to distribute 30,000 copies of Jackson's veto message, foolishly believing that it would aid the Second Bank's cause.

In the end, Jackson won reelection easily, albeit it with a smaller share of the vote than he had carried four years prior. That should have been the end of the matter: Jackson was reelected; the recharter was defeated; and the existing charter was set to expire before the end of Old Hickory's second term. But none of this was enough for Jackson, who wanted to see the Second Bank brought to its knees. To do that, he and his Kitchen Cabinet of intimate advisors adopted a plan to remove existing federal deposits from the Second Bank. Most of his official cabinet opposed that, including Secretary of Treasury William Duane, whom Jackson had installed because McLane had been too pro-Second Bank for the president.

By law, only the secretary of the treasury could remove the deposits, and only if he feared that they were not safe. But a recent inquiry had shown that the Second Bank was perfectly safe, with $79 million in assets to just $37 million in liabilities. The House of Representatives had even voted 109-46 to affirm that the deposits were secure. Duane had told Jackson that he would resign his office so the president could appoint somebody to carry out the order, but when the time came, the secretary refused to step down. So, Jackson fired him, replacing him with Roger Taney in an executive coup reminiscent of the "Saturday Night Massacre" during the Nixon administration.[67]

For Jackson, the legal niceties of the Second Bank charter were irrelevant. He had fought the Second Bank in the election, had won handily, and now had a mandate from the people to do exactly what he pleased, the law be damned. The Senate, controlled by Clay and the National Republicans, disagreed, and censured him by a vote of 26-20, the first and only such Senate act against a president.[68]

This, of course, did not deter Jackson, who instructed Amos Kendall, a key Kitchen Cabinet advisor, to find state banks willing to take on the public funds. Kendall was explicit that one of the criteria for selecting banks was that they were friendly to the administration, and an analysis of the historical record has demonstrated that approximately 79 percent of all "pet" banks selected to house government deposits were controlled by Jacksonians, with most of the rest being held by independents or National Republicans friendly to the administration. And so, in violating the law, Jackson not only destroyed his greatest political enemy, he also found a new form of patronage to secure his coalition.[69]

But Biddle had one last arrow in his quiver: a credit contraction. Inevitably, the federal assault on the Second Bank would have provoked some kind of response from the latter, if for nothing else than it was unsure of just how far Jackson was willing to go.[70] Nevertheless, historians have generally concluded that Biddle took matters farther than he needed to; what's more, there is Biddle's own admission to being motivated by politics to inflict economic pain on the country.[71] He wrote to one correspondent, "The relief, to be useful or permanent, must come from Congress and from Congress alone. If that body will do its duty, relief will come – if not, the Bank feels no vocation to redress the wrongs inflicted by these miserable people. Rely upon that. This worthy President thinks that because he has scalped Indians and imprisoned judges, he is to have his way with the bank. He is mistaken."[72] To another, he wrote: "Nothing but the affidavits of suffering abroad will produce any effect in Congress. . . . Our only safety is in pursuing a steady course of firm restriction – and I have no doubt that such a course will ultimately lead to restoration of the currency and the recharter of the bank."[73]

Thus, between January 1834 and October 1834 the Second Bank's reserve ratio rose from 0.371 to 0.670, and its specie reserve increased from $10 million to $15.6 million. The effect of this action was to drive the economy into a relatively mild recession, something on the order of the contraction experienced in 1949.[74] In the end, what stopped the Second Bank's squeeze was the widespread acknowledgment that the institution was sound, even with the deposits removed, and thus in a position to give relief, especially to New York investors. Still, even as Biddle loosened credit restrictions, he refused to help the banks in Washington and Baltimore, whose misfortunes traced back to the mismanagement of local pets (run by friends of Taney, no less).[75]

Biddle's lesson failed to take hold in the public mind, and his contraction meant the destruction of whatever credibility the Second Bank still had. Biddle slinked off the national scene; he secured for it a state charter in Pennsylvania, but it failed during the Panic of 1837. So complete was Jackson's victory, the United States would not implement anything approaching a sensible monetary policy until the Civil War.

Historians have remembered the period that spans Jefferson's inauguration in 1801 to the close of Jackson's presidency in 1837 in different ways. It has been called Jeffersonian Democracy and Jacksonian Democracy; it has been said to mark the rise of the market economy, the first full flowering of American nationalism, the birth of Manifest Destiny, and so on.

Here, we have examined it from a different perspective, tracking the demise of the Republicans' orthodoxy, their embrace of a more expansive government, and the corresponding rise of governmental corruption. The Republican Party had been organized to stop this growth of government, the loosening of the constitutional structures, and ultimately the corruption that followed; yet by the end of Monroe's tenure, they had accepted all of the Federalist agenda, and more.

Thus, less than a generation after his death, Hamilton's ideological triumph was all but complete. The reason for his victory should be clear enough by now: the Republican opposition of the 1790s was never more than that. It was a critique, a dire prophecy of doom and gloom, a jeremiad; it was not a positive program to deal with the nation's challenges. For all of its faults, at least Hamilton's agenda realistically addressed the problems facing America. How to establish real independence vis-à-vis the European powers? How to grow the national economy? How to bind the states into a permanent union? These are the questions that Hamilton obsessed over. His Republican opponents were not so burdened because, as an opposition party, they did not have the obligations of governance. When they finally got their hands on the levers of power, and faced the challenges that the former secretary of the treasury did, they discovered—sooner or later—the wisdom of the Hamiltonian perspective.

But—and herein lies the central paradox at the heart of American political corruption—none of this means the initial Republican critique of Hamilton was wrong. It simply means it was not suited to the demands of a would-be American empire. The Republicans, as we saw in Chapter One, were deeply concerned about retaining the balance among different forces in society for the sake of the public good; this was at the front and center of Madison's thinking. When Hamilton found its straightforward interpretation to be ill-suited for his national program, the Republicans warned that his innovations threatened the balance and would ultimately lead to corruption as factions within society would gain leverage to implement their own selfish ends. As we saw in Chapter One, that is precisely what occurred.

And, as we saw in this chapter, *it occurred again* when the Republicans mimicked Hamilton's program. Congress quickly turned internal improvements and protective tariffs into opportunities for electoral gamesmanship. Graft became an increasingly common phenomenon in the fast-expanding executive departments. Bad management, stockjobbing, political payoffs, and needless economic pain characterized the early management of the Second Bank of the United States. Jackson—the closest thing America has ever had to a caesar—shoved the Native Americans aside without regard to their treaty rights. And, worst of all, the Bank War between Jackson and Biddle was a fundamentally lawless test of wills that drove the country straight into an economic recession.

All of this can be traced—either indirectly or, in many cases, directly—to the growth of government beyond the Madisonian vision of the Constitution. Americans may have decided that they had no choice but to grow the government, that the demands of an Empire of Liberty required a more expansive view than that drawn up in Philadelphia in 1787. Nevertheless, in so doing, they effectively threw off a key tenet of Madison's thinking, that a considered delineation of political power across well-designed institutions was necessary to prevent corruption and protect a true republic. In other words, the problem was not so much that they abandoned their old ideas of limited government; it was, rather, that they did not update the government's institutions to handle these new powers responsibly.

Indeed, Jefferson's demurral from seeking a constitutional amendment for the Louisiana Purchase is illustrative. It was *inconvenient* for him to pursue such a structural update to the original design; better instead to seize the power before the unpredictable Napoleon changed his mind. While on the extreme end of the spectrum, this was not an isolated incident. In case after case during this period, we see Republicans behaving just as the Federalists did. The political externalities of national greatness were so pressing, they refused to consider whether the old structures of government could exercise these new powers responsibly.

Indeed, they could not. As a consequence, corruption came to the United States of America—and as we shall see, it was here to stay.

3

"The General Scramble for Plunder"

Patronage in Jacksonian America

A S WE HAVE SEEN, James Madison understood the framing of the Constitution as a search for republican balance. He sought to empower the national government to solve the pressing problems of the day, but he did not want to allow factionalism to overrun the system. Thus, he carefully tried to balance structures against powers to prevent any one faction from gaining too much power at the expense of the common good. As we saw in Chapter Two, the growth in the power of the national government beyond what the Framers intended threatened this balance, and led in due course to corruption. It was as if the Constitution was a scale, carefully calibrated when originally designed, but too much weight was added to one side, disrupting the equilibrium. Corruption was the inevitable result.

It was not just changes in power relations that would upend this balance. Changes in the institutions of government itself—independent of whether those institutions gained or lost power—could similarly disrupt the scale, and lend itself to corruption. Just as he carefully considered which branches of the government should possess which powers, Madison was just as attentive to how those branches should operate. As later generations altered those operations, the balance could be lost as well, creating new venues for corruption.

As we shall see, the democratization of the presidency and the rise of the two national political parties had precisely this effect.

At first blush, this might sound like a ridiculous assertion. After all, today's Democrats and Republicans, conservatives and liberals, all celebrate the Jacksonian revolution of popularly elected presidents. And furthermore, social scientists now uniformly recognize political parties as essential ingredients in democratic republics. How can benevolent developments such as these ever have become conduits of corruption?

Ultimately, the problem is that the Framers simply did not see either trend coming; thus, our governmental charter has nothing to say about political parties and implicitly assumes a government dominated by the Congress rather than the president. Did the Framers err in overlooking these developments? Perhaps. Durable political coalitions were already in existence in every state legislature of the union by 1787, and the very same democratizing influences that contributed to the Revolution ultimately led to a popularly elected president. On the other hand, the history of republican government up to that point had indicated pretty clearly that parties were not to be tolerated and managed, but rather squashed, and that legislatures—not executives—were the most dangerous institutions to republican governance.

Regardless of what they should have done, the Framers did not make provisions for these dual trends, which means that, benevolent or malevolent, they disrupted the original balance of the Constitution, altering fundamentally the way our government functions—in unanticipated ways.

These two developments—a democratized presidency and political parties—are causally related. The presidency has always been the greatest political prize in the republic. Democraticizing it changed the calculus of politicians seeking the office; to win, they must now mount nationwide electoral campaigns. This necessity facilitated the rise of national parties, as the state-based factions that had once characterized politics were not broad enough to accomplish this. The two major paries thus unite a broad array of actors in a shared quest for electoral victory; they rally like-minded voters all across the country, and they coordinate officials across federal, state, and local governments. This makes them important centripetal forces countering a very centrifugal Constitution.

As we shall see, by disrupting the way the Constitution anticipates the government will function, the combination of political parties and mass-based presidential elections has lent itself to corruption on an enormous scale. Whereas under the Constitution members of the Congress should be on the lookout for executive encroachment upon legislative prerogatives, the parties in pursuit of electoral victory undermine these institutional rivalries. Thanks to the party system, members of Congress of the same party often overlook such executive high-handedness insofar as it facilitates the party's electoral agenda, especially its quest for the presidency. Similarly, the president is now quite inclined to indulge members of Congress provided that they are affiliated with his own party. Because the Constitution has nothing to say about this dynamic, and indeed because this dynamic runs contrary to what Madison anticipated in *Federalist* #51, it is easy for such relations to devolve into corrupt devices that unbalance the republican experiment.

All of this helps us understand how the spoils system became rampant in the nineteenth century. The resources required to win a nationwide presidential election were too massive for parties to raise on their own, and so they turned to the public treasury for partisan purposes, rewarding their friends with jobs, contracts, sinecures, and so on as the spoils of victory. The Constitution anticipates that such corruption will not happen; the Congress is expected to check a president who abuses the public trust in such a fashion, or vice versa. But the political parties united these disparate entities in a shared quest for power, and therefore plunder. The result was an institutionalized form of corruption that would endure for generations, and indeed continues in one form or another to this very day.

———————

Political parties are integral to modern American democracy. As political scientist E. E. Schattschneider puts it, "they are in the center (of modern government) and play a determinative and creative role in it."[1] And not only in the United States, either; there is no democratic republic on the face of the planet that does not have a party system of one sort or another.

The reason, as scholars have come to understand, is that parties homogenize the vast diversity of opinions and interests within society, (hopefully) harnessing them in service to a greater good. In Congress, for instance, legislators confront a series of collective action and social choice problems, all of which relate one way or the other to getting a large, diverse body to work on behalf of shared goals. Political parties solve these problems by rewarding similarly minded legislators who work together.[2] Good partisans, for instance, who help advance the party's collective goals, often receive leadership positions, or plum committee spots; bad ones are sent off to backwater committees where their influence is minimized.[3]

Indeed, evidence suggests that legislative parties in Congress were in existence as early as 1791, and every state assembly during the 1780s had a legislative divide between the cosmopolitan coastal areas and the rough-hewn interiors. All of this should make sense: political parties seek to unify and harmonize groups of legislators into coherent coalitions, and in so doing help the legislature actually function.

Parties have uses beyond legislatures, as well. An important service they provide is regulating political ambition; would-be politicians who want to climb the career ladder ultimately must sacrifice their own interests to the goals sought by the whole party, at least to some extent. This ensures, again to an extent, that those who reach the upper echelons are reasonably qualified and disposed to serve the public good.[4]

Parties also regulate the scope of political conflict in the country. A nation as large as the United States has the potential for a limitless number of fights between the citizenry. Which become part of political conflict, and which are left out of the public sphere? It depends on how the parties respond—both individually and together—to these problems. Thanks to the work of parties, certain tensions become the source of political conflict while others remain latent. As we shall see, this was an important function that the Democrats and Whigs served during the Jacksonian period. The issue of slavery was always dangerous to the union between the North and the South; neither party had an interest in severing that union, so both conspired to keep the slavery problem at bay, at least for a time.[5]

Additionally, they serve an important function within the electorate. Mobilizing an electoral coalition in a nation as vast and diverse as the United States is no little feat. It requires tremendous effort by thousands of activists, not to mention the expenditure of vast fortunes. Who has the personal incentive to contribute so much? The answer is: nobody besides those who get to serve in office should the party win. That is certainly not going to cut it, and thus the challenge of party mobilization is a kind of public goods problem. The parties solve this similar to the way that the Public Broadcasting Service (PBS) does. Why donate during PBS pledge drives? It makes much more sense not to donate and enjoy the programming for free. This is why PBS offers you a tote bag, CDs, DVDs, or something, depending on your contribution. This is exactly what a political party does as well: it rewards people with private benefits when they contribute to the collective good of the party. In the modern era, contributors to the party often enjoy special access to officeholders; in Jacksonian America, many of them expected rewards like jobs or contracts. While the benefits have changed over time, the function of such benefits remains the same: for the donor, it is a private gift that only he can enjoy, thus giving him an incentive not to free ride and allow others to do the heavy lifting for the party.

Despite the many uses of political parties, the Framers of the Constitution were deeply suspicious of them. In Madison's view, the factionalism that had rent the state governments during the 1780s—between the coastal, commercial elites and the yeoman interior class—had nearly brought the nation's experiment in self-government to an end.[6] Political parties are, after all, organized factions, and Madison spoke for many when, in *Federalist* #10, he writes:

> By a faction, I understand a number of citizens, whether amounting to a majority or a minority of the whole, who are united and actuated by some common impulse of passion, or of interest, adverse to the rights of other citizens, or to the permanent and aggregate interests of the community. There are two methods of curing the mischiefs of faction: the one, by removing its causes; the other, by controlling its effects.[7]

In other words, no political party could have a truly public-spirited nature; inevitably, every last one of them was bound to favor some group over another, thus undermining the public interest.

An important purpose of the Constitution, per Madison in *Federalist* #10, is to "break and control the violence of faction." Rather than acknowledge the inevitability of political parties, the Constitution seeks to keep them from coalescing, by dispersing power far and wide. The hope was that no faction, or party, could possibly grab all the levers of political power for their own selfish purposes. While factions would inevitably form, they would not be able to attach themselves permanently to the government. Somewhere, somehow, an opponent would retain a toehold in the government to veto the designs of fractious majorities, and in time the partisan fever would break. This is why historian Richard Hofstadter calls the founding document a "Constitution against parties."[8]

It is thus quite surprising that the Framers would themselves become the originators of the party system. Why the change of heart? In fact, there was not really a change of heart at all, at least among the Republicans. They saw themselves as representing a truly public interest, that of the great majority of the country, and the Federalists as a minority faction, utilizing the preeminence of George Washington and, later, fear of war with the French, to confuse and beguile the public. Ultimately, the Republicans believed that they, and only they, were the representatives of the people, while the Federalists were suspicious of public opinion, and sought to separate the management of the government from the people. This is why Thomas Jefferson, Madison, and their allies could flip-flop so seamlessly from antiparty to proparty. They did not really see themselves as a party in the sense that we think of them today, and they certainly did not think of the Federalists as being a mass-based party like today's Democrats and Republicans. For them, Jefferson's triumph in 1800 heralded a restoration of the republican spirit of the Founding rather than the victory of one faction over another.[9]

Even though they would have denied that they were a party in the way we think of them today, they nevertheless acted like one. For instance, President Jefferson exercised tight control over his allies in Congress, prompting Federalist senator Timothy Pickering to complain, not without merit, that Jefferson "secretly dictates every measure which is seriously proposed and supported" in the Congress. The Republicans also developed a party organization that was a prototype of the modern variety. They believed that their restoration of constitutional principles required an active organization that would spur on the public; the Federalist threat, as they saw it, lay in the idleness of the great mass of people who were true Republicans. And so it was that the contest for the presidency in 1800 did more than any electoral battle in a generation to encourage the growth of party organizations in the states. While few states at this point had popular elections for the Electoral College, a series of battles for state government control in New Jersey, New York, Pennsylvania, and Virginia served as proxy battles for the presidency, and in these states the Republicans sought to organize a unified front.[10]

After Jefferson's victory, the Republican leadership hoped to separate the Federalist electorate from the party leadership. In his first inaugural, Jefferson declares, "We are all Federalists; we are all Republicans."[11] This was not meant as some kind of new age, gooey pabulum; instead, it signaled a policy of conciliation, an integral aspect to the Jeffersonian project. Much of this was covered in the previous chapter, as the Republicans increasingly adopted the Federalist domestic program. As we shall see later in this chapter, Jefferson and his Republican successors were relatively subdued (compared to the Jacksonians) in removing Federalist officeholders from the government. They hoped that they could peel off enough of their opposition to render this two-party system a dead letter.

While this strategy bore political fruit—as the Federalist position in Congress shriveled to virtually nothing and its capacity to contest presidential elections disappeared—not everybody on the Republican side was satisfied. John Randolph of Virginia and his "Quids" faction believed that the party's leadership had sold out its principles for the sake of political expedience. More often than not, the peculiar Quids were on the outside looking in during Madison and James Monroe's tenures, but New York political maven Martin Van Buren was a rising star who felt that the fusion policy of Monroe, which worked to further integrate Republicans with old Federalists, was handing power over to a crypto-Federalist contingency.

Van Buren has since been remembered as a founder of the two-party system, but like the early Republicans he denied the popular legitimacy of his opponents. The National Republicans, and later the Whigs (as his opponents would be called), in his view, were merely rebranded Federalists, who beguiled the public into voting against their own interests. As far as Van Buren was concerned, there was one party that represented the people's interests, the Republican Party. Where he differed from his predecessors was his opposition to reconciliation with the Federalists, believing that this weakened the party organization and thus undermined principled Republican governance. A robust party organization, clearly delineating what the party stands for and who are its standard-bearers, was the only true protection for the principles that Jefferson had rescued in 1800.[12]

The events of the 1820s seemed to vindicate Van Buren's suspicions. The "amalgamating policies of Mr. Monroe"—as Van Buren once put it—led to a collapse in party discipline on the national level in the early part of the decade, culminating in the death of the party caucus in 1824.[13] The Republicans could not agree on a presidential nominee, and so four candidates—John Quincy Adams, Henry Clay, William Crawford, and Andrew Jackson—all ran as Republicans, and all sought the White House via a personal following largely predicated on regional ties. The result was the election of Quincy Adams, himself a former Federalist whose ambitious political program would have been music to the ears of Alexander Hamilton.[14]

Van Buren had faced a similar situation in his home state of New York. Once essential to the Republican alliance, New York had fallen prey to factional rivalries predicated upon family ties. The Schuylers, the Livingstons, and the Clintons variably dominated New York politics during Van Buren's lifetime, which inevitably meant a corruption of the pure Republican faith as Federalists often held the balance of power. Van Buren and his "Bucktail" faction in New York lacked the family pedigree of their principal opponent, DeWitt Clinton, but they more than made up for it in political organization. By building a network of party operatives that stretched from the state capitol in Albany all the way down to the local precincts, they captured power in 1820 and even succeeded in rewriting the state constitution in 1821. The tight organization of this "Albany Regency" ensured that there would be no heresies to pervert the true Republican faith. When the New York legislature sent Van Buren to Washington as a senator in 1821, he resolved to take his ideas of party organization nationwide.[15]

But how to do that? In 1824, Van Buren thought that Secretary of the Treasury Crawford was the best candidate for the old Jeffersonian faith, but Crawford suffered a stroke before the election and ultimately finished third in the balloting. The surprising strength of Jackson pushed Van Buren and the Regency toward Old Hickory's side in the wake of the disputed outcome, and he worked behind the scenes to deliver the Crawford faction to Old Hickory. Twenty years earlier, Jackson's popularity might not have counted for much in the presidential contest, but by 1824 two-thirds of the states cast popular votes for the presidency, and the political power of Jackson's appeal was undeniable.

What Van Buren wished to do, and indeed what he basically accomplished, was unite the political popularity of Jackson to the old alliance of "the planters of the South and the plain Republicans of the North." Moreover, this new coalition would be solidified and maintained by an elaborate party organization, a nationwide version of what the Regency had already built in the Empire State, binding political elites to the grassroots in a shared quest for office.[16]

And the glue that would hold this new organization together? Political patronage. Van Buren and the Democrats (as this coalition would come to be called) would use the public treasury to reward their loyal supporters with jobs, contracts, considerations, and anything and everything they could to incentivize as many people as possible to help elect Jackson president. And in so doing, they would ring in a new era of political corruption, unlike anything the nation had seen before.

Article II, Section 2 of the Constitution declares:

> [The president] shall nominate, and by and with the Advice and Consent of the Senate, shall appoint Ambassadors, other public Ministers and Consuls, Judges of the supreme Court, and all other Officers of the United States, whose Appointments are not herein otherwise provided for, and which shall be established by Law: but the Congress may by Law vest the Appointment of such inferior Officers, as they think

proper, in the President alone, in the Courts of Law, or in the Heads of Departments.

This power, divided between the Senate and the president, was not handed over lightly by the Framers. In the lead-up to the Revolution, the colonists faced extreme hardship at the hands of royal agents. The Declaration of Independence argues that King George III "has made Judges dependent on his Will alone, for the tenure of their offices, and the amount and payment of their salaries. He has erected a multitude of New Offices, and sent hither swarms of Officers to harrass our people, and eat out their substance." It is little wonder, then, that the Framers sought to spread the power of appointment across two branches, and to give the lion's share of authority to the president, an agent they thought would be sufficiently dissociated from politics.

Little wonder as well that, during the administration of George Washington, the appointment power was not misused for political purposes. The great "Father of His Country" did not face the voters in either 1788 or 1792; his larger-than-life reputation meant that he was immune from the ebbs and flows of politics more than any of his successors; and the fact that he had well and truly earned his sterling reputation meant that his top priority as president was establishing the legitimacy of the new government, not enriching his friends and family. While he excluded opponents of the new Constitution, many of his appointees sided with Jefferson over Hamilton on the most consequential policy questions, without fear of reprisal from Washington. He also refused to allow special consideration for military officers or relatives; his highest priority was finding fit people to fill available positions.[17] Executive heads—like the postmaster general—who had the power to appoint inferior officers also followed Washington's lead in this regard.[18]

John Adams generally followed the same policy, although the increasing tensions between the Federalists and the Republicans meant that political considerations were more prominent.[19] As Adams wrote, "Washington appointed a multitude of Democrats and Jacobins of the deepest dive. I have been more cautious in this respect."[20] In particular, the Provisional Army the Federalists created to prepare for a potential war with France was dominated by supporters of the president, with Republicans on the outside looking in. Even so, patronage was not, by any stretch, a normative rule during this period; it is one thing to staff the government with those who view the world similarly to yourself, quite another to do so as a form of political payoff.

That concept first appeared on the national stage with the Jefferson administration, who not coincidentally was the first president to triumph in a competitive electoral contest. Granted, there were few direct ballot battles between Adams and Jefferson in 1800, but nevertheless many voters made a choice between the two, largely via a series of state-level proxy battles, especially in New York and Pennsylvania. This meant Jefferson faced a burden that his predecessors did not; he owed his victory, in part, to the campaign efforts of his supporters. How to repay them?

Electoral considerations were a key reason why Aaron Burr, a shady character by the standards of the day, was elevated to the position of vice president. He developed one of the first electoral machines in the city of New York to contest the state legislative seats that would determine whether the Empire State's electors would go for Adams or Jefferson. Burr was even influential in creating the Manhattan Company, an alternative financial institution to the pro-Federalist Bank of New York and the local chapter of the Bank of the United States. This pro-Jefferson institution made credit available to Republican business owners, paving the way for an all-out party effort in the spring of 1800. Little wonder, then, that Burr was rewarded with the vice presidential slot on the Republican ticket.[21]

There is also strong circumstantial evidence to suggest that Jefferson handed rewards to a key member of Congress in the wake of his election. The final tally in the Electoral College left Burr and Jefferson in a tie, even though the former was intended to be vice president. The Constitution requires the House to select a president whenever no candidate has an Electoral College majority. Burr refused to give way to Jefferson, and to create a ruckus, the Federalist representatives voted for Burr on ballot after ballot. Although Jefferson denied making any political deals, it seems probable that Federalist Richard Bayard, Delaware's lone member of Congress, received special consideration for his important vote. Each state receives one vote when the House chooses the president, so Bayard alone was as important as the entire New York or Virginia delegation. Bayard requested through intermediaries that a new administration retain local port collectors, who ultimately were indeed retained. Bayard later informed one collector, "I have taken good care of you."[22]

This would not have been the first time Jefferson used his official capacity for a partisan purpose. While the circumstances surrounding Jefferson and Bayard are somewhat hazy, the deal between the "Sage of Monticello" and Philip Freneau is clear as day. In 1791, as the battle between Jefferson, Madison, and Hamilton became increasingly partisan, the former were concerned that Hamilton was using Treasury Department printing contracts to subsidize John Fenno's proadministration *Gazette of the United States*. Jefferson and Madison countered by tasking Freneau to run a Republican newspaper, the *National Gazette*. To cover some of these costs, Jefferson secured Freneau a job as a translation clerk in the State Department.[23]

With Jefferson installed as president in 1801, he faced a conundrum. On the one hand, the precedents set by Washington and Adams clearly put limits on the extent that federal jobs could be used for political purposes. Moreover, as noted above, Jefferson honestly believed that the mass of the Federalist Party could be separated from its leadership, and widespread removal of Federalist officeholders would only impede that goal. On the other hand, the clamor for offices among Republicans was great, and Jefferson, as the first unabashed president/party leader, could not ignore such demands. And, anyway, Federalists greatly outnumbered Republicans in office (by Jefferson's estimate there were only six Republicans out of hundreds of presidential appointees, "and those were chiefly 'half-breeds'"), far out of proportion to their relative strengths in the public at large.[24]

Thus, rather than make a series of flat-out removals, Jefferson adopted several half measures for the first two years of his administration to achieve a balance of roughly 3:1 in favor of the Republicans. First, he refused to sanction Adams's last-minute appointments, or indeed any that went through after it was clear he had lost the election. He replaced Federalists who retired from office exclusively with Republicans. He fired the most obnoxious and politically active Federalists. He also dismissed marshals and attorneys to counter at least in part the Federalist control of the judicial branch. In all, Jefferson made about 100 nonmilitary removals on the presidential level from a total corps of roughly 400, with most of the removals coming from diplomatic consuls, attorneys, tax collectors, and justices of the peace.[25] That is more than double what Washington and Adams combined had done, but nevertheless many Federalists remained comfortably ensconced in office during the rule of the Republicans.

After roughly two years in office, Jefferson achieved the balance that he was seeking, and the removals process by and large stopped. Six more years of Jefferson as president, plus eight of Madison, then another eight of Monroe meant the temporary end of partisan politics, at least on the national level, so the Federalist tradition of keeping the appointing power separate from politics was basically restored. Over the course of sixteen years in office, Madison and Monroe made a combined total of just fifty-four civilian, presidential-level removals. Quincy Adams made just twelve during his troubled four years in the White House.[26]

This tradition of retention in office from administration to administration came to an end with the election of Jackson in 1828, the first candidate since Jefferson to take power from the opposition party via an electoral contest. Indeed, the increasing democratization of the presidency since 1800 made Old Hickory more of the people's choice than even Jefferson, which in turn created enormous political pressure from Jackson's coalition. After all, the electoral effort was absolutely enormous. Some 1.5 million people had voted in 1828, with ballots spread out over twenty-four states from Maine to Louisiana. Jackson's victory was not due to a private affair among elites in the Electoral College, nor a triumph in a few, localized proxy battles; the entire nation had placed him in office, via a popular vote that was three times the size of the total ballots cast in 1824. And while that had afforded the president a new source of power—he could claim to be the only tribune of the people—it also meant he had a new set of obligations, particularly to his campaign workers and agents who now expected to reap some of the spoils of victory.[27]

Importantly, Jackson brought with him to Washington politicos whose statewide political authority depended on tightly structured organizations that were built, in part, around political patronage. Van Buren's Regency was a prime example of such an organization, but to him could be added Thomas Ritchie of Virginia's "Richmond Junto," Isaac Hill of New Hampshire, and John Eaton of Tennessee's "Nashville Junto." All of them were established spoilsmen in their home states, and all of them would become influential in the new Jackson administration.[28]

But it was Old Hickory himself who promulgated a (somewhat passable) moral justification for raiding the federal government to pay off party workers. He judged rotation in office a principle in keeping with the republican founding. In his first annual message to the Congress, Jackson writes of long-tenured employees:

> [T]hey are apt to acquire a habit of looking with indifference upon the public interests and of tolerating conduct from which an unpracticed man would revolt. Office is considered as a species of property, and government rather as a means of promoting individual interests than as an instrument created solely for the service of the people. Corruption in some and in others a perversion of correct feelings and principles divert

government from its legitimate ends and make it an engine for the support of the few at the expense of the many. . . .

In a country where offices are created solely for the benefit of the people no one man has any more intrinsic right to official station than another. Offices were not established to give support to particular men at the public expense. No individual wrong is, therefore, done by removal, since neither appointment to nor continuance in office is a matter of right. The incumbent became an officer with a view to public benefits, and when these require his removal they are not to be sacrificed to private interests.[29]

Jackson, as we saw in the last chapter, had a unique talent for linking his own political interests to the public good, then defending his "principles" with unmatched zeal. So it was during the Bank War, and, as the above quotation indicates, so it was with the spoils system.

In all, Jackson removed roughly one-quarter of the presidential-level workforce, with the dismissals centered around federal attorneys, marshals, and counsels, as well as tax collectors, receivers, and public land agents.[30] Subpresidential appointees were also dismissed in large numbers, too. For instance, by the spring of 1830 Van Buren had been instrumental in ousting 131 postmasters in all of New York State, while Hill had ensured that 55 postmasters were removed from his tiny state of New Hampshire.[31] These removals were made possible after Jackson promoted the honest and able John McLean from the postmaster generalship to the Supreme Court, after McLean refused to play patronage games with the offices under his control. In McLean's stead, Jackson named William Barry, a loyalist whose incompetent six-year rule ultimately led to scandal, inefficiency, and embarrassment, until Old Hickory finally named him ambassador to Spain, a post where he could do much less damage.[32]

Soaring rhetoric about these offices belonging to the people aside, the intention of this activity should be obvious: by securing jobs for their own side, the Jacksonians held together and expanded their voting coalition in advance of the next election. This spoils system was their solution to the public goods problem they faced; it provided the hardest campaign workers with private benefits in exchange for their continued service to the party.

There were limits to the spoils system in its earliest incarnation, in no small part because Jackson was unpredictable and always independent-minded. Additionally, there were many strong Jacksonians already in the federal workforce by the time he took control. Moreover, his political opponents were a strong force in the Senate for most of Old Hickory's tenure, even controlling the upper chamber during the twenty-third Congress of 1833 to 1835.

Still, the turnover was substantial, unparalleled in comparison to his predecessors, and remarkable in and of itself. Roughly 40 percent of the presidential-level civilian workforce was removed during Jackson's tenure, with some departments facing more removals than others.[33] Of the thirty-seven district attorneys in office in 1830, only seven were left by the end of the decade. Only eight of the thirty-six district marshals remained. Among the diplomatic corps, just 35 of 131 original consuls held their jobs by the end of the decade. Only eighteen of the fifty-seven presidential-level customs officers in New York City, Virginia, Boston, and Charleston still held their jobs, and scores more subpresidential appointments in the customs offices were similarly wiped out. Ditto the post offices, land offices, and more.[34]

Van Buren followed Jackson in the White House, and with the government full of Democrats, he had little need to make removals, which is not to say that he abandoned the spoils system.[35] He just maintained the program that Jackson put in place. In fact, the real fate of the new spoils system would be decided by the anti-Jacksonian Whigs. They swept into the White House with William Henry Harrison that year, and enjoyed a 29-22 majority in the Senate, after years of complaining about how the Jacksonians had defrauded the public by paying off their most ardent supporters. With a firm grip on power, what would they do?

The Whigs had won the election that year in much the same way that the Democrats had in the previous three cycles: by mastering the art of the mass campaign.[36] As a consequence, the Whig leadership had scores of loyal campaign workers to reward, and the lust for office proved too much, previous caterwauling about the spoils system notwithstanding. What would they do instead of raiding the public treasury to pay back all those who helped pave the way to victory? Find private money? Hope that their campaign workers would be happy with a pat on the back and a "job well done"? Of course not.

Thus, the combined administrations of Harrison and John Tyler (who succeeded Harrison in the White House after the former died a month after his inauguration) saw the removal of more than 450 presidential officers, almost as many as every previous administration combined.[37] Removals on the subpresidential level were just as dramatic. Francis Granger, postmaster general for just six months in 1841, deserves special mention.

He swept out some 1,700 postal workers, and later claimed that if he had been in charge of the Post Office for a few more weeks, he would have dismissed 3,000 more. Unfortunately for Granger, Tyler—who was not a Whig in the same mold as Clay or Daniel Webster but rather an old-school Republican who hated Jackson's heavy-handedness—had fallen out with his one-time allies, and was soon angling to win an election in his own right under the Democratic banner. Tyler thus filled the civil service with Democrats sympathetic to his cause. In one of the more outrageous tales from this period, his son leaned on sympathetic postmasters to purchase fifty to sixty copies each of a sycophantic biography, *The Life of John Tyler* by Alexander Abell, to distribute on their routes.[38]

And so it went during the period of Jacksonian Democracy, from 1828 until the Civil War. Hundreds upon hundreds of presidential-level appointees were cleaned out during the administrations of James K. Polk, Zachary Taylor, Millard Fillmore, Franklin Pierce, and James Buchanan. The last, a Democrat, went so far as to remove the appointees of his own predecessor, also a Democrat. Whether this advanced the agendas of these later Jacksonian-era presidents is another matter entirely. The point of this exercise was to reward party workers so that they would remain loyal and motivated for legislative battles and the upcoming campaign. But only Polk was successful in Congress, and he was notoriously stingy in offering patronage to his coalition. Furthermore, none of these incumbents was even renominated for the presidency after having secured it originally.[39] Indeed, Polk perhaps came closest to the mark in recognizing that the spoils system actually weakened the president's standing as he had to say "no" to so many greedy office-seekers, who numbered in the tens of thousands by the 1850s.

Moreover, the utility of the patronage to hold a coalition together began to diminish as the slavery issue became unavoidable. Both the Democrats and Whigs were transregional parties that sought to forge a political coalition on both sides of this issue; early in the Jacksonian era, patronage was helpful in this regard, neutralizing discontents on both sides and keeping the issue from redefining electoral politics. But with the debate over Texas annexation, then the Mexican War, the admittance of California, and finally the Kansas-Nebraska turmoil, slavery came to the forefront, and no amount of patronage could push it to the background. Indeed, sometimes—as happened with the New York Democrats during the Pierce administration—the issue split parties *within* states, and there was little a president could do. By the 1850s, everybody seemed to resent everything that Fillmore, Pierce, and Buchanan did with patronage; either it was too much for this group or not enough for that group.

Still, for a time the spoils system was the glue that held together two sharply divided political parties. It was a way for presidents to unite a disparate and far-flung political coalition in a shared quest for the nation's top office, now firmly decided by the public at large. To accomplish this, the old Federalist and early Republican tradition regarding retention in office had to be tossed aside. In its stead came a system in which both parties raided the federal treasury for narrow and fractious purposes, and predictably, corruption became rampant and widespread.

There is a fine line that must be drawn when connecting patronage to political corruption. After all, a president should have the power to appoint agents who share his worldview, and who will act in good faith to carry out his instructions. Similarly, members of Congress whose districts or states are affected by a particular executive agent should have the right to make recommendations on behalf of people of ability. Moreover, if a certain campaign worker also happens to be well-suited for a job, there is nothing inherently wrong with rewarding him with that position after victory has been secured, nor in choosing him over an equally well-qualified applicant who opposed the victorious party.

The issue gets down to the public good: is it being served by a given appointment, or is it being sacrificed for the sake of a party's electoral standing? That must be the sine qua non of our analysis. It is not sufficient to say that the patronage system was corrupt simply because the parties rewarded their friends. They must *also* have done so at the expense of the national interest.

For the period under discussion here, there is copious evidence to that effect, which fully justifies the conclusion that the spoils system was a corrupting influence on our government during the Jacksonian period. A few general considerations, followed by some specific cases, will demonstrate this point quite easily.

On the broadest level, the spoils system expanded politics far too wide for the public good. Too many officers were subject to removal based on changing administrations, which meant turnover was too high, and the efficiency of the civil service was accordingly reduced. That is especially true for the period under discussion, when control of the presidency changed hands every four years between 1840 and 1852 (not to mention the intraparty sweep that Buchanan conducted against Pierce's men after his election in 1856). Ultimately, a handful of lower-level, permanent staffers had to manage the affairs of the government during this era, as every four years a new series of politically appointed agents would be brought into office with no experience of how the government was to operate.[40]

Additionally, the spoils system was not a one-way street. The president or his advisors did not simply hand out a partisan a job and expect nothing in return. They expected quite a bit, which meant that public resources were conscripted for the partisan campaign. We already noted above the pressure that President Tyler's son brought to bear upon postal workers in advance of the 1844 Democratic convention, and while that might have been a particularly tacky type of abuse, it was far from unique. Government workers were regularly expected to contribute copious amounts of time for the sake of the party campaign, leaving their public duties unattended. Moreover, there was a widespread practice of party assessments, wherein the state or local party would take a kickback from the employee, the size of which usually depended on his salary.[41]

Another type of kickback had to do with the party presses. As mentioned above, Hamilton and Jefferson both used public resources to subsidize friendly newspapers, but starting with the Jacksonians the relationship between the press and the government began to shift. Some presses became "administration papers" that had unique access to the party in power; their editors were often integral in party decision making. To finance these operations, the government often handed administration newspapers lucrative printing contracts. After 1860, the Government Printing Office took charge of printing the legislative record, executive rules, and so on, but prior to that the administration as well as both chambers of Congress each contracted with private printers, binders, and engravers. In the Jacksonian era, these became party jobs, and the fees that the printers charged for their services usually went well beyond market value, again with the expectation that the printers would kick some of the proceeds back to the party's electoral effort.[42]

Turning from general concerns to specific instances of outrageous behavior, there are a few departments that stand out above the rest in terms of venality and corruption. The Post Office is perhaps the most obvious example; unsurprising, since its massive size and geographical bigness made it a perfect source of patronage. When Washington was first inaugurated, there were only seventy-five post offices and just 1,875 miles of post road. When Jackson took office, there were more than 8,000 post offices and

115,000 miles of post road.[43] As mentioned above, Van Buren and other spoilsmen quickly seized on it for rewarding their cronies, and to make full use of it they expanded the Post Office beyond what was necessary. Postmaster General McLean had managed an extensive postal service with just thirty-eight clerks in early 1829. By 1834, Postmaster General Barry had ninety clerks on his staff. The Whigs (before they won the executive branch and became staunch advocates of the spoils system) derided this, with a Whig-dominated congressional investigation declaring, "The business of the office cannot have increased since the 1st of April, 1829, in the proportion of 38 to 90."[44] Quite right.

If the Post Office was useful because it was so vast, the customs houses were useful because of the money that flowed through them. This was a perfect place to install less-than-scrupulous agents who would skim a little off the top, taking care to kick back something to the party. By 1858, the collection of customs duties was a continental affair, stretching from Maine all the way to California. The major cities would have hundreds of customs officials, and New York had nearly 1,000 by the time of the Civil War. As Leonard White argues in his landmark study of public administration in the Jacksonian period: "The office of collector of the Port became one of the principal prizes in the patronage lottery."[45] And little wonder why: that officer had tens of millions of dollars pass through his office every year.

Little wonder as well that the New York collectors were outright crooked through much of this period. Jackson appointed Samuel Swartwout to the position in 1829, and in a letter to a colleague Swartwout wondered, "whether or not I shall get anything in the general scramble for plunder." He sure did. Swartwout pulled off a defalcation so great that it would make the Sopranos green with envy. By the time the federal government finally figured out what was going on, Swartwout escaped to England, having embezzled approximately $1.2 million in federal funds (or $25 million in today's dollars). Van Buren appointed in Swartwout's stead Jesse Hoyt—the recipient of the above-mentioned letter from Swartwout, no less!—who treated government investigators in a supercilious manner and was also guilty of embezzlement.[46]

The land offices were a locus of similar fraud, because they—like the ports—were far-flung outlets where money changed hands with little oversight from Washington. Land officers would borrow federal dollars to speculate in public lands, take advantage of exchange rates to engage in arbitrage, and loan government money out for their own purposes.[47] The most outrageous example of such fraud came from one W. P. Harris, a land receiver in Mississippi, who lost over $100,000 in government money by speculating. Harris recommended that his friend, Gordon Boyd, replace him, and the latter ended up losing $50,000 in a similar venture![48]

Corruption was not confined to the bottom of the rung, either. The Buchanan administration serves as a good case in point. Buchanan had to deal with the new Republican Party. Formed after the Whig Party collapsed, it won a House majority in 1858 and undertook an extensive investigation of the administration. The report of the Covode Committee (named after Congressman John Covode) was controversial in its day, but has since generally been accepted.[49]

The Covode Committee found a widespread abuse of the patronage system, some of which is consistent with frauds already mentioned, others that went above and beyond. It accused the Buchanan administration of greatly overcharging on printing and bundling, at a loss to the government of tens of thousands of dollars per year, with kickbacks naturally delivered back to the party. It found that the collector of the port of Philadelphia used patronage to advance the Pennsylvania Democratic Party, and gave his own brother a shadow job (where he received a paycheck for no apparent work). It also discovered evidence of levies placed upon customs officials to help Buchanan carry Pennsylvania in 1856. In several of these instances, it suggested that President Buchanan knew what was going on, and even approved of some of these actions.[50]

The most salacious charge from the Covode Committee, which if true would go beyond the sort of corruption discussed above, was that the Buchanan administration was responsible for distributing $30,000 to $40,000 worth of patronage to buy votes in Congress to pass the Lecompton Bill. This highly controversial measure would have approved the proslavery constitution written by a faction within Kansas; southern Democrats generally supported it, but northern Democrats and the Republicans were staunchly opposed. The main pieces of evidence in support of the Covode Committee's accusation were the bank records and testimony of Cornelius Wendell, a disgruntled former press agent of the Buchanan administration. Additionally, two House Democrats opposed to the Lecompton Bill claimed to have rebuffed bribes made to them.[51]

Whether the Buchanan White House was particularly corrupt, or if it just faced an intensely partisan opposition in the new Republican majority, is difficult to say. It is worth noting that one of the two minority Democrats on the committee agreed with the merits of the majority's charges, though he did not sign on to its report.[52] Even so, the broader story to tell here is how much patronage had corrupted the everyday functions of the government. Widespread inefficiency, the installation of second-rate characters in important positions, the skimming of government resources by party operatives, the many thefts, large and small, by governmental agents—all of this became par for the course by the time of the Civil War. The two parties had totally coopted the civil service, perverting public resources for their own ends. Buchanan and his henchmen might have quibbled at the margins of the Covode Committee's discoveries, but there is no denying these fundamental truths.

———————

The story told in this chapter is a straightforward one. The rise of the two party system, combined with the popular election of the president, put enormous pressure on the Democrats and the Whigs to mobilize tens of thousands of people for the quadrennial campaign. To do that required some way around the public goods problem that such mobilization faces: how do you incentivize somebody to work for a collective goal when his own interests suggest he should merely free ride, leaving others to do the work? The most effective answer the parties came up with was patronage. Let the government foot the bill for the party effort in the form of jobs, sinecures, contracts, and other gratuities. This, in turn, upended the old, highly ethical system of retention in office across one administration to another, and led to widespread inefficiency and theft. Put simply, it corrupted the bureaucracy. As we shall see in Chapter Four, this type of corruption would last for half a century before the first reforms began to clean up the mess.

There is a larger lesson to be learned from this story, as well as the story told in Chapters One and Two. In those earlier chapters, we saw the power of the government expand in ways that the Framers of the Constitution did not anticipate. Indeed, in the case of a federal power to charter corporations, the Framers had explicitly voted down such an authority. And for all of those innovations, there were no amendments to the Constitution ratified, which again was the mechanism by which the Framers anticipated the document would be altered. Even Madison himself came to adopt this attitude toward the Hamiltonian system, deciding that the precedent of a generation had vindicated the Bank. This bred corruption, as the original institutions were not capable of handling these new powers responsibly.

Here, we have seen how ad hoc institutional changes can also disrupt the Madisonian balance, even if they may seem sensible at first appearance. A democratized presidency sounds like an essential ingredient of any republic to modern ears, and indeed it had an ineluctable appeal as early as the 1820s. But even so, it was not something the Framers anticipated; in 1787, they had designed an executive branch based on very different premises. The succeeding generation altered this without a full consideration for what that would do to the Newtonian design of the Constitution. As we saw, it bred a two-party system—something the Framers thought was antithetic to republican government—as well as the spoils, which was really the first of many instances of institutionalized, broad-based corruption. In other words, altering the presidency in seemingly benevolent ways meant that the constitutional regime was unable to balance properly the vast array of social factions to ensure a public-spirited outcome. Checks and balances began to break down.

Thus, the story here is deeply consistent with our thesis. One cannot go altering this or that provision of the Constitution without serious consideration of how the change will affect the rest of the regime, for checks and balances are in fact quite delicate. This is true of creating new federal powers, like a national chartering authority, or altering structures, like democratizing the presidency. When these break down, corruption has room to grow.

And, as we shall learn, political corruption is like a cancer. Once it is introduced into a system, it tends to spread. The public eventually becomes used to certain corrupt innovations, which empowers politicians to introduce more innovations that spread the corruption, which are often accepted in turn, and therefore encourage even more innovations. We saw a hint of that here, as the spoils system became progressively worse. Jackson's use of the appointment power for political purposes was relatively limited, but twenty-five years later the fraud and abuse under the Buchanan administration was widespread.

Similarly, as we turn in the next chapter from Jacksonian America to the Gilded Age that spans the end of the Civil War to the rise of the progressive movement, we see politicians finding new and more wicked ways to undermine the public good for the sake of their own interests. In fact, politicians during this period will *combine* the abuses discussed in the last two chapters, using old-fashioned patronage along with tariffs and internal improvements to build impenetrable political machines that perpetrated widespread frauds against the public good.

4

"Permanent and Terrible Mischief"

Machine Politics in the Gilded Age

FOR GENERATIONS, historians have accepted a straightforward peri-
odization of American political history: the Federalist era gave way
to Jeffersonian Democracy, then Jacksonian Democracy, the antebellum
struggle, the Civil War, and later Reconstruction and the Gilded Age.[1] The
common consensus on the Gilded Age is that it was lost to corruption, as
professional politicians degraded public morals and ransacked the common
weal for their own benefit. Henry Adams's contemporary assessment still
holds, more or less:

> One might search the whole list of Congress, Judiciary, and Executive
> during the twenty-five years 1870–1895, and find little but damaged
> reputation. The period was poor in purpose and barren in results.[2]

It is not our purpose here to push back on conventional wisdom in this
chapter and the next, but rather to modify it: the period after the Civil War
was more corrupt than those eras that preceded it, but it did not spring
forth de novo. As we shall see, there is a continuity between the corrupt
practices of the first half of the nineteenth century and the perfidy of the
second half. The difference is that corruption was perfected, in terms of
both economic development and patronage.

The next chapter will examine the growing links between business and
government in the era, as Hamiltonian notions of governmental support
for the economy became increasingly corrupt. This chapter showcases the
increasingly sophisticated patronage regime. Here, we will not really find

politicians doing much new with the spoils system, but rather adapting and improving the practices of previous generations. There is little, for instance, that Roscoe Conkling did in New York State that Martin Van Buren did not do fifty years prior. It is just that Conkling did it better, having learned from his predecessors.[3]

Moreover, the nature of civil service became more complex, and thus more susceptible to corrupting influences. The president had historically dominated the appointment process, but as the size of the civilian government grew because of the Civil War, the expansion westward, and the expanding economy, it became more difficult for him to manage the public offices personally. This ultimately favored local politicians, and their patrons in the Senate, many of whom became dominant political bosses.[4]

In the subtext here is the idea that corruption is similar to gangrene or dry rot: if left unchecked, it inevitably spreads. What we shall see essentially demonstrates that point. Politicians initiated corrupt practices regarding the civil service in the 1830s, suffered no rebuke for their efforts, and slowly but surely expanded upon and perfected their operations.

———————

The spoils system was firmly entrenched by the time Abraham Lincoln was inaugurated in 1861, and for all of the ways that Lincoln revolutionized American politics and society, he did nothing to alter this status quo. In fact, he reinforced existing norms by dispensing more patronage than any predecessor, which is really saying something. Of the approximately 1,500 offices at Lincoln's disposal, he removed about 1,200 Democrats from these offices.[5] Moreover, this statistic does not take into account the thousands of subpresidential offices, like local postmasters and workers at the New York Customs House, who were likewise removed. Lincoln also used the extraordinary expansion in the size of the civilian government as a form of payoff; nonmilitary posts increased from about 41,000 jobs in 1861 to 195,000 in 1865, and the Republican Party had total discretion over who would get those jobs. As Carl Russell Fish notes, "The sweep made by the Republicans . . . was the cleanest in our history. Never before did so small a proportion of officers remain to carry on the traditions of the civil service."[6]

It is hard to fault Lincoln for this extensive use of patronage, even if his actions did contribute to the corruption of the civil service (which they most certainly did). The Republican Party of which he was now the leader was a hodgepodge of diverse interests: former antislavery or protariff

Democrats, Free-Soilers, members of the nativist "Know-Nothing" Party, most northern Whigs, German immigrants who feared competition with slave labor, and border state Constitutional Unionists. In general, they shared a commitment to economic expansion and the containment of slavery, but there was a vast degree of diversity within these broad boundaries.[7] Patronage was essential to holding this unwieldy coalition together.

With the exception of Andrew Jackson, Lincoln probably made the most successful use of the resources at his disposal. He was always ready to satisfy an important person by pulling some strings to get his son or nephew into West Point. He regularly consulted senators, governors, and House members on sensitive appointments. He vigorously courted newspapermen with patronage, displaying a keen understanding of their capacity to mold public opinion.[8] One time, he even appointed a man named "Schimmelpfening" because he thought it would be "unquestionably in the interest of the Dutch."[9]

In many respects, the homespun Lincoln was the embodiment of the natural aristocrat whom Alexander Hamilton might have envisioned using corruption to advance the national interest. In some instances, that meant buying off members of Congress. Charles A. Dana, editor of the *New York Tribune* and strong supporter of Lincoln, once recalled the challenges he faced in getting Nevada admitted to the Union as well as pushing the Thirteenth Amendment, which outlawed slavery, through Congress. The votes of two congressmen were purchased with internal tax collectorships while another was offered a $20,000 office in the New York Customs House.[10]

Of course, the weakness in the theory is the assumption that a natural aristocracy would be available to steer the ship of state. With Lincoln's assassination in April 1865, there began a generations-long drought in presidential leadership. Lincoln's successors lacked either the skills or the political capital to manage the factions that he had corralled, and the predictable result was rampant corruption.

Vice President Andrew Johnson assumed the presidency upon Lincoln's death. Johnson, first a congressmen from east Tennessee, then a senator, and later the military governor of the state during the Civil War, was a Democrat and throwback to the Jacksonian era. He despised the slaveocracy of the South, but for fundamentally different reasons than those of staunch abolitionists like Charles Sumner of Massachusetts or Thaddeus Stevens of Pennsylvania. In his infamous inaugural speech before the Senate as vice president, a seemingly drunk Johnson shouted again and again that he was a "plebian." That speech gravely damaged his reputation, but it was a fair statement of his political philosophy. He came from humble roots, resented those born of privilege, and saw himself as a defender of the average man. Initially, Johnson impressed the Radical Republicans who wanted to guarantee voting rights for the newly freed slaves and to disqualify scores of secessionists; it seemed as though both sides, while coming from opposite directions, had the same enemies.[11]

But Johnson quickly changed course as his tenure unfolded. He sought a term in his own right, and to do that he hoped to rebuild the old Jacksonian coalition of the urban ethnics, the hardscrabble farmers of the North, and the southern Democrats. He soon began promoting extremely lenient terms for the southern rebels, and moreover used his patronage power to install agents in government sympathetic to his ambitions. He removed nearly half of all the officeholders whose positions he controlled and saw to it that thousands of subpresidential positions were staffed with his sympathizers.[12] When the Radical Republicans brought impeachment charges to the Senate, Johnson at first angrily rebuked aides who suggested he use his patronage powers to secure his acquittal, but as time wore on he changed his mind. His supporters offered patronage, and at times even cash bribes, to prevent his removal from office. Meanwhile, his opponents busily promised jobs in a new, Radical Republican administration.[13]

Johnson's leniency toward the South, his general refusal to make compromises with his Republican rivals, and the obstinacy of the old Confederates generated widespread anger in the North, resulting in a Republican triumph in the 1866 midterm elections. The public gave the Republicans veto-proof majorities in both chambers, and the Radicals used this to good effect. They took control over Reconstruction policy and essentially stripped Johnson of his appointment powers via the Tenure of Office Act of 1867. Passed over Johnson's veto, it provided that presidential appointees subject to senatorial consent were to hold their positions until a successor had been appointed. The president could suspend such officers temporarily, but he had to seek approval from the Senate within twenty days of the suspension.[14]

The Tenure of Office Act represented a profound change in the way the removal power functioned. Granted, the text of the Constitution is silent on the question of removals. It declares, "the executive Power shall be vested in a President of the United States of America" and, "he shall nominate, and by and with the Advice and Consent of the Senate, shall appoint Ambassadors, other public Ministers and Consuls, Judges of the supreme

Do you believe the "Liberal Bias" myth?
Limbaugh, Hannity, Palin, Glen Beck, etc
love to accuse the media of liberal bias.
This is what's called "working the refs"
and it's a cynical, manipulative ploy.
Don't fall for it.

Ask yourself: If the mainstream media has
such a liberal bias, then why are they ignoring
these important news items & viewpoints?:
www.ProjectCensored.org
www.DemocracyNow.org

For the facts about media bias, please see:
www.Alternet.org/story/15187
www.FAIR.org

And tune into the Thom Hartmann show to
hear Thom debate Conservative guests at:
www.ThomHartmann.com

Court, and all other Officers of the United States, whose Appointments are not herein otherwise provided for, and which shall be established by Law." Nevertheless, those who were at the Constitutional Convention in Philadelphia and also in the First Congress strongly supported an absolute presidential removal power.[15]

And there the matter stood for over seventy years, until the clash between Johnson and the Radicals. The battle over Reconstruction is an important drama in American history, and the Tenure of Office Act a key moment in that story. But it also had consequences for the body politic that extended far beyond Reconstruction. James K. Polk was the first president to worry that patronage actually undermined the position of the president, for it made him too dependent on the office-seekers who had patrons in the Congress. The Tenure of Office Act would legalize this imbalance, ensuring that Polk's worst fears would be realized for another generation.

There were reasons to be hopeful when Ulysses S. Grant became president in 1869. As the victorious warrior in the Civil War, Grant reassured the North that he would not let the hard won victory be lost during the peace. Meanwhile, the South was encouraged by his declaration after his nomination, "Let us have peace!"[16] No president except George Washington entered the White House with so much goodwill. As Adams observes,

> Grant represented order. He was a great soldier, and the soldier always represented order. He might be as partisan as he pleased, but a general who had organized and commanded half 1 million or million men in the field, must know how to minister. . . . The task of bringing the government back to regular practice, and of restoring moral and mechanical order to administration, was not very difficult; it was ready to do itself, with a little encouragement.[17]

The earliest signs were encouraging, as Grant drew a line in the sand regarding the Tenure of Office Act, declaring that he would only fill offices that were already vacant until Congress revised the law.

Ultimately, the high hopes were dashed as Grant signed off on a compromise that preserved the essence of the original law.[18] Worse, his cabinet appointments indicated that, despite his wartime acumen, he was ill-prepared for the ebb and flow of politics. His nominee for the State Department, Elihu Washburn of Illinois, was thoroughly unqualified for the job; his only real recommendation was that he had been an early sponsor of Grant during the Civil War. Worse, Grant named Alexander Stewart as secretary of the treasury; his appointment was technically illegal because he was actively engaged in trade at the time of his nomination. The Republican-dominated Senate had to put Grant through the embarrassment of disapproving the appointment.[19]

These were harbingers of troubles to come. As Adams laments, "Grant avowed from the start a policy of drift; and a policy of drift attaches only barnacles."[20] The trends that had been developing since Jackson's day—spoils, graft, the frauds of professional politicians—all seemed to grow at a substantially quickened pace under Grant, so much so that by the time of his reelection in 1872, corruption was an issue in national politics. According to Republican Congresman George F. Hoar, "Selfish men and ambitious men got the ear of that simple and confiding president. They studied Grant, some of them, as the Shoemaker measures the foot of his customer."[21]

Two men who made a keen study of Grant were Jay Gould and Jim Fisk. In an effort to corner the gold market, they lured Grant's brother-in-law Abel Corbin and Assistant Treasurer Daniel Butterfield with lucrative gold offerings in the hopes that they could extract insider information. They also paraded the unsuspecting president about New York City, so their fellow traders would get the impression that they knew something nobody else did. Ultimately, their plan failed as Grant finally caught wind, but their scheme sparked the Black Friday panic of 1869 that damaged the U.S. economy for months thereafter.[22]

There was also the Belknap scandal. The wife of William Belknap, Grant's secretary of war, learned that military trading posts were leased through private contractors, all going through her husband's office. She won a bid for a trading post at Fort Still for a friend, who in turn agreed to share the profits with her. Though Belknap's wife died, the secretary continued to enjoy this tidy little kickback, having collected some $20,000 by 1876. When the scandal broke, Grant allowed Belknap to resign rather than face rebuke from the Congress.[23]

There was also the Whiskey Ring, a conspiracy all through the Midwest between thousands of Treasury Department officials and whiskey distillers to avoid tax payments. At the head of the ring was General John Macdonald, collector of internal revenue in St. Louis and a wartime buddy of Grant's. So fearful of the reaches of the scandal was Attorney General Benjamin Bristow—one of the few honest men still in government—that he barely spoke of it to anybody. When Grant learned of the crime, he demanded that the criminals be brought to justice, but he clammed up when his personal secretary, Orville Babock, another Grant associate from the war, was implicated. Grant submitted a sworn deposition on behalf of Babock, and later saw to it that Bristow was removed from his position.[24]

There were also the Sanborn contracts. Since Hamilton's time at the treasury, the government gave incentive payments to people who informed about delinquent customs duties or other revenues owed to the government. This moiety system was finally eliminated, but a provision in an appropriations bill allowed the secretary of the treasury to appoint no more than three people to help the Treasury Department collect delinquent revenue. A protégé of the notoriously corrupt Representative Benjamin Butler (a Grant loyalist), John D. Sanborn, won that contract and even induced Secretary of the Treasury William Richardson to give him oversight of all railroads. Sanborn went on to collect $427,000 worth of outstanding taxes, for a moiety of over $200,000. Amazingly, the government would have collected almost all of this money anyway, so this was little more than a kickback to the crony of a well-placed House member. Even more amazing is the contrast between Bristow and Richardson. The former did his job diligently and was dismissed; the latter was, at best, lax in his duties and was eventually appointed to the Court of Claims.[25]

There was also the Star Route fraud. The Constitution gives Congress the power to establish and maintain a post office; however, because the government could not always maintain certain routes, they contracted private firms to service them. Thomas Brady, the second assistant postmaster general, working in conjunction with Stephen W. Dorsey, a former carpetbagger senator from Arkansas and a protégé of Grant, presented sham petitions to service these routes at cut-rate prices; later on, they offered enhanced service for an extra fee, which Congress obligingly supplied. Only a fraction of the total money appropriated went to servicing these routes; the rest was distributed among the cronies. Some of it ended up in Indiana in the closely contested presidential election of 1880, as Dorsey, then an official at the Republican National Committee, used Star Route money to buy voters. In the end, Brady and Dorsey escaped prosecution.[26]

There was also the administration's lax implementation of Reconstruction, which bred corruption. Republican officeholders in the South were incorrigible spoilsmen, arguably more so than their northern counterparts. These carpetbagger and scalawag Republicans were shunned from mainstream southern society, making public jobs their only opportunities for gainful employment, and making civil servants even more avaricious.[27]

Moreover, rings of businessmen and officeholders who conspired to bilk the government regularly captured Republican-led governments in the South. For instance, a ring headed by Milton Littlefield, a former union general, and businessman George Swepson, an advisor to the governor of North Carolina, distributed about $200,000 in bribes to Tar Heel State legislators to obtain millions of dollars for new railroad lines. But instead of spending the money to do what they promised, they used it to buy stock in other railroads, speculate in state bonds, further their political connections, and even take a lavish tour of Europe. In the end, of course, the railroad was never built.[28]

The corrupted South was also the site for the greatest electoral fraud in the country in 1876. While Democrat Samuel Tilden won a comfortable majority in the nationwide presidential vote (thanks to suppression of the black vote in the South by Democrats), the vote in three southern states—South Carolina, Florida, and Louisiana—was close enough for Republicans to contest. The GOP probably won South Carolina, and Florida was genuinely too close to call, but Republican-run voting boards in Louisiana wiped out a six thousand–vote advantage for Tilden and ended up reporting a Rutherford Hayes victory of several thousand votes.[29]

Grant was not directly implicated in any of these scandals, but there is a pattern of presidential diffidence that is undeniable and damning. Too loyal to his friends, too sympathetic to old wartime buddies, too much in awe of men of wealth, too lax in the day-to-day business of governance, Grant was not so much guilty of sins of commission, but sins of omission. His overawing public stature would have given him political cover to reshape and reform the body politic, but Grant refused to do it. The result was that the sorts of frauds that had periodically marred the body politic from the Founding until the Civil War all seemed to happen at once, and in a much more dreadful way. If Lincoln's tenure represented the potential good that a natural aristocrat could do with the tools of corruption, Grant's demonstrated what happens if a man of immense natural talents instead chose not to do anything.

Grant's laxity in the executive branch had a profound effect on the body politic. In 1872, it sparked a division within the Republican ranks, as a faction of Liberal Republicans separated from the rest of the party to back the candidacy of publisher Horace Greeley, who also received the endorsement of the Democrats. While this challenge went nowhere—Grant slightly improved on his margin of 1868, despite the suppression of pro-Grant African Americans in the South—it presaged a split that would develop within the Republican Party. In time, a large number of Republicans would reject Grantism. These "Half-Breeds," as they would be known, would clash with Grant's Stalwart faction in the nomination battles of 1876, 1880, and 1884. Meanwhile, the corruption issue contributed to the Democratic rebound of 1874, when the party regained control of the House of Representatives for the first time since 1858. For the next twenty years, the Democrats would control at least one branch of Congress or the presidency for every cycle except for a brief Republican resurgence in 1888.

Grant's Stalwart faction did not merely represent a diehard clique of supporters, although they most certainly were that. At the 1880 convention, for instance, there was an effort to renominate Grant for an unprecedented third term. The effort lost steam as the anti-Grant forces coalesced around James Garfield of Ohio. Even so, 306 delegates—"the Immortal 306" as they were known—backed Grant on every ballot, an unusual twist, as historically a successful dark horse like Garfield usually enjoys a stampede in his direction at the end. The Stalwarts, embodied by the Immortal 306, were also the political beneficiaries of Grant's patronage policies. A look at the final roll call in the 1880 nomination is illustrative. Nearly 40 percent of these delegates came from the eleven states of the former Confederacy; the Republican Party in these states benefited enormously from Grant's military Reconstruction and his distribution of patronage. Roughly the same number came from just three states: Illinois, New York, and Pennsylvania. Not coincidentally, all three developed robust statewide machines, akin to Van Buren's Albany Regency, thanks to Grant's patronage policies.[30]

Actually, to say that Grant had a patronage policy is somewhat of a misnomer. Whereas other presidents had used patronage to manage their coalitions in pursuit of reelection or favored policies, Grant essentially ceded control of patronage to the dominant personalities of the Senate. The Tenure of Office Act bound the president to listen to the Senate, but as Johnson (and, for that matter, Grant's successors) demonstrated, the president could at least put up a robust fight for the sake of the appointment power. But not Grant. After his initial skirmish over the Tenure of Office Act, he backed down and effectively handed over much of the patronage power to a new class of senatorial satraps. The Senate, in turn, was transformed from the world's greatest deliberative body—as it was when Henry Clay, John C. Calhoun, and Daniel Webster debated the great issues of their day—into the meeting place of state party bosses.[31]

Adams best captures the unmatched power of the Senate bosses in *The Education of Henry Adams*:

> [O]ne day when Adams was pleading with a Cabinet officer for patience and tact in dealing with Representatives, the Secretary impatiently broke out: "You can't use tact with a Congressman! A Congressman is a hog! You must take a stick and hit him on the snout!" . . . He had to ask: "If a Congressman is a hog, what is a Senator?" This innocent question, put in a candid spirit, petrified any executive officer that ever sat a week in his office. Even Adams admitted that Senators passed belief. . . . Great leaders, like Sumner and Conkling, could not be burlesqued; they were more grotesque than ridicule could make them. . . . They did permanent and terrible mischief. . . . The most troublesome task of a reform President was that of bringing the Senate back to decency.[32]

Grant was not such a reform President, as Adams well knew. Little wonder that the machines these senators controlled stayed with Grant until the final ballot in 1880.

Who were these bosses? There was Oliver Morton of Indiana, an initial organizer of the Republican Party. A paralytic who had to be carried into the Senate chamber, he nevertheless was a shrewd political operative who used patronage, contracts, and licenses—all the tools of mid-nineteenth–century corruption—to build a machine in what was at the time the most uncertain of northern swing states. According to one local newspaper, "Morton ran the party . . . as a school master ran his school. He cared little whether his orders were liked or not, so long as they were obeyed. He controlled the politicians as a showman controlled his puppets."[33]

There was Zachariah Chandler of Michigan, of whom one early twentieth-century historian writes:

> [This] very fat, very rich, and very bibulous dry-goods merchant . . . the most belligerent of the older Republican leaders, who had become Mayor of Detroit and Senator before the war, also ruled over an irresistible machine for managing elections in his State. For twenty years there were but "Chandler legislatures" and "Chandler Governors" in Michigan, while this "political Leviathan" directed his subordinates and his local interests by means of an army of officials, Federal and State job-holders, collectors, assessors, petty postmasters. These could all be seen regularly making their march upon the State capitol in election seasons, "a retinue that might have been mistaken in its immensity for the Israelites who remembered longingly the flesh-pots of Egypt."[34]

In Illinois there was John "Black Jack" Logan. A former Democrat, Logan was one of the most brilliant political Civil War generals (i.e., those generals who owed their position to a political appointment). He emerged from the other side of the war an early leader of the Grand Army of the Republic, a veterans organization that lobbied successfully for ever-generous pension benefits for Union soldiers. He was also a staunch Republican, serving as one of the seven impeachment managers the House sent to prosecute the case against Johnson in the Senate. He was perhaps the best "bloody shirt" orator the Republicans had; every election season, Logan would tour contested districts and states to remind voters how the Democratic Party had stood for treason while the GOP had stood for the Union and the flag. Though Logan often clashed with his own party on economic issues like the tariff, he nevertheless was a staunch supporter of civil rights for the freedmen, one of Grant's best surrogates in 1872, and an unsurpassed spoilsman. After his chief rival in Illinois, Senator Lyman Trumbull, broke with Grant to join the Liberal Republicans, Logan became the undisputed master of the Illinois Republican Party.[35]

Two bosses above all are worth discussing in detail: Simon Cameron of Pennsylvania and Conkling of New York. While they were not necessarily more corrupt than Chandler, Morton, or Logan, they built machines that lasted for years beyond Grant's tenure. A closer examination of their records sheds light on the nature of political corruption during this era, and the extent to which President Grant facilitated it.

Cameron's reign atop Pennsylvania politics did not end until 1877 when he handed off power to his son, J. Donald Cameron, and his protégé, Matthew Quay. Because his career spanned the Jacksonian, Reconstruction, and Gilded ages, he underscores the point that later corruption differed only in degree, not in kind, from its earlier incarnations.

In 1822, a young Cameron took partial ownership of the *Pennsylvania Intelligencer*, the official mouthpiece of the state Democratic party and accordingly a recipient of patronage through state printing and binding contracts.[36] Around this time, state governments throughout the country began investing in public improvement projects—first canals then later railroads, and of course publicly chartered banks. The distribution of these contracts was decided by politically elected commissioners, and so Cameron shifted quite easily from partisan editor into government-sponsored businessman.[37] By 1854, Cameron was the head of three railroad companies, president of the Commonwealth Insurance Company, cashier of the Bank of Middletown, and a director or manager of many other businesses, all of which depended in some way or another on the commonwealth's blessing.[38]

His political activism landed him a patronage appointment to the Indian Commission under Polk, and it was here that the first of many whiffs of criminality would emanate from Cameron. As Indian commissioner, it was up to Cameron to settle the various claims of the Winnebago Indians, who were due a payment from the federal government. His efforts on behalf of the government were clouded by the fact that only a handful of tribesmen received any certificates, many received amounts much smaller than specified, and even those certificates originated from a bank that Cameron controlled. In the end, the details of exactly what happened are lost to history; still, the ignominious title "Great Winnebago Chieftain" would follow Cameron around thereafter, and his ascent within Democratic politics stalled for a while.[39]

Cameron eventually broke with the James Buchanan wing of the Pennsylvania Democratic Party, largely over the issue of tariffs. Nevertheless, he was elected to the Senate in 1857 by a Democratic-dominated legislature, thanks to a coalition of dissident Democrats, Whigs, and Know-Nothings. This feat was a testimony to what was at the time a carefully cultivated personal network greased by his wealth and willingness to do favors for his friends.[40] For instance, Cameron was able to induce Democrat William Lebo to defy President Buchanan to vote for him; four years later, Cameron saw to it that Lebo was named a major in the army.[41]

He was an early supporter of the Republican Party in the Senate, and he controlled the Pennsylvania delegation to the 1860 Republican Party convention in Chicago. There, his agents approached the representatives of Lincoln, who was in a pitched battle for the nomination against William Seward of New York and Salmon Chase of Ohio. Cameron's people promised that he would swing the Keystone State delegation to Lincoln in exchange for a cabinet post. Though Lincoln was not aware of this at the time, his representatives agreed, and Cameron soon found himself as secretary of war.[42]

In general, the war effort was run reasonably free from graft or corruption within the government. One might have guessed, having come as far as we have in this story, that it would be an easy opportunity for the Republican Party to entrench itself permanently in the government. As we shall see, that happened to some extent; however, the country was fortunate to have a trained cadre of quartermasters largely free of the patronage regime, who because of the Mexican War of the 1840s had already developed reliable bureaucratic processes.

Another big reason was that Lincoln quickly regretted his decision to appoint Cameron, effectively fired him, and replaced him with the able Edwin Stanton. Lincoln, of course, was warned ahead of time about the dangers of Cameron. Stevens visited Lincoln early on to argue against the selection, which promoted Lincoln to ask, "You don't mean to say you think Cameron would steal?" Stevens replied, "No. I don't think he would steal a red-hot stove." Lincoln, a master manipulator of those under his management, cleverly relayed this story to Cameron, presumably to keep him in line. Cameron was outraged and demanded a retraction from Stevens. The latter gleefully obliged: "I believe I told you he would not steal a red-hot stove. I will now take that back."[43]

It is fair to say that if Cameron thought he could profit, politically or financially, from stealing a red-hot stove, he assuredly would have. During his brief tenure at the War Department, he turned it into his own patronage fiefdom, expanding his network of political clients at the expense of the war effort, and therefore the Union itself. The number of examples of Cameron's perfidy that come down through history are too numerous to mention, but fortunately one illustrates exactly what his aim at War really was.

One of Cameron's agents at the Chicago convention was William Cummings; later on, Cameron paid him back generously for his assistance, naming him a codirector of the Union effort to procure supplies in New York City. Also in charge of this effort was George Morgan, a relative and business partner of the governor of the Empire State. These two executed a massive fraud upon the government that ultimately got Cameron censured by the House of Representatives. Historian Fred Shannon writes:

A fund of $2,000,000 was left at the disposal of the couple, subject only to nominal oversight by a committee of reputable citizens. A strange era of spending resulted. The sum of $21,000 was expended for *linen pantaloons and straw hats*. The firm of Benedict and Hall received a contract for 75,000 pairs of shoes at $2.20 a pair, which were worth much less. A member of the firm testified that Cummings received no pay from them for the transaction but that the contract was let to them in return for the kindness of an occasional temporary loan of $500 or $1,000. Along with other peculiar army supplies purchased by Cummings were large quantities of Scotch ale, London porter, selected herrings, and 23 barrels of pickles. Without being bound by oath or bond, Cummings spent

$250,000 during the summer of 1861. Even if honest he was thoroughly incompetent; his sole qualification being that he was a friend of Simon Cameron.[44]

It is doubtful that the pickles and pantaloons made it to Bull Run or Shiloh, where young men were dying in defense of the Union that Cameron was bilking. But that was the way it went for his entire political career: Cameron's allies always made out one way or another, and his opponents were left on the outside looking in.

Lincoln, as previously noted, was quite aware of the criticism directed at his secretary of war, but holding Pennsylvania within his coalition was an important objective. Even so, by early 1862, enough was enough. Ever the political diplomat, Lincoln offered Cameron the ambassadorship to Russia, which he was obliged to take, humiliating as it was.[45]

Cameron was not the first politician to be caught turning his office into his own patronage fiefdom, and he certainly was not the last. What makes him unique is the extent of his comeback, which was complete and total by 1867. His exile to St. Petersburg was short-lived, and though he was out of the government, his friendly relations with key officials like Stanton and Chase, as well as his personal organization that ran across the all-critical state of Pennsylvania, meant that he remained the point person for federal patronage disposal. Moreover, Cameron worked hard on behalf of Lincoln in 1864, even assisting him in getting the convention to nominate Johnson for the vice presidency.[46]

So powerful was the Cameron organization that he easily reclaimed a Senate seat by besting popular wartime governor Andrew Curtin in the Republican legislative caucus in 1867.[47] That marks the start of the Cameron political machine's complete control of Pennsylvania. It lasted across four bosses: Cameron ran the state until 1877; then he handed the reigns over to his son Donald and Quay. The latter dominated the state until his death in 1904. After Quay, Boies Penrose was the boss of the Keystone State until his death in 1921.[48] During this period, the Republican Party almost always controlled the governorship, the state legislature, the House caucus, and both Senate seats. And in most cases, the particular Republicans in charge of the state were ultimately answerable to one of Cameron's protégés, Quay or Penrose.[49]

We will have much to say about Quay in the next chapter, for he serves as a crucial link between the spoils system of the Grant administration and the wholesale domination of politics by industrial interests. For now, let us focus on Cameron's relationship with Grant, as it illustrates just how easily Grant was controlled by men whom Lincoln knew to keep at arm's length.

Grant gladly favored Cameron's machine in Keystone State appointments, even going so far as to withdraw nominees friendly to Curtin's faction after Cameron complained.[50] Cameron was also instrumental in making sure that reform-minded Republicans, like Attorney General Ebenezer Hoar and Secretary of the Interior Jacob Cox, had short stints in the administration. The *Cincinnati Times* suggested that over two hundred people in Washington owed their position to Cameron, in one way or another.[51] Perhaps this was an exaggeration, but Cameron held so much sway over Grant that he prevailed upon the president to name his son as secretary of war in 1876, despite the fact that Donald Cameron was unknown on the national stage and had served in no significant posts prior to his nomination.[52]

With Grant solidly behind Cameron, he was, according to the *Harrisburg Patriot*, "the undisputed master of Pennsylvania. Every department of the State government is at his feet. He is the fountain of all political honors and preferments, and the signs are that he will be able to transmit his rule."[53] Cameron-sponsored patronage held together a geographically and socioeconomically diverse affiliation across the more than forty-five thousand square miles that made up the Keystone State.[54] There were the rural Yankees, Scots-Irish, and German immigrants who made their livelihood through the farm economy. Once strongly Jacksonian, they had shifted into the Republican coalition in the 1850s, and they were represented by rural county organizations all across the state. There were the major cities of Philadelphia, the second largest American city by 1880, and Pittsburgh, the twelfth largest. Their (often fraudulent) vote totals virtually guaranteed the GOP would win Pennsylvania in presidential elections, though the urban bosses were independent of the Cameron machine, which meant they needed careful tending.[55] There were also Pennsylvania's vast economic interests: financial and trade interests in Philadelphia, as well as a growing industrial economy through the rest of the state. Cameron held these diverse forces together for over a decade.

If we put aside the moral outrage at seeing how Pennsylvania, the birthplace of the Constitution, perverted every noble purpose the Framers had set forth, we can appreciate the kind of elegance by which the Cameron machine operated. Even if its purpose was pernicious—the concentration of political, economic, and social power around one corrupt individual—its efficiency was a marvel of political innovation.

An examination of how the machine operated in 1872 and 1873 is illustrative. Its balanced use of patronage helped it best a potentially strong Liberal Republican movement, centered around Philadelphia-area journalist Alexander McClure. The speakership of the state house went to a member from Philadelphia County. A senator from Allegheny County was made speaker of the state senate. Next up, Cameron was, naturally, reelected to the Senate with virtually no competition. Lest the new governor develop any pretensions as a reformer, his salary was doubled to remind him who buttered his bread. Then, the state legislature passed a reapportionment bill guaranteeing that Democrats would never control more than nine of the state's twenty-seven House seats. With this business completed, the legislature went about passing private bills to pay off virtually every interest group or hard-working party member. This included a boon to the Pennsylvania Railroad, a vital machine partner, which received a 100 percent increase in its capital stock. The legislature debated all of these outside of public view, in the committees, and passed them only at the very end of the session.[56]

And so it went in the Keystone State for more than half a century. During that time, Pennsylvania produced not a single memorable reformer or public-spirited leader. The purpose of this machine was its own perpetuation, nothing more. And though it lasted for many years after Grant retired from public life, it was his generous attitude toward Cameron that allowed the latter to transform himself from a disgraced war secretary into the unmatched leader of Pennsylvania. Later presidents and national leaders would try to resist the Cameron machine, but by that point it was too late. In the end, the only thing that brought it down was the Great Depression.

———————

The Republican Party of New York never acquired the same stranglehold over statewide politics that its counterpart in Pennsylvania enjoyed; for all the power of the Empire State GOP, New York City and Brooklyn (separate entities until 1898) were staunchly Democratic, with the former under the control of Tammany Hall for most of the period between the rise of Boss Tweed in the 1860s and the Great Depression. Even so, the New York Republican machine, led first by Conkling and later by Thomas Platt, loomed large in the era, and was arguably more potent on a national level than the Cameron organization. New York was the most populous and economically powerful state in the Union, and its outcome in the presidential election was almost always in doubt. And so, Conkling and Platt, who combined had almost total control over the party organization for forty years, were never to be ignored.

Long ago, New York had been a state dominated by well-organized political factions. As noted in the previous chapter, DeWitt Clinton's personal organization controlled statewide politics during the early nineteenth century, sometimes aligning with the Federalists, other times with the Jeffersonian Republicans. In the 1820s, Van Buren's Albany Regency took over the state and kept it solid for Old Hickory.

However, Van Buren split with the party in the 1840s over the issue of slavery; this rift divided and destroyed the Regency, and the power vacuum would remain unfilled for decades. The Whigs, and later the Republicans, were initially ruled by newspaper editor Thurlow Weed and Seward, Lincoln's chief rival for the nomination in 1860. But Seward had stuck with President Johnson through thick and thin; his work behind the scenes to save the president from impeachment kept Johnson in office, but left Seward persona non grata in the New York Republican Party.[57] On the Democratic side, the party was split between Tammany Hall in New York City and the upstate operations that controlled Erie Canal patronage.[58]

It was Conkling who created order out of this chaos. The former mayor of Utica, a wartime member of the House and a judge advocate for the Department of War, he was elected to the Senate in the wake of the Radical triumph of 1866. In the upper chamber, he was a strong defender of Radical Reconstruction and voted to impeach Johnson. Well-dressed, handsome, and exceedingly arrogant, Conkling was by no means a people person, and he would eventually leave the personnel management of the machine to Platt. Nevertheless, he and Grant became fast friends. Grant admired his strong personality and inclination to tell the president what he really thought, and Conkling felt that Grant was a man in need of guidance through the unfamiliar world of American politics.[59]

This proved very important for Conkling in his political battle with fellow New York senator Reuben Fenton. Grant did not much care for Fenton, who struck him as obsequious, and the decisive move against Fenton came in early 1870. Professional politicians had become dissatisfied with the work of Moses Grinnell, a respected merchant and now the collector of the New York Customs House, who seemed not to realize that his main job was to keep their patronage flowing.[60] Vacationing the prior year in New York, Grant became friends with Thomas Murphy, who had a reputation as a shoddy contractor during the war. Regardless, they both loved horses, so that was enough for Grant to place him in the most important revenue job in the entire country. In doing so, Grant pushed out or demoted several of Fenton's appointments, all of which caused Fenton to put up a fight via the Tenure of Office Act. Meanwhile, Conkling, who previously had not been an ally of Murphy's, saw an opportunity to consolidate his position, and mounted a stiff defense of Grant's new appointee. The Senate overwhelmingly backed Murphy, Conkling, and Grant, and that was basically the end of Fenton's political career. The New York legislature replaced him in 1875 with Francis Kernan, one of Conkling's cronies from Utica. As for Murphy, he did such an awful job that New York City merchants demanded he be replaced, and Grant dutifully appointed a Conkling lieutenant, Chester Arthur.[61]

With Arthur installed in the New York Customs House, the Conkling operation was able to take a firm control over the Empire State. The value of the collectorship cannot be understated. All by itself, the Customs House collected some 70 percent of the country's customs revenue. It employed hundreds of workers whose combined salaries topped $2 million.[62] It was the single greatest patronage plum in the entire country, and Grant handed it over to Conkling for little more in return than friendship.

After Grant had left office, Hayes appointed a commission run by John Jay, the grandson of the great Federalist statesman, to investigate how the Customs House was run. The Jay Report is worth discussing in detail, for it illustrates how the Conkling machine defrauded the government and private businesses of millions of dollars.[63]

For starters, the moiety system lined the pockets of the top officials at the Customs House. Originally established to incentivize diligence in sniffing out tax cheats, the top federal agents at the Customs House were entitled to a cut of all federal revenue collected when they discovered concealment or fraud. As the tariff rates crept higher and higher after the War of 1812, the potential bounty to be won was enormous.[64] By the mid-1870s, the main agents at the Customs House were bringing home over $50,000 per year (or nearly $1 million in today's dollars), with a base salary of just $12,000.[65]

An easy scam for the party hacks at the Customs House was to undervalue imports, then make an "official" discovery of the fraud. Under law, the entire value of the import was forfeited, a steep punishment that induced many businesses to reach a settlement with the government. Thanks to the moiety system, half of the seized revenue went to the Customs House officials, eventually to be kicked upstairs to the Conkling machine.[66] An outrageous example of such a fraud occurred in 1872. That year, the Customs House informed the import house of Phelps, Dodge & Company that it had undervalued goods worth a total of $1.75 million. Horrified, William Dodge worked out a settlement with the government for a total penalty of about $270,000. After they made the payment, Phelps, Dodge & Company officials discovered that the actual amount of undervaluations was a little less than $7,000 and that the company only owed the government a paltry $1,664.68! Arthur, who generally had a good reputation (relative to his execrable predecessors), escaped identification with the scandal by claiming ignorance.[67]

The Conkling machine did not merely see a cut of the moiety bounty. It also drafted government workers at campaign time and took thousands of dollars from them as well. Each employee was generally assessed between 2 percent and 6 percent of his salary to the party's coffers, no exceptions admitted. According to George William Curtis, a Customs House official, who testified to the Committee on Civil Service and Retrenchment:

> On one occasion there was a very heavy assessment made in the New York custom house. A body of gentlemen connected with the service there, made representations to me of their absolute inability, with justice to their families, to pay this assessment in addition to others that had been levied at about the same time, during the same year. I replied, of course, that, officially, I had nothing to do with the matter, but, knowing the collector, I would wait upon him and see what could be done. I went to the collector, whom I knew personally very well. I stated the case of these gentlemen, and he heard me with politeness—with impatient politeness—and when I had ended he brought his fist down on the table with great emphasis and said, "Well Mr. Curtis, for every one of the gentleman in this office who are unwilling to pay this assessment, I know of at least 50, whose names are duly registered, who would very willingly take the place with all the encumbrances."[68]

On top of this, the employee turnover at the Customs House was extraordinary, as hundreds of employees were regularly turned out to make way for new workers, all to appease the latest political faction at the top of the heap. In fact, one contemporary critic estimated that in the five years before Arthur took over, there were over 1,500 replacements made at the Customs House, or nearly one person fired and another hired every day![69]

Unsurprisingly, all of this had a terrible influence on morale at the Custom House. Doing your job well had virtually no relation to whether you kept it; instead, it all came down to whether you were friendly with the right people. Thus, a climate of laziness and turpitude pervaded the

Customs House. Workers only actually worked a few hours a day, if they showed up at all, and many of them had the attitude that they should take what they could while they could. In addition to the top-down scams like that perpetuated upon Phelps, Dodge & Company, low-level employees were susceptible to bribes to look the other way or give a competitor an extra hard time. They also regularly bilked merchants on a penny-ante basis.[70]

All of this defrauded the government of revenues, hurt the city of New York as merchants went to other ports, and in general hampered the economic growth of the nation. The amount of money lost to these hacks might easily have topped today's equivalent of $1 billion, a terrible blow to the public interest.

But it was a boon for Conkling and his seemingly unstoppable political machine, all thanks to Grant. Amazingly, for all the fortunes that Grant made for so many unworthy cronies, he almost died penniless, saved only by signing a lucrative contract to publish his memoirs.

His autobiography makes no mention of Cameron or Conkling.

Writing to Lyman Trumbull in July 1870, former Republican senator James Grimes of Iowa complained:

> It looks at this distance as though the Republican party was "going to the dogs"—which, I think, is as it should be. Like all parties that have an undisturbed power for a long time, it has become corrupt, and I believe that it is to-day the (most) corrupt and debauched political party that has ever existed. . . . I have made up my mind that when I return home I will no longer vote the Republican ticket, whatever else I may do.[71]

Grimes would pass away before the election of 1872, but Trumball effectively carried out his threat by bolting the party banner that year to back the Liberal Republican ticket. Though the Liberals went nowhere, four more years of Grantism would mainstream their views. When the Republicans gathered in Cincinnati for the 1876 convention, many in the party were looking to make a change. Initially, the convention deadlocked between Conkling and Morton on the Stalwart side, Bristow, the prosecutor of the Whiskey Ring who was being presented as a reformer, and Speaker of the House James G. Blaine, the leader of the anti-Grant Half-Breed faction.

In many respects, Blaine was an obvious choice to replace Grant in the White House. The speaker of the House and perhaps the best orator of the period, he had struck out against Grantism during his tenure, but he was not as far gone from the Republican reservation as Bristow (hence the "Half-Breed" designation affixed to him). But Blaine and Conkling had clashed over the years and were by this point political enemies. Moreover, Blaine had the stink of corruption on him as well, which we shall discuss in Chapter Five.[72] On the seventh ballot, the anti-Blaine forces coalesced around Hayes, governor of Ohio. The Democrats, meanwhile, nominated Governor Samuel Tilden of New York, who had built a national reputation as a crusader against the Tweed Ring. The Democrats inserted a strong civil service reform plank in their platform and ran against Republican corruption.

Hayes ultimately prevailed in the 1876 contest, but he entered the White House with a cloud hanging over him. The Republicans had undoubtedly stolen the presidency in Louisiana and possibly Florida, but in fairness to them, the Democrats stole it first by suppressing the black vote (they also stole the elections of 1880, 1884, and 1916 in precisely the same manner). Regardless, Democrats christened Hayes "His Fraudulency," an ironic appellation seeing as how he had genuine reformist intentions. Hayes believed that the spoils system had undermined the constitutional regime, and he placed civil service reformer Carl Schurz in charge of the Department of Interior. Per Hayes,

> The offices . . . have become not merely rewards for party service, but rewards for services to party leaders. This system destroys the independence of the separate departments of the government. It tends directly to extravagance and official incapacity. It is a temptation to dishonesty.[73]

In the end, Hayes ultimately disappointed reformers and Stalwarts alike as he sought a middle path between the two poles within the party.[74] Still, he would come to great grief by taking on the New York Customs House and the Conkling machine.

Without the Tenure of Office Act, decapitating the Conkling machine would have been easy. All Hayes would have to have done is fire Arthur and the others directly under his command, and nominate somebody else. But because of that law, as well as Grant's prior refusal to risk his political capital on killing the machine in its infancy, Hayes found himself in a fight that exacerbated the divisions on display in Cincinnati.

After the Jay Commission began to reveal its findings, Hayes sent word to the leaders of the New York Customs House—Arthur, Naval Officer Alonzo Cornell, and Surveyor George Sharpe (all Conkling men, naturally)—that he wanted them to resign. However, they refused to budge.[75] Not only that, but Cornell, who was also a member of the Republican National Committee, continued to hold both positions, despite an order from Hayes that federal employees could not also be party appointees simultaneously.[76] So, Hayes suspended them, as was his privilege under the Tenure of Office Act, and sent replacement nominations to the Senate. Yet these nominations failed, and in fact Hayes only garnered the votes of six Republicans, with the rest joining Conkling.[77]

Facing pressure from dispirited and disgruntled reformers, Hayes once again pushed the issue in 1879. He sent a letter to the Senate arguing that Arthur had "made the customhouse a center of partisan political management. The customhouse should be a business office. It should be conducted on business principles." This was somewhat unfair, as the Customs House had been corrupt since at least the days of Jackson and Van Buren. Nevertheless, Arthur maintained the old crooked practices, even if he dressed better and curried favor with the business elite. Hayes again submitted alternative nominations to the Senate and managed to defeat the Conkling nominations, although most Republicans once again opposed him. The measure passed by the support of the southern Democrats, who were more than happy to see their political opponents tear themselves to shreds.[78]

Hayes had forsworn a second term, which probably saved him the ignominy of being defeated by the still-powerful Stalwart factions at the 1880 convention in Chicago. As noted above, the Stalwarts proffered Grant for an unprecedented third term. The old general had been busy touring the world for most of Hayes's tenure and had cleaned off some of the grime that had collected on his reputation during his presidency. Blaine was again in pursuit of the nomination, although again he had failed to unite the anti-Stalwart vote around his banner, as a decisive minority of it sided with Secretary of the Treasury John Sherman. For ballot after ballot, the convention remained deadlocked. On the thirty-fourth ballot, matters remained largely where they had been on the first one: Grant with over 300 delegates but consistently short of the 379 needed to win, Blaine stuck around 280 delegates, Sherman trailing with about 100, and the rest scattered. At this point, movement began toward Garfield as a compromise candidate for the anti-Grant forces. Though he was no saint himself (having been caught up in the Crédit Mobilier scandal, which we shall discuss in the next chapter), he nevertheless entered the convention opposed to Grant. By the thirty-sixth ballot, most of the Blaine and Sherman delegates had rallied around him, giving him a narrow 399-306 victory over Grant.[79]

The party platform included a plank that read "The Republican party . . . adopts the declaration of President Hayes that the reform of the civil service should be thorough, radical and complete." This was an exceedingly ironic statement, considering that most of the Senate Republican caucus had opposed Hayes's efforts to reform the New York Customs House. Irony soon devolved into parody as the Republicans, to appease the Stalwart faction, actually nominated Arthur to be vice president.[80]

Conkling and his machine went into overtime to win New York for the Republican Party, knowing full well that the all-precious stream of federal patronage was on the line. And they succeeded. Against former Union General Winfield Hancock, Garfield won the Empire State by twenty-one thousand votes out of more than one million votes cast. That difference was greater than his national popular vote plurality over Hancock, which was a paltry nine thousand votes out of nine million cast. Moreover, New York's thirty-five Electoral College votes were the difference between victory and defeat for the Republican Party. It appeared that the Conkling machine would be safe.

But appearances can be deceiving. Garfield wanted to appease all factions within his badly divided party, but the supercilious Conkling refused to negotiate. As such, Garfield named William Robertson, a Blaine ally, as the head of the Customs House. Like Hayes before him, he won the battle with support from a majority of Senate Democrats. In a bold gamble, Conkling and Platt (who by then had succeeded Kernan in the Senate) resigned their seats, with the intention of being returned to the upper chamber by a statement of purpose from New York Republicans.[81]

Whether this gamble would have worked will never be known, for fate intervened through the work of a deranged office-seeker named Charles Guiteau. On July 2, 1881, while waiting at the Sixth Street Station in Washington, Garfield was shot by Guiteau. Shortly after his arrest, authorities found a letter in his pocket, which read in part:

> The president's tragic death was a sad necessity, but it will unite the Republican party and save the Republic. I have no ill will toward the president. His death was a political necessity. I am a lawyer, theologian and politician. I am a Stalwart of the Stalwarts. I was with General Grant and the rest of our men in New York during the canvas.[82]

This letter, though a testament to Guiteau's deluded state of mind, gravely damaged the reputation of the Stalwart faction. Garfield lingered for several months, then passed away, leaving Arthur as president. As far as the voters were concerned, enough was enough with the GOP. The Democrats won 60 percent of the House seats in the 1882 midterm, enjoying a seventy-three-seat advantage over the Republicans.

In the nineteenth century, lame duck sessions of Congress were extremely long. A new Congress would not be seated until a year after its election, leaving defeated members plenty of time to legislate even after their rebuke. The Republicans took advantage of this opening after their 1882 shellacking to pass the sweeping Pendleton Civil Service Act, which Arthur dutifully signed into law.

The Pendleton Civil Service Act was a tough piece of legislation. It outlawed assessments on civil servants and set up a classified list of positions that were not open to patronage appointments, instead to be governed by regularized examinations. The law also allowed presidents to expand the classified list, grandfathering employees who were originally appointed for patronage purposes. This had an important, though unexpected, effect on the civil service. After twenty-four years of Republican dominance, the presidency changed hands in every election between 1884 and 1896, and so every outgoing president had an incentive to place his patronage appointees on the classified list. Thus, by the end of the century, some one hundred thousand civil servants were protected from patronage politics.[83]

This was a fitting conclusion to the patronage era in federal politics. Though Jackson had claimed it was a principled response to elite control of the government, the reality is that raw political calculations brought it into being, and nurtured it for half a century. In the end, it was the same sort of raw political calculation that ultimately destroyed it. Politics drove the Republicans to adopt the Pendleton Civil Service Act in 1883, and politics forced Republican and Democratic presidents alike to expand its scope dramatically over the next twenty years.

———————

By all accounts, Grant was an honorable man who never took a dishonest dollar out of politics. Reformers at the time thought he was a dullard, a fool, and a drunk. Yet his brilliant autobiography reminded the nation what it had learned at Appomattox Court House in 1865: he was an extremely intelligent, albeit plainspoken and taciturn man who, unlike the generals who preceded him, had the will to save the Union.

Unfortunately, Grant's personality and skill sets were ill-suited to the world of politics, and he was soon captured by machine bosses like Cameron, Chandler, Conkling, and Morton. For whatever reason, Grant was the first to see how General Robert E. Lee could be defeated, but he could not see how these men used him. He could not understand how his administration facilitated corruption, birthed vicious political machines, diminished faith in the government, and eventually undermined the project of Reconstruction.

At this juncture, it is worth remembering the dinner Hamilton had with Thomas Jefferson in the early days of the republic. Hamilton dismissed the notion that corruption was a problem for a well-governed republic; indeed, it could be a boon if it was wielded by the right person. Lincoln, in many respects, proved Hamilton's point. If Lincoln had to buy off a handful of hack New Jersey pols to secure the passage of the Thirteenth Amendment and outlaw slavery once and for all, so be it. In fact, following Hamilton, perhaps we should be *grateful* that Lincoln had such corrupt tools at his disposal. If such a momentous vote could not be won on principle, then thank goodness Lincoln could win it through bribery.

Yet if Lincoln seemed to prove Hamilton's point, then Grant proved the point of Jefferson and James Madison. The latter, writing in *Federalist* #10, warns that the natural aristocracy was no hedge against the corruption that factionalism can breed:

> It is in vain to say that enlightened statesmen will be able to adjust these clashing interests, and render them all subservient to the public good. Enlightened statesmen will not always be at the helm.

Grant had proven himself to be an inspired warrior, but he was not an enlightened statesman. Under his helm, patronage was transformed from a system to reward campaign workers into a massive structure propping up party bosses in the Senate.

Returning to first principles, ultimately the problem was that the country had by this point effectively abandoned much of the original constitutional regime, without replacing it with something of equal value. Instead, subsequent generations of Americans venerated the Constitution while simultaneously ignoring inconvenient provisions, never realizing that maintaining the republican balance required careful consideration of each change that was made.

That never happened, obviously. As we saw last chapter, the country had created two extra-constitutional parties by the middle of the 1830s to pursue a newly democratized presidency; these two parties in turn began to loot the government to pay off their political contributors. The Constitution anticipated none of this, and these new arrangements were surely a challenge to a system Madison hopes will check "the violence of faction." Nevertheless, the country did not redesign the original charter with an eye to managing parties, and thus did not retain the balance that Madison sought to enact. In this chapter, we saw the perfection of the party system; absent countervailing forces, the Republican Party constructed massive and unstoppable statewide machines that raided the public treasury merely for its own perpetuation.

As we shall see in the next chapter, the destruction of the patronage system did not thwart these party machines. Once created, they could not be so easily destroyed, and they soon found new ways to aggrandize themselves at the expense of the public interest.

5

"The King of Frauds"

Business and Politics in the Gilded Age

THE GILDED AGE after the Civil War is usually remembered as an anomalous era of unprecedented corruption. Morals fell to shambles, avaricious politicians rose up, and there was an epic collapse in public ethics. None of this had ever been seen before, so the thinking goes.

In an important sense that is most definitely the case, for the country had never seen corruption quite as bad as existed in the two or three generations following the Civil War. But in another sense, that is not true. As we saw in the last chapter with the spoils system, while the level of patronage-based corruption may have increased, there was no qualitative difference between the Gilded Age and the Jacksonian period. Instead, the spoils system was perfected, in a perverse sense of the word. Politicians became more adept at using government jobs to grow and maintain political organizations, and in turn to bilk the public more efficiently than Andrew Jackson's cronies ever did.

The story is the same when we consider the other main theme of Gilded Age corruption, currying favor with big business. In Chapter One, we saw corruption spring up over governmental efforts to support the economy, in the case of the Bank of the United States. A former Treasury Department official used insider information to game the system, members of Congress were on the take, and even the stately Hamilton allowed details of his plans to become known to speculators. As we saw in Chapter Two, these trends continued through the Jeffersonian and Jacksonian eras; as government did more to grow the economy, business-oriented corruption similarly grew. This "progress" continued apace in the Gilded Age. It was not that this form of corruption—of public officials and business-men conniving for private goals—was unheard of prior to the 1880s. Far from it. Instead, as rapid economic growth depended more and more on governmental policies, the incentives and opportunities for businessmen to involve themselves in politics became greater. Meanwhile, with federal jobs no longer an available patronage outlet, and the costs of campaigns ever-growing, politicians sought new sources of funds to manage their po-litical empires. Thus, new forms of corruption did not emerge; instead, old forms proliferated and became more sophisticated, organized, and even accepted.

So commonplace were the new ways of doing business that, when hauled before a Senate investigative committee about the Sugar Trust's influence on Congress, Senator Matthew Quay unabashedly admitted that he had been speculating in sugar while the Senate was modulating the tariffs on refined and raw sugar, that he would continue to do so, and there was not a damned thing anybody could to do to stop him. And he was right.[1]

Why did this happen? In a word: money. As we shall see, the economic program that business wanted—lax regulations, the gold standard, and high tariffs—made vast classes of the citizenry worse off. Harm was espe-cially concentrated in the agricultural sector, which by this point was still the most populous of all working groups. This should not have happened, at least in theory; after all, the system as understood by James Madison was intended to prevent factions from dominating public policy for their own interests. Majority factions would be checked by the complicated structure of the Constitution; minority factions would be checked by the majoritarian principle at the heart of all true republics. If business interests were pursuing policies that helped the few at harm to the many, then they should have failed.

But money was the way around this. Money bought off key gatekeep-ers within the government, especially the Senate. Members of the upper chamber oversaw executive and court nominations, and thus ensured that only nominees friendly to business would get through. They dominated their state delegations to nominating conventions, meaning that presiden-tial nominees were never heretical. They also had great sway within their states, many of them operating as bosses who could squash unfavorable legislation even at the subnational level. Senators, as we shall see, were purchasable during this period, and this was why business could thrive even at the expense of the public at large.

During the Bank War of the 1790s, Madison and Thomas Jefferson worried that the Bank was buying off members of Congress so as to circumvent the will of the people. This happened to some extent, as we saw, but their worst fears went unrealized; Hamilton's steady leadership prevented calamity from happening, and the Bank was generally beneficial to the country. The same cannot be said during the Gilded Age. During this period, the country enacted every aspect of the Hamiltonian agenda and expanded upon it in significant ways, regardless of whether the government created by the Constitution was competent to carry out these tasks. It was not, and as we shall see, the result was Jefferson and Madison's worst nightmare. An interested clique of financial and industrial elites grabbed hold of the government and channeled public policy to their own ends, often at the expense of the public good. The stockjobbers that so worried Madison and Jefferson in 1791 look like penny-ante pikers compared to the corrupt politicians and well-heeled financiers who took the reins of the government in the Gilded Age.

By the middle of the 1880s, the Stalwart political bosses who built powerful machines because of Ulysses S. Grant's patronage policy were no more. The Pendleton Civil Service Act of 1883 had begun the process of creating a permanent bureaucratic class, and more importantly outlawed party assessments of government workers. President Chester Arthur, who was a true supporter of Ulysses S. Grant while serving as the collector of the New York Customs House, charted an independent course after President James Garfield's assassination, effectively destroying what remained of the Stalwart-dominated New York machine. Meanwhile, Grant's rock-ribbed supporters—Levi Morton, Roscoe Conkling, John Logan, Simon Cameron, Zach Chandler, and Stephen Dorsey—had all left the Senate. And, to add insult to injury, their mortal enemy, James G. Blaine, the Half-Breed Republican from Maine whom they so staunchly opposed in the 1876 and 1880 nomination battles, had finally won that prize in 1884.

Still, Grantism was essentially a solution to the collective action dilemma we discussed in Chapter Three, and this problem remained. That is, in an age when electoral campaigns cost exorbitant sums to carry on, how does one actually raise the cash? Federal patronage had been the solution to this challenge; with that avenue now closed, the political class searched about for an alternative.

Ironically enough, it was Blaine who was an innovator on this front; he was one of the first major party leaders to see the advantage of courting big business. Of course, Stalwart machines like Conkling's operation ran interference for businesses, but they remained essentially independent. By and large, Conkling had his own revenue streams in the form of federal patronage and skimming from the Customs House. Sometimes he allied with business; sometimes he didn't. Blaine was one of the first major political leaders in the Republican Party to forge a permanent relationship with the burgeoning class of well-heeled industrialists.

Between 1860 and 1890, the rate of growth in the industrial economy was astounding: the production of anthracite coal increased by 525 percent, bituminous coal by 2,358 percent, crude petroleum by 9,160 percent, and pig iron by 1,713 percent. The farm economy also expanded rapidly, as wheat production increased by 339 percent and corn by 301 percent. Even cotton, grown largely in the war-ravaged South, expanded by 261 percent.[2] The railroad network developed by leaps and bounds: in 1865 there were approximately thirty-five thousand miles of track; by 1897 there were two hundred thousand miles. Trunk lines connected all the eastern ports with growing midwestern cities like Chicago and St. Louis, a network of main and branch lines connected these cities to the farming areas of the Great Plains, several intercontinental rail lines had been built, and even the South's railroad infrastructure was growing.[3]

This era has often been called a laissez-faire period of history. The phrase suggests a lack of governmental interference in the economy, but in fact the government was a major player in it, strongly supporting certain industries with favorable policies. After the southern Democrats bolted from Congress in 1861, northern Republicans were free to pursue whatever legislative program they liked. As most of them were former Whigs, it should come as no surprise that they instituted a version of Henry Clay's American System. They passed strong protective tariffs, homestead laws to encourage westward expansion, and, most important for the railroads, legislation to promote their development. In particular, railroads received extensive land grants (roughly totaling 130 million acres), which they could sell to homesteaders at a profit. Those firms building the intercontinental railroad also received loans on generous terms from Uncle Sam.[4]

The railroads, created in part by government fiat, were of course very interested in ensuring that favorable policies would continue. And here Blaine would become a trusted ally. By 1877, several railroads had failed to pay back overdue loans, totaling about $65 million. Senator Allen Thurman, a Democrat from Ohio, offered legislation to establish a schedule of repayment, which the railroad barons—above all Jay Gould of the Union Pacific and Collis Huntington of the Central Pacific—most desperately wanted to avoid. As such, they turned to Blaine, at that point a senator and a once and future presidential aspirant, to kill the bill. He did so successfully, prompting liberal Republican Senator George Edmunds of Vermont to complain privately:

> It is my opinion that Mr. Blaine acts as the attorney of Jay Gould. Whenever Mr. Thurman and I have settled upon legislation to bring the Pacific railroads to terms of equity with the government, up has jumped James G. Blaine, musket in hand, from behind the breastworks of Gould's lobby, to fire in our backs.[5]

Blaine's continued efforts on behalf of the railroads did not come cheaply. In 1869, he had saved a land grant for a southern railroad, and as a gratuity the company offered him special privileges, giving him more than $150,000 in land grants and bonds for selling securities to his friends. Later, when the railroad went belly up, Tom Scott, the baron whose career included the presidencies of both the Pennsylvania Railroad and the Union Pacific, bought $75,000 worth of those securities back from Blaine's friends. He paid $64,000 for them, far more than the market share. These dealings became public prior to the 1876 nomination battle, killing Blaine's chances. And, naturally, the Democrats made use of them in the 1884 general election campaign, dubbing him "James G. Blaine, the continental liar from the state of Maine."[6]

If men like Gould and Huntington represented a new form of businessman—the captain of industry who had under his control tens of millions of dollars of capital and thousands of workers across dozens of states—Blaine represented a new form of politician. Previously, businessmen interested in grabbing something from the government usually had to deal with an endless horde of avaricious, grasping legislators. This was especially true on the state level; in the past, the relationship was such that it was unclear whether they were bending public policy to their whims or whether greedy government officials were simply extorting money from them. But Blaine, a leader with an enormous following both inside and outside the government, was offering the railroad barons a simplified form of transaction: they dealt with him, and he dealt with his followers. This is a model that other industry leaders would endorse, even after the railroads were eclipsed.

For all his shady dealings, Blaine was somehow not involved in one of the greatest acts of malfeasance in the nineteenth century: the Crédit Mobilier scandal, which broke in 1872 and dominated headlines for much of 1873. It implicated dozens of government officials, including Vice President Schuyler Colfax, future Vice President Henry Wilson, and future President Garfield. The heads of the Union Pacific Railroad created Crédit Mobilier as a dummy corporation that was supposed to do construction work for the railroad (at a handsome profit for its owners). To cover up this obvious conflict of interest, the owners of Crédit Mobilier made common cause with Representative Oakes Ames of Massachusetts, who sold shares of Crédit Mobilier to members of Congress. In fact, several members paid nothing, using the dividend from the stock as payment.[7]

The *New York Sun* blew the lid off the story in September 1872, hoping to embarrass Grant. Its headline read:

THE KING OF FRAUDS
How the Credit Mobilier
Bought Its Way Through Congress
COLOSSAL BRIBERY
Congressmen who Have Robbed the People, and who now Support
the National Robber
HOW SOME MEN GET FORTUNES
Princely Gifts by the Chairmen of Committees In Congress[8]

A congressional investigation ensued, which came down very hard on the railroad executives for trying to bilk the government, but unsurprisingly went very easy on members of Congress. In the end, Ames was censured for bribing congressmen, but no congressmen were censured for having accepted bribes. Historians who have examined this after the fact have concluded that Ames was certainly trying to peddle influence, that he offered the stock to members of Congress friendly to the Union Pacific, and that they only grabbed it after learning that a generous dividend would be paid them.[9]

Crédit Mobilier was the most notorious example of railroad influence peddling, but it was far from the only one. As we saw in Chapter Four, the Reconstruction South was particularly rife with corrupt dealings between would-be railroad tycoons and carpetbagging legislators.[10] Similarly, the Erie Wars in New York saw railroad tycoon Cornelius Vanderbilt pit his bought-and-paid-for pols against those in the pocket of Erie Railroad Treasurer Daniel Drew.[11] And all across the country, railroads regularly distributed free passes to members of Congress, state legislators, governors, reporters, and anybody else who could help their cause. Railroad executives were always ready to loan money to legislators who were strapped for cash and would be very forgiving whenever repayment ran a little late; they would throw junketing parties that wined and dined important members of the government; they would give family members hot stock tips, jobs, or other sinecures.[12] As Huntington once said, the railroads saw three types of legislators: the clean (who would do "the right thing" without being bribed), the commercial (who needed bribes), and the communists (who could not be bribed and who would not back the railroads). In a letter to a colleague, he was unabashed about the practice of bribery:

> If you have to pay money to have the right thing done, it is only just and fair to do it. . . . If a man has the power to do great evil and won't do right unless he is bribed to do it, I think the time spent will be gained when it is a man's duty to go up and bribe the judge. A man that will cry out against them himself will also do these things himself. If there were none for it, I would not hesitate.[13]

In the wake of Crédit Mobilier, the position of the railroads in the political process began to decline. On the federal level, the scandal soured the country's appetite for more land grants to the railroads. Meanwhile, on the state level, farmers, especially in the Midwest and Great Plains, had turned against the railroads. Often, executives would water their stock down, and to continue to pay dividends they would raise rates. In areas of high competition, like the Northeast, that was simply impossible, so rate hikes usually punished midwestern farmers outside the trunk lines. On top of that, railroads often controlled grain silos and other storage units that farmers needed to store their crops, and would charge a fortune for their use. For some hard-pressed farmers, it became cheaper to burn their crops rather than ship them to market. Widespread agrarian unrest eventually prompted state governments to begin regulating railroads; the Supreme Court eventually upheld these Granger Laws.[14]

By the end of the nineteenth century, the age of dominant railroad barons was basically at an end; governmental regulation, popular disapproval, and rampant overdevelopment meant the industry's growth began to slow markedly. Consolidation was inevitable, and eventually tycoons like J. P. Morgan began to control them as parts of much larger economic empires.

Other business enterprises would emerge to replace the railroads at the pinnacle of politics. Many of the corporations of this new age had been transformed by the opportunities and constraints of the industrial economy. No longer was the dominant form of organization a single owner or a partnership; instead, large pools of capital were required, with ownership distributed across a vast group of anonymous people and day-to-day decisions made by a professional management class. Moreover, high fixed costs put enormous pressure on businesses to combine, either vertically or horizontally, in a way to regulate prices and production.[15] All of this put businesses on a potential collision course with government, at the state and federal level. There were an infinite number of ways in which the interests of this industry or that corporation might conflict with the public good, be it in one of the several states or the nation at large. What would business do then?

The answer, as we shall see, is that it would dominate politics in ways that are to this day unparalleled. In particular, its vehicle for dominance was the Republican Party, which followed Blaine in abandoning the Stalwartism of Grant, Logan, and Conkling in favor of a policy agenda that unified the interests of the financial sector in the Northeast with manufacturing interests in the Midwest, key agricultural factions, and Civil War veterans.

The alliance between business and the GOP was similar in essence to the alliance between the financial sector and the Federalists, and later with early industrial concerns and the Whigs, in that the two worked to secure each other's interests. The difference was that the government could simply do *more* for big business in the Gilded Age, and so the relationship between a party and corporations was tighter than it had ever been. Moreover, Republican policies were hegemonic for more than a generation; even if the Democrats usually controlled portions of the government, they never succeeded in implementing alternatives to the probusiness GOP.

In particular, the Republican alliance with the business community depended on the promotion of three policies: a lax regulatory structure, the gold standard, and high protective tariffs. On any given policy, some Democrats in some places could be counted on to support the interests of business, but only the GOP leaders provided blanket support; for instance, Democratic presidential candidates from Samuel Tilden in 1876 through Grover Cleveland in 1892 were all strongly progold and opposed strenuous regulation of business, but they were weak on protection. Many Republicans were weak on at least one of these issues, especially on the state level in the West. But the upper echelons of the GOP were dominated by northeastern conservatives and business-friendly midwesterners, and they could deliver all three policies.[16]

First and foremost, businesses wanted government not to restrict them, on the state or federal level.[17] This hands-off approach was protected by the Court, dominated overwhelmingly by conservatives in this period (the four Court nominees of Cleveland, a Democrat, were indistinct from their Republican counterparts on this issue). In particular, the Court carved out three important principles for business interests. First, it used the Commerce Clause to squelch state regulation of interstate commerce, taking a very broad view of what constituted the latter. Second, it interpreted the Interstate Commerce Act and the Sherman Antitrust Act (the two major pieces of federal regulation during this period) in ways most beneficial to business. Finally, and most importantly, it reimagined the Fourteenth Amendment's Due Process Clause as a license for the Court to review state regulations of intrastate business activity.

As late as 1880, it was not at all clear that the Court would take this approach. After all, in the *Slaughter-House* cases of 1873, the Court explicitly rejected the idea that the Fourteenth Amendment limited the ability of state governments to regulate business. Moreover, in *Munn v. Illinois* in 1876, the Court upheld the authority of state governments to regulate grain silos in Illinois, declaring that the state had the power to regulate a business that directly influences the public interest. Yet the conservative appointees of Rutherford Hayes, Garfield, Arthur, Cleveland, Benjamin Harrison, and (later on) William McKinley eventually reshaped the Court, so that by 1886 it began walking back its expansive view of state regulation. The Court also took a very negative view of labor unions, and even reversed an earlier ruling that had upheld the income tax.[18]

Political scientist Richard Bensel calls the Court's actions here the "judicial construction of the national market." Although it was an integral part of Republican economic policy, Bensel contends that it was essential for the Court to carry this program out because it was so unpopular. State after state, including many with Republican majorities, enacted new regulatory laws during this period, and despite the best efforts of conservatives in Congress, even the federal government instituted new regulatory laws like the Interstate Commerce Act. It was only the Court that was sufficiently isolated from public opinion to carry on this program.[19]

The same was basically true of the gold standard. While this policy did not directly benefit the manufacturing class, it was nevertheless essential to its prosperity. The gold standard enabled the integration of New York and European money markets, which allowed for government bonds and railroad securities to be exported. It also encouraged financiers to invest their capital in American manufacturing concerns, rather than sending it abroad.[20] Like laissez-faire, however, this was an extremely unpopular policy, at least in certain quarters. As such, the secretary of the treasury, who was relatively removed from the ebbs and flows of public opinion, took charge of maintaining the gold standard during this period.

Because gold was in relatively short supply during this period, the maintenance of the gold standard meant a slow but steady deflation. A pair of Levi Strauss jeans that cost $1.12 in 1875 would have cost just $0.92 in 1885. In our consumer-centered society, this may sound a great deal, but it led to disaster for the agricultural classes in the South and West, which were heavily indebted, largely to northeastern creditors. Every year, farmers had to produce more and more just to pay back their loans. That made them desperate for inflation, above all the printing of cheap silver dollars.[21] Prosilver sentiment was widespread in the country during this period, and in many sessions a majority of Congress was at least somewhat disposed to silver. While the conservatives always managed to squash the idea of unlimited coinage of silver (which would have driven gold entirely out of the country), they nevertheless had to compromise at several points to allow for the limited coinage of silver. The Bland-Allison Act of 1878 and the Sherman Silver Purchase Act of 1890 required the Treasury Department to mint a fixed amount of silver coins every month.[22]

As gold dollars were more valuable than their silver counterparts, the efforts of the government to put the silver coins in circulation were unsuccessful, as they were quickly exchanged for gold coins. Thus, the onus was on the executive branch, and in particular the secretary of the treasury, to ensure that the gold standard was maintained despite the silver coinage.[23] This meant in effect keeping the gold reserve at or greater than $100 million, a signal that all government money was exchangeable for gold. Maintenance of this standard was generally a pretty easy feat to accomplish, given how the tariff generated such a large surplus for the treasury. But the Panic of 1893 drastically reduced federal tax revenues. On top of that, the Court outlawed the federal income tax in 1895, dealing another blow to projected federal tax revenues. Soon enough, uneasy investors began to fear that the gold reserve might not be sufficient, and a panic depleted the reserves. Congress rebuffed President Cleveland's proposal of a bond to purchase new gold, and finally, with nowhere left to turn, Cleveland, a staunch gold bug, embraced a plan from Morgan and the Rothschilds House to import gold from Europe.[24]

The final policy, a strong protective tariff, was not so much an economic necessity as it was a political one. The tariff benefited key electoral constituencies, keeping them with the GOP even if other aspects of its program did not aid them. For that reason, the tariff was the responsibility of the Congress, the branch closest to the people. In essence, the tariff became a massive congressional logroll, the largest in history up to that point. With it, the Republicans could effectively buy off capital owners in selected industries, as well as their workers. They also expanded it to certain agricultural sectors, like the wool industry, to shore up their support in the key midwestern battlegrounds where gold was deeply unpopular. On top of this, the tariff—in particular, the tariff on refined sugar—was so large that it created enormous annual surpluses. Republicans dedicated those spare revenues to ever-generous pensions for Union veterans. In particular, the Dependent Pension Act of 1890 opened the pension rolls up to any disabled Union veteran, regardless of whether his wounds occurred during the war, and by 1895 some 74 percent of veterans were receiving a pension (compared to 17 percent just ten years prior). Veterans were a crucial electoral constituency, especially in Ohio, Indiana, and New York, all of which were uncertain states in the presidential election.[25] Thus, the pension program captured yet another vital electoral group in the logroll.

While responsibility for these policies was spread out across all three branches of government, the Senate was the keystone of the operation. Senators obviously played a large role in the formulation of tariff policy, and they were useful in watering down House sponsored efforts to regulate business or inject silver coinage into the economy.[26] They also exercised oversight over the Treasury Department and the Court, by virtue of their authority to advise and consent on nominations. Furthermore, because senators were selected by state legislatures, they had a strong incentive to organize state parties in the hopes of dominating them. This, in turn, meant that they were an important point of contact for business interests eager to influence national *and* subnational policy. Finally, because of this state dominance, senators usually carried great sway with delegations to the presidential nominating convention; in many cases, they controlled them altogether. This meant that senators had great influence in deciding who was and who was not a viable candidate for the nomination.[27]

And so it was that dozens of senators during this period were in hock to business interests. Among them were Orville Platt of Connecticut; William Allison of Iowa; Eugene Hale of Maine; James McMillan of Michigan; Thomas Platt and Chauncey Depew of New York; Joseph Foraker and Mark Hanna of Ohio; J. Donald Cameron, Quay, and Boies Penrose of Pennsylvania; Nelson Aldrich of Rhode Island; Stephen Elkins and Nathan Scott of West Virginia; and Philetus Sawyer and John Spooner of Wisconsin.

How was this connection solidified? For starters, there was a lot of intermingling between the groups. Aldrich's daughter, for instance, was married to John D. Rockefeller, Jr. Also, many senators doubled as captains of industry. For instance, Elkins was a mine owner, Sawyer made his fortune in the lumber lobby, and McMillan was a railroad magnate. Still others were lawyers or counselors for the business elite. Most famously, Depew was the right-hand man to Vanderbilt for years. Additionally, Allison and Spooner worked as lawyers for big corporations.[28]

Of course, professional crosspollination was no substitute for money when it came to influencing politics. Money paid for campaign organizations at the grassroots; it paid for literature and its distribution; it paid for the speaking fees of thousands of surrogates; and it enabled politicians to grant the kinds of favors necessary to run powerful political machines. After the money from federal patronage disappeared, money from corporate America is what made up the difference.[29]

The 1884 election was really the first time big business played a front-and-center role with the Republicans, as Blaine socialized prominently with captains of industry like Andrew Carnegie. In 1888, and above all in 1896, the Republican National Committee made great inroads in soliciting contributions from big business—"frying the fat," as one Republican operative put it. Indeed, by 1904, some 39 percent of reported contributions to the Republican presidential effort were in amounts of $50,000 or more, which works out to be roughly $1.3 million or better today. In all, such mega donations accounted for $900,000 of the party's reported receipts, or $23 million in today's dollars.[30]

How were Republican politicians responsive to the needs and interests of the business community during this period? We have already answered this question in the aggregate: the party elite promoted three core policies for business and took in contributions hand over fist because of it. While this is instructive, it only tells part of the story. What about individual politicians? What did they give, and what did they get in return?

Unsurprisingly, politicians were loath to keep accurate records of their dealings, which is why it was such a big deal when William Randolph Hearst got his hands on the correspondence between John Archbold of the Standard Oil Company and various politicians on the state and federal level. Such a scoop was it that Hearst, despite acquiring the letters some time earlier, held off on publishing them until the 1912 campaign season, and then dripped them out month by month in *Hearst's Magazine*.

The Standard Oil Letters implicated over a dozen public officials, but probably none was caught with his hand farther into the kitty than Foraker, Republican senator from Ohio.[31] Hearst's scoop indicated that Standard Oil gave Foraker at least $44,000 in 1900 alone (which works out to be nearly $1.2 million in today's dollars). The letters Hearst revealed did not detail an explicit quid pro quo, but they certainly suggested as much. Archbold would send thousands of dollars to Foraker "in accordance with our understanding," as he once wrote. Importantly, he would also send along detailed opinions about various politicians, and often even make a request for intervention. For instance, in January 1900, he wrote:

> The matters regarding which I wanted to talk with you this afternoon are those of threatened and very objectionable legislation at Columbus. The first is a bill introduced by Mr. Russell of Meigs, amending the so-called "anti-trust" law in a way that would be most objectionable to every corporate interest in the state. Probably you are familiar with this bill.
>
> The second is a most malicious resolution for an investigating committee to be headed by Griffin, of Lucas, giving them power to investigate pretty much everything within the state, from the Supreme Court down. The resolution does not limit the expense of the investigation, and authorizes the employment of counsel. It is said to be the intention of the committee to employ [Ohio Attorney General] Mr. [Frank] Monnett[e] as its counsel. We want to enlist you actively and promptly to the defeat of these measures. They are undoubtedly inspired by Monnett[e] and his followers, and their purpose is unquestionably of the most vicious character. That appointment of the "marauding" committee comes up by agreement on the 25th, so that it, as well as the other, should be attended to very promptly. Will you do everything to compass their defeat? Shall be glad to hear from you promptly.[32]

What is most notable about this is the familiarity of it all, not just in this letter to Foraker but in all the letters that Hearst revealed. There is no apologizing, no sense of embarrassment, not the slightest hint that this is an extraordinary request. That strongly suggests that correspondence such as this was very common; politicians and well-heeled donors would trade favors for contributions with such regularity that nobody involved thought anything of requests such as this.

While Foraker came off looking terrible because of the Standard Oil Letters, he was hardly the worst offender of the era, nor was he the most industrious. While he acted improperly, he never leveraged his favoritism into his own political fiefdom. Throughout his career, he always played second fiddle, even in Ohio, first to John Sherman and later to Hanna, who were much better at the game than Foraker.

The political entrepreneurs who did dominate the era are worthy of special consideration, for in many respects they equaled the likes of Vanderbilt, Rockefeller, and Carnegie. They not only used corporate support to enrich themselves and ensure their reelections, but to create indomitable political organizations. There were probably a half dozen or more such bosses who spanned this era, ruling either their state or the Senate or both, but two in particular stand out as archetypes of power. Quay in Pennsylvania was the prototypical state boss whose tight relationship with business interests helped him control a diverse, populous, and important state. Meanwhile, Aldrich had little interest in controlling the politics of Rhode Island, but instead set his sights on dominating the Senate itself. Let's take a closer look at both men.

––––––––––––

Quay of Pennsylvania might very well have been the greatest politician of the Gilded Age. Though the Keystone State was exceedingly diverse, the Democrats never came close to cracking it during his reign. The state was never up for grabs during the presidential election contests, its congressional delegation was always strongly Republican, and the Democrats only once held the governorship. So durable was the Pennsylvania machine that, when Quay died in 1904, control transitioned seamlessly to Penrose, his top lieutenant, who in turn commanded it until his death in 1921.

Yet neither Quay nor Penrose is remembered for any great feat of public service. The vast powers they concentrated were never dedicated to anything but the perpetuation of those powers. Quay served in the Senate for fifteen years, but his name was never attached to any great piece of legislation. Ditto Penrose, whose service lasted for almost a quarter century. Today, these titans of Gilded Age politics are largely forgotten. Insofar as they are remembered, it is only in venues such as these, where their turpitude is the main interest.[33] Still, Quay's political acumen cannot be understated. Though he was once an opponent of Simon Cameron, he nevertheless became, by the time of the latter's retirement, one of his most trusted allies. And though Cameron had hoped to pass control of his machine to his son, in fact it was Quay who took charge. The younger

Cameron had a somewhat imperious temperament and was not the adept manipulator of men that Quay would prove himself to be. Quay had the right kind of mind to balance the various forces within Pennsylvania politics, and to do so without cracking heads.[34]

When Quay inherited the Pennsylvania machine in the mid-1880s, he understood what only a handful of other Republicans, like Blaine, were coming to terms with. The old methodologies were no longer working; bosses could no longer count on federal patronage to meet the demands of the machine. No president since Grant had been friendly to the bosses, not even Arthur, who had been a lieutenant of Conkling in New York. Moreover, the Pendleton Civil Service Act had outlawed many easy sources of party revenue. Meanwhile, there were still tens of thousands of men on the machine's payroll in Pennsylvania, with a cost of over $20 million.[35] What to do?

Like Blaine, Quay would get in very tight with the business interests, not only in the state of Pennsylvania (a key industrial cog in the nation's economic machine) but also the country at large. They could fund his machine, and his machine in turn would ensure that their interests were well tended to in Harrisburg and Washington. In reorienting the machine this way, Quay became one of the first bosses to act as an intermediary between business and government. Rather than bribing dozens of legislators, who might not even vote the way they were instructed, businesses could bribe Quay, who in turn would make sure that his troops in the statehouse did what they were supposed to do. In this way, Quay helped make corruption a much more tidy, sophisticated affair.[36]

It should thus come as little surprise that Quay's name was mentioned many times in Hearst's Standard Oil expose. In fact, Quay somehow manages to stand out amidst all the perfidy by asking *too much* of Standard Oil! In a letter dated July 18, 1898, Archbold wrote Quay to inform him: "I have your favor of the 15th and will do as you request, provided that you finally say that you need so much. Please ask for it in installments, as needed, from time to time, not all at once."[37] The details of Quay's demands have been lost to history; one can only imagine just how much cash he wanted that the mighty Standard Oil needed to spread it out.[38]

With "the Interests," as muckraker David Graham Phillips calls them, supplying Quay the resources needed to take control of his state, Quay attacked at the point of greatest impact: the state treasury. As Penrose would later explain: "Quay made it his policy to keep at least one hand on the public purse. Only once in twenty years was there a state treasurer he could not control while he was in power. That state treasurer was Matthew Stanley Quay."[39] With control over the treasury, Quay was able to send state funds to pet banks, where his machine in turn was able to take unsecured loans out on those revenues. That money was then used to fund campaigns, buy off local party bosses and newspaper editors, or bankroll speculative schemes by machine agents, especially Quay himself. Over the course of his career, Quay lost millions of dollars in this sort of speculation, and was almost sent to prison, saved only by a bailout from the Camerons.[40]

Quay's career also demonstrates that the avenue between politics and business was not a one-way street. Yes, politicians effectively gave businesses more (i.e., favorable legislation) than they received in return (campaign contributions, graft, etc.), but in many cases businesses were simply extorted by state leaders. This occurred with less regularity after the rise of machine bosses like Quay, but such men were still quite capable of scamming the wealthy when they thought they could get away with it.

One such example with Quay concerns the streetcar lines in Philadelphia. At one point, a businessman from Cleveland approached Quay and Penrose with an offer to expand the lines in Philadelphia and charge less than the current holders of the licenses, Peter Widener and William Elkins, were offering. Widener and Elkins were away in Europe, so Quay and Penrose acted quickly to pass a law through the state legislature providing for charters for new Philadelphia lines. Rather than give the new lines to the man with the original idea, the state machine quickly snatched them up via a series of dummy buyers with neither the intention nor the money to build the lines. When Widener and Elkins returned home, they had no choice but to buy the licenses from the machine, with a tidy profit going to the latter. Powerful and wealthy as they were, there was really nothing else the two could do. The reality was that their economic position depended upon the benevolence of the state government, which meant they had no choice but to acquiesce when Quay extorted them.[41]

Far from rebuking Quay, the national Republican Party in fact depended on him when it mattered most, in the hotly contested presidential election of 1888. For the first time in a quarter century, the Republicans were running a presidential campaign from the outside looking in. With Cleveland in the White House, the Republicans could not use the executive branch to fill up their campaign coffers, so they turned to Quay. He was instrumental in shifting the party's national message away from the Bloody Shirt and toward an economic appeal centered around protective tariffs. When

Cleveland proposed reductions in the tariff schedules in 1887, he handed Quay a golden opportunity. The latter was relentless in his pursuit of business contributions, warning industrialists all across America the harm that would befall them if the Democrats succeeded in rolling back protection. In total, the Republicans officially raised about $1.2 million, with over 40 percent of the contributions coming from Pennsylvania and $50,000 coming from Quay himself.[42]

When Quay passed away in 1904, the control of the state went to Penrose, who continued the same methods. Penrose, who was born into a Philadelphia patrician family, never much saw the appeal of graft. His vices had more to do with hard drinking and loose women, but like Quay he also lusted after power.[43] After the state auditor revealed that massive graft had accompanied the construction of the new state capitol in 1902, reformers thought they might finally get proof that Penrose was on the take. Yet they were sorely disappointed. While there can be little doubt that Penrose knew his cronies were bilking the government to the tune of millions of dollars in construction costs, he himself stayed away. As he said at the time:

> A long time ago I decided I didn't want that kind of money. It screams too loud when grasped. I decided to get far enough along to be able to control legislation that meant something to men with real money and let them foot the bills. Never commit yourself but always be in a position where you can if you choose. The men with money will look you up then and you don't have to worry about campaign expenses.[44]

The famously blunt Penrose had a way with words, and here he captures the ethos of the era as well as anybody ever has.

Like much of New England, Rhode Island was rock-ribbed Republican for the entire period in question. Prior to that, it was usually to be found in the column of the Whigs. Given the fact that it was dominated by proto-populist agrarians in the 1780s, this might come as a bit of a surprise. But the commercial and industrial revolutions that transformed New England into a wealthy shipping and manufacturing hub swept Rhode Island along with it. By the time Aldrich entered the Senate in 1881, it was solidly Republican and quite comfortable with governance by and for the Interests.

Rhode Island in fact was a very easy state to control. The Constitution requires each state to have a "republican" form of government; if most southern states made a mockery of this principle by disenfranchising African Americans, Rhode Island was not much better. Each township counted as one political unit, and therefore enjoyed one seat in the statehouse. What this meant was that the most populous cities, like Providence, had as much representation as towns that had just a few hundred residents. In all, a political faction that won as few as one-eleventh of the public's support could control the entire state government. Moreover, the votes of many Rhode Islanders were, to put it bluntly, up for sale. The "purchaseables," as they were known, leveraged their outsized political power to pull in some extra cash at election time, and more often than not would solicit bribes from both sides of the aisle.[45] Thus, when Aldrich was elected to the Senate, he was set for life, provided he kept the right people happy. Of course he did, and his efforts on this front were minimal enough that he could turn his attention to acquiring power in Washington.[46]

The Senate of the Gilded Age lacked the formal leadership structures that it exhibits today, but there were nevertheless men who dominated the body. In the 1890s, a select group of senators met regularly for a poker game at Senator McMillan's home. This game came to be known as the "School of Philosophy," and its members were the informal leaders of the Republican Party in the upper chamber. Within this group was a central clique of four men who were the leaders among the leaders: Aldrich, Allison, Orville Platt, and Spooner.[47] Each served an important purpose in the Republican Party. For instance, nobody was better than Spooner at defending the party's positions. Meanwhile, Allison was a key liaison between the Interests and Republicans in the Midwest; he more than anybody else worked to dilute proposals that would be bad for the Interests, like free silver or federal regulation of businesses. As for Aldrich, he was the "Head of it All," as Phillips puts it.

Aldrich's greatest asset was his acute understanding of tariff laws, and his domain was the Senate Finance Committee. From Arthur's first efforts to systematize tariff laws in 1883 until the Payne-Aldrich Tariff law of 1909, there was nobody in the Senate who better understood the arcana of tariff laws (in the whole government, probably only McKinley was his match), and nobody who so diligently worked to protect the interests of the Interests.

For instance, when Arthur established a tariff commission in 1882, it surprisingly suggested that tariff rates be reduced as part of an overall reform of the schedules. But after a tariff law wound its way through the Senate Finance Committee, it neither reduced rates significantly nor rationalized the code. This "Mongrel Tariff," as it was known, was transformed due to the efforts of Aldrich.[48] A quarter century later, Aldrich was doing the same thing. To blunt the populist-progressive message of William Jennings Bryan, the Republican platform of 1908 declared "unequivocally for a revision of the tariff by a special session of the Congress." With William Howard Taft's victory that year, the Congress got to work on precisely that. The bill that emerged from the House did lower rates, but Aldrich's Senate enacted over eight hundred amendments, so that the final bill did not reduce rates significantly from their prior levels. When pressed on the party's betrayal of its platform, Aldrich retorted "Where did we ever make the statement that we would revise the tariff *downward*?"[49]

As the chief architect of the tariff for almost thirty years, Aldrich was not just close to particular industries in his home state that relied on favorable governmental policy. He, rather, was essential to all of them. As Phillips asserts:

> Various senators represent various divisions and subdivisions of this colossus. But Aldrich, rich through franchise grabbing, the intimate of Wall Street's great robber barons, the father-in-law of the only son of the Rockefellers—Aldrich represents the Colossus.[50]

Aldrich was explicit in his belief that businesses had a right to be represented in government. If public policy was going to affect private enterprise, then in Aldrich's opinion it was essential that private enterprise not only got a say, but the final say. As Lincoln Steffens argues, he was "the commercial ideal of political character."[51] That this was a firmly held view of Aldrich's, rather than an attitude that the Interests purchased, there can be no doubt. But there is also no doubt that Aldrich was very well paid by the Interests for articulating that view, and defending it so ably in the Senate. In fact, it netted him millions of dollars by the time he died.

One of Aldrich's key clients in the Senate tariff battles was the sugar interests, in particular Henry Havemeyer, the president of the American Sugar Refining Company. The Sugar Trust had two controversial stands on the tariff: first, it wanted the tariff duties on raw sugar to be kept low, and the duties on refined sugar to be kept high. Louisiana sugar growers hated the competition with foreign sugar, so keeping the duty on raw sugar low was not particularly easy. Moreover, the duty on refined sugar was one of the greatest moneymakers for the federal government, accounting for a sizeable portion of the annual surplus, which by 1890 had become something of a national embarrassment. Still, Aldrich combined a deep understanding of the tariff schedules with unmatched parliamentary adroitness to deliver for Havemeyer.

By the 1890s, Aldrich was growing tired of life in the Senate. He had expensive tastes—for instance, he had taken a shine to Persian rugs—and he always dreamed of owning a grand country estate on Warwick Neck. So, he was thinking of leaving politics for a more lucrative career in business. This was a loss that the Interests, and especially the Sugar Trust, simply could not afford.[52]

It was then the Sugar Trust intervened to keep Aldrich where it wanted him. John Searles, Jr., the chief industry lobbyist who had worked closely with Aldrich during the legislative battle over the Mongrel Tariff, offered an unbelievable business opportunity. He would stake between $5 and $7 million in cash to form the United Traction and Electric Company, of which Aldrich was made president for no money down. Their business would be to modernize the street railways in Rhode Island, with Aldrich furnishing the votes in the state legislature to grant the new outfit very generous franchises. So successful were they that $100 par value shares of United Traction and Electric Company sold for $40 in 1896 and $110 in 1901. Without investing any money of his own, Aldrich was made a millionaire several times over.[53] And thus he could stay in the Senate to represent the Interests, which he did most expertly.

———————

Even if we define corruption in the narrowest of terms, it is still more than evident during this period in American history. There is no way to define Quay's raiding of the Pennsylvania state treasury as anything but corruption. Similarly, we can be as charitable as we want to Aldrich, but we still must conclude that there was something deeply inappropriate in his dealings with Havemeyer, Searles, and the American Sugar Refining Company.

But such a slim view of things fails to capture the greater fraud of this era. Recall Chapter One, with Jefferson worrying about Bank shares influencing members of Congress to vote against their constituents' interests. Similarly, recall Madison's worries about certain factions legislating at the expense of others. Neither was supposed to happen in the American system, and yet during the period under study here, both did.

While there is much to celebrate about the American Industrial Revolution, it is important to remember that federal support of it was far from rational, systematic, or fair, as Clay envisioned his American System would be. Clay's program sought an explicit balance between the various factions within the country. In his schema, the country would develop economically, but in a way that explicitly benefited all Americans in roughly equal terms. This was not the case in the Gilded Age. The tariff may have been advertised as an agent of economic growth, but in fact it was a massive logroll that politicians fell into after inheriting the emergency tariff levels from the Civil War. Similarly, the gold standard was retained even though deflation during the period surely hampered the prosperity of the whole country, and the lax regulatory regime of the era was underwritten almost exclusively by the Court *against* the wishes of the mass public.

Moreover, the phrase "Industrial Revolution" is kind of a misnomer. Industrialism was far from a nationwide process, and the benefits did not accrue equally to all classes of people. It favored the Northeast and Midwest over the South and West, workers over farmers, capital owners over workers, and rich over poor. So it went with federal policy as well. If you were a farmer whose crops were exported worldwide, you probably did not enjoy any sort of protection for your product, the equipment you needed for your farm cost much more because its manufacturers were protected, and deflation meant that your crops were worth less and less every year, even as the mortgage on your farm remained the same. On top of that, the Supreme Court time and again struck down attempts by your representatives to regulate the railroads that were jacking up your shipping rates or the industrial plant that insisted your brother work twelve-hour days. Gilded Age public policy created winners and losers, and you were a loser.

As Democratic representative Hilary Herbert of Alabama put it:

> If the farmer in the Northwest and in the South will ponder upon these things he will understand why it is that in America there are so many rich manufacturers, who pile in money to swell the corruption fund in political campaigns, who give dinners in America that eclipse the world in extravagance, who ride in bedizened coaches and four over the turnpikes of Europe, who rent castles in Scotland and on the Rhine, and whose highest ambition seems to be, spurning the plain ways of the American people, to marry their daughters to these seedy scions of spendthrift aristocracy who are ever on the watch to trade their titles of nobility for the fortunes of foolish American women; and they will understand, too, how it is that there are so many impoverished American farmers.[54]

This is fundamentally inconsistent with what Madison envisions in *Federalist* #51. The federal government should not be able to pursue policies that so relentlessly favor some factions of the country over others. So, how did this come about? The answer parallels the complaint Jefferson and Madison leveraged against the Bank: the Interests corrupted the people's representatives. In a fair vote, the gold standard, laissez-faire, and much of the tariff regime might very well have fallen. As we saw, the Interests made sure that members of Congress, not to mention state representatives, were well tended to, so that a fair vote was never actually cast.

The result was that whenever the public good went against the demands of the Interests, the solid bet was on the latter. More often than not, politicians would either ignore public demands, or, better yet, pass measly pieces of legislation like the Bland-Allison Act, the Sherman Antitrust Act, or the Interstate Commerce Act. Perhaps Penrose put it best in his advice to Henry Clay Frick during the Homestead Strike. Give the strikers "a little extra gravy until they settle down," Penrose suggested, "then raise prices or the tariff to pay for it."[55]

While the Republican critique of Hamiltonianism missed the mark in important respects, the corruption of the Gilded Age vindicated the essential argument. For by that point the country had, in the main, adopted every one of Hamilton's major proposals for government support of the economy, and had created novel ones in addition. And the result? A Pennsylvania senator conspiring with a steel magnate to hoodwink the masses. This is the sort of thing that Jefferson and Madison warned about; a government that overstepped its boundaries to support a faction—even for the ostensible sake of the public good—was bound to be captured by that faction, with corruption the inevitable result. Hamilton might have been right that such policies were essential to the development of an American empire, but his opponents were right to point out it would threaten the very soul of the republic.

6

"To Dissolve the Unholy Alliance"

The Progressive Response to Corruption

T HE PROGRESSIVE MOVEMENT, which dominated American politics from 1901 to 1921, drastically changed the functions of government, and in doing so altered the relationship between the individual and the state. The impulses of the progressive movement—articulated in, for instance, the Progressive Party's 1912 platform and Woodrow Wilson's first inaugural address—remain the animating spirit of American liberalism, which now dominates the Democratic Party.

Though the progressive movement was a highly diverse political force, it had a handful of central ideas. Above all, progressives believed that the body politic was in need of drastic reform. Not all progressives suggested a reevaluation of the Constitution, but important ones did, and almost all progressives promoted policy innovations that had previously been the domain of radical agrarians or socialists. Their specific formulations varied, naturally, but most of them had in mind the same goals: to expand the powers of the national government to realize the public good, particularly in regulating the new industrial titans, and also to force the government to behave responsibly, rather than currying favor with small factions of society.

This idea of responsibility has an important relationship to James Madison's "great desideratum" of government, which as we noted in Chapter One, is "such a modification of the Sovereignty as will render it sufficiently neutral between the different interests and factions, to controul one part of the Society from invading the rights of another, and at the same time sufficiently controuled itself, from setting up an interest adverse to that of the whole Society." One can see how responsibility as an idea fits into this schema at least in some ways: an irresponsible government is one that is not neutral. And indeed that was a key critique of the progressives against Gilded Age government; it had been captured by a perverse combination of corporate malefactors and machine hacks, transforming the great middle of the country into its victims. The movement was thus an effort to reorder the body politic for the sake of the public interest, and from this perspective progressivism can be viewed as a reimagining of American republicanism.

Still, a wide intellectual gulf separated Madison from the progressives. Heavily influenced by European historicism, especially the writings of G. W. F. Hegel, many progressives came to eschew the notion of abstract right, which of course formed the bedrock of the constitutional system. Instead, they embraced the view that truths as we know them are contingent upon reason as revealed through history.

From the progressive standpoint, the Framers had not so much erred in their efforts as subsequent events had rendered their formulations moot. Madison had been particularly worried about a fractious majority violating the public good or minority rights for selfish ends. That is why, to accomplish this great desideratum, the Framers relied upon the popular will in only one half of one of the three branches, the House of Representatives; they believed that majorities could be as dangerous to true republicanism as anything. In contrast, the progressives believed that history had finally forged a national consciousness that could only be expressed by the unchecked will of the majority. In Madison's day, the thirteen far-flung former colonies barely had identifiable common interests beyond defense against the European powers, but the nineteenth century had created a people with a shared identity and common purpose. Standing in its way, the progressives reasoned, was Madison's most cherished doctrine, the separation of powers. Originally intended to keep fleeting majorities from undermining the public good, it was now inhibiting an enduring national majority from using government to realize the public good. Thus, whereas Madison sought to separate power as broadly as possible, the progressives— Wilson in particular—sought to concentrate it. Only by locating power in a single place could that power be made responsible to the public at large, and therefore reflect the newly developed national consciousness.

In the end, however, the progressive imposition of responsibility upon the government was more apparent than real. Much of this has to do with Wilson. While he originally supported the idea of transforming our system into something akin to the British model, where the executive and legislative functions are practically located in the British House of Commons, he abandoned that approach in the 1890s. Instead, he began calling for strong, vigorous presidential leadership, which, he claimed, could unite the powers that the Framers had separated, and thus induce the government to be responsible. Wilson's vision of the presidency has proven to be quite durable, inspiring scholars and the public at large to clamor for a presidential superman to force a recalcitrant Congress to put aside its petty squabbles for the greater good. But in practice, it has rarely existed. The main problem is that the modern vision of the presidency was never formally amended into the Constitution. Legally speaking, the relationship between Congress and the president is basically the same today as it was at the Founding. Instead, the modern president's mastery over Congress is wrapped up in the political context of the moment. When that context is favorable for executive leadership, the president can manage the government toward the sorts of responsible ends Wilson envisioned. But more often than not such a context is lacking.

Worse, the progressives *did* succeed in expanding the power of the federal government, which acquired the authority to regulate more intimately private business for the public good. Absent institutional reforms, this expansion in power would only increase the potential for corruption in future years. Following the core thesis of this book, growing governmental power without altering its institutions is a blueprint for corruption, as the government can be expected to exercise those powers irresponsibly, or corruptly. That is what we saw as the Hamiltonian (and, later, Whig and Republican) ideals of economic promotion were perverted into the machine systems of the Gilded Age. Expanding government's power to regulate the economy, without forcing it to do so responsibly, was bound to have a similar result.

Wilson also called for a bureaucracy that could pursue scientific principles of management to address policy problems without interference from political agents, but again he overpromised and underdelivered. As we shall see throughout the second half of the book, the bureaucracy has never been as independent of politics as the progressives claimed it could be. Moreover, members of the bureaucracy were quick to develop professional solidarity, organize themselves politically, and join the vast array of pressure groups actively participating in the public space. Thus, the progressives—to be followed by the New Dealers and the Great Society liberals—facilitated a new institution, largely unanticipated by the Constitution, that would become susceptible to corruption in the twentieth century and beyond.

The thesis of this book is a fundamentally Madisonian one: the structure of the government must correspond to the power it wields. Wilson, at least during his academic career, seemed to assent to a version of this hypothesis and called for an updating of the Constitution to meet the expectations of the power it should wield. But he and his allies never followed through, meaning that while they cut down on certain forms of corruption, like the corporate-dominated Senate, the essential sickness remained, and would manifest itself in different symptoms down the road.

––––––––––––––

The common conception about the Gilded Age—in its own day as now—is that something had gone afoul with America's civic morality. Corruption proliferated because the people had gone lax in their republican responsibility. As we have endeavored to show here, that thesis is problematic; the types of corruption that dominated during the Gilded Age were in fact present in previous eras, and the differences were instead of degree. But there is another problem with this idea: contrary to the suggestion of lax morals, reformers were almost always on the political battlefield during this era. The Liberal Republicans arrayed against Ulysses S. Grant; the Mugwumps opposed James G. Blaine; the populist movement refused to be crucified on what William Jennings Bryan called a "Cross of Gold." All of these groups had some grievance with the status quo, and there is barely a moment during the Gilded Age when they were not threatening upheaval of some sort or another.[1]

What sets the progressive movement apart from these previous efforts is its breadth of appeal, in particular its capacity to unite reformers of all stripes. The Liberal Republicans and Mugwumps were mostly northeastern elites who had little sway in the West. The populists, on the other hand, were a southern and western coalition that northeasterners feared. The Progressives linked these groups together by combining the Liberal/Mugwump appeal to good government with the populist desire to redistribute the national wealth (leaving aside their complaints about the currency). And so, the progressive movement had strong adherents in all quarters of the nation. Counted among its leaders were northeasterners like Wilson and Theodore Roosevelt, midwesterners like Wisconsin senator Robert LaFollette, westerners like California governor Hiram Johnson, and southerners like Georgia governor Hoke Smith.[2]

These men and others like them also came from both parties, which were internally divided along ideological lines. Conservative Republicans like Nelson Aldrich refused to cede an inch of ground, but Tammany Hall Democrats were just as opposed to the progressive movement. This created a level of confusion that we today—with a liberal Democratic Party and a conservative Republican Party—do not experience. In fact, 1904 was an election year when the Republican nominee, Roosevelt, was arguably farther to the left than his Democratic opponent, the Tammany-backed Aldon Parker.

There were not a lot of differences between the Republican and Democratic varieties of progressivism, and in historical retrospect it is much better to link Roosevelt's presidency to Wilson's than to fellow Republicans like Warren Harding or even William McKinley. That is not to say he and Wilson did not quarrel when they squared off for the presidency in 1912; they certainly did, but the disagreements turned out mostly to be rhetorical. About the only substantive differences between Roosevelt's "New Nationalism" and Wilson's "New Freedom" were mild disagreements on tariff reform (though both opposed the levels set by the Payne-Aldrich Act of 1909) and whether the trusts were socially useful. Roosevelt thought they were, and that the government should regulate them. Wilson railed against this kind of bigness and promised to squash them altogether. By and large, however, Wilsonian progressivism was basically identical to the Rooseveltian version; once in office, Wilson produced more progressive accomplishments than Roosevelt did in his two terms, and as many as the "Rough Rider" ever could have hoped to achieve in a third.[3]

In terms of policy, the progressive movement—Northeast, Midwest, South, West, Democratic, Republican—can be fairly summed up as an assault on the forces that had ruled politics more or less since the Civil War. These were the Senate bosses we discussed in the last chapter, the (Irish-run) urban political machines of the major American cities, and the giant corporations that now dominated so much of the American economy and, increasingly, society and politics. Thus, socioeconomically speaking, the progressives sampled most heavily from native-born, Protestant, middle class Americans, who were feeling squeezed by both the very wealthy and the very poor. Henry Demarest Lloyd spoke for many in the movement when he imagines that the middle class would "absorb the other classes."[4]

On the local level, the progressives tried to root out corruption in the cities by advocating nonpartisan elections, unelected city managers, ever-stricter regulations of patronage, and so on.[5] Many progressives also pushed for prohibition, a fairly obvious attack upon immigrant Catholics. Similarly, the eugenics movement that many progressives endorsed had not-so-subtle ethnic implications to it.[6] By and large, however, the progressives met with little success in their war against corrupt city machines and morally "suspect" immigrants. As we shall see in the next chapter, Tammany's preeminence in New York City would not be undone until the Great Depression and Franklin Delano Roosevelt's crafty distribution of patronage.

On the state and federal level, the progressives turned their attention to what Teddy Roosevelt calls "the malefactors of great wealth," who they believed were keeping the whole country from enjoying the fruits of industrial development. Henry George aptly sums up what had so disturbed his progressive brethren:

> We plow new fields, we found new cities; we girdle the land with iron roads and lace the air with telegraph wires; we add knowledge to knowledge, and utilize invention after invention . . . yet it becomes no easier for the masses of our people to make a living. On the contrary, it is becoming harder.[7]

In their pursuit of a more level playing field, progressives sought to expand vastly the powers of the federal government, which until that point had largely refrained from restraining economic activity among private citizens. Borrowing from Herbert Croly's influential *Promise of American Life*, it has often and rightly been said that the progressives pursued Hamiltonian means for Jeffersonian ends. That is, they advocated the use of a powerful national government to promote greater equality among the citizenry.

In general, progressives successfully advocated three types of reforms on the federal level.[8] First, they pushed for more aggressive regulation of businesses. These powers were already nominally on the federal books—thanks to the Sherman Antitrust Act and the Interstate Commerce Act, both passed in the 1880s—but the progressives were the first to take those laws seriously. The dominance of conservative Republicans in Congress generally stymied Roosevelt's legislative push in his first term, but in 1902 he famously opened up a suit under the Sherman Antitrust Act against the Northern Securities Company, a railroad trust belonging to such magnates as E. H. Harriman, James J. Hill, J. P. Morgan, and John D. Rockefeller.[9] Roosevelt also managed to get the Elkins Act passed in 1903. This only slightly increased the powers of the Interstate Commerce Commission (ICC) to regulate the railroads, but it was a prelude to the more powerful Hepburn Act of 1906, which allowed the ICC to set maximum railroad rates and beefed up its investigative and regulatory scope.[10] Later on, the Mann-Elkins Act of 1910 extended the power of the ICC to telecommunications.[11] The Federal Trade Commission Act of 1914 empowered a new regulatory agency to issue cease and desist orders to business combinations believed to be engaging in anticompetitive practices.[12] The Clayton Antitrust Act of 1914 further expanded federal power over trusts.[13] Beyond the trusts and the railroads, the Pure Food and Drug Act and the Meat Inspection Act, both passed in 1906, mandated truth in advertising for food and drugs shipped across interstate lines.[14] And the Federal Reserve Act of 1913 created the Federal Reserve, an institution that exists to the present day to regulate the currency.[15]

Second, the progressives extended the civil service regime and more generally worked to make government responsive to the public interest. The Tillman Act of 1907 prohibited federal candidates or parties from receiving corporate money. The Lloyd-LaFollette Act of 1912 clarified the grounds by which federal employees could be removed from office. The Seventeenth Amendment required the direct election of senators, and the Nineteenth Amendment extended voting rights to women.

Third, progressives sought to redistribute the national wealth toward the farming, working, and middle classes, away from the owners of capital. The Sixteenth Amendment legalized the income tax, and the corresponding Underwood Tariff lowered tariffs while imposing a modest income tax on top earners.[16] Progressive legislation also began supplying certain interests with new federal privileges; this idea was relatively limited during the progressive era, but it would become a dominant concept in American liberalism a generation later. The Federal Farm Loan Act of 1916 provided rural farmers with banking credits. Perhaps the most significant, and at the time most controversial, measure in this vein was the Adamson Act of 1916, which mandated an eight-hour workday for railroad workers.[17]

The progressives offered a vast array of solutions to address many national problems, but their agenda also had a deeper philosophical import. For starters, they called for a reconceptualization of liberty itself. As Roosevelt argues in his famous speech in Osawatomie, Kansas:

> The essence of any struggle for healthy liberty has always been, and must always be, to take from some one man or class of men the right to enjoy power, or wealth, or position, or immunity, which has not been earned by service to his or their fellows. That is what you fought for in the Civil War, and that is what we strive for now . . .

In our day it appears as the struggle of free men to gain and hold the right of self-government as against the special interests, who twist the methods of free government into machinery for defeating the popular will. At every stage, and under all circumstances, the essence of the struggle is to equalize opportunity, destroy privilege, and give to the life and citizenship of every individual the highest possible value both to himself and to the commonwealth.[18]

This is a substantially different definition of liberty than the Founders would have assented to. As Croly puts it, Roosevelt's progressivism substituted "a frank social policy for the individualism of the past."[19] That runs contrary to the conventional understanding of liberty as absence from restraint, but Roosevelt and the progressives argued that their agenda was deeply consistent with liberty.

In their view, just how free were people with a government that, by staying out of their way, facilitated their oppressors? This hands-off approach had in fact undermined the people's capacity to determine their collective fate through the government, a much more meaningful type of freedom than the scope of a state's police power. In the Framers' day, there was no such trade-off between governmental regulation and the freedom of the people to rule, but now there was. As Croly argues:

It is the economic individualism of our existing national system which inflicts the most serious damage on American individuality; and American individual achievement in politics and science and the arts will remain partially impoverished as long as our fellow countrymen neglect or refuse systematically to regulate the distribution of wealth in the national interest.[20]

Other notable progressive thinkers like John Dewey, Frank Goodnow, and William Allen White similarly called for the reconceptualization of liberty.[21]

In addition to rethinking liberty, the progressives hinted at an essential change in the constitutional structure. The government, as currently conceived, was simply incapable of advancing the public interest. Instead, as the Progressive platform of 1912 declared:

Behind the ostensible government sits enthroned an invisible government owing no allegiance and acknowledging no responsibility to the people.

To destroy this invisible government, to dissolve the unholy alliance between corrupt business and corrupt politics is the first task of the statesmanship of the day.

The deliberate betrayal of its trust by the Republican party, the fatal incapacity of the Democratic party to deal with the new issues of the new time, have compelled the people to forge a new instrument of government through which to give effect to their will in laws and institutions.[22]

In a certain sense, then, progressivism was really a reimagining of American republicanism, and the Progressive Party in 1912 saw itself as the vehicle to bring this about. In and of itself, the forging of a new political party represented a substantial challenge not just to the powers of government, but its very structure, for the sake of promoting responsibility.

Of course, Madison had dedicated much of the constitutional infrastructure to this very task, but the progressives believed that the problems of a modern, industrialized economy required new institutional solutions. As Roosevelt argues in his 1905 inaugural address:

Such growth in wealth, in population, and in power as this nation has seen during the century and a quarter of its national life is inevitably accompanied by a like growth in the problems which are ever before every nation that rises to greatness. Power invariably means both responsibility and danger. Our forefathers faced certain perils which we have outgrown. We now face other perils, the very existence of which it was impossible that they should foresee.[23]

So, while the progressives were pushing for a substantial expansion of federal power over the original grant of 1787, they had some fairly traditional reasons for doing so. The constitutional solutions of 1787 were no longer sufficient to protect the republican principles of 1787. The only way to save American republicanism, many progressives reasoned, was to revise the Constitution.[24]

Importantly, Wilson also was of the view that core principles had to be reconsidered, without regard to their historical provenance:

The Constitution is not honored by blind worship. The more open-eyed we become, as a nation, to its defects, and the prompter we grow in applying with the unhesitating courage of conviction all thoroughly-tested or well-considered expedients necessary to make self-government among us a straightforward thing of simple method, unstinted power, and clear responsibility, the nearer will we approach to the sound sense and practical genius of the great and honorable men of 1787.[25]

Wilson's views merit special consideration, for several reasons. While some men of this era were progressive philosophers and others were progressive politicians, Wilson was both. From the mid-1880s until his election to the New Jersey governorship in 1910, Wilson was a professor of political science and then president of Princeton University. And while, as we shall see, there are significant differences between Wilson's earlier work and his later writings, his core critique of the Madisonian system remained basically the same. In many respects, his presidency represents his efforts to realize the changes to the constitutional system that he prescribed some quarter century earlier.

———————

To understand what exactly frustrated Wilson about the Constitution, we have to understand his view of history and the role it played in philosophy itself. Heavily influenced by European historicism, especially the writings of Hegel, Wilson eschewed the idea that abstract principles are permanent.[26] Instead, he saw such concepts as being contingent upon the rational working-out of history. What was right or just in 1787 might not have been so in 1902, when Wilson published *A History of the American People*. In it, he writes:

> A full century had gone by since the government of the nation was set up. Within that century, it now began to appear, fundamental questions of governmental structure and political authority had been settled and the country drawn together to a common life. Henceforth matters were to be in debate which concerned the interests of society everywhere, questions of the modern world, touching nations no less than communities which fancied themselves to lie apart.[27]

For Wilson, the development of a national identity and the challenges of the modern world had obviated central principles of the Founding, above all Madison's separation of powers. This form of government might have made sense given the identity of the nation at the time, when it was a disparate and divided young republic. But there was no longer any reason to fear a fractious majority unjustly imposing its will upon a helpless minority; now, that majority could be expected to be animated by "the common consciousness, the common interests, the common standards of conduct, (and) the habit of concerted action."[28]

From this perspective, the separation of powers was not simply a vestigial organ harmlessly attached to the body politic; it was rather a cancer rotting the country from the inside out. It destroyed the possibility of democratic oversight of the government, which in turn meant that the government would never be responsible to the public will:

[L]arge powers and unhampered discretion seem to me the indispensable conditions of responsibility. Public attention must be easily directed, in each case of good or bad administration, to just the man deserving of praise or blame. There is no danger in power, if only it be not irresponsible. If it be divided, dealt out in shares to many, it is obscured; and if it be obscured, it is made irresponsible. But if it be centered in heads of the service and in heads of branches of the service, it is easily watched and brought to book. If to keep his office a man must achieve open and honest success, and if at the same time he feels himself intrusted with large freedom of discretion, the greater his power the less likely is he to abuse it, the more is he nerved and sobered and elevated by it.[29]

In his early writings on the subject, Wilson compared the American system unfavorably to the Commons. Because of the separation of powers, nobody could be held accountable, in either Congress or the executive branch. Worse, Congress parceled out responsibility to obscure committees that were further insulated from responsibility. In the end, the public may want one thing, but Congress is free to produce something quite different:

Without leaders having authority to guide their deliberations and give a definite direction to the movement of legislation; and, moreover, with none of that sense of responsibility which constantly rests upon those whose duty it is to work out to a successful issue the policies which they themselves originate, yet with full power to dictate policies which others must carry into execution,—a recognition of the need of some sort of leadership, and of a division of labor, led to the formation of these Standing Committees, to which are intrusted the shaping of the national policy in the several departments of administration, as well as the prerogatives of the initiative in legislation and leadership in debate . . . in practice, (this) subverts that most fundamental of all the principles of a free State,—the right of the people to a potential voice in their own government. Great measures of legislation are discussed and determined, not conspicuously in the public session of the people's representatives, but in the unapproachable privacy of committee rooms.[30]

The House of Commons, on the other hand, possessed the executive and legislative functions united under a strong political party led by the ministers of the government. Party members ran for election on an explicit program, which they were then empowered to legislate and execute. Their successes or failures were clear for all to judge for themselves, and so the actions of government could be said to embody the national will. Wilson asserts:

Responsible ministries . . . form the policy of their parties; the strength of their party is at their command; the course of legislation turns upon the acceptance or rejection by the Houses of definite and consistent plans upon which they determine. In forming its judgment of their policy, the nation knows whereof it is judging; and with biennial Congresses, it may soon decide whether any given policy shall stand or fall. . . . But, above and beyond all this, a responsible Cabinet constitutes a link between the executive and legislative departments of the Government which experience declares in the clearest tones to be absolutely necessary in a well-regulated, well-proportioned body politic.[31]

Wilson's complex relationship with Madisonian republicanism should be apparent in his comparison of Congress to the Commons. Like Madison, he was above all concerned with the realization of the public good. However, he had a different understanding of what that good requires of the government, and exactly what threatens it. Deeply worried about the unreliability of a majority to govern for the public interest, Madison separated power as broadly as he could while still creating a functional government. On the other hand, Wilson exhibited great faith in the wisdom of the majority, and as such believed power must be concentrated so that the majority can monitor its exercise. Put another way, the two start from basic republican premises, but their subsequent judgments led them to polar opposite conclusions.

Wilson's confidence in the public will and his belief that power must be centralized never wavered during his career in the academy or politics. What changed was his prescription to bring this about. In the 1880s, as a young academic, Wilson called for drastic reforms to transform Congress into a kind of American House of Commons. But as his reputation grew, and a political career became a possibility, he softened his tone, instead calling for the comparatively moderate idea of a strong president to promote responsibility. Historians judge that strategic considerations were at play here; it would have served his political purposes poorly if he advocated radical changes to the Constitution. However, Wilson was also impressed with the presidential leadership exhibited both by Grover Cleveland and Roosevelt.[32]

The influence of Roosevelt is worth another mention here, for no president until Wilson ever did as much to expand the scope of the executive office. Roosevelt insisted that he was swimming in Abraham Lincoln's wake, but there was a qualitative difference between Lincoln's efforts to win the Civil War and Roosevelt's threat to seize the coal mines during the anthracite strike in northeastern Pennsylvania in the winter of 1902. As political scientist Jean Yarbrough argues persuasively, Roosevelt came to espouse a new view of the role of the executive, that of a steward of the national interest who could on behalf of that interest draw upon inherent powers of government. Though Roosevelt always claimed to be following the example of Lincoln and the *Federalist Papers*, in fact he was searching for ways around the limits of the constitutional presidency.[33]

Wilson published *Constitutional Government* in 1908, the last full year of Roosevelt's presidency and just two years before his election to the governorship of New Jersey. It is clear from this work that the vigor of Roosevelt's administration had impressed him greatly:

> The makers of the Constitution seem to have thought of the President as what the stricter Whig theorists wished the king to be: only the legal executive, the presiding and guiding authority in the application of law and the execution of policy. . . . As a matter of fact he has become very much more. He has become the leader of his party and the guide of the nation in political purpose, and therefore in legal action. The constitutional structure of the government has hampered and limited his action in these significant roles, but it has not prevented it. The influence of the President has varied with the men who have been Presidents and with the circumstances of their times, but the tendency has been unmistakably disclosed, and springs out of the very nature of government itself. It is merely proof that our government is a living, organic thing, and must, like every other government, work out the close synthesis of active parts which can exist only when leadership is lodged in some one man or group or men.[34]

Moreover, Wilson put his money where his mouth was. Upon his election as governor of New Jersey, he actively involved himself in the policymaking process, using a combination of legislative bargaining and public advocacy to accomplish four major reforms: a direct primary law, a corrupt practices law, a workmen's compensation law, and the creation of a public utilities commission.[35] Wilson's success as New Jersey governor—an important northeastern state that Democrats had struggled to win for twenty years—made him an early favorite for the Democratic nomination in 1912. After he won the White House that year, he again employed this idea of strong presidential leadership, heavily involving himself with Congress and regularly making direct appeals to the public to accomplish his legislative goals.[36]

Wilson's success, along with the victories of other strong presidents like Franklin Roosevelt, Lyndon Johnson, and Ronald Reagan, have validated the Wilsonian concept of the presidency with much of the academy and the public at large. The country has informally expanded the scope of the presidency beyond what is formalized by Article II of the Constitution.[37] Today, among other things, the president plays the role of chief diplomat, legislative leader, party leader, advocate of prosperity, and popular tribune.[38]

As political scientist Jeffrey Tulis notes in *The Rhetorical Presidency*, this has amounted to a kind of second constitution. None of these responsibilities is enunciated in the founding document; instead, they hinge on the president's ability to use his prestige to coordinate various officers of the government. Presidential advisors, historians, and political scientists identify two main types of presidential influence, both of which Wilson utilized. The first is legislative bargaining. As presidential advisor Richard Neustadt puts it:

> Effective influence for the man in the White House stems from three related sources: first are the bargaining advantages inherent in his job with which to persuade other men that what he wants of them is what their own responsibilities require them to do. Second are the expectations of those other men regarding his ability and will to use the various advantages they think he has. Third are those men's estimates of how his public views him and of how their publics may view them if they do what he wants. In short, his power is the product of his vantage points in government, together with his reputation in the Washington community and his prestige outside.[39]

Neustadt sees the president dominating the inside game by his mere presence, and in recent years scholars have noted that presidents also rely on an outside game of direct public appeals. Political scientist Samuel Kernell calls this second strategy going public. Whereas Neustadt's bargaining president would bring pressure to bear directly on legislators, a president who goes public applies indirect pressure, through the medium of public opinion. In this thinking, the president rallies people to his cause, the clamor for his agenda shows up in polls and other metrics of the public mood, and then Congress finally relents to his will. While extant since the days of Roosevelt and Wilson, it has become a more dominant force of presidential leadership since the Reagan administration.[40] Most recently, Barack Obama's view of presidential leadership has been more heavily tilted toward outside persuasion than probably any of his predecessors.

This is the theory of strong presidential governance, hinted at by Cleveland, developed by Roosevelt, championed by Wilson, and clarified by subsequent politicians and academics. But how well does it work in practice? Are the informal powers of the presidency sufficient to impose the responsibility upon the government that Wilson thought was so necessary?

In a word, no. As Wilson's close advisor, Colonel Edward House, wrote in his diary:

> [Wilson and I] talked much of leadership and its importance in government. He has demonstrated this to an unusual degree. He thinks our form of government can be changed by personal leadership . . . [but] no matter how great a leader a man was, I could see situations that would block him unless the Constitution was modified. He does not feel as strongly as I do.[41]

House was right, as Wilson would learn firsthand in his failed attempts to force the Senate to ratify the League of Nations. He embarked on a vigorous speaking tour to pressure the upper chamber to assent, but he failed.[42]

In fact, the juxtaposition of his early successes with this later failure is illustrative. At the height of Wilson's mastery of the political scene, Congress had overwhelming Democratic majorities: 291-134 in the House and 51-44 in the Senate. By 1919, at the climax of the battle over the League, Republicans controlled both chambers: 240-192 in the House and 49-47 in the Senate. This suggests that the president's powers to manage the Congress are in fact contingent upon other factors, in particular the composition of the legislature he is supposed to be able to bend to his will.

And indeed, we see this again and again throughout history. Franklin Roosevelt, Johnson, and Reagan all exhibited the qualities of powerful presidents because they enjoyed strong party or ideological majorities backing their programs. When those majorities faded away, as they did for Franklin Delano Roosevelt in 1938, Johnson in 1966, and Reagan in 1982, the leaders struggled to rein in Congress. Importantly, most of the time, presidents face divided government of some sort or another, meaning that their capacity to be strong (in the Wilsonian sense) is severely hamstrung.

The fact that congressional majorities sometimes line up for presidents but usually do not undercuts the strong presidential leadership model. Instead, it supports a view that political scientist Charles O. Jones advocates, a diffusion of responsibility model. Per this theory, the country regularly sends mixed or even conflicting mandates to the government, usually resulting in divided powers and thus a highly constrained president. The president's opportunities for leadership have relatively little to do with his mettle, but instead are presented when the public occasionally produces unified party government.[43]

Other contextual factors weigh on a president's ability to exhibit Wilsonian strength, even when he might enjoy solid majorities in Congress. For starters, there is his place in the larger ideological structure of his age. Dwight Eisenhower may, for instance, have wanted to roll back the scope of government, but the political settlement of his day pretty strongly favored continuing it at New Deal levels. Bill Clinton faced similarly constraints as a Democrat holding office when, facing staunch Republican resistance, he conceded that "the era of big government is over."[44] The president also runs into trouble because of the Twenty-Second Amendment, which limits presidents to two terms. Lame duck presidents have trouble leading because legislators have little to fear from a presidential tenure with a quickly approaching expiration date.[45]

Perhaps the greatest limitation the president faces is public opinion itself. In Wilson's telling, the president has the potential to inform, direct, and mobilize the people. But in practice, this is rarely true, as Wilson saw in his failed efforts to leverage public support into ratification of the League. Subsequent presidents have similarly struggled, and the history of public opinion polling on the presidents shows the same thing again and again: presidential support almost always declines over time. As political scientist Theodore Lowi puts it, "the harder presidents try to please their mass constituency, the more alienated that constituency becomes."[46]

All told, perhaps John F. Kennedy summarized the limitations of the modern president better than anybody:

> The fact is that I think the Congress looks more powerful sitting here than it did when I was there in the Congress . . . When you are in Congress, you are one of a hundred in the Senate or one of 435 in the House . . . but from here I look at Congress and I look at the collective power of the Congress . . . and it is a substantial power.[47]

The Wilsonian president remains a powerful ideal in both the academy and the public at large, but that does not alter the fact that it remains a mythical creature, meaning that Wilson essentially failed to re-create the Oval Office as the place where governmental authority is centralized and finally made responsible to the public at large.

As we have seen, Wilson's primary hope for responsibility hinged first upon a parliamentary-style Congress, and later on an overawing presidency. But he had a secondary prescription, developed from the work of the Liberal Republicans and the Mugwumps: that of an independent bureaucracy run on scientific principles. This presents a bit of a tension in Wilson's thought, as well as in the progressive movement in general. On the one hand, they called for a democratization of politics; on the other, by advocating an enlarged bureaucratic class, they called for a narrowing of the scope of politics.[48] In their schema, politics would settle broad questions about the direction of the country, but afterward a cadre of professionally trained bureaucrats would have discretion to determine the best way to pursue that direction. Per Wilson:

> The field of administration is a field of business. It is removed from the hurry and strife of politics; it at most points stands apart even from the debatable ground of constitutional study. It is a part of political life only as the methods of the counting house are a part of the life of society; only as machinery is part of the manufactured product. But it is, at the same time, raised very far above the dull level of mere technical detail by the fact that through its greater principles it is directly connected with the lasting maxims of political wisdom, the permanent truths of political progress.[49]

Much like his views on the presidency, Wilson's elevation of the bureaucracy—as somehow being above politics—has taken great hold in the public imagination in the intervening years. It was a core assumption Wilson made when he handed so much discretion over domestic affairs to the War Industries Board during World War I. Faith in the bureaucracy to realize the public good was also a central premise in Franklin Roosevelt's economic planning agencies, especially the National Recovery Administration and the Agricultural Adjustment Administration. And Johnson's promise that poverty could successfully be combated ultimately hinged upon the idea that experts in the government could distribute money in such a way as to defeat it.

This ideal, while attractive, also falls short of reality. For starters, Congress, not the bureaucracy, is ultimately in charge of determining which functions are and are not transferred to bureaucrats. Scholars have found that the legislature makes those determinations based upon political, not economic or social, efficiency. In other words, Congress outsources some

functions, like airplane safety, to the bureaucracy because it believes retaining those powers will do its members no political good. Meanwhile,
other functions—above all the distribution of benefits to constituents or
donors through, for instance, the tax code—are jealously guarded by the
legislature. Thus, the bureaucracy is capable of imposing responsibility on
the system only in those policy domains where members of Congress doubt
that irresponsibility would gain them much.[50] That is hardly comforting
for advocates of responsible government.

Moreover, as we shall see in later chapters, the bureaucracy itself is far
from immune to politics. On politically sensitive subjects where the bureaucracy does have discretion, we should expect members of Congress to
pressure it, and that pressure is often successful. Even more troublesome
for the Wilsonian ideal is the fact that shortly after the great increase of bureaucratic responsibility during the Great Depression and World War II, bureaucrats developed a kind of class consciousness. Politicized labor unions
followed thereafter, and bureaucrats now count as some of the most potent
political agitators in the country, regularly giving millions upon millions
of dollars every campaign cycle to the Democratic Party.

———————

By situating their demands for reform in terms of the public good, the
progressives invoked the spirit, if not the logic, of the republicanism of the
late eighteenth century. And, like Madison before them, they tended to
eschew the idea that public morals were the cornerstone of good government, though of course the progressives were not above trying to reform
morals. Instead, their main focus was, like Madison, on the structure of
the government itself. They appreciated that the government had become
corrupt in the same way that Madison might have understood the term,
and that as a consequence public policy had tilted inexorably toward the
interests of well-positioned factions rather than the people as a whole.

But they diverged at key points from the Madisonian system. Whereas
Madison feared the proclivity of a temporary majority to trample upon the
common good or the rights of the minority, the progressives believed that
the march of history had profoundly shifted the concept of majority rule.
In 1787, the national interest was a largely inchoate concept, as the far-
flung nation had little by way of a collective identity. But the progressives
thought that the political, social, and economic development of the nineteenth century changed all that. There was now a public good in a sense

that simply did not exist a century earlier, and the only way that good could be achieved was by letting the majority well and truly rule. This caused important progressives not only to call for the expansion of federal power, but the reorganization of its distribution through institutional reform. The Framers had separated that power to shield the public interest; the progressives sought to unify it to realize the public interest.

How does this disagreement fit into our own schema here? The thesis of this book is that systematic political corruption—or, as the progressives might have put it, irresponsibility—stems from a mismatch between the powers of the government and the structure of that government. The government as the Framers designed it in 1787 was thoughtfully balanced between the two, but politicians almost immediately began adding powers to the national government beyond the initial enumeration, without due regard for structural reforms. What's more, they created new institutions, like the political parties and a democratized presidency, in an ad hoc fashion; these were meant to solve pressing political problems and their influence on the constitutional structure was barely, if at all, considered. All told, these changes disrupted the Madisonian balance, yielding the corruption that had come to be a dominant issue by the turn of the nineteenth century into the twentieth. By promulgating constitutional reform as a tonic for corruption, some progressives overlap in part with our thesis. While they did not explicitly identify the structure/power mismatch that we have fingered as the central culprit in corruption, the acknowledgment of the need for institutional reform to make the government responsible is a roundabout way of making the same point: that the structure of the government is no longer suited for the powers it seeks to wield.

Following our thesis to its logical next step, we arrive at the following critique of the progressives: they are to be faulted because they never followed through on their promise of institutional reform. Perhaps the fact that they acquired power, and indeed so much of it for so long, convinced them that root and branch changes to the Constitution were not really necessary, that they could make the government responsible by their very presence. If this is true, they committed the same mistake that Thomas Jefferson and Madison did after the election of 1800, overemphasizing the personalities temporarily in office and underemphasizing more durable power relations. Regardless, while some progressive institutional reforms served to tamp down on the particular instances of corruption of the day, like the machine-dominated Senate, they did not fundamentally reorder the government to fit the powers that it had acquired since the Founding. Thus, it should come as no surprise that political corruption would, in due time, reappear.

And, in important respects, it would worsen. The Hamiltonian power to develop the national economy was the source of much political corruption in the nineteenth century; the progressives retained it. The party system as developed over time similarly facilitated corruption; again, the progressives largely kept it intact. But they did more than this: they effectively added another type of power to the federal array. Not only was the government allowed to promote the national economy, it could now also regulate businesses for the public interest. Ordinarily, we might not think of this as a source of corruption, but as we shall see in the next chapter it most certainly is. Just as there is a lot of money to be made by facilitating this or that business for the sake of "economic development" (real or imagined), there is a similarly large fortune to be won by regulating this or that business for the sake of the "public good" (real or imagined).

Moreover, the progressive era hinted at yet another power that would be more fully realized during the New Deal: that of providing direct benefits to interest groups. We see this with the first hints of organized labor protection, especially the Adamson Act of 1916, as well as payoffs to the farmers through devices like rural banking credits. Again, as we shall see in Chapter Seven and beyond, there is money to be made from a government that is granting particular groups unique privileges or immunities. And where there is money to be made, corruption is sure to follow.

All told, by ignoring the issue of balance between governmental structure and power when they finally got their hands on power, they harmed the cause of responsible government that they had championed. They certainly eliminated the worst excesses of the Gilded Age, but they laid the groundwork for more costly frauds during the twentieth and twenty-first centuries.

7

"A Grand Political Racket"

Corruption in the New Deal

THE PROGRESSIVE ERA was an important milestone in the growth of the state, as the federal government successfully claimed for itself new powers that the Framers had never imagined. Even so, it fell far short of the kind of communitarian vision espoused by Herbert Croly in *The Promise of American Life*, whereby the American people would substantially revise their individualist ideology to join together in a collective effort for the betterment of all.

It was not for lack of progressive leadership in Washington, Woodrow Wilson was narrowly reelected president in 1916, but was reelected nonetheless. Moreover, he was returned to Washington with Democratic majorities that, while not quite rivaling the progressivism of the Congress elected in 1912, were certainly interested in reform. The roadblock turned out to be the conflict in Europe; Wilson had promised to keep America out of it, but Germany's policy of unrestricted Atlantic warfare was intolerable. Congress declared war in April 1917, barely a month after the president was inaugurated.

The war dominated the rest of Wilson's tenure. Public opinion on the war was far from uniform, and Republicans regained control of the Congress in the 1918 midterms. They delivered Wilson a stinging defeat by rejecting his League of Nations proposal, and in 1920 the old guard of the Republican Party was triumphant for the first time in a generation. Ohio senator Warren Harding was elected with the largest share of the popular vote in the country's history.

The progressive agenda was to lie dormant for the ensuing decade, and the new powers that the government had previously claimed for itself went basically unused. Thus, while political corruption was salacious and titillating during the decade, there was not anything particularly novel about it. Indeed, Harding's posthumous reputation suffered immensely because of the Teapot Dome scandal, but it had the same kind of feel to it that the scandals of the Ulysses S. Grant administration did: a languid executive sat idly by while his underlings robbed the country blind. Secretary of the Interior Albert Fall was tasked with leasing the Teapot Dome Oil Field in Natrona County, Wyoming, to a private contractor to provide oil for the navy. He gave the contract to Mammoth Oil, which in turn provided Fall with loans and gifts that today would be worth millions of dollars.[1]

The conservative ascendancy would endure this disgrace in part because Harding died in 1923, thus saving the Republicans from the embarrassment of running or rebuking him in 1924. Furthermore, flinty Vice President Calvin Coolidge, the former Massachusetts governor whose previous claim to fame was ending the Boston police strike of 1919, was above reproach. He cruised to victory in 1924 and handed Herbert Hoover a solid Republican congressional majority in 1928. By that point even the Democrats seemed to have moved beyond progressivism. Their nominees in 1924 and 1928—John Davis and Al Smith, respectively—would both later become vehement critics of the New Deal.

The Great Depression upended this equilibrium for good. Considering that it had total control of the government for nearly a decade before Black Friday in 1929, the Republican Party took the entirety of the blame, and after the 1932 election was totally removed from power in Washington and most of the states. Moreover, the progressive faction within the Democratic Party came roaring back to life.

The party nominated Franklin Delano Roosevelt for president in 1932; here was a man with solid progressive credentials. He had served as assistant secretary of the navy under Wilson, had been the vice presidential nominee in the last progressive Democratic presidential campaign in 1920, and had promoted governmental efforts to mitigate the hardship of the Depression while governor of New York. To win the nomination in 1932, FDR beat out the Tammany Hall–backed Smith by rallying the old progressive forces in the South and West. While he was decidedly cagey during the 1932 campaign about what an FDR presidency would be like, there was little doubt that when he and his surrogates talked about a "New Deal," they had in mind a shift leftward in public policy.

The New Deal as a policy program was the single greatest peacetime expansion of government in the country's history. It was certainly progressive by the standards of its time, and even nowadays some of its programs might shock the individualistic sensibilities of Americans. It defies easy characterization, reflecting the shambolic interests and goals of FDR. The president charmed and courted intellectuals, like Rexford Tugwell of Columbia University, but he was certainly no deep ideological thinker, nor was he well-grounded in the minutiae of public policy problems.[2] As such, the purposes of various New Deal programs were often hazy and its means often contradictory.

Still, we can make general conclusions about the thrust of governance during the period. In general, the New Deal vitiated the traditional notion of a government constrained by enumerated powers in the Constitution. While nominal limits remained, the boundaries of civic discussion shifted notably. The federal government came to be the main focal point for solving public problems, rather than states, communities, or individuals. In particular, the New Dealers claimed for the government an essentially unlimited power to regulate economic activity, to distribute social welfare benefits to broad classes of society, and an expansive notion of how the feds could stimulate economic growth and national development. These powers had been promoted by the Progressive Party, but the New Dealers put their platform into practice.

Following the thesis we have laid out here, this new acquisition of power facilitated political corruption to an enormous extent. The government designed in 1787 was simply incapable of regulating the vast, sprawling American economy, or at least doing so in a way that advanced the public good above all else. Ditto the provision of social welfare. Social Security was something that the Framers never intended when they designed the Constitution, and if they had, they surely would have built a different foundation for such a federal authority. Absent institutional reforms, retrofitting such comprehensive designs onto this system of government was bound to create problems. In particular, the administration's efforts were often captured by the most powerful interests—southern plantation owners, industrial magnates, Wall Street profiteers—who used the government as a vehicle for their own agendas.

What's more, under the guises of internal improvement, economic development, and employment programs, the New Deal also greatly expanded traditional forms of political corruption. As we saw in Chapters Two and Five, partisan politics and federal aid to the economy can easily combine to facilitate corruption, as federally backed projects become po-litical payola. That is exactly what happened during the New Deal, to a degree rarely seen before. The Democratic Party's efforts to stimulate the economy through works programs and the like were captured for partisan purposes. Moreover, harkening back to Chapters Three and Four, the New Deal marked a real step backward from the old Mugwump vision of good government, as the Pendleton Civil Service Act became a dead letter for a while, as the old patronage regime again dominated public administration.

On balance, we shall see that the New Deal was not a good period for honest government. Expansion of governing authority opened new avenues for corruption and substantially widened old ones. While scholars continue to debate the efficacy of the New Deal in combatting the Great Depression, the evidence unequivocally shows it made political corruption a bigger problem than it already was.

Before examining the novel forms of political corruption during the New Deal, it is appropriate to look at how the FDR administration greatly en-hanced old-fashioned methods. Up to this point in our story, corruption has had two dominant features: the misuse of federal jobs through the patron-age system and the inappropriate channeling of resources under the guise of economic development. Both styles of corruption featured very heavily during the New Deal, despite the reformist pretensions of its advocates.

For starters, the New Deal brought back the old spoils system that the Mugwumps and Liberal Republicans thought they had eliminated in the 1880s with the Pendleton Civil Service Act. In vastly expanding the num-ber of governmental programs, the New Dealers simply suspended the old civil service rules. The Democratic Party had been on the outside looking in for over a decade by the time Roosevelt was inaugurated, and it was hungry for the spoils of victory. By the end of 1934, Congress had exempted nearly sixty agencies and about one hundred thousand workers from the old rules.[3] By 1939, nearly 40 percent of the federal workforce, and nearly one million workers, were all but exempt.[4] One scholar calls the period a "new gold rush" for spoilsmen, and the National Civil Service Reform League declared at the time, "Not since Grover Cleveland's administration has the merit system had to face such a serious challenge to its existence as it faces now upon the late change of the administration."[5]

Though FDR hailed from the reformist tradition of the New York Demo-cratic Party, he heartily obliged the spoilsmen. In fact, he did more than any predecessor to systematize and organize the distribution of patronage. He installed Jim Farley, his chief political fixer, as postmaster general; from FDR's inauguration until his attempted purge of disloyal Democrats, Farley stood at the nexus of New Deal policy and Democratic politics. It was Farley's job to run interference between the New Deal agencies, Democratic members of Congress, local party leaders, sympathetic newspapers, and more.[6] Here was an unabashed patronage man, in the old school of politics. He avers:

> My conception of politics is that it is the mechanism through which the program of a political party is translated into legislation. . . . The most important thing in any organization—industrial, governmental, or political—is the loyalty of its workers. We are more likely to get that loyalty for the Administration if we appoint Democrats than if we appoint Republicans.[7]

Farley mandated that job applicants receive an endorsement from members of Congress, an easy way to both manage the onslaught of unemployed job seekers, ensure that good New Dealers got the jobs, and keep congressional Democrats in the loop. In fact, Farley developed a clever workaround to the problem of congressmen having to tell would-be workers no: their honest endorsements would be submitted to him in one color paper, and phony endorsements in another.[8] Even so, the flood of applications was simply too much for the administration to handle, just as it had been for presidents during the Jacksonian era. Furthermore, with widespread unemployment, it was virtually impossible to keep all factions of the Democratic Party satisfied.[9]

Congress also heavily politicized the relief and recovery programs. These borrowed heavily from the Whig/Republican tradition of federal spending for internal improvements. Democrats had traditionally opposed these measures, but FDR and the New Dealers embraced them wholeheartedly. They spent millions to employ people building roads, bridges, public buildings, dams, and so on. Whether this had a significant effect on unemployment remains a matter up for debate. What is not contestable is that politicians on every level of government used the funds for their own political purposes. Democrats in Congress were especially aggressive in using the New Deal to solidify their political coalitions. Early relief programs like the Public Works Administration (PWA) and the Federal Emergency Relief Administration (FERA) depended heavily upon specific congressional allocations, and politics became an inevitable factor in two ways.

The first was in terms of timing. Relief rolls invariably expanded right before a national election and contracted shortly thereafter. By maximizing the workforce right at Election Day, the Democrats could give the impression that the economy was better than it actually was. And, of course, newly added workers, grateful to their Democratic patrons for the paycheck, could express their appreciation through their votes.[10]

The second was in terms of distribution. Scholars have long investigated patterns of New Deal relief spending, and generally conclude that, while economics played a part, so also did politics. In particular, the dispensing of relief depended upon per capita electoral votes, the uncertainty of Democratic political support in a district, as well as the stature of the member of Congress who represented a district (House appropriators were particularly adept at directing money to their districts). In other words, the distribution of relief was set up not simply for the purpose of economic recovery, but also to secure the political positions of congressional Democrats.[11]

This was not necessarily a good thing for President Roosevelt. Of course, the president had an interest in keeping his coalition together; why else would he install a fixer like Farley at the Post Office? However, the logroll forming around relief efforts was often too much. After all, Congress was dispensing relief programs based on its own interests, not necessarily FDR's, yet his administration had to take the blame for the inevitable cries of cronyism that rang out from Republican critics. After the 1934 midterms, FDR renegotiated the terms of the relief programs with congressional Democrats. While the latter would retain the appointment power over program administrators (or anybody who made more than $5,000 per year) as well as aggregate funding levels, the administration would make determinations about where money would be appropriated.[12] After 1935, the old PWA and the FERA programs were rolled into the Works Progress Administration (WPA), run by a diehard New Dealer, Harry Hopkins.

Hopkins was not a professional politician. His background was in the nonprofit sector, working on behalf of the poor and later as a public health official for New York City. He had entered FDR's orbit during the latter's tenure as New York governor, and when Roosevelt went to Washington he installed Hopkins in the FERA. As Arthur Goldschmidt, one of Hopkins's associates at the FERA, comments, "When I first knew him, he was completely nonpolitical except for a very deep commitment to Roosevelt. He hadn't gotten Potomac Fever."[13] However, Goldschmidt adds, "He did get it later."[14] As the central agency charged with relief efforts, Hopkins was inevitably drawn into political fights, and he would later come to initiate more than a few on his own.[15]

The problem, for starters, was structural. While Hopkins had independence in terms of program initiation, he was not entirely immune to Congress. After all, the New Deal was at that point still an ongoing reform effort that depended upon enabling legislation from Congress. Legislators could not simply be ignored, and indeed Hopkins became a cultivator of congressional opinion, using the WPA as a tool to build and maintain goodwill between key congressional Democrats and the White House.[16]

Beyond that, Congress retained control over the administrators of the WPA at the state level, and some enterprising party leaders used that to maximum effect. Pennsylvania was a notable example. The Keystone State had stayed Republican in the 1932 election, and the position of the Pennsylvania Democratic Party remained in doubt. It was in this context that Democratic senator Joseph Guffey, first elected in 1934, sought to use WPA funds to secure his political position. He installed his crony Edward Jones as state administrator, and the two used the WPA to try to build a statewide machine. They padded the rolls before elections, leaned on relief workers to vote Democratic, and even brought back the long-condemned practice of party assessments. The corruption was so bad that it induced WPA field representative Lorena Hickock to complain in a letter to Hopkins:

> They believe in the patronage system. . . . Eddie Jones has run WPA in Pennsylvania as he thought it ought to be run. . . . I do know . . . his show is a Hulluva lot better than it generally gets credit for being. But, my Lord, it's political![17]

It was not simply members of Congress using the WPA for politics. There is solid circumstantial evidence that the administration began to do so as well, especially after FDR's court-packing plan failed in 1937. The president felt burned by members of his own party, and he wanted to intervene in Democratic primaries in 1938 to purge recalcitrant members of Congress.[18] To that end, one of his point persons in this effort was Hopkins, who around this time was alleged to have said of the New Deal, "We shall tax and tax, spend and spend, and elect and elect." Many historians, especially those sympathetic to the New Deal, dispute the provenance of this statement, but it nevertheless comports with his views at the time about the utility of the WPA.[19] Thomas Stokes, Pulitzer Prize–winning journalist and self-avowed New Deal sympathizer, argues that his "friends within the New Deal . . . sought refuge in the seductive philosophy that the end justifies the means and, under this philosophy, they condoned the political organization of relief workers."[20]

There were hints of this effort in the public statements of WPA administrators. After FDR had publicly endorsed a purge (in so many words) of conservative congressional Democrats, Assistant WPA Director Aubrey Williams told the Workers Alliance, the WPA union, that its members should vote to "keep our friends in power."[21] The Oklahoma WPA administrator similarly urged workers to back Senator Elmer Thomas, whom Harold Ickes had publicly endorsed.[22] Hopkins himself tossed in his two cents in the Senate primary in Iowa, telling the *Des Moines Register*, "If I voted in the Iowa primary, I would vote for Otha Wearin on the basis of his record."[23]

All across the country, conservative Democratic leaders—including Senate stalwarts such as Burton Wheeler, Patrick McCarran, Champ Clark, and Carl Hatch—heard rumors and innuendos that the WPA was being utilized to wage an internecine war. Undoubtedly, the most explosive story came out of Kentucky, where staunch New Dealer Alben Barkley was in a tough primary against Governor Albert "Happy" Chandler. After hearing the same rumors that had troubled conservative Democrats, Stokes went down to the Bluegrass State to see things for himself. His exposé on political fraud there won him a Pulitzer, and in his autobiography he recalls:

> For two weeks I travelled through the length and breadth of the state, talking to politicians on both sides, WPA directors, WPA workers, state officials and employees. When I had completed my investigation I wrote a series of eight stories in which I reported what I had found, which was that the WPA was deep in politics on behalf of Senator Barkley and that Chandler's state political leaders were using state employees in every possible way and levying upon their salaries. I called it "a grand political racket" in which the taxpayer is the victim.[24]

The worries about WPA politicization in Kentucky and other states finally induced Congress to take action. It created the Sheppard Committee to investigate fraud in the relief efforts, and found, per Stokes, "a far more extensive political use of WPA than I had disclosed."[25] In particular, Kentucky WPA officials engaged in what the Sheppard Committee called a "systematic canvassing of WPA employees" to pass out campaign materials, solicit funds, and pressure them into voting. In western Kentucky, the Committee found evidence that the instructions were given by the regional director himself.[26] Roughly a year after the Committee released its report, a former WPA worker from Kentucky named Earnest Rowe released letters he had received from State Director George Goodman, who instructed Rowe on how workers were to be solicited for funds (2 percent of their salaries was requested), and that he should keep records of who contributed and who did not. Moreover, four days after the Sheppard Committee was authorized to conduct its investigation, Goodman wrote Rowe to tell him to get rid of their correspondence.[27]

An important consequence of the WPA scandals of 1937 and 1938 was new, tough civil service laws, in the form of the Hatch Acts of 1939 and 1940, as well as the Ramspeck Act of 1940. The Hatch Acts strictly limited political activities by federal appointees or state employees paid for by federal funds; the Ramspeck Act of 1940 instituted a new merit system for federal workers. The political motivations of this were similar to the Republican calculus behind the Pendleton Civil Service Act. Democrats at this point were under fire for patronage. After seven years in office, their supporters occupied almost all of the worthwhile federal posts, so why not outlaw the practices they were engaging in so as to secure for their workers permanent positions?[28]

The Sheppard Committee never traced Kentucky WPA corruption up to Washington, or even to Barkley. And in retrospect, what we are left with is a hell of a coincidence that lacks the smoking gun: FDR declared a purge against conservative Democrats; Hopkins helped develop the strategy; insofar as the WPA was used as a political tool in 1938, it was only on behalf of candidates FDR and Hopkins preferred; even so, no direct evidence back to Washington. Strange indeed! The scandal harkens back to the Crédit Mobilier, where Oakes Ames was rebuked for bribing members of Congress, though nobody was rebuked for accepting them. Here, FDR and Hopkins could claim that their underlings all across the country spontaneously began using federal resources to back their favored candidates.[29]

Where there is no doubt about White House politicization of relief work is in the case of the urban machines, especially Tammany Hall in New York.[30] Roosevelt's political coalition in 1932 was so large that he would have won easily without New York, but victory was no guarantee in 1936. Would the typically Republican voters of the Midwest stick with him?[31] The answer turned out to be yes, but that was far from certain by the middle of FDR's first term, which meant that he had to ensure the old Democratic constituencies were as solidly behind him as possible. That meant a major problem for the president in the Empire State.

With forty-seven electoral votes, New York was by far the most important state in a presidential contest, and it was regularly divided between the Democratic-dominated New York City and Republican-dominated upstate. Tammany had been lukewarm on Grover Cleveland and Wilson, and in both instances nearly undermined their electoral prospects. As a Cleveland-style Democrat, the young FDR had tussled with Tammany in 1911, famously taking charge of a faction of insurgent Democrats in the state legislature to oppose Tammany's choice for the U.S. Senate. Tammany had repaid him in kind by thwarting his attempts to win first the governorship and then the other Senate seat in 1914. Worse for FDR, Tammany had swung the New York delegation to Smith over FDR at the 1932 convention in Chicago. Put simply, Tammany Hall was a problem for FDR.[32]

It was also struggling mightily by 1933. Charles Francis Murphy, Tammany's longtime boss who had more or less brought the machine to respectability, died in 1924, and the organization had never found competent leadership to replace him. Moreover, the Depression put great strains on Tammany's resources just when more people needed help. Progressive Republican Fiorello La Guardia had mounted a mayoralty campaign in 1929, though Tammany-backed Jimmy Walker had defeated him. Walker's term was plagued by scandal, and he was forced to resign in 1932. La Guardia was running again in 1933 and New York Democrats believed he would win in a head-to-head battle against Tammany-backed John O'Brien.

Meanwhile, Roosevelt had allied with Ed Flynn, boss of the Bronx, and he hoped to work behind the scenes to elect a mayor who would elevate him at the expense of Tammany. So Flynn and Farley, with FDR's active encouragement, pushed former acting mayor Joseph McKee into the race against La Guardia and O'Brien.[33]

Thanks to a split in the Democratic ranks, La Guardia would win the election with less than 50 percent of the vote. This was a defeat for New York Democrats but not, as it turned out, for FDR. The new mayor was a strong supporter of urban political reform and the New Deal, which made him—like Wisconsin Republican Robert La Follette—the very sort of Republican Roosevelt had hoped to draw into his coalition. When the WPA was formed in 1935, FDR resisted pressure from upstate Democrats to place control over New York relief spending in the hands of Albany, which surely would have used it to remove La Guardia from office (and thus hand Tammany a golden opportunity for a comeback). Instead, Roosevelt and

Hopkins made New York City its own district for WPA purposes, effectively handing control over relief to La Guardia.[34]

FDR's use of relief money to intervene in politics was not limited to New York City. In fact, Roosevelt had an active hand in shaping the urban political scene in Philadelphia and Pittsburgh, both of which went from being Republican cities to Democratic ones, with the latter developing an FDR-sponsored machine run by David L. Lawrence.[35] In Chicago, FDR favored the incipient political machine of Edward Kelly, which later was run by William J. Daley.[36] Frank Hague of Jersey City was the boss of a relatively small metropolis, but he could deliver votes in a closely divided New Jersey, so he was also given control of local patronage.[37] In general, politics played a role in determining which urban bosses controlled relief funds and which did not. Those who supported the New Deal, and more importantly could deliver votes on Election Day, were favored; everybody else was on the outside looking in.

As we have seen, the idea of government promoting economic activity traces back to the 1790s, with Alexander Hamilton's agenda. On the other hand, government regulation of industrial activity is relatively new, with the first major pieces of legislation not enacted until the 1880s, and even then not really enforced with vigor until the early 1900s. Thus, the potential for corruption in regulation was latent, but that is not to say it did not exist. It all comes down to what government decides to regulate and how it goes about the regulation. The potential for profit for businesses in such decisions is at least as great as any decision about tariffs, land subsidies to railroads, or charters for new canals. If businesses or interest groups can manipulate governmental regulations—maybe to favor themselves, maybe to disfavor their competitors, maybe both—they can draw a rent from the public.

The National Industrial Recovery Act (NIRA), passed toward the end of the spring legislative session in 1933, represented a capstone to the progressive drive for greater regulation of the economy. It called for an effective merger between government and industry for the sake of economic harmony. Little wonder, then, that the NIRA would realize much of the potential for corruption in the progressive program to control the economy.

Exactly how this harmony was to be achieved, the New Dealers were not entirely sure.[38] In fact, the NIRA was a grab bag of policies from a variety of sources. Business interests, like Henry Harriman of the Chamber of Commerce and Gerald Swope of General Electric, had been advocating a suspension of the antitrust laws so that businesses could stabilize the economy by coordinating with one another. Similarly, big businesses often sponsored think tanks that similarly praised the virtues of trade groups. Progressive academics like Tugwell wanted the government to manage actively the economy. Old Progressives like Donald Richberg felt similarly about democratizing industry. Labor leaders like John L. Lewis of the United Mine Workers were also demanding governmental management, as well as labor protections. Congressional Democrats on the left like Hugo Black were calling for limitations in weekly hours. And supporters of economic stimulus through public works, like Ickes, wanted a robust stimulus program.[39]

One point upon which they generally agreed was that the experience of World War I was a good one. The record of the War Industries Board (WIB) was particularly influential. Government and industry had partnered together through the WIB to coordinate the war effort on the home front. Leading the charge were the so-called "dollar-a-year" men, the famed financier Bernard Baruch, Robert S. Lovett of the Union Pacific Railroad, and philanthropist Robert S. Brookings, who (so the mythology went) put aside personal gain to save the country.[40] As FDR said when he signed the NIRA:

> Many good men voted this new charter with misgivings. I do not share these doubts. I had part in the great cooperation of 1917 and 1918 and it is my faith that we can count on our industry once more to join in our general purpose to lift this new threat and to do it without taking any advantage of the public trust which has this day been reposed without stint in the good faith and high purpose of American business.[41]

With the WIB serving as a vague template, the NIRA called for a grand bargain whereby the government would suspend antitrust laws to allow businesses to write codes governing industrial production. In return, businesses would work with labor groups and consumer advocates to protect the rights of unions and keep prices from rising too high. In other words, government, business, labor, and consumers would all work together to bring about a responsible return to economic growth.[42]

In fact, the benevolent experience of World War I was overstated, which presaged problems for the NIRA. Large businesses were extremely profitable during the United States' neutrality period during the war—the House of Morgan in particular made a fortune brokering Allied war bonds and facilitating the delivery of matériel—and one of the unspoken purposes of business leaders who helmed the WIB was to keep the profits flowing.[43] That's exactly what happened. While the dollar-a-year men of the WIB certainly served their country at a troubled time, they also directed lucrative business contracts to their companies and allies, learned the details of their competitors, and made connections that could endure over time. Much as would be the case with the National Recovery Administration (NRA), this was possible because the government did not coerce businesses; rather, it negotiated with them, enabling the latter to use their bargaining power to make a profit at the expense of the government.[44] The experience with the NIRA would be similar.

In keeping with the coalitional nature of the NIRA, it was worded ambiguously in key spots, so as to give everybody the impression they would get exactly what they wanted.[45] Thus, the NIRA as passed did not so much represent a comprehensive plan, but a plan to have a comprehensive plan. This was the weakness that big business exploited.

In many respects, the NIRA was supposed to be pluralistic, even Madisonian. The government would give everybody a seat at the table and manage them toward a socially constructive end, at least in theory. In practice, the government lacked institutional mechanisms to make sure the final judgment was fair to all sides. The NIRA gave the NRA licensing authority to coerce businesses to toe the line, but NRA Administrator Hugh Johnson believed (correctly, as it turned out) that it would not be judged constitutional. So instead, he pitched the idea that coordination would be good for business, and that they should join the new regulatory regimes. He also used moral suasion, even rallying the public to get industries to adopt codes as swiftly as possible.[46]

The bargaining over the development and implementation of industry codes gave big business the upper hand over its smaller competitors, organized labor, consumers, and even the government. Nobody, including government regulators, had sufficient knowledge about the industries they were regulating, and they were inevitably dependent upon business input. Moreover, business groups were well organized, much more so than laborers or consumer interests. And the rush to get codes adopted put extra pressure on the government to accede to business demands. Thus, concessions to unions and consumers in most codes were incommensurate with the gains big business won from them. More often than not, provisions that protected unions and consumers were riddled with loopholes while businesses had iron-clad guarantees.[47] Importantly, the NRA was not really an enforcement body; rather, industrial code authorities were tasked with interpreting the rules and then ensuring that companies followed them. Big business dominated these boards, giving them yet another advantage. Thus, insofar as labor unions or consumers won protections in the codes, it was often difficult for them to realize the gains in practice.[48]

Moreover, the price and production regulations written into the codes often worked for big businesses, whereas small businesses were hard pressed to make any sort of profit. Worse, small businesses were often hesitant to appeal to the code authorities about violations, fearful that their bigger competitors would get an insider look at their businesses.[49] As Nebraska Democratic Congressman Henry Luckey complained in a letter to FDR:

> The multiple restrictions placed on the small business man have resulted in an unfair and unnecessary discrimination against him to the advantage of a rapidly growing, monopolistic group of big business concerns. The small business man has little time to familiarize himself with the complicated rules and regulations which change frequently, and only too often as a result of these rules, finds himself compelled to close his business rather than carry on the unequal struggle.[50]

Worse still, while Johnson was not prepared to use the heavy hand of the government to regulate big businesses, the big business–dominated code authorities were not so demure when it came to small businessmen. The facts of the *Schechter Poultry* case, in which the Supreme Court unanimously struck down the NIRA, are illustrative. In a sting operation, the code authorities governing chicken wholesalers accused the Schechters of selling ten unfit chickens. The Schechter brothers were fined $7,425 and sentenced to months in jail, but a closer look at the chickens revealed that only one chicken was conclusively unfit! Similarly, a maker of batteries from York, Pennsylvania, spent weeks in prison for not paying $5,000 in bail. His "crime" was not paying the forty cent hourly wage the code demanded; that he could not afford it was irrelevant.[51] In Jersey City, a dry cleaner spent three months in jail for charging thirty-five cents to press a suit when the code authorities said forty cents was the minimum.[52]

For all of these unfair practices, the NIRA did virtually nothing to help the economy. The average worker's earning power did not increase, nor did unemployment decrease measurably. Even the big businesses that dominated the codes did not see much more stability in their economic outlook.[53] The problem was a simple matter of economics. Even if government could get businesses to write codes to benefit everybody, which it could not, profit margins were so low in 1933 that there was simply not enough wealth to spread around. Scholars from the Brookings Institution fairly argue what has since become an academic consensus:

> In so far as the NRA purchasing power theory called for a general increase in income of employees at the expense of the earnings of employers, it was, we believe, ill suited to the conditions prevailing when it was advanced. . . . [T]his attempt to squeeze blood from the turnip would have aggravated the stagnation of business and investor expenditures, thus still further delaying the release of purchasing power impounded for such expenditures.[54]

When the Court struck down the NIRA in 1935, it was probably doing FDR a favor, though he would never admit it. The only value of the program, in the long run, was its lesson that grand bargains between business and government in our particular system ultimately favor business, often at the expense of everybody else.

———

Though the Democratic Party broke historical precedent by picking up seats in the 1934 midterm elections, there was an undeniable sense at the beginning of 1935 that the New Deal had hit upon rough times. The NIRA was coming under fire and was soon to be struck down by the Court. The Agricultural Adjustment Administration, which we shall review in detail in Chapter Nine, had not turned out to be the transformative program that many liberals hoped it would be. Ditto the Tennessee Valley Authority. And with the economy having turned a corner (though still weak), the business community was complaining about governmental interference. Eventually, FDR would win a landslide reelection in 1936, but in the winter and spring of 1935, this was not at all clear.

It was at this point that Roosevelt made a surprising about-face. His First New Deal had deep roots in Wilsonian progressivism, but the Second New Deal would focus on tasks that had made Wilson blanch. In particular, it would emphasize benefits distributed directly to classes of citizens (not coincidentally those whom FDR deemed indispensable to his political success), paid for by other classes of citizens (not coincidentally those whom FDR deemed indispensable to his opponents' success). Thus, it imposed new taxes on the wealthy as well as new regulations on banks and utility companies, while simultaneously bestowing new entitlements upon the elderly and organized labor.

As we have seen throughout our story, at critical points national politicians have either expanded the powers granted by the Constitution or reimagined them for novel purposes. Hamilton and the Federalists claimed for the government the power to develop the national economy by building a financial and tax infrastructure. The National Republicans and later the Whigs expanded upon this claim to justify government support of physical infrastructure. Republicans after the Civil War amplified these powers to develop an expansive pro-business platform. The progressives of the early twentieth century claimed for the government an expansive power to regulate private property for the sake of labor, consumer, and environmental protection; the New Deal took this advance to its ultimate conclusion in the NIRA.

Roosevelt's Second New Deal, in particular its dispensation of benefits directly to the citizenry, amounts to another expansion of power. Granted, this had been exercised in the past, but the scope was quite limited. The Civil War pension program was similar, but even at its most expansive and wasteful, the core justification of the program was payment for services rendered. It was not open-ended; sooner or later, all of the pensioners would die, and the government obligation would be finished. The Wilson administration took a few steps toward general welfare programs, like banking credits for small farmers, but these were tentative at best. The Second New Deal was a broad, durable, and transformative grant of new benefits directly to whole classes of citizens.

And, like each expansion of power before it, these programs would do much good; however, they would also be manipulated in novel ways to secure the status or privilege of factions of society at the expense of the public interest. We have defined that as political corruption. Just as we saw with policies like the tariff, the devil is always in the details. The idea of a protective tariff to support and grow American industry seemed eminently sensible as a public policy, but matters become much more controversial when we look at which industries received support and which did not. So it went with this new form of power created by the Second New Deal. Politicians could easily toggle benefit streams to favor some groups and punish others. And, much like tariff rates, they could do it quietly, via legislative arcana that only a handful of initiates could really understand.

This problem would become more pronounced later on, decades after the New Deal. Chapter Eleven will look in depth at Medicare, which has since become the poster child of social welfare corruption. Still, we can see political abuse in such programs almost immediately, with the passage of the Social Security Act. Long heralded as a triumph of liberal policy-making, and eagerly expanded over the years by both political parties, Social Security nevertheless had embedded within it quiet payouts to key interest groups. In particular, the southern gentry class, which had been the Democratic Party's bedrock for nearly a century, made out like bandits.

Passed in 1935, the Social Security Act provided disability and old-age pensions to *qualified* workers, which is where the southern aristocracy manipulated the law to keep their largely black tenant farmers in place. The conventional thinking about the Jim Crow South for blacks is that it was a lot like *Road Warrior*, a kind of postapocalyptic dystopia where there was no law and the weak were dominated by the powerful. This is not exactly the case. While it is true that there was an absence of law to safeguard poor blacks, they nevertheless built protective patron-client relations with their landlords. Landowners faced an uncertain labor market, with precious little room for error; they could not risk their crop by hiring bad wage earners at harvest time, nor could they chance not finding any labor should the market get too tight. To guard against this, landowners had an interest in building such relationships. The tenants offered reliable labor; the landowners offered benefits like schools and churches, medical care, legal assistance, housing, gardening plots, and old-age assistance.

By any standard, these benefits were paltry, which is why landowners did not want the federal government swooping in to offer a separate source of income through Social Security. Thus, the original act excluded vast classes of agricultural workers to protect what economists Lee Alston and Joseph Ferrie call an "elaborate system of paternalism"[55]:

> A powerful patron can be viewed as a substitute for the state. . . . For protection to remain valuable to workers, planters had to prevent substitutes from emerging for their services. Local and state governments, by providing civil rights and greater welfare benefits, could have reduced the value of planter protection. However, planters either controlled the judicial, legislative, and enforcement branches of local and state governments outright or allied themselves with these forces. The federal government was more of a threat.[56]

That was where southern Democrats in Congress came into play. While far from a legislative majority, they nevertheless dominated key access points in Congress, thanks to their seniority. As a one-party region, southern

Democrats who won election hardly ever lost thereafter, which meant they could rise through the ranks to control important committees like Rules in the House or Finance in the Senate. They leveraged these positions to exempt agricultural workers from Social Security, to ensure that the paternalistic regime in the South would be sustained.

A similar logic directed their behavior on the Fair Labor Standards Act (FLSA), which set the first national minimum wage law. Like Social Security, the FLSA was a direct provision of welfare to workers, only it would be paid for by employers rather than the government. Southern planters could not abide a wage floor set above what they offered, otherwise the quality of their patronage would be substantially reduced. Thus, southern Democrats in Congress made sure to carve out broad exemptions for farm workers here as well.

That was far from the end of carve-outs in the FLSA. In fact it was festooned with special considerations for well-positioned interests, all written into the law as exemptions from the mandated wage floor. So complicated were the FLSA exemptions that the law became a kind of domestic tariff, protecting certain regions at the expense of others. And while it shielded southern agricultural interests, southern manufacturers found themselves getting bowled over by a massive logroll.

By 1937, northern industries had come to terms with the emergence of organized labor as a dominant force in the economy. Labor had already unionized the auto, rubber, and steel industries, so at that point there was no turning back. Yet the South resisted unionization, often through extralegal means. Northerners feared a flight of capital to Dixie, and thus conspired to set the FLSA wage floor so low that, for all intents and purposes, only the South was affected. As H. C. Berckes of the Southern Pine Association claimed at the time:

> Frankly, I have found most of these businessmen anticipating a larger degree of influence by labor in their business, and the attitude of many of them would not be appreciated by the members of our industry. Much of this comes from the fact that there is plenty of agitation with respect to the necessity for curbing the trend of industry southward. A great many industrialists in the North, and especially politicians, believe that the South has an undue advantage and that labor is being sweated to the extent of destroying entire Northern industrial communities, which are already moving South because of wage differentials and agitation from foreign labor elements in the North.[57]

Though liberal Democrats held an overwhelming majority in the Congress at that point, the House Rules Committee, dominated by southern Democrats, put the brakes on the FLSA, at least for a time. It was only through a discharge petition passed on the House floor that the bill got around them. In the end, the North got to impose its penalty on the South for resisting the unionization trend.[58]

The experience with Social Security and the FLSA is relatively small potatoes compared to the corruption and waste Medicare would eventually produce, but then again this was just the beginning of a new federal power. This is hardly the first time corruption started out slowly and built over time. Malfeasance in connection to the Bank of the United States was nothing compared to what happened with the Second Bank, or with the tariff during the Gilded Age. It often takes time for special interests to figure out how to maximize their private benefits. Moreover, these early provisions, while important developments in the government's growth, are small compared to the powers that were soon to come. With more money and authority comes more opportunity, and greater incentives, to bilk the government. As we shall see in Chapter Eleven with Medicare, the corruption in New Deal social welfare programs turned out to be just a taste of what was to come.

The New Deal was an explosion in the size and scope of government, far beyond what the country had previously experienced at any point during peacetime and certainly more than what the Framers had ever envisioned. Thus, following our thesis that corruption stems from a mismatch between institutions and power, we should expect the New Deal to be a hotbed of corruption. And indeed it was.

For starters, it revisited the two principal forms of corruption the country had dealt with by that point: patronage and economic development. With the New Deal, these two forms were actually linked. A crucial goal was to provide employment building infrastructure, meaning that politicians could benefit by selecting loyal workers (and leveraging their loyalty at election time) and designing the works programs for maximal political benefit. Congress gleefully participated in this, but so also did the executive branch. There is strong circumstantial evidence suggesting that top-level New Dealers tried to use the WPA to oust conservative Democrats; moreover, FDR most certainly did use patronage to favor loyal urban machines and punish disloyal ones.

Beyond that, the New Deal also vastly expanded upon a governmental power that had been utilized modestly up to that point: restricting private enterprise for the public good. Of course, the Constitution allows for congressional regulation of interstate commerce, but the Framers never had in mind the sorts of intimate restrictions that the NIRA entailed, and the government they built was simply not up to the tasks set forth in the law. Predictably, corruption was the result, and the program was an abject failure. Liberals wanted to make the American economy a more equitable bargain, but they really just gave business the tools to secure the privileged position that the left had so detested.

Finally, the New Deal was revolutionary in identifying the federal government as the guarantor of basic social welfare. While the government had provided direct benefits to citizens before, these had only been limited or conditional. Social Security and the minimum wage were much broader in scope. Again, the Founders never anticipated this, and the structure of the government is ill-suited to the task. Parochial interests with key representatives in Congress used the FLSA and the Social Security Act to secure their economic positions, largely at the expense of poor southern farmers.

What to make of all this? A pluralistic system of government such as ours is not meant to rebuild the economy, regulate every sector of industry in the most intimate of ways, and redistribute millions (later, billions) of dollars between classes. It is, rather, intended to be a place where different factions meet up, fight each other, and come up with a consensus on how to exercise a limited number of powers. It is a bottom-up design to make sure no group gets the short end of the stick; it is not meant to bring about top-down visions of a better society, especially when those visions deal with every intimate aspect of American economic life or involve massive transfers of wealth. When politicians start believing otherwise, they ask this government to do more than it is capable of doing, and it becomes prey to manipulation.

The point here is not to criticize the principle of industrial regulation, to promote a laissez-faire view of political economy, or to argue against social welfare provisions like Social Security. The point, rather, is that such programs must be evaluated within the context of the particular government that is implementing them, and the American government was never designed with such actions in mind. It was meant to balance powers among institutions, and when new powers like economic regulation or social welfare provision are introduced without structural redesign, that balance is prone to be disrupted. Just as Hamilton never thought a national bank would plunge the economy into recession via corrupt mismanagement, FDR never thought the NIRA would advance industrial interests at the expense of labor or consumers. Nevertheless, that is precisely what happened because the government could not behave responsibly. Similarly, neither Gilded Age advocates of Civil War pensions nor liberal promoters of Social Security and the FLSA saw how they could become political payoffs, but retrofitting such powers on to our system produced exactly that result.

Of course, there was no turning back after the New Deal. These powers were here to stay, and so too was the corruption they bred.

8

"Clear it with Sidney"

Modern Liberalism and the Interest Group Society

A S WE HAVE SEEN, government tends to grow over time. This is not simply because it does more of what it has long since done, and at greater cost; it also acquires new powers that it did not previously possess. Our government does this despite the limitations set forth in the Constitution; Article I, Section 8 explicitly delineates the powers granted to the Congress, but as early as 1791 politicians began reading new powers between the lines. Writing in opposition to the Constitution during the ratification debate, its Anti-Federalist opponents warned that the federal government would never stay within the boundaries the new structure set, and they turned out to be correct on this point.

The thesis of this book is that the power of government has grown much too vast for the institutions designed to manage it, and the result has been corruption. The power of a government grown too big favors narrow interests rather than the public good in general, as the institutional mechanisms designed to forestall such favoritism break down. An important corollary to this hypothesis is that the government tends to become worse at exercising its powers responsibly as time goes on. Corruption, as we have suggested, is like a cancer. It does not stay in one place; absent explicit efforts to combat the contagion, it spreads throughout the government, infesting new areas that had been previously uninfected.

The carrier of this disease is the organized faction. Responding to some new governmental beneficence or imposition, a faction organizes itself to apply pressure to the government. Through campaign contributions and lobbying, it induces the government to tilt public policy to its favor, at the expense of the public good. This, in turn, creates a vicious cycle. The success of a given faction induces another to organize, then another, then another, so that the original effect is multiplied.

We have seen this several times so far. Consider the evolution of the patronage regime, which started out as a way for President Andrew Jackson to secure his position within the government. This action spurred a reaction from people who saw that there were benefits to be had from favorable government hiring policies, and it prompted the development of an increasingly sophisticated party organization to gain and dispense patronage. Thus, a half century after Jackson's tenure, patronage went from being a side benefit of power to the whole point of power itself. We also saw this with protective tariffs; originally proposed by Alexander Hamilton and later Henry Clay to stimulate economic development, they prompted business interests to organize to maximize their benefits. Eventually, these interests gained control over important politicians and rewrote the whole tariff system to benefit themselves, rather than the country at large. Even Civil War pensions had a similar story; originally meant to remunerate disabled veterans, they turned into a fraudulent raid upon the treasury by the Gilded Age Republican Party to reward its most loyal voters.

This is the context for understanding what comes after the New Deal, which is an inflection point in our story. Government grew during the nineteenth century, and its growth facilitated this spread of corruption, but even so there was a consensus that the government possessed fundamentally limited powers. Neither of the major parties thought the federal government could do whatever it wanted. The exceptions to this consensus were the Progressives, who lost the 1912 presidential election but came to power as the New Dealers in 1932. Their eventual successes meant that their view of government finally triumphed. The old view, of a constitutionally limited government, essentially died with the New Deal.

The political debate in the intervening years has not so much been about whether the government can do certain things, but how it should do them. Sure, conservative Republicans still hew to the idea that the Constitution is but a limited grant of power. Occasionally, they can muster a bare majority of the Supreme Court to remind Congress that Article I, Section 8 does not grant a general policing power, but for the most part this is still a minority position. By and large, the New Dealers accomplished an inversion of the original Constitution: once upon a time, the government could only exercise powers explicitly granted by the Constitution; now, it can do whatever the Constitution does not explicitly forbid.

Following our hypothesis, we should expect corruption to spread and multiply following this growth in power, because institutions have not been updated to manage these vast new powers. In particular, factions should be stimulated to organize by this newly activist government, tilt public policy in their favor, and then induce others to mimic their success. And why shouldn't they organize? After all, the newly limitless powers of the federal government had the capacity to affect, positively or negatively, a vast array of factions in society. They would be fools not to try to protect their own interests. Organized factions are not the problem; the problem is the system in which they operate. It lacks the capacity to balance and check such aggressive, tenacious lobbying to ensure the public good is protected.

This is how the New Deal facilitated what is usually called the interest group society, or the idea that organized interest groups now serve as mediators between the government and the citizenry, influencing both elections and public policy. Often, defenders of this development make arguments reminiscent of James Madison's *Federalist* #10, in which he imagines a vast coterie of factions checking and balancing one another, so that the public interest is preserved. In fact, Madison's original vision bears little resemblance to today's situation. Contemporary interest groups do not necessarily check each other to preserve the public good; just as often, one group dominates or, worse, multiple groups coordinate their efforts to redirect public resources to their private ends. That's not a pluralistic version of republicanism; it is, rather, a pluralistic style of corruption.

The difference is not to be found in social changes, nor is there a flaw to be discovered in Madison's thinking. The difference is with the government—or, more specifically, the *growth* of governmental power. Stretching beyond its original limits, government now has the capacity to affect virtually every facet of every American life. This has induced the development of interest groups; they multiply and become more professional so as to ensure that their members get a "fair share" of the federal pie. They encamp at Washington, applying constant, organized, highly effective pressure. This is not what Madison originally foresaw in society, and his system is not capable of dealing with such intensive lobbying. The result is corruption, as interest groups gain private benefits at the expense of the public good.

This chapter will develop the above argument more fully, although its trajectory will differ slightly from previous entries. Whereas we have usually tracked corruption by the development of governmental power, here we shall pocket the lessons learned about the New Deal in Chapter Seven and instead focus on how this government expansion stimulated factions to organize into sophisticated interest groups. Organized labor and its transformation in the middle of the twentieth century shall be our point of entry. From there, we shall transition to a general discussion of how interest groups in contemporary America function, and then conclude with an overview of what this means for the rest of our story.

Before the New Deal, organized labor was a different creature than what it would become after, or what we know of it today. Of course, modern organized labor had been around since the nineteenth century, and the American Federation of Labor (AFL) was a key player during World War I. However, whereas the AFL generally preferred Democrats over Republicans for president, it was hardly active politically. Between 1906 and 1928, the AFL shelled out just $95,000 on political campaigns.[1]

Franklin Delano Roosevelt had been mostly uninterested in the labor question during the First New Deal, and his 1932 electoral coalition—anchored, like Woodrow Wilson's, in the South and West—did not depend heavily on organized labor, which had been in decline since the end of World War I. The National Industrial Recovery Act (NIRA) had labor protections written into it, but they had been ambiguously worded and corporations had found easy ways around them. Even so, labor had strong advocates on the left, most notably Senator Robert Wagner of New York. When the NIRA fell apart, Wagner swooped in with an alternative proposal that Roosevelt embraced.

The National Labor Relations Act (or Wagner Act), which passed in 1935 during the Second New Deal, gave organized labor unequivocal protection. Laborers gained the right to organize unions, which were authorized to bargain collectively on their behalf. Meanwhile, business efforts to undermine unions were severely curtailed. The act also established the National Labor Relations Board (NLRB) to enforce the new rules and settle disputes between workers and companies. With members appointed by the president and confirmed by the Senate, the first NLRB was extremely favorable to unions.

This innovation did not spark much interest from the bulk of the AFL, which was dominated by high-skilled craft unions like the carpenters. Yet a handful of officials—notably John L. Lewis of the United Mine Workers and Sidney Hillman of the Amalgamated Clothing Workers—recognized the potential of the Wagner Act. They split with the AFL to found the Congress of Industrial Organizations (CIO), which helped form new unions in the steel, auto, rubber, and electrical industries.

But the CIO did much more than this. Recognizing that its fortunes now depended upon continuing favorable policy from Washington, the CIO committed itself entirely to the 1936 presidential election. Lewis was particularly aggressive, effectively abandoning his unionizing activities in 1936 to work on behalf of FDR via the CIO's deceptively named Non-Partisan League. As Lewis put it:

> With the guarantee of the "right to organize," such industries may be unionized, but, on the other hand, better living standards, shorter working hours and improved employment conditions for their members cannot be hoped for unless legislative or other provisions be made for economic planning and for price, production, and profit controls. Because of these fundamental conditions, it is obvious to industrial workers that the labor movement must organize and exert itself not only in the economic field but also in the political arena.[2]

Labor's Non-Partisan League was unprecedented. Before 1936, interest groups had, of course, contributed heavily to political campaigns before, but none had committed itself to mobilizing voters directly, and at such a cost. The CIO and its affiliated unions spent upward of $775,000 to help elect Democrats, with the United Mine Workers alone chipping in about $470,000.[3] Meanwhile, grassroots organizing by Hillman helped flip the city of Philadelphia to the Democratic Party for the first time since the Civil War, and Lewis's United Mine Workers was integral in maximizing FDR's vote in mining-heavy areas in Idaho, Pennsylvania, and West Virginia.[4]

FDR's landslide victory codified a durable alliance between the president and the CIO. Indeed, when Lewis—angry because FDR had not done enough for labor—balked at supporting him in 1940, the rest of the CIO stuck with the president.[5] It was the smart move; after all, labor had grown from about three million members in 1933 to eight million in 1939, with about half of that total belonging to CIO unions.[6] Beyond that, the Democratic Party had committed the federal government to the promotion of economic stability, social welfare, and workers' rights. All of these assisted labor's members indirectly.

Labor's participation in the Democratic coalition did not go unnoticed, by either side. The Republican Party's posture toward labor had varied from indifferent to slightly amenable prior to the Second New Deal. Herbert Hoover, for instance, signed the Norris-LaGuardia Act in 1932, which barred yellow dog contracts and prohibited courts from issuing injunctions against nonviolent labor strikes. But the rise of the CIO and its connection to the Democratic Party was a bridge too far. When the Republicans gained effective control over the Congress, by allying with conservative southern Democrats, they passed the Smith-Connally Act of 1943 over FDR's veto. This wartime provision temporarily prohibited direct union contributions to political parties or campaigns (similar to what the Tillman Act of 1907 had done for corporate giving). In 1947, the Taft-Hartley Act made the ban permanent and limited the Wagner Act by giving states the right to restrict collective bargaining. Republican hostility toward labor was a key part of what induced the AFL and CIO to merge in the late 1950s.[7]

If the GOP grew hostile to labor, the Democrats only grew closer. In response to Smith-Connally, Hillman and the CIO devised a legal workaround called a political action committee (PAC). Nominally independent of labor, it would support its favored political candidates by channeling voluntary union donations to them. Desperate for all the help they could get in what they feared would be a tight race, FDR and the Democrats gladly joined forces with the CIO PAC, which spent almost $1 million that cycle (mostly collected from the Amalgamated Clothing Workers, the United Auto Workers, the Electrical Workers, and the United Steel Workers).[8]

Labor, in turn, won unprecedented access to a political party. FDR's poor health was an open secret among party insiders heading into the 1944 presidential campaign, and there was great controversy over whom to put on the ticket. Urban political bosses, southern Democrats, and organized labor all had a say. In fact, labor's influence took on mythological proportions, as a *New York Times* report claimed that, when it came to who the vice president should be, the president said, "Clear it with Sidney." The line is probably apocryphal, but in reality Hillman was immensely influential. He did not have the final say on the eventual nominee, Harry Truman, but he almost assuredly had the authority to veto the candidacy of Jimmy Byrnes of South Carolina, who had an antiunion record.[9]

In the postwar era, labor shifted from an entity concerned about organizing workers to a professional, bureaucratized lobbying and campaign arm of the Democratic Party. George Meany, the first president of the merged AFL-CIO, was hugely important in facilitating that process.[10] He became a critical player in the Great Society period of Lyndon Johnson's presidency, serving as a vital link between the White House and congressional Democrats and as a power in his own right.[11] For instance, in 1966 the White House proposed expanding the minimum wage's eligibility, but not increasing the wage itself. Meany was not happy about that, and in front of Democratic bigwigs in a Florida meeting, was heard to have said, "We can make our own way without the Democratic or Republican party. I don't buy the idea that we have to toady along behind any particular party." Shortly thereafter, he flew back to Washington for an impromptu meeting with the president. Johnson, who was famous for working over members of Congress to see things his way, was duly worked over by Meany. The president quickly agreed to a thirty cent raise immediately, with another twenty cents the following year. Speaking afterward, AFL-CIO lobbyist Andrew Biemiller would say, "Johnson went out of his way to bring George down immediately to act on this thing. There wasn't any question that our relations with Lyndon were so good as to be almost incredible."[12]

How does organized labor fit into a story about political corruption? Of course, labor in the 1950s was suspected of being broadly corrupt, and that view survives among some to this very day, but it is overstated. Even when Congress passed the Landrum-Griffith Act, which placed tighter controls on internal union operations, venality was isolated to relatively few unions. It goes without saying Lewis was no Matthew Quay. Lewis comes down through the pages of history as a rough-around-the-edges guy prone to shoot first and ask questions later, but his motivations are entirely different from Quay's. Lewis was in it for the mineworkers, perhaps the most put-upon workingmen in all of American history; Quay was in it for Quay.

So why is labor in this discussion? It gets back to how we understand the idea of corruption itself. It need not be a product of venality, although it certainly can be. The frame of reference here is not necessarily personal corruption, but system-wide, governmental corruption. That takes us right back to Madison in *Federalist* #10. Any faction can have virtuous motives or venal motives; what they share in common is the potential to be "united and actuated by some common impulse of passion, or of interest, adverse to the rights of other citizens, or to the permanent and aggregate interests of the community." In our understanding of corruption here, public policy is said to be corrupt when such factions can inform governmental policy so that it is bad for the public at large but good for the faction. The motives of the factions do not directly enter into it.

Labor, therefore, is not venal. It is factional. And insofar as it enjoyed the capacity to dictate the terms of public policy for its own benefit, rather than everybody's collective good, it can be understood as participating in a corrupt practice. Importantly, this is no indictment of labor itself; it is responsible to its members and its members alone, not the public good. Rather, this is a criticism of the system of government as a whole. The government should not allow factions like labor to influence policy unduly, but in fact labor was able to do so many times over from 1936 until 1980, and then sporadically thereafter.[13]

Moreover, labor only came to be that way because it was stimulated by the government. Organized labor had existed through much of the nineteenth century, and the AFL had been extant since 1886, but never had it been so political. It was only after the powers of the government expanded so dramatically after the Great Depression that organized labor became a permanent political force. And who can blame it? By that point, the government had claimed for itself the authority to regulate union elections, set minimum wages, oversee working conditions, and provide old-age pension insurance. All of this was of maximal interest to labor, and as the above quotation from Lewis suggests, it would be foolish not to enter the fray as an interest group.

Federalist #10 is often understood as the framework to understand groups like labor, but such analyses elide crucial distinctions. Labor as a type of social faction has always been extant, and while Madison in *Federalist* #10 does not mention it by name, he certainly implies its existence by demarcating the line between property holders and non-property holders, noting how the two are wont to engage in political combat. The new government, as he argues, would be a venue for various social factions like capital and labor to battle it out. Because the system was designed to balance and check such forces, the final result would be in the public interest. But as we have seen, the actions of the federal government—above and beyond the constitutional boundaries that Madison was defending in 1787—transformed labor from a social faction into a modern-day pressure group: a permanent, organized, sophisticated force that exists within Washington for the express purpose of maintaining and expanding the policy benefits it receives. Madison's system does not anticipate this development, and the schema he endorses in the *Federalist Papers* essays is simply not reconcilable with such an agent.

Labor was not the first such faction to become an interest group. In the first half of the book, we saw the rise of an aggressive business lobby during the nineteenth century, also in response to favorable government policies. Again, Madison in *Federalist #10* envisions capital owners being a faction that the government must balance against others, but he never anticipates this development, let alone asserts that the regime can resist such a force. There is an enormous gap between the factional give-and-take in *Federalist #10* and the behavior of Standard Oil or the American Sugar Refining Company. Just as with labor, the difference was the transformation of business from faction to pressure group by the intervention of an activist government.

Indeed, we have seen that the earliest such example dates back to the initial days of our history. Recall from Chapter One how Madison and Thomas Jefferson worried that the Bank of the United States was buying off members of Congress. As Jefferson argued to George Washington in 1792, an honest accounting of legislative preferences would have brought about the demise of the Bank. However, Jefferson thought enough members had developed an interest in the Bank that they basically voted against their constituents. Thus, the friends of the Bank cannot simply be understood as the financier faction in a Madisonian schema. They were, rather, creations of the government, uniquely dependent upon it for their continued prosperity and taking aggressive actions to secure it. Madison called them a "pretorian band," which is how we should understand business and labor groups in the modern era.

This account goes a long way to explaining why interest groups have proliferated since the Great Depression: they have sprung up in response to the federal government's acquisition of new powers. As we saw in Chapters One, Two, and Five, the federal government has long taken responsibility to develop the domestic economy, both in terms of building internal infrastructure and actively supporting businesses, a power which it of course still claims. Since the Great Depression, it has enormously increased the resources committed to that task. Economic development is now a top priority of a multitrillion dollar government.

As we saw in Chapters Six and Seven, since the Sherman Antitrust Act and the Interstate Commerce Act, the federal government has also claimed the power to regulate commerce for the public interest. This authority harkens back to the Constitution itself, but under the New Deal it expanded in ways far beyond what the Framers originally anticipated with the Commerce Clause. The government has the power to interfere with private property for the sake of consumer safety, labor protections, environmental concerns, and a whole host of justifications. For all intents and purposes, the government essentially possesses a general police power to interfere with any private behavior, as long as it is not explicitly forbidden to do so via some other provision in the Constitution.

As we saw in Chapter Seven, since the New Deal the government has also taken care to provide direct social welfare benefits to the citizenry. The programs started out relatively small during FDR's tenure, but now there is a vast array of benefits: Medicare, Medicaid, Social Security, food stamps are all income or in-kind transfers directly from the government to the populace, whereas innovations like the minimum wage and union protections use businesses as a medium for securing benefits for certain citizens.

Each of these powers was claimed for the sake of the public interest, but none has been used exclusively for that purpose. Collectively, they amount to a virtually limitless capacity to intervene in affairs that the Framers had deemed either private or under the purview of state and local governments. This means that, just as it did with the Bank faction in the 1790s, big business in the Gilded Age, and big labor in the New Deal, the federal government uses its powers to create winners and losers. That may not be the intention of the public-spirited laws that enact these policies, but it is nevertheless inevitable. When the government establishes eligibility rules for Medicare or Social Security, builds a dam in that congressional district or a bridge in this one, or allows states to determine union membership rules, it necessarily helps certain people but not others. Thus, it gives a wide variety of factions an incentive to organize in ways akin to what labor did. And each seeks the same goal: to have policymakers "Clear it with Sidney" before they make the final decision.

This proliferation of interest groups has utterly transformed the American political process. One of the earliest politicos to recognize this development and its implications was James Rowe, a New Dealer who was an integral part of Truman's reelection brain trust. In a private memo in 1948, he wrote:

> The truth is that the old "party organization" control is gone forever. Better education, the rise of the mass pressure group, the economic depression of the 30s, the growth of government functions—all these have contributed to the downfall of "the organization." Tammany, Hague,

Kelley and the rest of the straight party leaders, while still important, are no longer omnipotent, no longer able to determine the issue. For practical political purposes they are moribund; they cannot be relied on to do the job alone.

They have been supplanted in large measure by the pressure groups—and the support of these must be wooed since they really control the 1948 election.[14]

It might be an overstatement to claim that these groups controlled the 1948 election, or any other. Indeed, the party system has proven itself to be incredibly durable, in no small part because parties make alliances with sympathetic interest groups, just as the Democrats committed themselves firmly to organized labor. Even so, pressure groups have become a dominant part of the political system, not just in the electoral arena but also in the legislative and administrative processes.

What sort of groups are we talking about? As we have seen here, one group is organized labor; though it predated the New Deal by many years, its politicization was a consequence of governmental action under FDR. Another such example is the intergovernmental lobby. The New Deal committed Uncle Sam to helping the cities deal with the social welfare and employment challenges they faced. The federal stream of revenue flowing into cities predictably influenced the latter to organize, with the U.S. Conference of Mayors created in 1932. By the time of the Dwight Eisenhower administration, this group would become, as one scholar puts it, a kind of "secretariat" for the federal government's urban policies.[15]

Postwar governmental policies also provoked a shift in the posture of big business. It had long been a participant in policymaking, but with the government claiming more authority for itself, business had every incentive to amplify its influence. Moreover, the election of Eisenhower in 1952 signaled a more business-friendly environment in the nation's capital, and firms began opening up offices in Washington to see what a Republican would do with the powers set forth by the New Deal.[16]

The Great Society also provoked business interests to organize more aggressively, although this time for defensive purposes. It was during this period that the New Left began to exert itself. Historically, the left had been associated either with the Progressives, New Dealers, or organized labor, all of which were primarily concerned about bread and butter issues like employment and working conditions. The New Left, which sprang forth in large measure from the postwar middle class, was more interested in quality of life issues, like pollution and consumer safety, which posed a new challenge to businesses' bottom lines. In 1971, future Supreme Court Justice Lewis Powell, then an attorney for the Chamber of Commerce, privately warned the organization's leadership about the need to meet this threat:

> Business must learn the lesson, long ago learned by Labor and other self-interest groups. This is the lesson that political power is necessary; that such power must be assiduously cultivated; and that when necessary, it must be used aggressively and with determination—without embarrassment and without the reluctance which has been so characteristic of American business.[17]

Powell's memo has a certain ahistorical quality to it. After all, it was, "labor and other self-interest groups" that had first learned *their* lessons from businesses, the original organized interests. Nevertheless, if we take Powell to mean it was time for business to step up its game to match its new competitors, then his thesis is indisputable. By that point, labor and other groups had developed new and sophisticated techniques to lobby the government to restrict business. It was time, Powell asserted, for business to counter its antagonists.[18] Indeed, they did.

Meanwhile, those New Left groups were busy supplanting organized labor as the dominant interests on the left. By the late 1960s, labor had peaked as a social force, and while its clout would remain enormous within the Democratic Party, it would have to share space with the environmentalist left, the consumer rights movement, the feminist left, and various other groups, most of whom were relatively new to the scene.[19] As of 1986, better than three-fourths of the citizens' groups were less than a quarter century old.

How do these groups operate on the political process? The first and perhaps the essential answer is, they use money. The modern political campaign is vastly different than that waged a century ago. Back then, what was needed above all was volunteers to get the message out door to door. Money mattered, of course; after all, somebody had to pay for all those pamphlets or offer cash to the purchaseable vote in Rhode Island. Yet the proliferation of modern communications technology, particularly television, fundamentally shifted the burden from volunteers to donors. In addition, the modern campaign has grown much more professional, and even scientific. Candidates are compelled to hire paid consultants to tell them how to talk and even dress, to hire media mavens to craft their mass communications, to hire public opinion experts to figure out exactly what the public wants, and most recently social media gurus to exploit other forms of mass communication like Twitter and Facebook.

Meanwhile, changes in campaign finance laws have given interest groups opportunities quite unlike any they enjoyed a century ago (at least, not legally). The culprit is the Federal Elections Campaign Act (FECA) of 1971, which remains the foundational law of campaign finance.

Like the Pendleton Civil Service Act and the Hatch Acts before it, the FECA's origin story is inextricably linked to politics, which might help explain why it has clearly failed to regulate properly the role of money in politics. As mentioned earlier, the CIO had exploited a loophole in the Smith-Connally and Taft-Hartley Acts by forming CIO PAC. When the CIO merged with the AFL, the two created the Committee for Political Education (COPE) to manage its political affairs. By and large, businesses were hesitant in following labor by creating a PAC for fear of its questionable legality. They were right to hold back. In 1968, a federal trial judge ruled that COPE violated the terms of Taft-Hartley, even sentencing labor officials to jail time. Fearing that the Supreme Court would uphold the district court, labor leaned hard on its allies in Congress to legalize PACs.[20]

Enter the FECA. The original law, plus its subsequent amendments of the 1970s, are still the framework by which political money legally flows between parties, interest groups, and candidates. The FECA established individual donation limits ($1,000 per federal campaign) and PAC donation limits ($5,000 per federal campaign), limited the amount of direct or coordinated assistance candidates could receive from political parties, established public financing of presidential campaigns, strengthened disclosure requirements, and empowered the Federal Elections Commission to monitor campaigns and enforce the law.[21]

Labor figured that it was preserving its political position by lobbying for the FECA, and in the short term it most certainly was. Yet over time, labor's PAC activity was totally subsumed by the proliferation of business and professional association PACs. Knowing now that PACs were perfectly legal, and seeing over the years just how successful COPE had been, virtually every group under the sun formed a PAC. Businesses led the charge. In 1978, there were about 1,500 PACs, of which 785 were corporate PACs that gave almost $10 million, about 450 trade association PACs giving about $11 million, and roughly 200 labor PACs giving $10 million. In 2004, there were more than 4,000 PACs, of which about 1,600 were corporate

PACs that gave nearly $120 million, 900 trade association PACs that gave $80 million, and 300 labor PACs that gave $50 million.[22]

This money flows overwhelmingly to incumbents, in no small part because the cost of running a campaign has increased enormously, while limits on PAC giving have been constant. It makes more political sense for a PAC to fund a friendly incumbent, to help him scare away would-be challenges, than to toss a measly $5,000 to a challenger who will likely have to raise at least $1 million to win a House seat.[23]

Thus, PACs are, per political scientist Paul Herrnson, the "electoral arm" of an interest group.[24] The best groups combine PAC money with grassroots agitation and lobbying of Capitol Hill and the executive branch.

Professional lobbying is an often misunderstood practice of modern politics. The average person is wont to think of it in terms similar to the quid pro quos suggested by the Standard Oil Letters uncovered by William Randolph Hearst: a politician writes a letter requesting cash or some other consideration, the lobbyist obliges, and then later writes back requesting favorable legislation. But that is not really how it works in the modern age.

Above all, lobbying is about the provision of information from a trusted source. In almost every field of public policy, legislators and administrators are faced with mind-bending complexity. Our government seeks to do so many things, that in turn have so many second-, third-, and even fourth-order effects, it is simply impossible for a legislator to develop expertise on all the areas on which he or she is required to legislate. The legislator has trouble predicting what consequences a law will have, both in policy terms (how it will affect my constituents?) and in political terms (how will it affect my reelection prospects?). Enter the lobbyist. From the first to final stages of lawmaking, lobbyists are there to provide legislators with crucial information. They help them write bills. They help them mark them up during committee hearings. They provide feedback during conference committees. They provide technical information to executive agencies looking to clarify legislative intent. They do it all.[25] And they are everywhere. In 1968, there were fewer than one hundred registered lobbyists working the House side of Capitol Hill. In 2000, there were approximately fifteen thousand lobbyists working both sides. In 2006, there were more than thirty thousand.[26]

Some pressure groups play both sides of the aisle. For instance, the pharmaceutical industry was highly influential when Congress passed the Medicare prescription drug program in 2003, under Republican leadership, *and* the Affordable Care Act in 2009, under Democratic leadership. Yet many interest groups align closely with the parties, depending on how well each side's goals line up with one another. For instance, the drug companies can play both sides because Republicans and Democrats are both interested in managing health care, from which the drug makers can profit. On the other hand, organized labor's interests are often indistinguishable from those of the left, which means labor has allied with the Democratic Party. Similarly, the probusiness Chamber of Commerce usually finds itself opposed to labor, and thus on the same side as the Republicans. Some interest groups, like the National Rifle Association (NRA), used to play both sides, but have shifted with broader electoral forces. Rural voters most inclined to support the NRA used to be in both parties, but now they side with the GOP, and the NRA has all but followed suit. Such interest groups have come to serve important roles within their parties. They coordinate activities between branches of government (as labor did in the 1960s), filling out party coffers (PACs gave less than $5 million to the parties in 1980 but more than $40 million in 2004), and even recruiting and training candidates (as groups like Emily's List and the Club for Growth often do).[27] While party leaders tend to downplay the centrality of interest groups in their electoral and legislative campaigns, as that does not sit well with the broad public, they are nevertheless major players.[28]

Though this system of influence is not nearly as coarse as the behavior discovered by Hearst in the Standard Oil Letters, it is just as pernicious. While lobbying is most effective when there is a trusting relationship between the lobbyist and the legislator, this does not mean that the information the lobbyist provides is impartial.[29] That's not to say that lobbyists outright lie to legislators; it is to say that they present them with their employer's perspective on the truth, one that is inevitably tied up in private interests, and not necessarily the public's interests. The real danger for the public interest is to be found therein: if legislators lack the expertise to determine whether a policy is in the public interest, and the only ones who know are those whose interests are private, then how can legislators be sure that the public interest is served? Of course, they cannot.

When discussing the Gilded Age in Chapters Four and Five, we noted that the patterns of corruption during that period were more sophisticated than a half century prior. Today, they have been further refined by an order of magnitude. In the modern system, organized interests have instituted ordered, predictable protocols that inoculate them personally from public contempt, even though the effect upon the public interest is the same today as it was in the Gilded Age. Nowadays, lobbyists and politicians can look themselves in the mirror and feel good without temporizing, but the public interest is still undermined all the same.

Indeed, the political science literature of the last quarter century has shown that lobbying works, albeit it in roundabout ways. Early studies of the effect of lobbying upon Congress and the executive often turned up no substantial evidence; it was not until the late 1980s and early 1990s that experts found quantitative evidence providing the link.[30] The reason is that it is often subtle, as this anecdote from two political scientists illustrates:

> A lobbyist from a major defense contractor speaking to a class on interest groups was asked, "What was the most important vote you influenced?" The lobbyist responded, "Do you mean the most important vote, or the most important thing I did for (the firm)?" She went on to explain that her most significant achievement was obtaining a 25 percent increase in the price of her firm's missile. But a recorded vote never took place. The price increase occurred during committee markup of an omnibus defense bill. Although this outcome boosted the firm's profits by $50 million over five years, no legislator voted directly on the price increase.[31]

This is the sort of influence that a straightforward analysis will never detect. Thus, it was only after political scientists sharpened their methods of inquiry that they found the real effects of lobbying.

In general, the state of research suggests a few general conclusions. First, lobbyists struggle to win floor votes in either chamber of Congress, especially when the issues are highly salient, legislator preferences are well known, or partisanship is an important factor. For instance, businesses tend to be more effective on influencing roll call votes on tax and regulatory policy, where their interests are harder to detect, than on direct subsidies, where they are more obvious.

Next, lobbyists do much better in the committee and the subcommittee universe. They are adept at steering legislators toward issues that help their employers and away from issues that do not. Additionally, they use their political contacts in the legislature to influence the bureaucracy. Heavy contributions to well-placed members of committees can signal to bureaucrats that an industry is prepared to use its political muscle to fight regulatory incursion, and this often scares away regulators who are politically sensitive.

Further, aggregate analyses show that lobbying yields policy payoffs. For instance, firms that spend more money on lobbying per year tend to pay less in taxes, all else equal. Additionally, firms that spend more on lobbying are less likely to be scrutinized by the Environmental Protection Agency, all else equal. Also, hedge funds that are connected to lobbyists trade more heavily in politically sensitive stocks, suggesting that their connections supply them with insider information.

Finally, legislators also seem to profit from lobbying. For instance, the stock portfolios of legislators tend to run ahead of the market insofar as members invest in companies that either have headquarters in their districts or give campaign contributions. Moreover, legislators who plan to leave Congress for a lobbying career are more likely in their final term to offer favorable legislation to woo prospective employers. This is significant because the percentage of former members who are now lobbyists is 50 percent in the House and 43 percent in the Senate, compared to just 3 percent in 1974.[32]

Labor, or at least labor as it came to be after the New Deal, serves as a metaphor for the interest group society that has developed in the last eighty years. The New Deal, and subsequent governmental efforts like the Great Society, so thoroughly involved the government in every aspect of American life that a seemingly limitless number of factions mimicked labor. They organized, they set up headquarters in Washington, and they began pressuring public officials into adopting favorable policies.

Is this proliferation of interest groups a good thing? Some argue yes, drawing on ideas reminiscent of Madison in *Federalist* #10. Per this theory, no one group is able to dominate another, so the end result must be policy that does not harm the public interest. Just as Madison seeks to pit faction against faction to secure the public good, we can be confident that when the Chamber of Commerce squares off against the AFL-CIO, the two will balance one another so that the final product of the policy process is good for everybody.[33]

Yet this is a fallacy of composition. Just because all of the organized interests at the table have signed off on a proposal does not mean that it serves the public interest. Alternatively, it could be that the process of policy development is much too favorable to certain groups over others; in that case, the give and take among interest groups inevitably favors the wealthy over the poor, the organized over the unorganized, the active over the latent. None of this need be consistent with the public good. Similarly, what is to stop the various interests in this pluralist system from coordinating a massive logroll, such that each group is bought off by a particular benefit? Far from advancing it, this could be more detrimental to the public interest than if a single interest group dominated the body politic.

These are the sorts of considerations that prompted political scientist Theodore Lowi to pen a very pessimistic take in *The End of Liberalism*. Writing in the late 1960s, just as it became clear that this new interest group society was here to stay, Lowi warns that the new regime is inconsistent with truly public policy. He contends:

> The expansion of government that helped produce sustained prosperity also produced a crisis of public authority. Why? Because the old justification for that expansion had so little to say beyond the need for the expansion itself. The class of objects to which a new and appropriate public philosophy should first have been applied, it seems obvious, was to the purposes to which the expanded governmental authority should be dedicated.[34]

But, according to Lowi, no alternative public philosophy ever emerged. Government acquired new powers with ease, but there was never a serious attempt to grapple with the problems of how, why, and when those powers should be used. Instead, Lowi argues, what developed is an "ersatz political formula" that essentially offers no insight on these questions; it justifies policy decisions not by whether the proposal in question accomplishes some agreed-upon public purpose, but whether it follows old notions of pluralistic give and take. His name for this new mode of government is *interest group liberalism*:

> It may be called liberalism because it expects to use government in a positive and expansive role, it is motivated by the highest sentiments, and it possesses strong faith that what is good for government is good for the society. It is "interest-group liberalism" because it sees as both necessary and good that the policy agenda and the public interest be defined in terms of the organized interests in society.[35]

Per Lowi, the problems with this system are that it distributes power to the most interested groups in society, setting up an inevitable conflict between the public good and private demands; it creates new pathways of privilege that usually reinforce the prerogatives of existing interests; and it resists most change, even in the face of declining public confidence.[36]

The rest of this book will explore these themes in detail. As we shall see, interest group governance is regularly not public spirited. While there have been instances when government acts according to the public interest, too much of its business is wrapped up in rewarding the factions that have mobilized to pressure it. In many cases, these benefits undermine whatever public-spirited purpose the formulators of the original policy had in mind. Put bluntly, interest group liberalism has bred corruption in the body politic. It may be more socially respectable than what Hearst uncovered in the Standard Oil Letters, but today's corruption is at least as widespread and pernicious as anything seen during the Gilded Age. There may no longer be a grubby quid pro quo between Foraker and the agents of John D. Rockefeller, but make no mistake: the interests of today's Standard Oils are just as well served by today's William Forakers.

This is why the parallels drawn between interest group liberalism and Madisonian pluralism are unsustainable. Madison never intended any of this; in fact, he envisioned a polity that worked in exactly the opposite manner. In the *Federalist Papers*, he was justifying an eighteenth century government of discrete, limited powers by arguing that, properly designed, it could successfully play referee among the various factions in society. What we have today is a universe dominated by what Madison called "pretorian bands," created by, personally interested in, and seeking everywhere to manipulate public policy to their own ends. These groups are not balanced by our system; instead, government has stimulated them to become aggrandizing clients, whose "violence" Madison feared would destroy the republic.

The remainder of this work shall examine policy areas where the operation of the interest group society has undermined the public good. In doing so, it shall follow the core thesis of this book. The expansion of governmental power into the domains of economic development, regulation, and social welfare has undermined the capacity of checks and balances to operate properly. As a consequence, interest groups can capture public policy and pervert it to their own ends. In the cases to be discussed, this process has bred inefficiency and inequity, as the government wastes money on those in socially or economically advantageous positions. In some instances, the results have been even more pernicious.

9

"A Grab Bag of Subsidies"

The Politics of American Agriculture

Virtually nobody is interested in farm subsidies. The average voter, even a politically engaged one, does not want to hear about how Congress raises consumer prices through support of the domestic sugar industry or a dairy cartel in the Northeast. Indeed, if there is a chapter in this work that you, dear reader, are most likely to skim or skip, it is this one. But, of course, that is how political corruption so often functions. Recall our review in Chapter Five of Nelson Aldrich's tenure in the Senate. He mastered an immensely boring subject—Gilded Age tariff schedules—that almost nobody else had the patience to learn, and used that vast public ignorance to funnel princely sums to his political benefactors in the sugar lobby. In turn, they helped him become an exceedingly wealthy man.

This kind of informational asymmetry—parties with particular interests possess knowledge that those whose concerns are more general simply lack—is a common way by which corruption occurs. Following the republican principle, the final arbiter of the public good must ultimately be the public itself, but what if it lacks the knowledge or the attention span to arbitrate? A too-common answer: special interests whose fortunes depend on government policy will dominate. That is what we shall see in this chapter on farm subsidies. Widespread public ignorance or apathy to the quadrennial farm bill has enabled lobbyists and legislators to turn it into a massive giveaway to well-heeled special interests whose moral claims to public subsidies are measly at best.

Moreover, this chapter will highlight another theme that has continued throughout this work. Programs designed to help a needy class of people, or to serve the public at large, are often transformed into payola for the privileged. We saw this again and again in our review of nineteenth-century political economy, with both patronage and tax laws transforming from relatively noble institutions into corrupt logrolls among the elite. Here, as we shall see, direct federal support of the American farmer, which began during the New Deal, came about because he was in truly desperate straits. But that was soon to change. Over the course of the twentieth century, the spread of agricultural technology combined with the rise of large agribusinesses meant that there were fewer farmers than ever, that family farms were fewer still, and that those who remained tended to be better off economically than nonfarmers. And yet farm subsidies not only persisted, they proliferated, as interest groups dependent upon those subsidies lobbied Congress aggressively to keep the public funds flowing their way.

The story here, then, is eerily similar to the tale of nineteenth-century tariff laws. Originally designed to protect nascent American industry, they remained in place even as industry developed and outgrew the protection offered by the law. Indeed, as industry grew more powerful economically, it developed more political power and, perversely enough, was able to lobby for more protection even though the economic justification for it evaporated. Ditto the farm subsidies, as once they were in place, Congress has been unable to eliminate them because it lacks the capacity to defy the special interests who dominate the issue.

The American farmer has long been central to the nation's political economy. The early partisan divide in the pre-constitutional era could largely be understood as a contest between wealthier farmers and merchants on the one hand, and yeoman farmers on the other. Ditto the early contest between the Republicans and the Federalists, and later the Democrats and the Whigs. The battles over the First and Second Banks of the United States, in particular, pitted poor farmers against the wealthy.

Because the farmer was such a politically potent force in American electoral politics, constituting a majority of the workforce until about 1880, he inevitably attracted much attention from politicians. Henry Clay's American System was meant to balance protective tariffs (good for industry) with internal improvements (good for farmers). The Lincolnian Republican Party put an expanded version of this program into practice, facilitating farming through the Homestead Act and the promotion of land grant colleges that would support agriculture. In the Gilded Age, as we saw, the farmer was often pitted against railroad executives and later northeastern financiers, as he bid for tighter restrictions on railroads and inflationary monetary policy. The farmer-capital divide reached its broadest with the election of 1896, when the Democrats nominated agrarian populist William Jennings Bryan of Nebraska. Bryan lost, of course, and the tension between the two sides quickly eased thereafter as farmers prospered over the next quarter century.[1] During this period, the political class settled on a program for the farmer that included tariff protections, banking assistance (the Woodrow Wilson administration set up a system of twelve banks to deliver credit to farmers), extension services, marketing help, irrigation and drainage projects, and education.[2] The best times for farmers were during World War I; at their high point, farm prices were greater than at any time until the 1950s.[3]

The recession that followed the cessation of hostilities hit farmers especially hard. For most of the 1920s, they would never really recover. This new farm crisis facilitated the rise of an organized interest bloc in Washington, made up of groups like the American Farm Bureau Federation and politicians in both parties.[4] This new alliance, led by men closer to the polished lobbyists of today than the agrarian radicals of the 1890s, promoted a new kind of assistance to the farmer: direct intervention in commodities markets. Until that time, farm policy revolved around ways to help the farmer grow more crops or get them to market easier, but the McNary-Haugen Bills of the 1920s introduced the idea of tinkering with the market to get the farmer a better deal. Popular in Congress, this program was nevertheless vetoed by President Calvin Coolidge.[5]

The Great Depression would change this calculus for good, shifting U.S. public policy in ways that endure to this day. There are reams of statistics to describe the hardships that the American farmer suffered during this awful period, but nothing captures his misery more vividly than John Steinbeck's *Grapes of Wrath*:

> [T]he dispossessed were drawn west—from Kansas, Oklahoma, New Mexico; from Nevada and Arkansas families, tribes, dusted out, tractored out. Carloads, caravans, homeless and hungry; twenty thousand and fifty thousand and a hundred thousand and two hundred thousand. They streamed over the mountains, hungry and restless—restless as ants, scurrying to find work to do—to lift, to push, to pull, to pick, to cut—anything, any burden to bear, for food. The kids are hungry. We

got no place to live. Like ants scurrying for work, for food, and most of all for land.

　We ain't foreign. Seven generations back Americans, and beyond that Irish, Scotch, English, German. One of our folks in the Revolution an' they were lots of our folks in the Civil War—both sides. Americans.[6]

Franklin Delano Roosevelt was deeply sympathetic to the plight of the farmer. This fact is often overlooked, for the political coalition that FDR eventually forged was predominantly industrial and urban. Regardless, farming was a major policy interest for him, and in New York State he had put tremendous effort into a recovery program for upstate farmers. It is not coincidental that, as president, his first major reform effort was the Agricultural Adjustment Act (AAA), a comprehensive program to revitalize the farm economy.

The AAA was similar to the National Industrial Recovery Act (NIRA), discussed in Chapter Seven, in that it sought a grand bargain for the sake of economic stabilization, though the actual deal was different in its specifics. The economic logic behind the program often seems tenuous to modern minds, and it's fair to say that the AAA was at times a triumph of ideology over common sense; for instance, late implementation of the AAA relative to the growing season meant that in 1933 thousands of planted acres were torn up, and at one point the government even ordered millions of baby pigs to be slaughtered.[7]

FDR and his New Dealers explicitly built the program to please the farm bloc that had formed in the 1920s. The Farm Bureau was particularly influential, so much so that after the AAA was announced, the Bureau claimed that the program was really its invention. This was not actually true, but the interest group pretty much got everything it wanted in the legislation. And when the Supreme Court struck the AAA down, the administration worked closely with the Farm Bureau to build an alternative.[8]

What did the Farm Bureau want? It wanted farmers in the catbird seat, and that is exactly what it got: local governance was essential to the AAA. As historian and New Deal enthusiast Arthur Schlesinger writes:

> The "lifeblood" of AAA, in [FDR advisor Rexford] Tugwell's phrase, was furnished by the count production-control committees, made up of farmers who elected their own officers and actually administered many of the control programs. As the county committees made acreage allotments, as they checked the execution of the programs, the farmers subjected themselves to a novel process of economic self-government.[9]

This approach would characterize American farm policy for generations to come. In essence, the New Deal empowered the farmers to manage their own affairs, subsidized by generous taxpayer contributions.

How did it all work? The goal of the AAA was to get farm prices back to parity, defined as the prices that agricultural products fetched during the heyday of 1910 to 1914. To do that, farmers were paid not to farm and raise livestock. New Deal economists believed that an overabundance of commodities had driven prices down, but farmers had no choice but to keep producing more and more. The AAA would step in and offer them a bargain: refrain from producing too much and the federal government would subsidize them. The hope was that this would reduce the oversupply of agricultural goods, increase their prices, and thus restore some portion of farmer income, which at that point was much more essential to the broader economy than it is today.[10] The details were worked out on the local level. The federal government would set broad commodity targets and leave it to local organizations of farmers to figure out how to meet them.

As we shall see through the rest of this chapter, this would more or less be the contour of American farm policy until the 1970s, and it would create an inordinate number of problems during the postwar era. But even during the Depression, the program was extremely troublesome. The main problem, like the NIRA, was that the wealthiest and best-organized factions had an advantage in the seemingly democratic processes both programs used to draft rules. And these elite interests totally undermined the goals established by the government.

It was in the South where the gap between wealthy and poor farmers was largest, and in the South the injustice of the AAA was so flagrant. At its base, the AAA was built on a voluntary alliance between farmers and Uncle Sam, which meant that the government had to write the terms of the deal in such a way to get farmers to buy in. Simultaneously, it hoped also to protect the interests of the poor tenants and sharecroppers who worked the land of others, but when push came to shove, the interests of the plantation owners had to come first, given the design of the legislation. Moreover, many of the AAA administrators—as well as key members in Congress—were either plantation owners or had a background in the southern plantation economy. Little wonder that they wrote and implemented a bill that favored their interests.[11]

Poor farmers under the AAA were disadvantaged in several ways. For starters, the implementation of the program, left to local committees, placed them on the outside looking in, as interest groups such as the Farm

Bureau came to dominate the local levels. After the AAA became law, the Bureau took to membership drives at the local level, especially in the South where it was relatively weak, so as to solidify its role as the key mediator between government and farmers.[12] Similarly, the statewide extension services, which also generally reflected the views and interests of the wealthy farmers, were heavily represented in the programs. Beyond that, it took time to participate in local meetings on acreage reduction, which poor tenants could not spare but wealthy landowners could. Moreover, the calculations of specific reduction targets were difficult to understand, working to the disadvantage of illiterate croppers.[13]

The policy itself also worked directly against southern tenants and sharecroppers. For instance, the 1933 contract made no provision whatsoever for how tenants were to receive federal payments. Instead, Uncle Sam sent a lump sum to plantation owners and merely hoped that they would pass on the appropriate amounts to their tenants. This problem was rectified for the 1934–35 contract, but the definitions of the various tenant classes were vague enough to leave landowners with wriggle room to stiff their tenants. Beyond that, the tenants were often little match for landowners who wanted to pocket the cash. The latter could manipulate their books, or apply the cash to "debts" the tenant had racked up. And then, what was the tenant to do? Appealing to the local board, dominated by the plantation class itself, was hardly a solution. Appealing to the courts was similarly a hopeless proposition, at least for poor African Americans whose second-class status was written into the law itself.[14]

More broadly, the incentive structures of the AAA simply worked against poor farmers, in several respects. First, it was often up to landlords to decide which acres would be reduced and which would not be. So, landlords often reduced acres that they farmed (via wage earners, who were not eligible for AAA support), pocketed the cash, and redistributed the farmed land to their tenants. As one South Carolina tenant complained, "Our landlord wouldn't plow up any of our cotton. He plowed up his own so that he could get the pay for it."[15]

Second, the AAA facilitated a transition from tenancy to wage earning. Historically speaking, the tenancy system existed in the South because it served as a hedge against the unreliability of labor. Landlords did not want to find a labor shortage come harvest time, or perhaps worse hire unreliable wage earners. So, they hired more reliable families as tenants or sharecroppers, leaving them the responsibility for maintaining the land. But the cash payments of the AAA gave the landowners an insurance policy against unreliable farm labor. Moreover, the acreage reductions increased the available labor supply from which owners had to choose. So, many of them used their AAA payments to replace their tenants with wage earners. They also bought farm machinery, which cut down on the need for any labor at all, tenant or wage.[16]

The hardest hit in this schema were African Americans. The most vulnerable in southern society, they were always the last hired and first fired.[17] Between 1930 and 1940, the number of black tenants and sharecroppers decreased by over two hundred thousand. Some of this decline can be attributed to the effects of the Great Depression, but the bulk of it happened after the farm economy was already in recovery. The AAA's incentive structure is primarily what pushed African Americans off their tenant plots.[18] Worse, mechanization dealt a double blow to their standing. Not only did it cut down on the need for farm hands, African Americans were simply not trusted to run the equipment. As sociologist Gunnar Myrdal notes in *An American Dilemma*, his classic study on African Americans, "To operate an expensive machine is to have a position of responsibility, which, even in the rural South, must draw 'white man's pay.'"[19]

At least in the South, the AAA made a bad situation worse. As economists Price Fishback, William Horace, and Shawn Kantor write in *The Journal of Economic History*:

> [The] New Deal public works and relief grants indeed stimulated local economics. . . . In contrast, the AAA program . . . had little or no positive effect on retail sales and, perhaps, incomes. In fact, the AAA might have had a substantial negative effect. Historical analysis of the AAA suggest that non-landowners at the lower end of the agricultural distribution suffered declines in income as a result of the AAA. . . . The structure of the AAA altered landowners' incentives in such a way that income was redistributed from laborers at the lower end of the skill distribution to landowners.[20]

This truth was not unknown back in the 1930s. A handful of lawyers and policy analysts in the Department of Agriculture, which managed the AAA, were quite aware of these problems, and were deeply sympathetic to the sharecroppers and unions like the Southern Tenant Farmers Union. When their boss was out of town, this group of insurgents proposed a new rule to redistribute farm income to the poorest farmers. When the brass at the AAA, including progressive icon Henry Wallace, found out, they were apoplectic. So also were congressional Democrats from the South, who organized a delegation to complain directly to the president. In the end, the upstarts were unceremoniously sacked.[21]

Just as it did with the NIRA, the Court struck down the AAA, in early 1936. However, the AAA had built up a strong constituency, especially among the nation's (relatively) wealthy farmers and their powerful interests like the Farm Bureau. Thus, the government quickly passed temporary legislation to keep key programs in place, and then in 1938 passed a new, permanent farm bill that satisfied the objections of the Court. Agricultural subsidies were here to stay.[22]

This was much to the chagrin of the first four presidents to serve after World War II—Harry Truman, Dwight Eisenhower, John F. Kennedy, and Lyndon Johnson—as farm subsidies would become expensive, inefficient, unfair, and yet politically undeniable. The war deserves much of the blame. When the conflict began, the government's posture changed from pursuing price supports and supply management to encouraging farmers to produce as much as they possibly could.[23] Prices soared and farmers reaped the benefits, but their representatives in Washington feared a repeat of the postwar bust of the 1920s. Accordingly, Congress adopted the Steagall Amendment of 1941, which required federal support at 90 percent of parity for two years following the war, and also expanded the number of commodities protected by the government.[24]

It would be very hard to roll back this expansion, even after the war, despite the fact that it cost the government a lot of money. Price supports led to increased production, and thus lower market prices, and therefore more government expenditures. The main ways to control this dilemma are through reduction in or reform of support guarantees, output restrictions like production quotas, or attractive incentives to retire land from use. From 1948 through 1973, the government tried all of these methods, and they all failed, one way or another.[25] As a consequence, farm prices stagnated from a continued supply glut, farm incomes similarly stalled, and government payments ballooned.[26]

To provide a perspective on just how much this cost Uncle Sam, consider the value of the stocks held by the Commodity Credit Corporation (CCC), the main entity through which the federal government managed prices until the 1970s. Farmers could take out loans from the CCC using their harvest as collateral, with the total value of the loan equaling the target value of their harvest. If the target price was matched or exceeded in the marketplace, farmers could sell their crops on the open market and pay back their loan.[27] If the target price was not matched, they could simply forfeit their crops as repayment. In 1952, the inventories held by the CCC were valued at $1 billion. By 1960, they peaked at $8 billion and were still $5 billion as of 1966 when a new export surge was underway. Meanwhile, government payments per farm averaged $44 in 1948, but rose to $123 in 1956 and $974 in 1967.[28] And all this was despite the efforts of four consecutive presidents to get control of this runaway program.

Truman was the first postwar president to tackle farm prices, but as was so often the case with this cantankerous chief executive, partisan bickering ultimately undermined reforms that might otherwise have been salable. The 1948 farm bill was a document that nobody really liked, but it did plant the seeds of reform by calling for flexible price supports. Basically, it would give the secretary of agriculture the capacity to toggle support levels for certain commodities; this was hardly a free marketer's ideal, but it would still mark an improvement over the absurdity of supports at 90 percent of parity, regardless of conditions.[29] Ultimately, this foundation was undone by Truman's quest for reelection. Labeled the underdog by just about everybody in 1948, Truman took to the campaign trail and viciously demagogued the GOP through the Farm Belt, even though there was not a lot of daylight between the two sides. It worked. Truman won a lower share of the vote overall than FDR earned in 1944, but he improved on his predecessor's margins in the Farm Belt.[30]

The Truman administration, and its new Agriculture Secretary Charles F. Brannan, took that as a mandate for a major reform program. But Republicans were deeply offended by the campaign (not to mention disappointed by the results) and in no mood for a compromise that might deliver the corn and wheat farmers of the Midwest—historically rock-ribbed Republican— to the Democratic Party. Brannan compounded this error by developing his plan with his own staff in the Department of Agriculture. The agriculture committees in both chambers of Congress, not to mention the interest groups to which they were in hock, were used to having free hand over farm policy and did not take kindly to this transgression.[31]

Brannan's plan would have replaced price supports with income supports, with the typical family farm as a baseline. The idea was to keep farm income stable while letting prices find an actual market equilibrium.[32] In its initial draft, Brannan's idea of a target income was too generous for conservatives in Congress, and using the family farm as a baseline was a nonstarter for the agribusinesses and large farms that were coming to dominate the industry. Moreover, the Brannan Plan would replace an inconspicuous subsidy (price supports) with an apparent one (income supports); this drew the ire of the Farm Bureau, which did not want to expose its constituents to a public backlash for being on welfare.[33] Even so, these problems had potential workarounds, but Congress never gave it a real try. Farm policy was bipartisan, congressional, and deeply flawed. Credit to Truman and Brannan for trying to fix the problems, yet by pursuing a partisan plan from the executive branch, they failed to deal with the power relations that had created the problems in the first place.

Eisenhower did not endorse Brannan's idea of income subsidies, but he did strongly support flexible price supports, and his choice of agriculture secretary—Ezra Taft Benson—sent a clear signal to Washington that he was serious about changing the status quo. Benson himself was a farmer and a staunch advocate of free market reforms; if he had his druthers, he would have totally upended the twenty-year consensus of federal meddling in farm prices. This made him wary of Eisenhower, who had placed himself in the political middle, but on this issue there was little difference between the two. Both solidly backed adjustable supports with a goal toward weaning the farmer off federal subsidies altogether.

Unfortunately, Eisenhower and Benson would face congressional opposition from their own party. Like Truman before him, Ike would learn that on farm policy there was a bipartisan consensus to keep authority housed in Congress and keep the subsidies flowing to the politically powerful farm bloc. So, despite GOP majorities in both chambers in 1953 and 1954, Eisenhower failed to get his flexible price support plan through Congress, which had already suspended the provisions of the 1948 bill to phase them in. The president had to twist arms to get a measly compromise through the Congress, and even then the contempt from the Farm Belt was so palpable that there was talk among *Republicans* about forcing Benson out of the cabinet.[34]

Democrats took control of the Congress in 1955, and by 1959 the legislature sported the most liberal membership since the mid-1930s. They demanded high and fixed price supports, which Eisenhower had to veto twice over.[35] Thus, Ike's emphasis shifted toward production controls. He embraced wholeheartedly the Soil Bank program designed to aid farmers in efforts to retire land from production. Much like the AAA efforts to stem production through acreage restrictions, this was bound to fail. Farmers had every incentive to put the least productive acres into retirement, and moreover innovations in scientific agriculture, fertilizer, and pesticides, (often subsidized by the very same federal government looking to restrict output) meant that farmers could grow more and more with fewer and fewer acres. By 1962, nearly sixty-five million acres were retired under the Soil Bank, but the surplus was still unchecked.[36]

When Kennedy succeeded Eisenhower in 1961, he brought with him a similar desire to put a stop to the open-ended nature of Uncle Sam's support of the agriculture class. His main approach was to target output directly, rather than indirectly through flexible supports. With Kennedy's blessing, the Food and Agriculture Act of 1962 gave farmers a choice: they could receive generous subsidies for strict production controls or take their chances in basically a free market regime. The critical test of the new policy came with a vote by American wheat farmers in 1963. Interest groups like the Farm Bureau lobbied heavily against the deal, arguing that the government would blink and restore the subsidies if the farmers voted down the output limits. That is exactly what happened. Wheat farmers voted overwhelmingly against the new contract and Congress dutifully backed down, fearful of the political consequences of defying farm interests.[37]

For twenty years after World War II, the farm problem was intractable. The country was on the hook for the farmers' bottom line, but could not take necessary steps to keep costs from running out of control. Truman tried shifting the basis of payments from parity to income support; Eisenhower tried flexible payments; Kennedy tried output quotas. In each instance, the factions opposed to the president enjoyed the upper hand.

And then, out of the blue, the problem disappeared, at least for a time. The reason: an export boom that the policy mavens in Washington had nothing to do with.

Granted, Truman, Eisenhower, Kennedy, and Johnson had all emphasized exports as a way to get rid of the surplus. The Marshall Plan gave food to a devastated Europe. Eisenhower's Food for Peace program, expanded by Kennedy, offered surplus commodities for national security purposes. And all these leaders were anxious to expand foreign markets. None of this made an enormous impact, although exports did begin to tick up noticeably in the mid-1960s.[38]

The big difference came in 1973 when the Soviet Union began importing massive quantities of grain. Prior to 1972, trade with the Soviet Union was less than $10 million per year. It expanded to $1 billion in 1973, and then doubled to $2 billion by 1985. Meanwhile, Richard Nixon successfully opened China up for trade, creating another market for U.S. agricultural products. By the end of the decade, exports accounted for about 40 percent of all American farm output.[39]

This gave the political class a decade to declare victory in the fight against the farm problem, as if their policies had anything to do with it. In reality, the export boom drained the surplus and therefore eased the costs Uncle Sam had to bear to prop prices up. The 1973 farm bill took advantage of the return of farm prosperity to alter the subsidy program in a substantial way. Whereas farmers historically received payments through the CCC via price supports, the government transitioned to deficiency payments, whereby farmers would receive direct subsidies if the real prices dropped below mandated targets. This had the advantage of bringing out into the open exactly who was getting what. Deficiency payments were much more transparent than CCC loans, meaning that Washington could also put caps on how much any given farmer could receive (although there remained plenty of loopholes). Farm groups opposed these innovations, but with times so good there was little fight.[40]

Alas, the salad days were not to last. A combination of factors brought misery to farmers by the mid-1980s. The new demand for exports prompted increased competition in the world grain market, especially from France. Meanwhile, the oil crises of the 1970s hit farmers especially hard because of their reliance on petroleum-based products like fertilizers and pesticides. Finally, runaway interest rates put the squeeze on farmers; always highly leveraged relative to nonfarmers, they had taken on greater debt loads during the 1970s.[41] All of this led to the farm crisis of the mid-1980s, which is why Ronald Reagan—a small government advocate who tried (unsuccessfully, like his predecessors) to reduce farm payments in the first half of his term—ended up setting a record for payments sent to farmers by 1986, when they totaled $26 billion.[42]

By the mid-1990s, the farm crisis had abated. Times were once again good, and conservative Republicans (now in control of Congress) tried to bring the farm program to heel. To that end, they passed the Federal Agriculture Improvement (FAIR) Act. The FAIR Act sought to move beyond price supports of any kind. Rather than set target prices for key commodities, the FAIR Act embraced freedom to farm: farmers would receive a subsidy based on the historical record, liberating them to plant whatever they wanted. Over time, the FAIR Act would lower the subsidy levels, thereby easing the farming community back into the free market. It worked—for a time. The first few years after it passed, farm subsidies declined. Then farm prices started dropping, interest groups started agitating, and Congress started passing a series of "emergency" appropriations to prop the farmer back up. By 2000, farmers were receiving $23.3 billion, up from just $6 billion in 1996.[43]

Subsequent farm bills followed this trend, funneling more and more money to the farmer. The 2014 farm bill—the most recent legislation as of this writing—promises to lower subsidies over the next decade, but most of the cuts are in the out years, which will almost assuredly be governed by new policies. In the short term, there are payment hikes and a movement toward subsidies via insurance support. In this schema, the federal government helps farmers by covering a portion of their premiums for disaster insurance and shallow loss insurance that protects them from too-low prices. Unlike direct payments, these are once again inconspicuous, protecting farmers from close scrutiny of just how much they are receiving from Uncle Sam.[44]

Between 1933, the first year of the AAA, and 2013, the taxpayers spent about $800 billion supporting American farmers, despite multiple efforts by almost every postwar president either to end these programs or substantially reform them.[45] The fact that presidents so consistently wanted to change the regime of farm supports strongly suggests that much of this princely sum was spent corruptly, per the definition we have been using in this book. That is, the money was spent for the benefit of select interests at the expense of the public interest. But, in and of itself, reform efforts are inconclusive. We still must ask, why did presidents oppose these policies so consistently? What is wrong with them?

Plenty. On paper, the farm bill is supposed to maintain a stable domestic farm economy, promote U.S. agriculture abroad, promote nutritious food, subsidize research, support the diet of the poor, and protect farmland.[46] In reality, it does none of these efficiently, and many of them not at all. So universally reviled is the farm bill that economists as varied as Greg Mankiw, former George W. Bush advisor, and Paul Krugman, liberal New York Times columnist, hate the farm subsidies.[47] Generally speaking, economists now believe that agricultural commodity markets can work on their own, without supports from Uncle Sam. Sure, the government should still tend to public goods, like maintaining roads and providing timely information, but otherwise the farmer should take care of himself.[48]

Economists have identified several major problems. First, on net the farm program is actually incomprehensible. Some policies push in one direction; others pull in the opposite way. For instance, for generations the government tried to eliminate the surplus through programs like the Soil Bank while *also* promoting research to help increase crop yields. The two policies cancel each other out, so why spend money on either? Similarly, direct payments to the farmers are meant to keep farm prices high, while programs like crop insurance encourage farmers to plant on marginal land, thus increasing supply and lowering farm prices.[49]

Second, the farmer really can compete in the market himself nowadays. Agricultural economists used to think that the farmer had no ability to toggle output to meet perceived demand. Thus, the farmer was essentially a victim of a vicious cycle: farm prices fell, inducing the farmer to grow more, which caused farm prices to fall further. Farmers today, however, do not have this sort of problem, at least on average. So advanced are the science and economics of agriculture that the farmer can adjust to market signals and manage supply accordingly, which helps explain why investments on well-run farms yield roughly the same returns as investments in the nonfarm economy. This is exactly what we should expect in an economically efficient market.[50]

Third, there is the issue of waste. Farm subsidies keyed on particular commodities produce surpluses as farmers direct resources toward the subsidized crops, rather than where an efficient market would have them be directed.[51] Add in the cost to the taxpayer of managing the program and the costs to the farmer to understand the program, and there is a substantial loss to society. For instance, consider the program that subsidizes ethanol product for use as a fuel additive. Ethanol producers would not turn a profit without federal subsidies, which cost the federal government roughly $5.91 per gallon. At that rate, it would cost $181 billion in taxpayer subsidies to reduce U.S. oil imports by two million barrels per day. There are better ways to spend money, and certainly better ways to reduce oil consumption.[52]

Closely related is the problem of deadweight loss. This is the result when the net benefits to farmers are less than the net costs to taxpayers and consumers. Estimates on deadweight loss are hard to make because they require modeling an alternative marketplace without federal interventions subsidizing the farmer (and driving up prices for consumers). Still, the data at hand suggests that deadweight loss is substantial. In 1973, it was about $2 billion, and it had risen to $5 billion by 1990. Recently, economists have estimated that the crop insurance program alone creates a deadweight loss of nearly $1 billion.[53] Again, this is money that is simply lost; if the farm programs were repealed in their entirety, national income would increase on net exactly by the total amount of deadweight loss.[54]

Fifth, there are public health concerns. For instance, consider the U.S. sugar program, which costs about $3 billion per year. Not only has this doubled the cost of sugar for the average American consumer relative to the world consumer, it has also facilitated the production of high fructose corn syrup. Annual consumption of this alternative sweetener now exceeds sugar consumption, and multiple studies have linked it to obesity.[55]

Finally, there is the issue of distributional justice. The mythology of farm subsidies is that they support the family farm through its trials and tribulations. Nothing could be further from the truth. In fact, farm subsidies are linked to agricultural output—be they in the form of crop insurance, commodity price supports, or deficiency payments—meaning that, the more you farm, the more you can get from Uncle Sam.[56] So unsurprisingly, farm subsidies benefit the wealthiest of farmers.[57] Today, the small family farm is economically a nonentity; big farms produce most of the output and therefore receive most of the benefits. In 2008, for instance, more than 60 percent of payments went to the largest 12 percent of farms. In 2010, the top 1 percent of farmers received more than 20 percent of the subsidies.[58] Across society as a whole, this means that farm payments tax the relatively poor to give to the relatively wealthy. About twenty years ago, the average farm family started making more money per year than the average nonfarm family. Seeing as how farm payments go to the wealthiest of the farmers, the net result is socially perverse.[59]

In fact, the winners of the farm subsidy game are even narrower than this analysis suggests. Owners of elastic inputs (e.g., laborers, suppliers of fertilizers, etc.) tend not to gain anything because supply simply increases. Consider an average farm worker. One would think he would win from subsidies as his wages increase, and he might at first. But over time, a better farm wage will attract workers from outside the farm sector, or induce workers within the farm sector to shift their labor to the subsidized product. So, he loses much of the wage increases he might have temporarily gained. Only owners of relatively inelastic inputs will gain, and in farming that means landowners. Not only this, but over time, the subsidies will be capitalized into the cost of doing business, through higher land values and therefore mortgage payments. Thus, the *real* winners of farm subsidies are those who own the land at the time the new subsidy level is mandated. They will collect windfall profits, but after that the value of the subsidies will be priced into the land.[60]

So if farm subsidies are so bad for the country as a whole, why have they been sustained despite regular efforts to reform or reduce them? One incorrect answer is that farmers are still an electorally potent force. They were at the time of World War I, constituting about 40 percent of the total workforce, and still at 20 percent by the time of the Great Depression. Today, however, there are only about one million farm workers, constituting just 1 percent of the total workforce.[61] Relatedly, representatives from farm districts have declined from 37 percent of total House members in 1950 to less than 1 percent today.[62] The big farmer organizations are also a fragment of what they used to be. The Farm Bureau was untouchable in the 1930s, but in the postwar era it came to be identified with the Corn Belt and Republican agricultural policies, and its influence began to decline, never to return to the glory days of the '30s.[63]

So, why does the subsidy program persist, even if its targeted beneficiaries—those poor souls described in *The Grapes of Wrath*—are now long gone? One answer is probably inertia. Federal programs rarely disappear. The federal government is still operating a Railroad Retirement Board, and railroad workers are now even scarcer than farm workers.[64] Relatedly, there is the organization of Congress, which doles out policy domains to specific committees. This creates the incentive for specialization, not just in terms of knowledge but also preferences. If the handful of agricultural interests, though electorally puny, can influence key committees where the handful of farm congressmen are all concentrated, there is relatively little the floor of either chamber can do about it. After all, committees not only originate bills but hold sway during conferences between the chambers.[65]

Still, this can only furnish a portion of the explanation. The balance of the cause has to do with interest group mobilization, akin to the story we told in Chapter Eight. As general interest groups like the Farm Bureau declined, commodity-specific groups rose to take their place, demanding particular payoffs for soybeans, wheat, corn, whatever. Moreover, a vast array of interest groups now have a stake in the farm bill, which touches a whole host of issues, from food stamps to conservation, land use, environmental issues, food prices, nutrition, world hunger, farm worker rights, agribusiness regulation, and more.[66] If the farm bloc of the 1920s was a tightly knit circle of interest groups and members of Congress, the interest groups that care about today's farm legislation are fragmented, and no organization or entity has the clout like the Farm Bureau had in the 1930s to unify these diverse interests into a single, coherent demand.[67]

This has lent itself to a logroll, or the process by which minority groups whose preferred legislation cannot win on a straightforward up or down vote unite to create a winning coalition. The farm bill is now, according to economist Matthew Mitchell, a "grab bag of subsidies" whose purpose is to ensnare enough particular interest groups and factions to win majority approval in the Congress. In 1981, there were 121 farm assistance programs; today there are almost 300, even as the farm population has declined. On top of this, numerous other programs have been created to attract support from non-farm interest groups.[68] Alone, most of the programs would assuredly fail, but together they form an unbeatable majority on the House and Senate floors to raid the public treasury for their private purposes. As political scientist William Browne puts it:

> Agricultural policy works, not because it is exclusionary, but because it is very accommodative to diverse and even conflicting member interests. Lots of members can win by playing but not by sitting on the sidelines or by just voting against farm programs.[69]

Perhaps the most famous alliance embedded within the farm bill is the union between rural farmer organizations and the urban poor. The trade is straightforward: relatively conservative members from rural areas vote for food stamp legislation while the urban representatives of the poor vote for farm subsidies that otherwise increase food prices. This coalition has been in place more or less since the mid-1960s, and the two programs were actually fused into a single bill in the early 1970s. The alliance between these groups is purely political. There is no policy linkage between food stamps and farm subsidies; the connection exists because rural representatives were looking to build legislative support for their high-cost subsidies in the middle of the 1960s, and the new liberal bloc demanding food stamps made for an easy ally. This is why the Department of Agriculture manages the food stamp program, even though similar programs are in the wheelhouse of other outlets like the Department of Health and Human Services. The logroll between the two factions means that the agriculture committees are in charge of food stamps, and they have placed the program in the department that they have the most experience overseeing.[70]

To put the story told in this chapter into context, it is worth revisiting a point already made. As noted previously, most of the gains from farm subsidies are to landowners who possess the property at the time the new programs are implemented. Everybody else loses because they hold elastic inputs, or because the gains are lost through higher mortgage payments. Since the farm programs were implemented in 1933, the United States has spent nearly $1 trillion in contemporary dollars in subsidies. Where has this money gone? If we follow the logic of agricultural economics, we must conclude that *it has mostly gone nowhere*. The original landowners from eighty years ago reaped a bounty (but still a pittance of the total sum of $1 trillion), and those who were in possession of the land when subsidies increased at various points similarly benefited to some extent, but other than that the benefits have simply evaporated. Virtually nobody was made better off by all this money.[71]

What makes this fact disturbing is that there is very little disagreement on this point, at least among those who do not have a direct interest in this or that provision of the farm bill. Disinterested economists now tend to agree that the farm bill is worse than useless; it actually harms the public good. And yet it is unable to be repealed. Even when Congress has come close to major reforms, like the 1996 FAIR Act, it never can seem to follow through. At the first sign of "hardship" for (relatively wealthy) farmers, it folded like a deck of cards, handing over more money than had been given in years.

Why? The answer is exactly the thesis we are defending in this book: the government was never designed to implement a policy such as this. Instead, the government was a compromise between various political groups extant in 1787; some wanted virtually unlimited federal power while others wanted to retain (more or less) the status quo under the Articles of Confederation, so they split the difference by creating a government of expanded, yet still discrete powers. Importantly, they built a structure to manage those powers and those powers alone. Yet generation after generation has seen fit to expand the powers of government without altering the structure to handle the new tasks responsibly. Now we simply ask too much of the government, and when we do that, it disappoints us.

In the case of farm subsidies, it is simply asking too much of this government to deal fairly with a program such as this. Even if we admit the economic case for a limited, or substantially reformed, version of farm subsidies, this government in particular could not execute it well at all. It would manage it to the interests of the well-connected and well-off, just as the New Dealers did with the AAA. It would resist commonsensical reforms, just as generations of postwar politicians did. If it did suddenly discover the courage to fix the programs, it would shrink from those reforms at the first sign of trouble, just as happened with the FAIR Act. It would expand the program for political, not economic, purposes, just as the most recent Congress did by expanding crop insurance, which helps well-heeled farmers hide how much they are actually receiving from Uncle Sam. It would do all this, and much more, so that within a generation the original program would be widely criticized, yet virtually unassailable.

It would do all of this because it is especially subject to the pressures of interest group appeals. In *Federalist* #10, James Madison envisions a grand clash of competing interests in our system of government, all battling each other for their own ends but in so doing ensuring the public good would win out. But this was for a government that did not do things like directly provide for the welfare of certain classes of citizens. Grant this government that power, and you also embolden interest groups to seek rents as aggressively as they can, perverting and twisting whatever noble purposes a policy might have had toward their own private ends. And the conflict that Madison argues would save the republic becomes the logroll that bankrupts it: why should interests fight each other, when instead they can coordinate to make sure everybody gets a payoff? A government such as ours, uniquely sensitive to those rent seekers, will do their bidding even at the expense of the public good. Even when that expense must be counted in the hundreds of billions.

This is how a country could waste so much money supporting the historically small and long since deceased coterie of farmers who happened to own land in 1933. Outrageous? Yes. Perverse? Certainly. Surprising? *Absolutely not.* To bring matters full circle: no, farm subsidies are hardly a "sexy" topic of public policy, but when it comes to political corruption in the current era, they are a metaphor for everything that is wrong with the body politic.

10

"The Parochial Imperative"

The Politics of the Pork Barrel

A T THE CENTER OF OUR STORY in this book is a tension, a centuries-old contradiction between the attitudes of the citizenry. On the one hand, Americans want a government that speaks for the entire public as it attempts to solve complicated problems that are national in scope. On the other hand, they want their representatives to have clear and unambiguous connections to local communities, and thus never be far from the needs and wants of their own neighborhoods.

This tension, as we saw, was apparent at the Constitutional Convention, which ultimately resolved it via Roger Sherman's Connecticut Compromise. Ours would be a government that utilized localized institutions to wield limited national powers. A great idea, but for one problem: the document did not go far enough to satiate the nationalistic demands of the people, or at least their leaders. So, the national government has acquired powers over the generations that dwarf the original grant offered in Philadelphia in 1787. All the while, the old localistic institutions remain largely unchanged. As we have argued, this has produced corruption, as our institutions are incompetent to handle these expansive powers responsibly.

Nowhere is this tension more apparent than in pork barrel politics, or the tendency of members of Congress to use federal resources to enrich their districts, often in ways that line their pockets or secure their reelections.

The pork barrel's origins trace back to the nation's commitment to develop its economic potential. The federal government would use tax dollars to help build roads, bridges, canals, and later on railroads; later still it would build highways and airports. This was not on the political agenda at the time of ratification, and the nationalistic Federalist Party did not emphasize this during its heyday in the 1790s. It really became a pressing concern after the calamitous War of 1812, when the country learned the hard way that it simply did not have the infrastructure to win a war such as that. This was unacceptable for a young, restless nation eager to make a claim to world greatness. As James Monroe intones, "We cannot go back. The spirit of the nation forbids it."

The problem, of course, was that the spirit of the Constitution, at least as understood by James Madison at the time of ratification, did forbid it. By this, we are not making a legalistic claim, but rather a philosophical one. (Although, on the legalistic issue, it is not for nothing that, at the end of his presidential term, Madison vetoed on constitutional grounds a bill that would have created a fund similar to today's highway trust fund.) When the Constitution was constructed, its authors never really considered that the government would use tax dollars to fund local projects that could serve a broader national purpose. If they had, they probably would not have built Congress the way they did, for the legislature is uniquely incompetent to handle such a task. This basic incompetence will drive the story in this chapter. Congress simply does not have the institutional capacity to allocate efficiently funds to local communities for national purposes; too often, that money will be wasted as legislators fund projects of dubious national value, but of monetary or political value to themselves.

And moreover, nobody really has the capacity to check the legislature on this. No member of either chamber can claim to represent the people at large; only the president occupies such a lofty position. Yet his hand is weak in this area. Inevitably tied to a significant faction of the Congress through the legislature, it is a politically costly move for him to rebuke his own side. Moreover, the veto is an extraordinarily inefficient way to drain the congressional pork barrel. After all, wasteful programs are nowadays embedded in enormous pieces of legislation that allocate tens (if not hundreds) of billions of dollars; these take months for Congress to put together. And all this happens with a deadline: if Congress does not pass its annual appropriations legislation, the government shuts down. Is it really worth it for a president to veto an entire bill for, say, highway transportation because of a few billion dollars of pork? More often than not, the answer is no.

What we have then is an obnoxious form of corruption. It may cost less per year than the amount wasted in Medicare, which we shall discuss in Chapter Eleven, and it may not put the broader economy at risk as did the corruption surrounding financial regulation, to be discussed in Chapter Thirteen. Still, it is a frustrating waste of money because it is so obvious and yet very little can be done about it.

To begin, we need a solid definition of the pork barrel, a peculiar phrase if there ever was one. In the *National Municipal Review* in 1919, Chester Collins Maxey writes:

> On the southern plantations in slavery days, there was a custom of periodically distributing rations of salt pork among the slaves. As the pork was usually packed in salt barrels, the method of distribution was to knock the head out of the barrel and require each slave to come to the barrel and receive his portion. Oftentimes the eagerness of the slaves would result in a rush upon the pork barrel to grab as much as possible for himself.[1]

Political scientists today are as wont to use the phrase pork barrel as they are distributive politics. And a more technical definition comes from Richard Andrews: "the practice of seeking expenditures of federal funds to benefit one's own region at the expense of another." This definition indicates that the pork barrel really belongs in our discussion of political corruption, as it elevates a factional interest, in this case, a geographical one, at the expense of the common good.

Indeed, political scientists have isolated the geographical nature of the pork barrel as one of its key identifying marks. Another is its divisibility; that is, funds can be toggled to meet the political or economic needs of any one district without affecting the distribution of funds to another.[2] Moreover, scholars usually look at the distribution of benefits against the coercive nature (or cost) of a policy. In this way, the pork barrel targets benefits narrowly while disbursing costs broadly, which gives it an obvious political appeal: the winners know they have won, and thus are grateful, while the losers are the taxpayers, who barely, or perhaps not at all, perceive that they have lost.[3]

The types of policy most susceptible to the pork barrel are those that Congress decides on a discrete basis. Benefits distributed by congressionally dictated formulas or bureaucratic decision-making processes are not as useful. Still, there are exceptions to this rule. For instance, congressional formulas can often have a distributive effect by prizing political variables while ignoring more relevant economic factors; the formula Congress uses to allocate highway trust funds relies heavily upon population, something that appeals greatly to the House of Representatives but is not necessarily indicative of need. Plus, as we shall see, Congress is often able to pressure bureaucrats into facilitating the pork barrel.[4]

As the quote from Maxey suggests, the pork barrel has been around for quite a while. He links it back to the 1826 omnibus rivers and harbors legislation, which was one of the first to combine parochial programs into a single appropriation, which is commonly called logrolling. As we saw in Chapter Two, Andrew Jackson railed mightily against this practice, though during his administration spending on internal improvements increased markedly, and his decision to accept or veto appropriations often had a political motive. In Chapter Seven, we noted how the New Deal became a pork barreler's paradise: congressional control over early projects meant that well-positioned legislators received more than their fair share, and later on the Roosevelt administration used the Works Progress Administration as a type of political machine.

In general, the problem with the pork barrel gets to the heart of our thesis. When the Constitution was hammered out in 1787, there was not really much thought given to the prospect of Congress using tax dollars to develop the nation. Indeed, the level of federally sponsored public works was quite muted until after the War of 1812. The upshot is that Congress is simply not well designed to take on this kind of task. And, following our theory, the greater the authority of the government, plus the more money at its disposal, the larger and larger the pork barrel. In other words, the real change since the early nineteenth century is that Congress can waste money in more policy domains.

From a republican perspective, what is so bad about all this? Three problems stand out, the first being inefficiency. The costs of these programs so often exceed their benefits because Congress distributes the funds via political calculations.[5] A secondary problem is a lack of optimization. Even if a project yields benefits that are greater than the costs, there are often alternative uses of that money that could provide an even greater return. Similarly, Congress spends an inordinate amount of its collective time and effort distributing these benefits, rather than focusing on national concerns. Finally, there is the problem of profligacy. As we shall see, the pork barrel thrives if and only if members who want to participate in it are somehow afforded that opportunity. This lends itself to the government spending more than it otherwise should, given the constraints that a large and persistent budget deficit imposes. For instance, Citizens Against Government Waste began publishing its *Pig Book* in 1991, when it catalogued some $4 billion in waste, despite a budget deficit of some $270 billion. By 2004, the pork barrel had increased to $23 billion, despite a deficit of $412 billion.[6]

There are a number of books, articles, and websites that catalogue the most ridiculous pork barrel projects as a way to spark the outrage of the reader. The following will indeed offer such a catalogue, one that is quite outrageous. Still, our goal is not simply to shock the reader's sensibilities; rather, it is to understand how the pork barrel actually operates. How is it that our governmental institutions continue to produce such policies? The problem cannot be reducible to personalities like Robert Byrd of West Virginia and Ted Stevens of Alaska. While they were among the greatest pork barrelers of all time, the reality is that they were simply better at a game that plenty of legislators have been playing since the 1820s. The deep historical roots of the pork barrel, and its seeming immunity to most reform movements, suggest that its origins are embedded within the structure of the government. As noted, the blame rests primarily with Congress, but it is time to dig a little deeper to see exactly what the problem with the legislature is.

The pork barrel has been around for ages, but political scientists did not really get a handle on it until they began to embrace the assumptions and methodologies of economists. One of the big breakthroughs on this front came from David Mayhew of Yale University in the 1970s. His *Congress: The Electoral Connection* begins with the assumption that members of Congress are above all interested in reelection, and they can be understood as pursuing that goal rationally.[7] Writing the same year, John Ferejohn of New York University notes that the pork barrel is electorally useful for members of Congress for three reasons: it builds a record upon which to run, it maximizes a legislator's freedom in other areas (i.e., if he brings home the bacon, he can get away with defying his constituents on other issues), and it robs potential opponents of an issue.[8] Members of a commission appointed by Ronald Reagan to study the pork barrel called this, "The parochial imperative . . . an excessive preoccupation with the local impact of spending decisions at the expense of the national interest."[9]

In the 1970s and '80s, scholars began to emphasize that the pork barrel was closely connected to the committee system. Vote trading on the floor of the legislature is actually a very difficult proposition. There is always the problem of cheating. Suppose that Bob and Tom are legislators. Bob agrees to support Tom's project if Tom supports Bob's project. But what obliges Bob if his project is voted on first? Nothing. He could cheat on Tom without consequence. As we saw in Chapter Nine, the vote trading between advocates of farm subsidies and food stamps took years to hammer out, and was only locked in once the agriculture committees corralled the programs into a single bill.

Something like this characterizes the pork barrel. Committees in Congress have enormous institutional power to guide legislation through the process, and can thus secure the gains from trade that a floor-based logroll simply cannot guarantee. In other words, committee power can keep legislators from cheating on their commitments to one another and ensure that participating members get their share of the pork. What follows from this is that legislators will flock to the committees with oversight over the policy domain that interests them—usually the committee that authorizes the expenditure or the appropriations subcommittee that appropriates the money.[10] So, for instance, a House member who wants to bring home highway-related pork will head either to the Transportation Committee or the Transportation and Housing and Urban Development Subcommittee of the Appropriations Committee. Highway pork will thus accrue predominantly to members of these committees, and especially to the more senior leadership.[11] As political scientists Barry Weingast and William Marshall argue:

> Instead of trading votes, legislators in the committee system institutionalize an exchange of influence over the relevant rights. Instead of bidding for votes, legislators bid for seats on committees associated with rights to policy areas valuable for their reelection. In contrast to policy choice under a market for votes, legislative bargains institutionalized through the committee system are significantly less plagued by problems of ex post enforceability.[12]

Put simply, the committee system helps members of Congress secure deals with one another, making sure that logrolls are durable over time.

Members of these committees also can use the power of oversight to extract concessions from bureaucrats, ensuring that when the latter put together their budgets, they reserve special privileges for the former. The Wilsonian ideal was for a bureaucratic class to be immune from politics, but that is quite often a myth. In reality, bureaucrats have to form and build coalitions to protect their policy turfs and maximize their budgets, which often means they have to curry favor with well-positioned members of Congress. As one bureaucrat in the Department of Energy told the Grace Commission, which Reagan formed to study government waste and inefficiency: "Long after your report is gone and forgotten, we'll still have to live with those people up on the Hill."[13] In his classic study on the relationship between Congress and the bureaucracy, Douglas Arnold finds that the latter's efforts to woo the former often contribute to the pork barrel.[14] Perhaps the most infamous example of this was the Model Cities program, enacted at the end of the Great Society. Originally meant to provide large, systematic grants to help rebuild a half dozen cities, it morphed into a socially useless logroll. Some 150 cities received small grants that did little to improve civic life, as bureaucrats attempted to build, then maintain, their legislative coalition.[15]

This distributive theory of legislative organization received pushback from several different directions in the late 1980s and early 1990s. Keith Krehbiel of Stanford University posits an alternative way to understand Congress. Members are not principally interested in acquiring pork barrel benefits, he argues, but rather in acquiring information. Thus, committees specialize in policy fields to ensure that the majority on the chamber floor gets the best deal possible. Krehbiel writes:

> Long before national or state governments became involved in the wholesale distribution of geographically targeted benefits, legislatures struggled with the problem of obtaining independent sources of information and expertise. Only by extricating themselves from dependence upon information from the executive branch were legislative bodies able to play distinctive and effective deliberative roles within separation-of-powers systems.[16]

Another group of scholars argues that the political party, rather than locking in gains from trade, is the prime organizing force in Congress. Majority parties function as legislative cartels that control committee membership and the floor agenda to protect the interests of their members.[17]

Compounding these challenges to the distributive theory is the fact that, in the years following its initial articulation, scholars had found, at best, mixed results in support of its core hypotheses.[18] So, it seemed as though what was an elegant theory may not have been an accurate one. Still, the anecdotal evidence in favor of the distributive theory is strong. The *Pig Book* is not highfalutin political science, sure, but it cannot be dismissed out of hand. Neither can the findings of the Grace Commission. What was going on?

In recent years, the distributive theory has made a bit of a comeback, as scholars have improved their hypotheses and developed more sophisticated datasets. On the theory front, scholars have increasingly come to realize that competing ideas about congressional organizations may not be all that inconsistent with one another. Congress can pursue multiple ends at the same time, and so some committees can follow an informational angle (e.g., the Intelligence Committee), others a distributive angle (e.g., the Transportation and Infrastructure Committee).[19] Furthermore, not all members of Congress are equally interested in the pork barrel; many—for instance, those in safe districts—simply do not need to acquire benefits to hold on to their seats and can instead focus on other goals like policy entrepreneurship.[20] Moreover, partisanship and the pork barrel can go hand in hand; parties can organize committees to secure electoral benefits primarily to their own members. On the data front, scholars have done a better job of figuring out exactly who benefits from programs—like, for instance, looking beyond primary contracting for military acquisitions to secondary contractors. They have also done a better job of looking at mediators within congressional districts, like interest groups.[21]

Thus, recent scholarship vindicates a modified form of the original distributive theory. As we shall see in the following section, certain committees are more likely to engage in the pork barrel than others, and certain members of Congress will be more interested in it and more capable of practicing it to maximum effect. Even though Congress has other interests, like information and partisan dominance, the consensus at this point is that subsets of the institution are indeed organized to lock in gains from trade.

When looking at the modern pork barrel, the place to start is the military. It is probably the best studied form of the pork barrel, and certainly the most expensive. We'll start with defense procurement, then transition to the politics of base closures.

There are the classic cases of military pork that are remembered from the news. There is the the Seawolf sub, the Osprey helicopter, and the F-22 stealth fighter. There is also the B-1 bomber, perhaps the most famous example of military pork, about which it was said that it was invulnerable to attack because it had parts made in all 435 congressional districts.[22]

Military pork often has only a tenuous relationship to the actual military. For instance, in the 1990s Congress allocated some $8 million to the military for mitigation of environmental impact on Indian lands.[23] More recently, antipork crusader Tom Coburn, Republican senator from Oklahoma, has found billions spent on nonmilitary purposes, including $37 billion for excessive overhead and support, $15 billion for education, $9 billion for military grocery stores, $6 billion for nonmilitary research and development, and $700 million for alternative energy.[24] A lot of this has to do with the military's outdated procurement policies, not to mention a lack of good central planning within the Department of Defense (DOD), but a lot of this is forced upon the military by a Congress interested in turning the national defense into the pork barrel.

A few examples from the 2004 *Pig Book* will illustrate the parochial nature of the problem. That year, Dianne Feinstein of California used her position on the Senate Military Construction Appropriations Subcommittee to secure nearly $28 million to update the Los Alamitos Joint Forces Training Base and March Air Reserve Base, and build a new gate complex at the Los Angeles Air Force Base. Hawaii senator Daniel Inouye, of the Senate Defense Appropriations Subcommittee, won a whopping $371 million for his state to overhaul the USS *Portsmouth*, expand the Hawaii Federal Health Care Network, and fund the Hickman Air Force Base Alternative Fuel Vehicle Program as well as an undersea vehicle testing and training environment.

Perhaps the most extreme case of pork for pork's sake came in 1996. House Minority Leader Richard Gephardt lobbied hard for McDonnell Aircraft, based in St. Louis, Missouri, where his district was centered, to be the prime contractor for the Pentagon's Joint Strike Fighter. He argued to the DOD that the fighter was an "affordable solution to our future strike warfighting needs." In the end, the DOD picked Boeing and Lockheed for the job, which prompted Gephardt to withdraw his support for the entire program *the very next day.*[25]

Considering the early history of the United States, it is peculiar that the military would be such an essential element of the pork barrel. During the debate over the Constitutional Convention, Madison warned about the "standing military force" that has become such a valuable form of pork. He argued:

> A standing military force, with an overgrown Executive will not long be safe companions to liberty. The means of defence against foreign danger, have been always the instruments of tyranny at home. Among

the Romans it was a standing maxim to excite a war, whenever a revolt was apprehended. Throughout all Europe, the armies kept up under the pretext of defending, have enslaved the people.[26]

For more than 150 years, the United States basically heeded Madison's warning. After every war, the United States demobilized its military. And in the early twentieth century, the government spent about 1 percent of gross domestic product on the military, about what it spent one hundred years prior.[27]

World War II changed all of that. Defense spending approached nearly half of gross domestic product, which had an important effect on the politics of the military. Historically, armaments were produced in the major cities in the East, but the necessity for more and more supplies—not to mention a strategic concern about concentrating production near the Atlantic Coast—pushed production into the rural and suburban areas, and into the South and West. Much of this had to do with politics, as well. During World War II, southern Democrats dominated the key points of access in the Congress, and ensured that their districts were well tended to.[28]

These new beneficiaries created enormous pressure for the government to keep military expenditures at an elevated level. Moreover, President Harry Truman thought that sustained military spending would help smooth out the business cycle, promote full employment, and prevent a return to the Depression that the war had ended.[29] And so, since the end of World War II, military expenditures during peacetime have been roughly four-and-a-half times (as a share of gross domestic product) what they were during the twentieth century prior to the war. Much of this has to do with the nation's commitment to promoting its interests worldwide against various threats like the Soviets or Islamists, but a lot of it also has to do with distributive politics. As South Dakota senator George McGovern commented in the early 1960s, the military had become "frozen into a permanent [Works Progress Administration]."[30]

Scholarly studies have shown that members from districts with undiversified economies and a military presence lobby hard to get on the defense committees, and use these perches to retain and expand their districts' share of the military establishment.[31] Members of the majority party, especially the most senior members, are the ones who derive the most benefits.[32] This often means protecting outmoded weapons that the Pentagon does not want, insisting on excessive production of munitions, and so on.[33] One of the most extreme examples has to do with a congressional requirement that the military power an installation in Kaiserslautern,

Germany, with inefficient anthracite coal that is shipped all the way from northeastern Pennsylvania. This policy is still in place today despite the fact that its architect, Daniel Flood of Wilkes-Barre, left Congress in 1980 after being censured for bribery.[34]

In the immediate aftermath of the Cold War, there was a peace dividend that President Bill Clinton wanted to use to reduce the budget deficit. The problem from a congressional standpoint was that this hurt local economies, so members regularly added expenditures to DOD requests, including House Republicans after their victory in 1994. While conservatives were generally interested in reducing the size of government, they nevertheless tacked on an additional $3 billion to $11 billion above what the DOD asked of them in the 1990s.[35] Members also exhibited a bias toward salvaging existing, outdated programs that contributed to local economies at the expense of research and development of advanced weapons that the DOD preferred.[36]

Congressional obstinacy on procurement is impressive, but it cannot hold a candle to the challenges the legislature gave the executive branch over military base closures. Historically, this power had been under the purview of the president, but starting in the late 1960s Congress began tying the hands of the commander in chief, partially in reaction to the fact that Lyndon Johnson had used base closures to punish his enemies.[37] Base closures are thought to be bad for local economies, and thus especially bad for members. As military historian Paul C. Koistinen notes, "Unlike contracting, these are very tangible and visible operations, often employing large numbers of nearby residents."[38]

By the time of the Jimmy Carter administration, Congress had effectively seized control of the base closure process and balked at even the slightest efforts to modernize the system. It was a classic tragedy of the commons. Members collectively may have known that base closures had to happen, but nobody wanted to be burdened by it. In 1983, Republican senator John Tower invited his colleagues to propose a list of military bases that could be cut back or closed. Only six senators responded and proposed cuts amounting to a measly $200 million.[39]

Finally, congressional irresponsibility became too much for the public at large to bear. As political scientist Kenneth Mayer aptly notes, the whole system "bordered on the preposterous, and it was increasingly difficult to argue that every base was essential to national security."[40] So in 1988, Congress finally implemented a process to close bases, called the Defense Base Realignment and Closure (BRAC) Commission. The system essentially cuts Congress out of the loop; the BRAC Commission formulates its suggestions independent of Congress and submits them to the secretary of defense, who in turn makes recommendations to the president; Congress can stop the closures only by voting to disapprove of the entire package.

Interestingly, the process may have broken the logjam, but it did not stop the logroll. For starters, congressional leaders have slowed or otherwise stopped new rounds of the BRAC Commission, often in a bipartisan manner.[41] Moreover, return to the theory of congressional-bureaucratic relations put forward by Arnold: solicitous of ever-larger budgets and anxious to protect and expand their domains, bureaucrats often curry favor with well-placed legislators. Arnold's study was finished a decade before the BRAC Commission, but recent scholarly literature indicates that it favors key members of Congress. If you are a senior member of one of the committees with authority over the military, you are less likely to see your district's bases closed, all else equal.[42]

––––––––––

Military pork might be the most costly form of distributive politics, but it is hardly the oldest. That "honor," as we saw previously, goes to internal improvements, especially expenditures on rivers and harbors. As William Safire writes: "The classic example of the pork barrel is the Rivers and Harbors bill, a piece of legislation that provides morsels for scores of congressmen in the form of appropriations for dams and piers."[43] The political appeal of rivers and harbors is twofold: first, every congressional district can have use for such projects; second, they are visible projects that enable members to claim credit.[44]

It remains a big business. For instance, in 2004 Senate Energy and Water Appropriations subcommittee member Thad Cochran secured $15 million worth of rivers and harbors pork for his home state of Mississippi, including $12 million for the Backwater Pump, $2 million for Gulfport Harbor, and $1 million for the Wolf and Jordan Rivers. Cochran joins a long, petty tradition, stretching back to the 1820s.

Typically, the manner in which Congress has supplied this pork is through the Army Corps of Engineers. It was founded nearly two hundred years ago to build canals and improve the nation's water transportation system. Today, it also protects wildlife, helps build parks, improves the water supply, and more.[45] The Corps' agenda has been taken over in part by the relevant authorizing committees and appropriations subcommittees; this means its fate is similar to the DOD's. Members on these committees increase the number of jobs the Corps is tasked to do, give it more money than the president requests, and tilt the extra work toward their own districts. In his seminal study on the subject, Ferejohn finds that membership on the House Public Works Committee, which has since been rechristened the Transportation and Infrastructure Committee, buys a member's state 80 percent of the cost of a new project per year. More senior members get more. Ferejohn shows a similar result for the appropriations subcommittee.[46] Moreover, Arnold's study of Congress and the bureaucracy discovers congressional leaders can influence the budget proposals of the Corps.[47]

None of this is to say that economic factors do not play a role in how these projects are allocated; for instance, scholars find that the outlays for public works projects run contrary to the business cycle, which is what we should expect if the government is pursuing Keynesian policies.[48] Still, politics is a factor and makes a difference. One scholar demonstrates that wasteful spending on rivers and harbors cost the taxpayers $3.6 billion in 1986 alone. That works out to be nearly $8 billion in today's dollars.[49] Little wonder, then, that Congress has been extremely protective of its turf. When Carter became president in 1977, he tried to leverage his overwhelming partisan advantage in Congress to cut the rivers and harbors pork, but Congress resisted. In the end, it agreed to eliminate only eighteen projects—far less than what Carter wanted and basically an insult to the president, who signed the appropriation into law nonetheless.[50]

Closely related to rivers and harbors pork is the waste in the National Park Service (NPS). The two most infamous examples of this are probably the Presidio in San Francisco, California, and Steamtown in Scranton, Pennsylvania. The Presidio, a former military installation, was a pet project of California Congressman Phil Burton. In 1972, he used his position as chairman of the interior appropriations subcommittee to fold the Presidio into the NPS, at a cost of $40 million in 1995. The Steamtown park was the brainchild of Congressman Joe McDade, who had a collection of old steam engines (imported from Maine, no less!) somehow declared a national park, at a projected cost of $60 million.[51] The tradition continues to this day. The 2004 *Pig Book* reports that Colorado Republican senator Ben Nighthorse Campbell won $15 million for park projects in his state, including $7 million for the Baca National Wildlife Refuge and $2.4 million for the Beaver Brook Watershed.[52]

The NPS has long been a domain of pork, and for good reason. Today, it oversees more than eighty million acres, which gives members plenty of opportunity to do visible good for their districts. Even so, there was a noticeable shift during Burton's stewardship over the agency. During his tenure, the appropriations subcommittee was often derided as the Park of the Month Club for its inclination to turn questionable sites into national parks. And, of course, the NPS receives more funding than it asks for, but this nevertheless burdens the agency.[53] Its purpose is to tend to genuine national treasures like Yellowstone, not the old trains that Joe McDade turned into a park.

Transportation is another policy domain that has long been susceptible to pork barrel spending. In 2004, the *Pig Book* noted that Kentucky Senator Mitch McConnell acquired $103 million for transportation projects in his state. A long list of projects were funded with this money, including $2 million for a Daviess County parking garage, $1 million for Kentucky Scenic Byways, and $500,000 for the University of Kentucky Academy for Community Transportation Innovation.[54] This sort of waste has been common for years. In fact, the United States has not had a comprehensive transportation strategy since the 1950s, when the federal government created the interstate highway system. Today, neither party is much interested in reimagining our infrastructure development program, instead they are content to indulge in the pork barrel.[55]

Highway funds are normally paid out of a trust fund from the gasoline tax. The money is distributed according to a formula; this itself is political in part because it takes into account population, which need not have any bearing on the worthiness of a state for highway funds.[56] But above and beyond that, members of Congress have been wont to insert demonstration projects into the highway bill. In theory, these are supposed to showcase innovative ideas on transportation and infrastructure, but in practice they are simply pork. In 2005, they cost the taxpayers $13.5 billion.[57]

These are probably the biggest policy domains of pork barrel—military, rivers and harbors, parks, and highways—but it is worth noting that, the closer you look at government expenditures, the more you notice: pork is everywhere. For instance, the 2009 American Recovery and Reinvestment Act—the stimulus put forward by President Barack Obama and congressional Democrats—was riddled with pork. Anecdotal accounts at the time reported on scores of parochial programs—like $30 million for Nebraska hospitals, $50 million for the National Endowment for the Arts, billions for Amtrak, and even a requirement that the Transportation Security Administration buy one hundred thousand uniforms from American textile plants.[58] Recent scholarship has validated these claims. A 2013 study in

Public Choice concludes that spending per district was significantly related to membership on the relevant authorizing committees and appropriations subcommittees, and more senior members received more.[59]

Of course, the pork barrel is a bipartisan game, and Republicans give as good as they get. A cornerstone of the George W. Bush domestic agenda was his faith-based initiatives, designed to provide federal funds to religious charities. Scholars find it had a distinctly electoral purpose as well. Fund distribution was significantly related to how states voted in 2000, and also to the size of the black and Hispanic populations, suggesting that Bush wanted to shore up his position with minority voters ahead of the 2004 presidential election.[60]

The perennial boondoggle of Amtrak is also a source for pork. In 1971, the federal government rolled the remaining handful of profitable passenger railroad lines into the National Railroad Passenger Corporation, or Amtrak, a for-profit corporation that receives public funds. It has struggled mightily to be profitable, and there is constant pressure to cut lines that are not generating enough revenue. Enter Congress. Members predictably vote against any cuts to lines that run through their districts, prompting Stanford economist David Baron to conclude:

> The political support for Amtrak should persist as long as service extends to enough districts, and the principal threat to Amtrak is that federal budget pressures may lead to reductions in appropriations which would force Amtrak to reduce service schedules or eliminate routes thereby eroding its political support.[61]

Even the academy is not immune from the pork barrel. Two trends have stood out over time. First of all, the ways that the government funds research and development "introduce predictable, systemic biases," according to scholars who have studied it.[62] The parochial imperative induces the government to favor projects that can be finished over a short time horizon, that promise net benefits early on, and that can be fragmented into many, independent subprojects. Writing for the Brookings Institute, Linda Cohen and Roger Noll study six federally sponsored research and development programs from the 1970s and 1980s, and discover only one—commercial satellites—to be an unequivocal success. Three of them—supersonic transport, the Clinch River Breeder Reactor, and synthetic fuels—failed. The photovoltaics program was not a commercial success but was a technological breakthrough, as was the shuttle program.[63] All in all, government funding of research and development "is so severely constrained by political forces that an effective, coherent national commercial [research and development] program has never been put in place."[64]

Second, universities have recently begun appealing straight to Congress for funding, rather than going through the normal channels of peer review. The first big breakthrough came in the 1970s with a $10 million bounty for a vet school at Tufts University, and it snowballed from there. In 1980, Congress allocated some $16.5 million to 21 programs through this system; in 1996 it gave more than $300 million to 417 programs.[65] The 2004 *Pig Book*, for instance, shows Nevada Democratic senator Harry Reid securing $2 million for the University of Nevada, Las Vegas Research Foundation, and another $2 million for the University of Nevada, Reno.[66] The political upside for such projects is not so much their visibility, but that they curry favor with academics and administrators, who are socially important and well-connected members of the local community.

Finally, consider the Government Printing Office (GPO). The pork barrel there is small, but illustrative considering the trajectory of our story. As we saw in Chapter Three, government printing contracts were once a way for politicians to reward their cronies, and Congress finally authorized the GPO in 1861 to reform the crooked system. Things are much better now, obviously, but politics is never far afield from any government endeavor. The Grace Commission notes that the GPO, which is overseen by an insignificant congressional body called the Joint Committee on Printing, had twenty-seven regional bookstores that sold government documents. In 1981 the GPO wanted to close or consolidate many of these offices, which were not heavily trafficked, but it had to back down when employees of the stores complained to the Joint Committee on Printing. Again, small potatoes, but in a way that makes it all the more significant; Congress dragged its heels to reform something because it would affect just a handful of people. And when considered in light of the ancient congressional irresponsibility on printing, the old aphorism is particularly apt: "plus ça change, plus c'est la même chose."

No discussion about the pork barrel can be complete without a consideration of congressional earmarks. Over the last couple years, they have been in the news, and the odds are good that they will be once again.

An earmark is a metaphor that refers to the cutting the ear of a pig or cattle as a mark of ownership. Earmarks have often been called "spending with a zip code attached to it." Congress makes the choice about what to spend and how to spend it by somehow circumventing the normal budgetary process, be it an agency proposal, the derivation of a distributive formula, hearings to determine the worthiness of an outlay, or competitive bidding among contractors. Instead, members of Congress prevail upon committee leaders to insert a specific appropriation into the legislation, or more often the accompanying reports on the legislation.[67]

Earmarks are the quintessential form of distributive politics, really stripping away all pretensions of responsible budgeting and arriving at the simple, most basic essence: sanctioned by committee and party leaders, members of Congress send money home for political purposes.[68] In fact, earmarks are really more valuable than other forms of distributive politics because they are clearly identifiable with members of Congress. A member who works the normal budgetary process—by, for instance, persuading the bureaucracy to include a favored project in its submission—delivers pork back home, but it is mediated. The earmark is direct and immediate, which gives it a special political salience.[69] In particular, earmarks can serve as a signal to the privileged and well-connected residents of a district, and political scientists find that elites who receive earmarks are more likely to contribute campaign money to incumbents.[70]

Earmarks have been around for quite some time, but by the end of the 1990s, the process had become institutionalized, with members communicating their requests either to appropriations subcommittee or authorizing committee staffers.[71] As one account puts it:

> An annual Spring ritual in most congressional offices . . . is the writing of a letter to each of the subcommittee cardinals in which the member spells out in detail each special funding request that falls within the jurisdiction of that subcommittee. Subcommittees are literally deluged with requests. As a rule a member can expect that at least a portion of his or her request will be deleted by the Subcommittee Chair. This being the case, the member without being too ham-fisted, will often make requests for more money or projects than are actually needed.[72]

"Deluged" is the right word. For instance, in 1994 there were 1,574 earmarks in the energy and water development bill, at a cost of $2.7 billion; in 2005, there were 1,722 earmarks at a cost of $9.5 billion. The transportation bill had 140 earmarks costing about $900 million in 1994; in 2005, there were 504 earmarks costing $6.6 billion. The appropriations bill for Veterans Affairs and Housing and Urban Development had 30 earmarks that cost $10 million in 1994; in 2005, there were 2,080 earmarks costing $1 billion.[73]

So committed was Congress to its earmarks that it long resisted repeated attempts to reform the process. In 1988, the Reagan administration tried to organize agencies to defy earmarks, arguing that appropriations reports did not have the force of law. But the revolt quickly lost steam as the bureaucracy realized just how dangerous it was to defy members of Congress on such a politically important matter.

In the end, the earmark regime was (seemingly) undone for the same reason the BRAC process was initiated: Congress just began to embarrass itself. Congressional scandals tied members of Congress to influence peddler Jack Abramoff via earmarks, and Congressman Randy "Duke" Cunningham was bribed by defense contractors to put earmarks into legislation.[74] Congressional Democrats put in place new reporting requirements for earmarks in 2007, and finally congressional Republicans imposed a moratorium on them in 2011.[75]

So, is the issue dead? Hardly. Despite the moratorium, Citizens Against Government Waste still shows 109 earmarks in fiscal year 2014 with a price tag of $2.7 billion. In fact, the moratorium could have adverse effects because it has made the process less transparent:

> Since earmarks were deemed to be non-existent in the FY 2014 omnibus bill, there are no names of legislators, no list or chart of earmarks, and limited information on where and why the money will be spent. Earmarks were scattered throughout the legislative and report language, requiring substantial detective work to unearth each project.[76]

Moreover, the moratorium is simply that: a moratorium. As we saw in Chapter Nine with agricultural subsidies—and as we shall see in Chapter Eleven with Medicare—Republicans in Congress often implement reforms that, later on, they simply cannot sustain. When the public stops paying attention, they quietly undo them.

———————

Members of Congress find all sorts of ways to profit personally from corruption. As we saw in Chapter Eight, there is solid evidence to suggest that members planning to join the lobbying corps will tilt their activity in the final years of their tenures to favor prospective employers. We will encounter this again in Chapter Thirteen when we look at Fannie Mae and Freddie Mac. This is not technically illegal, but it is nevertheless corrupt. It should not happen in a republic.

A more direct way for members to profit is via the pork barrel. Because it so often funnels money to districts to improve roads, harbors, rivers, and so on, it can positively affect property values, and it just so happens that members often own property near projects they initiated.[77] A few examples from recent history will explicate this point and show just how frequently these sorts of underhanded dealings occur. We'll focus in particular on powerful members within Congress to illustrate that such actions are far from considered below-board, although of course they should be.

- In 2004, House Speaker Dennis Hastert bought a plot of land in Plano, Illinois, for $15,000 an acre. Shortly after this purchase, he inserted a $207 million earmark into the highway transportation bill to build an interchange near his new property. The improvement caused the property value to double to more than $36,000 per acre.[78]
- Former House Speaker Nancy Pelosi was a strong advocate for the Third Street Light Rail Project in San Francisco, despite its high cost: about $660 million for just a six-mile route. She secured a $532 million earmark to initiate the project and another $200 million to complete it. She and her husband own a four-story office building two blocks from Phase Two. Experts think that could increase the value of the property by more than 150 percent.[79]
- In 2004 and 2005, Reid, who at the time was Senate minority whip, won $21.5 million to build a bridge over the Colorado River, connecting Laughlin, Nevada, to Bullhead City, Arizona. Reid owns 160 acres of land in Bullhead City.[80]
- In 2008, Norm Dicks, then a member of the House Appropriations Committee, and often called "the congressman from Boeing," won a $1.8 million earmark for a Washington State environmental agency, the Puget Sound Partnership, where his son worked as executive director. Over the next three years, he funneled more than $14 million to the Environmental Protection Agency, which turned it over to the Partnership.[81]
- Darrell Issa, who recently served as the chairman of the House Committee on Oversight and Governmental Reform, won nearly $1 million in earmarks between 2007 and 2008 to widen a road less than a mile from a medical building in Vista, California, that he owned.[82]
- Jerry Lewis, former chairman of the House Appropriations Committee, acquired $2.7 million in funds to redevelop Barracks Row in Washington, just four blocks from his home. Bill Young, another former Appropriations chairman, secured $73 million over a decade for several companies that hired his sons.[83]

This is all reminiscent of the soliloquy of Tammany Hall sachem George Washington Plunkitt, who was quoted at length in the preface. He famously said: "I seen my opportunities and I took 'em." That is exactly what happened in these instances, and it is a stark reminder of one of the core theses of this work. There have been many reform movements since Plunkitt's day, and the sorts of honest graft that were legal then are illegal now. Still, honest graft perpetuates over time, despite the best efforts of reformers. Today, it is often wrapped up in distributive politics: members funnel money to their districts to secure their reelection and also to line their own pockets.

It is a fair question to ask, and we are sure that you, dear reader, have pondered the query as we have swum through the grimy backwaters of our nation's political history: has corruption in America gotten worse over time? This chapter illustrates the two senses in which it has in fact gotten worse.

The first is that there is simply more money to be had. In 1826, the first year that an omnibus (and pork-ridden) rivers and harbors legislation was passed, the total value of the nation's gross domestic product was approximately $20 billion (in 2004 dollars). That is about $3 billion less than the amount Citizens for Government Waste discovers in its 2004 *Pig Book* alone. The reality is that, as the country has gotten larger and wealthier, the opportunities to take more and more money from the national till have increased. This is compounded by the fact that the government now takes on more tasks than it has ever done before. An ambitious politician on the make today has many more ways to undermine the public interest than would have been available in 1826 simply because there are so many more policy domains to meddle in.

The second way is more subtle, but becomes evident when we compare the misuse of the pork barrel for personal gain in this chapter to the practices of the Gilded Age. Back then, corruption had become more professionalized relative to past eras, but it still had a decidedly roguish quality to it. Everybody knew what Boies Penrose and Matthew Quay were up to, and even the surreptitious forms of it were not so surreptitious. The Standard Oil Letters unearthed by William Randolph Hearst laid bare the transactional nature of politics in that day, in language plain as day. Indeed, that is perhaps one reason why Plunkitt is still widely read today: he may have been a scoundrel, but he was a frank scoundrel.

Today, as we saw, this kind of corrupt behavior—"I seen my opportunities and I took 'em"—perpetuates, but with a legalistic veneer of plausible deniability. Politicians have gotten increasingly better at covering up exactly what they are doing. Today's pork barrel is embedded in legislation that runs thousands of pages in obscure legalese that virtually nobody can decipher. And, should some intrepid soul actually figure out what is going on, the politician in question can always issue the rote, totally unbelievable, and yet legally decisive denial. As Reid's assistant explained to the *Washington Post* about that bridge to Bullhead City:

> As has been stated before, Senator Reid's support for the bridge has absolutely nothing to do with the property he owns and is based on the fact that the project is good for southern Nevada, and nothing else.[84]

Sure thing, Senator Reid! And, conveniently, the same goes for the forty-plus other members, who were shown to have a personal stake in some public project by a recent *Washington Post* report. Not a single one of them did anything untoward. Absolutely not. In other news, when you finish reading this book, dear reader, be sure to give the author a call. He has a bridge for sale that you might be interested in—in Brooklyn, not Bullhead City.

At least Plunkitt had the decency to admit that he was engaged in graft.

But that is exactly the point: politicians today have professionalized the pathways of corruption so thoroughly that they can more easily defy detection, and, barring that, retain plausible deniability. This is so much the case that pols must wonder what is wrong with people like Cunningham or William Jefferson, two members of Congress who were actually convicted of accepting bribes in the last decade. There are now so many ways to enrich yourself or secure your reelection without getting noticed, let alone ending up in the slammer.

Outrage aside, there is a broader point to be made here. Thomas Jefferson and Madison were acutely worried about corruption not simply because it was bad in and of itself, but because it spreads. This is what we have seen, time and again. Corruption spreads not only because the government grows in size and scope, but because politicians get better at it when their dealings are not being actively thwarted by a watchful citizenry. This is how the Jacksonian spoils system devolved into the out-and-out debauchery of the Gilded Age. It is how the government today wastes more money every year than the country's national wealth when the pork barrel began. It is how politicians today can glibly dismiss obvious conflicts of interest, and nothing at all comes of it. Indeed, they can become leaders of the entire Congress.

"A Big, Dumb Price Fixer"

Medicare and the Politics of Entitlements[1]

A S WE HAVE SEEN, the New Deal ushered in a vast expansion of government powers, not just in terms of quantity but also of quality. It is not just that the government was doing more of the things it had used to do, it was now also doing new things. One of the most important new tasks it set for itself was the provision of direct social welfare to the citizenry. Of course, this had happened in ages past, with Civil War pensions, for instance. But the New Deal represented an important break with tradition in that the benefits provided by the federal government were not contingent upon military service and did not have an expiration date. The government commitment to direct social welfare became universal and unlimited.

While this was a new sort of power, it had a familiar potential for corruption. It all gets down to a conflict of interest, similar to that which occurs with economic development and regulation. In both cases, the government claimed new authority for the public good, but private interests gained control of the levers of power to channel federal efforts to their own ends. And so it goes with the direct provision of social welfare. For instance, suppose the government commits to fighting poverty among senior citizens. Does that mean that its interests align with those of seniors? Not necessarily. Instead, we should expect seniors—just like those who lobbied members of Congress for more spending on internal improvements—to try to bid upward their federal support, regardless of whether such increases are in the public interest. From the public's perspective, seniors should provide such amenities for themselves, and the government should be able to draw the line properly.

As we have seen time and again, that is easier said than done in our system, which was simply never intended to manage so many diverse tasks. Factions within society can be expected to organize to maximize their gains or minimize their harms, regardless of whether that is in the public interest, and the government as designed struggles in vain to resist. We have seen this happen with economic development and regulation, and so it goes with social welfare programs. In this chapter, we shall take a close look at the Medicare program, whose ostensible purpose is to provide seniors with efficient care for essential medical problems. In practice, however, it has been captured by the wealthiest seniors, doctors, hospitals, and a vast array of medical service providers, whose private interests are promoted, often instead of the public interest.

What are these private interests? There are two. First, providers demand essentially unlimited discretion in dispensing care to seniors, and they react negatively whenever any restrictions are placed upon them. Insofar as the government does regulate what they can do, these limits are quite weak, and providers claim outsized influence in deciding what those limits ultimately are. Second, senior citizens, or at least those who claim to represent them as lobbying groups, will not truck any alteration of the original Medicare contract, despite how outdated it may now be. Similarly, they refuse any and all requests from the federal government that seniors contribute a greater share for their care. Instead, they want more and more care paid for by somebody else.

The result, as we shall see, is a grossly inefficient program that often produces socially indefensible results. And its costs are set to increase at such a rapid clip that they will choke off almost every other federal priority within the next two generations.

This chapter will lay out this case in a largely historical fashion. First, however, it will establish a theoretical basis to understand the unique challenge Medicare poses for public-spirited government. It will then trace the experiences of early postwar liberals in their efforts to implement national health insurance, which failed because of staunch opposition from the medical service industry. This immensely influenced the construction of the original Medicare program in 1965, whose structure was, and remains, generous to the point of absurdity with providers. Congressional efforts to regulate the costs of the program were entirely ineffective for almost twenty years, despite the fact that the price tag grew precipitously. And, when reform finally came, Congress, heavily lobbied by providers, balked at straightforward regulation, despite the failures of the program to date and the fact that it was costing so much money. Instead, it adopted loose, general spending guidelines that have created enormous new problems. Meanwhile, senior citizens organized actively in response to the new benefits and have successfully checked most efforts to reform what is now an unsustainable program.

Medicare is a unique public policy in the United States, though it does share similar components with other programs. Medicaid, which serves the poor and was instituted in the same legislation as Medicare in 1965, is similar in that it provides medical care to a specific population. However, unlike Medicaid, Medicare is paid for in part by worker contributions to a trust fund, which creates a sense of public ownership. In this important regard, it is like Social Security. Yet, unlike Social Security, which is a reasonably straightforward pension program, Medicare does not guarantee a certain monetary amount to each beneficiary, but a minimum amount of care to be provided by third parties, namely medical service providers.

This makes Medicare a theoretically challenging program, and it is worth exploring its nuances, for they will help us understand why the government has to date failed miserably in managing it for the public interest. Medicare, like Social Security, provides its recipients with a kind of wealth, or property. But this property is not actually owned by the recipients, even if they think their contributions mean they are owed benefits from the federal government. Instead, the recipients enjoy it conditionally, depending on the political situation, rather than on the basis of the common law or the constitutional protection against seizure of property without due process. This makes for a kind of feudal arrangement between the governing class in Washington and the recipients of care.[2]

Adding further difficulty is the fact that the government does not provide this benefit itself, but rather delegates private agents to supply it. Politically and economically, this makes a lot of sense, as the government would otherwise have to build the capacity to provide care to seniors. Nevertheless, it makes medical service providers, broadly defined, a party to this contract as well.[3]

The result of all of this is a very complicated principal-agent problem, one that is animated by a diverse array of interests. The government has a public interest in providing necessary care to senior citizens in the most efficient way possible. It wants to make sure seniors are taken care of, but not pampered, and not at an exorbitant cost, for there are other important tasks to which federal dollars could be dedicated. Seniors, meanwhile, have an interest in maximizing the value of the care they receive; importantly, this could be over and above what the government deems to be necessary and efficient. Doctors and other providers have an interest in maximizing their private benefits (the same goes for nonprofit hospitals, which today have taken on many of the characteristics of their for-profit counterparts); again, this may be in conflict with the government's interests.[4]

Even in an ideal situation, the government would have an enormously difficult time making sure that the public's interests are triumphant. There are, after all, literally millions of Medicare transactions that happen every year. The logistics of creating an effective monitoring system to ensure that care is medically necessary and cost-efficient would be daunting, to say the least. In our system of government, however, the problem is insuperable. Those in government who are supposed to represent the public interest are heavily influenced by senior citizens and medical service providers. They lobby aggressively to ensure that such regulatory oversight is never developed, that the private interests of seniors and providers win out over the public concern for necessity and efficiency.

This is not to cast moral aspersions on those who do the lobbying. After all, as noted previously, the property they possess is conditional in nature. A Medicare recipient's claim is not protected by common law or the Constitution, but rather by the Social Security Amendments of 1965, which can be repealed or modified at any time. Meanwhile, the providers that service those claims gets reimbursed at rates updated every year by the government in a highly political process, not according to the forces of the market. Why would these groups not organize to protect their benefit streams? They would have to be foolish indeed simply to hope that the government will never alter the contract in ways that leave them worse off. So, they organize, they lobby, and they succeed in making sure the terms of the contract remain immensely favorable to their private concerns.

As per usual, Congress is the real problem, not those who seek to influence it for their own interests. And it is not the personalities within a particular Congress, but the institution itself. As of this writing, there are but two members of Congress still serving who also served when Medicare was implemented. Yet Congress today is no more able to stand up to these interests than it was in 1965. In particular, authority over Medicare is principally housed in a handful of congressional committees, which are consistently lobbied and plied with money from the medical service industry, rendering them highly indisposed to monitor providers effectively. Meanwhile, the senior lobby is ready, willing, and able to activate a vast network of elderly voters to lobby Congress to thwart attempts to update the program, especially in ways that would make wealthy seniors pay more.

The result, as we shall see, has been measly reforms that promise more cost controls than they actually deliver and create a vast array of unintended perverse effects. In some sense, the public interest is served—after all, seniors are getting care—but at an unreasonably excessive cost to society at large. That is the price of asking this government in particular to implement a program that it was never designed to implement.

The political origins of Medicare trace back to Harry Truman's Fair Deal agenda, which, despite being largely unsuccessful, came to serve as the blueprint for postwar American liberalism. Truman proposed a national health insurance program modeled along the lines of Social Security; workers would pay a portion of their wages into a trust fund, which would fund medical, hospital, nursing, and dental care, as well as laboratory services. In a message to Congress in 1947, he calls this, "a logical extension of the present social security system, which is so firmly entrenched in our American Democracy."[5]

From a policy standpoint, mimicking Social Security was problematic at best, as outlays for medical care could empty the fund of contributions from wage earners (as has nearly happened several times with Medicare Part A). However, from a political perspective, it was sensible indeed, for the social insurance model had proven itself invincible. When his advisors pushed back on this scheme to finance Social Security, arguing that it was regressive, Franklin Delano Roosevelt responded, "I guess you're right about the economics, but these taxes were never a problem of economics. They are politics all the way through. We put those payroll contributions there so as to give the contributors a legal, moral, and political right to collect those pensions. . . . With those taxes in there, no damn politician can ever scrap my social security program."[6] He was right; no damn politician ever has.

Even so, Truman's program was a nonstarter, despite the decision to tap into the popularity of Social Security. The American Medical Association (AMA) hired a professional public relations firm, Whitaker and Baxter, to coordinate an attack on the proposal after Truman's surprise reelection. The AMA opposed the program because it feared it was a stalking horse for government rationing of care, thus interfering with doctors' ability to practice medicine as they saw fit. In its first year, the AMA's campaign spent $1.5 million and distributed over fifty million pieces of literature against Truman's proposal; this was financed by a $25 assessment upon AMA members.[7] It spent another $2.6 million in 1950, but as Frank Campion notes in his history of the AMA, this was probably an "exercise in overkill." Staunch opposition from the dominant conservative coalition in Congress, a combination of northern Republicans and southern Democrats, virtually assured its failure, regardless of what the AMA did.

The defeat of Truman's national health insurance plan taught liberal reformers several important political lessons that would serve them well during the Great Society. Above all, liberals came to adopt the strategies of incrementalism and consensus-building. The push for universal health care, they realized, could not come all at once. Instead, their desired goal would have to be broken down into parts and passed gradually so as not to arouse the ire of the vast array of interests opposed to the project. Reformers would also need to win over affected interest groups and gain the support of the public to pass even these smaller pieces. This is why they came to embrace a medical care program for the elderly as a first step on the path toward universal coverage. The aged in the early 1960s were markedly poorer and sicker than the younger generations and evoked a great deal of public sympathy.[8]

Despite this strategic thinking on the part of reformers, Medicare still went nowhere prior to the 1964 election. John F. Kennedy tried to implement something like it during his brief tenure, but met with no success. Lyndon Johnson also tried between the time of Kennedy's assassination and his own election as president, but again the proposal failed. In both instances, the liberals had the full backing of organized labor, which wanted to shift health costs from company books, where they inhibited labor's ability to bargain for higher wages, and onto the federal budget. They also had the support of senior citizens, whom labor assiduously organized.[9] Yet the AMA once again opposed the initiative, and again shelled out millions of dollars to defeat the program.[10] In the end, the sustained conservative tilt of Congress gave the AMA the edge.

The results of the 1964 election changed all that. Johnson won an overwhelming majority, and he provided congressional Democrats with long coattails. The Eighty-Ninth Congress, which convened in January 1965, had 295 House Democrats, including 205 from outside the conservative states of the former Confederacy. This was the most liberal Congress since the one elected in 1936; LBJ and Wilbur Cohen, his Medicare point man, believed that they had a political opening, albeit a brief one, to pass a Medicare bill. Though the conservative coalition was weakened, it would certainly come back, and the provider community still wielded enormous power. Johnson and Cohen recognized that they had to act fast.

To capitalize on the opportunity, the Democrats pushed the legislation through Congress as quickly as possible. The bill that ultimately succeeded came together in an executive session of the House Ways and Means Committee on March 2, 1965. It passed the Committee on March 29, then the entire House on April 8, and it was signed into law on July 30. From a political standpoint, this haste made a great deal of sense. On a policy level, however, this quick turnaround did not allow time for the thought and debate necessary to build a well-functioning program.

In their hurry, Johnson, Cohen, and House Ways and Means Committee Chairman Wilbur Mills made at least two fateful choices that would haunt Medicare's future. First, they elected to implement what Mills called a "three-layer cake" approach. The original Democratic plan for the Medicare program looked like what today is known as Medicare Part A: hospital insurance for the aged paid out of a trust fund that collects revenue from a dedicated payroll tax, like Social Security. Republicans, after their drubbing in the 1964 election, sought to base their opposition in a positive alternative, so they put together their own plan. Representative John Byrnes of Wisconsin, the ranking Republican on the Ways and Means Committee, proposed a substitute to Medicare called Bettercare, which used premiums and general revenues to pay for an insurance program that covered doctor visits, nursing care, and other services. The AMA followed a similar tactic and proposed a third plan called Eldercare, through which the government would subsidize care for the indigent. Why did the AMA support Eldercare but oppose Medicare? The target population in Eldercare lacked resources to pay for their own care, so the AMA celebrated federal support for them, as it would expand doctors' business. On the other hand, Medicare was planned as a universal program, and thus it feared federal limits on existing activity.[11]

Liberals worried that their political momentum would be lost if the effort to pass Medicare became bogged down in a debate over these plans' relative merits. To preempt this problem, Mills executed a remarkable act of political cunning: he combined all three proposals into a single bill. He described the final product as a three-layer cake, with hospital insurance as the first layer (Part A), doctor visits as the second (Part B), and subsidized care for the poor as the third (Medicaid). As Cohen later remarked, "It was the most brilliant legislative move I'd seen in thirty years. . . . Mills had taken the AMA's ammunition, put it in the Republicans' gun, and blown both of them off the map."[12] Mills's three-layer cake passed through Congress speedily.

The liberals won their political battle, but the long-term policy implications were profound, and over the years the government has been stuck with a law much more unwieldy and more costly than it otherwise might have been. The programs that the AMA and the Republicans suggested were not meant to be implemented as they were originally proposed in committee. Medicaid has been an underperforming program from the start, and for all the money spent, it is unclear that it does much to improve the health outcomes of the poor.[13] As for Bettercare, which became Part B, Robert M. Ball, the commissioner of Social Security, would later remark:

> The provisions of the hospital insurance part—Part A—were really honed over several years during the early 1960s. . . . Part B, on the other hand, came out of an unexpected Ways and Means compromise. Mills took the physician part of John Byrne's voluntary plan based on an Aetna health insurance policy and made it a voluntary part of the new federal program . . . it really wasn't a good proposal . . . There were very few handholds for any kind of cost controls in Part B.[14]

As we shall see, this lack of consideration would have severe consequences for the federal budget.

The second important decision made by Johnson and the Democrats to force Medicare through Congress quickly was intended to garner the support of the medical service lobby. They gave the legislation a weak regulatory structure for governing the providers. Indeed, the act itself proclaims:

> Nothing in this title shall be construed to authorize any Federal officer or employee to exercise any supervision or control over the practice of medicine or the manner in which medical services are provided, or over the selection, tenure, or compensation of any officer or employee of any institution, agency, or person providing health services; or to exercise any supervision or control over the administration or operation of any such institution, agency, or person.[15]

This was not mere boilerplate to win a political battle. The regulatory structure of the program was shockingly weak, considering how much money it would soon come to spend. For starters, the law made clear that provider participation was voluntary and open to any licensed practitioner, which would become problematic in the future as the government today lacks the capacity to discriminate between providers on the basis of quality. What's more, the government employed intermediaries like BlueCross BlueShield to serve as claims processors. Thus, medical service providers did not even have to interact directly with the government. They dealt instead with third parties who, thanks to frequent interactions with the providers, were naturally disposed to their interests.[16]

Importantly, the law also adopted the permissive structure of indemnity insurance that BlueCross and BlueShield offered at the time. Medicare thus reimbursed doctors and hospitals not based on negotiated rates, but "usual, customary, and reasonable fees," as the law put it. As we shall see, the private insurance industry would change substantially in the years to come as new tools were developed in the private market to control costs, but Medicare remained anchored in a wasteful structure. The program also set in stone a distinction between doctors and hospitals, one that has since become quite arbitrary and, as we shall also see, led to a great deal of gamesmanship by providers to maximize their payoff from the government. Adopting the structure of BlueCross and BlueShield also turned out to be bad for seniors, as the model often was a poor fit for their actual needs. For instance, dental care and prescription drugs were uncovered, and Congress was slow to update the basic contract.[17]

To make good on its commitment to laissez-faire, the federal government put little effort into creating a sufficient regulatory apparatus after the bill became law. For starters, management of Medicare was housed in the Social Security Administration, which was very good at cutting checks to seniors in a timely fashion but had absolutely no experience in regulating the behavior of doctors and hospitals in their millions of interactions with patients. Decades later, Medicare would be spun off into a new department, the Centers for Medicare and Medicaid Services (CMS), but its institutional capacity remains weak. Today, CMS spends more money per year than all but twelve of the world's richest economies, yet its staff consists of about five thousand people. By comparison, Social Security's staff is roughly sixty-six thousand.[18]

Interest group politics, broadly defined, was the decisive factor in the structure governing Medicare. The government feared that, if the program was too restrictive of providers, the lobbies for the doctors and hospitals would have ammunition to kill the legislation before it became law, or, perhaps worse, refuse to participate in it after it became law. So, they wrote it explicitly in a way to win their support, and the consequence was an incredible expansion of health spending, well beyond what the program's creators had ever imagined.

Part of this had to do with the fact that senior citizens who once lacked access to medical care now had it and made use of it. Part of it also had to do with general inflation, which was quickly on the rise during the early years of the program. But much of it had to do with the permissive structure of the program itself. As one scholar puts it: "There is a general consensus among students of Medicare that until recently the methods by which it paid providers encouraged an unnecessary and unjustified increase in the intensity of treatment provided beneficiaries."[19] Indeed, the numbers are striking. During its first fifteen years of existence, Medicare averaged more than 10 percent growth per capita per year. While inflation as a whole was high for much of this period, especially in the health industry, Medicare outstripped these general price increases.[20] Put simply, doctors and hospitals were paid whatever they charged the government, so they charged more and more. Additionally, the ill-conceived financing mechanism for Part A, a Social Security–style trust fund, proved itself incompetent to handle the complexities of Medicare hospital payments. Between 1967 and 1984, there were two crisis periods (1969 to 1972 and 1982 to 1984) when the program's actuaries warned that the trust fund would go bankrupt within ten years, forcing legislators to scramble to patch the program.[21]

Medicare's out-of-control costs forced legislators' hands in 1972, when they authorized professional standard review organizations (PSROs) in that year's amendments to the Social Security Act. Medical service providers fought the PSROs tooth and nail, although they turned out to be weak institutions premised on the false hope that doctors could police themselves. They were miserable failures, doing nothing to check spending in the program.[22]

During this period, the AMA's political capacity grew more sophisticated. By 1974, it was arguably the second-most-powerful political action committee in Washington, behind only the AFL-CIO's lobbying operation.[23] Often working with the hospital lobby, it served as a powerful bulwark against government efforts to control costs. Jimmy Carter would learn this the hard way in the late 1970s. He proposed a 9 percent cap on hospital spending increases per year, which prompted furious lobbying from the AMA and the hospitals. They countered with a voluntary effort to stem costs, which, combined with their generous campaign contributions, scuttled the Carter proposal in Congress.[24] Of course, the voluntary efforts failed just like the PSROs before them.

The budget deficit became such a problem by the first term of Ronald Reagan that policymakers had to take another stab at reform. The solution they landed on is known as the prospective payment system (PPS). No longer would the government reimburse hospitals based on their usual, customary, and reasonable fees, but rather based on a payment schedule built for hundreds of diagnostic related groups (DRGs). The upshot of this complicated structure is that the government pays hospitals based on an estimate of how much their services really cost.[25] Hospitals grudgingly accepted the program in 1983 because budget reconciliation acts (which required fewer votes in the Senate) passed in 1981 and 1982 put even more strenuous caps on Medicare Part A expenditures.[26] What's more, the hit to the hospitals was mitigated because the PPS used a false baseline, whereby inflation under the program was projected to increase by much more than it ever would. This enabled the government to claim that it cut hospital spending more than it actually did, and made the cut to hospital payments less bad than it seemed.[27]

In 1989, the government followed up with a similar program to curb doctor expenditures, known as the resource-based relative value scale (RBRVS), once again through budget reconciliation.[28] This followed an ill-considered freeze of doctor rates in the mid-1980s that did nothing to curb costs because doctors responded by increasing volume.[29] The RBRVS was a system designed by academics that had enjoyed some success in trial runs, for instance in New Jersey. Similar to PPS, its goal is to reimburse doctors based on an estimate of how much value a given procedure adds, filtered annually through a conversion factor whose formula is set by Congress. Just as with the hospital regulations, the RBRVS is meant to impose some restraint on Medicare spending indirectly; it does not mandate what doctors must do, just what they can charge for their services.

Combined, the PPS and RBRVS did indeed check the growth in Medicare expenditures, at least for a time. From 1983 until 1991, with PPS in effect, total per capita Medicare spending grew by 75 percent

—still a lot, but less than health spending growth outside Medicare. The RBRVS helped to cut the growth rate in Medicare Part B, but after 1992 the annual average growth rate in the overall program ticked upward slightly, though it remained below the crisis-levels of the 1970s and early 1980s.[30]

Medical service providers did not love the new regime, but the reality was that Medicare remained a very good deal for them. Above all, they retained virtually untrampled autonomy, despite the fact that they were receiving billions of dollars in federal money every year. Here, it is appropriate to keep these new regulatory regimes in perspective. The restraints they placed upon providers constituted a notable break from past precedent, but prior to that point the providers had basically no supervision whatsoever. They could essentially charge whatever they wanted, and the government would foot the bill. The PPS and RBRVS provided top-down oversight, but only in an extremely limited sense. They were basically just budgetary measures that imposed limits on what providers could charge for a given procedure or examination. Considering how much money they were receiving, providers remained largely untouched in terms of how the government regulated their behavior.[31]

Compare Medicare, for instance, to the federal acquisition regulations, the process by which the government procures products and services from the private sector; there is an extensive and often time-consuming bidding process and review of the bidders to make sure the feds get the best value for their dollar (at least, in theory). Medicare, on the other hand, has never had anything of the sort, before or after the PPS and RBRVS, so careful are politicians not to impinge upon the freedom of medical service providers. In fact, the government lacks any real leverage over them whatsoever. It cannot force them to compete for its business, nor reward those who offer better care at lower prices. That is because Medicare is still legally required to accept any willing, licensed provider. The government even struggles to weed out bad providers who may be defrauding the taxpayer.[32] As Tom Scully, the former administrator of Medicare puts it, the program is a "big, dumb price fixer. . . . We are very good at fixing prices and paying quickly. But we have zero ability to monitor utilization or understand or differentiate payment based on quality."[33]

A recent example illustrates the severity of this limitation. In 2011, federal agents arrested a ring of service providers in Detroit for running a fraudulent Medicaid scheme. Two of the doctors were suspended from the Medicaid program, but continued to bill Medicare. In fact, Medicare paid them more than $1 million combined in 2012. A report from public interest group ProPublica identified dozens of doctors in a similar situation, who collectively received about $6 million from Medicare in 2012.[34]

Moreover, the PPS and RBRVS may have been innovative at the time of their implementation, but the government has been exceedingly slow in updating the fee schedules. There is an informational asymmetry at play here: the providers know how much these services really cost while the government does not, and the latter has not built up the institutional capacity to develop that knowledge. So, scholars generally find that the reimbursement rates in the PPS and RBRVS to be downward-sticky, meaning that they are rarely reduced, despite many efficiency gains in the provision of care. For instance, until 2003, Medicare's payments to ambulatory surgery centers were based on a 1986 survey of their costs, despite the fact that in the intervening years there were a wealth of productivity-enhancing innovations.[35]

Compounding the informational challenge is the age-old problem of whether the government has the will to be an arbiter for the public good, let alone the capacity. In particular, there are now a vast array of interest groups with a financial stake in these programs—no longer just doctors and hospitals, but home health care providers, skilled nursing centers, insurance companies, drug companies, information technology companies, senior citizen groups, and more. These groups have developed crackerjack lobbying efforts that utilize the complete array of tools discussed in Chapter Eight, and have been extremely successful in influencing congressional policy. So, even though the government may have (partially) broken free of their grip in 1983 to pass the PPS and in 1989 to pass the RBRVS, those groups have not disappeared. In fact, they remain in place and are working constantly to shift the law in their favor.[36]

As a consequence, the government has indeed managed to control spending rates to a degree through the PPS and RBRVS, but the limits of these programs have created a number of bad side effects. This is to be expected from any regime that uses price controls without monitoring the behavior of those whom it affects, either through the marketplace (e.g., competitive bidding) or regulation (e.g., licensing providers explicitly for Medicare or more stringent auditing). Price limits that come from the top will invariably induce unexpected behavior down below, and if there is nothing down there to guide provider and patient actions toward the preferred outcome, then surprising—and, often, socially perverse—results will occur. Of course, the providers would raise hell over any such limits to their autonomy, so the consequences of the PPS and RBRVS have often been perverse.

For starters, the PPS as originally designed induced hospitals to cut muscle, not fat. The incentive structure behind the program was to get hospitals to reduce costs, but there was no way to ensure that hospitals targeted waste. And so, one way to lower the cost per Medicare patient was to eliminate nursing staff, which many hospitals did. Another way was to release patients earlier, "quicker and sicker" as the phrase at the time went. Yet another way was to shun cases that hospitals expected to cost more than the anticipated fee.[37] Similarly, hospitals had an incentive to shift patients between different types of care to take advantage of the antiquated nature of the Medicare structure. For instance, outpatient services were not regulated under the PPS, so hospitals had an incentive to release patients from the hospital to continue care under a different, more generous price regime.[38]

The system also created incentives for what became known as provider silos. Medicare's PPS paid a lot more for some DRGs than their actual cost to provide the service, like orthopedic and cardiac care, so doctors had an interest in setting up hospitals that dealt only with those forms of medicine. The real problem with this was that general hospitals counted on the extra money generated by these DRGs to make up for others that left the hospitals with a deficit.[39]

Considering this, it should come as no surprise that the new systems also created incentives to provide unnecessary care. Whenever providers find a lucrative loophole in the PPS and RBRVS systems, it is in their interests to exploit it. For instance, experts now estimate that about half of the nearly half million spinal fusions performed every year are unnecessary; it is not coincidental that Medicare pays handsomely for them. Also, there has recently been a peculiar increase in the percentage of hospice patients who survive, which has led experts to suspect that Medicare's generous reimbursement rates are resulting in patients being sent to hospice even though they do not need end-of-life care.[40]

One of the most extreme examples of overcare has to do with how blindness in the elderly is treated. In many cases, doctors have a choice between several drugs, Lucentis (Novartis, Basel, Switzerland), which costs $2,000 per injection, and Avastin (Genentech, South San Francisco, CA), which costs $50. The drug of choice is Lucentis, despite the fact that the two work about as well, because doctors are reimbursed under the RBRVS for

6 percent over the average price of the drug. Thus, on a per-injection basis, a doctor can make an extra $117. Little wonder that Medicare's top biller in its most recent report turned out to be a doctor whose billings totaled $20 million, of which Lucentis accounted for $12 million.[41] All told, experts estimate that as much as 20 percent of the total cost of Medicare is attributable to highly expensive care that is of questionable value; meanwhile, essential care is often underprovided.[42]

In fact, studies find vast discrepancies in the quality of care that are traceable to problems with the RBRVS; it values high-priced specialists over primary care physicians, yet the latter seem to be more essential to good health outcomes. Researchers find that areas with higher per capita Medicare spending tend to have worse health care results than areas with lower per capita spending, and that these discrepancies correlate with the concentration of specialists versus primary care physicians. Areas that emphasize specialty care over primary care cost Medicare more, but produce worse results for patients.[43]

Just as worrisome as inefficiency is the challenge of fraud and abuse, whereby providers use less than honorable means to game the pricing systems. A common problem is "DRG creep" or upcoding, where hospitals code patient care under more expensive DRGs, even if the care provided actually qualifies under a less expensive one.[44] For instance, one study finds that between 1989 and 1996, the percentage share of the most generous DRG for treating pneumonia rose by ten points among not-for-profit hospitals, and twenty-three points among for-profit hospitals.[45] All told, the Center for Public Integrity estimates that upcoding cost Medicare $11 billion from 2001 to 2010.[46] A related practice is known as unbundling, whereby providers break services into multiple units rather than a single one to maximize the reimbursement. For instance, Medicare reimbursements for stroke patients include speech therapy, but in many instances such patients are released to have the therapy occur off-site, and thus billed to Medicare separately.[47]

The CMS estimates that "improper" payments to providers amounted to $28.5 billion in 2012, or more than 8 percent of all Medicare expenditures. It is worth noting that this metric is relatively narrow and does not include many of the aforementioned practices, so the real cost of impropriety is higher than this figure.[48] Importantly, the CMS may have the capacity to estimate that this money was wasted, but it has precious little capacity to do anything about it. Perhaps the most extreme example of its limitations came a few years ago, when Tenet Healthcare paid $42.8 million to settle allegations from the Department of Justice that it had taken $1 billion improperly from Medicare. Who discovered this gigantic overpayment? Not the Department of Justice, not the CMS, but Tenet Healthcare! In fact, the whole story broke because it turned itself in.[49]

Despite such a massive problem with cutting down on improper payments, the CMS suspended 80 percent of its recovery audit contractor program at the end of 2013. Moreover, in March 2014, Democrats and Republicans in Congress barred recovery audit contractors from postpayment reviews of improper hospital claims for eighteen months, and all claims for another six months. They did this despite the fact that recovery audit contractors had recovered $2.3 billion in 2012 alone.[50] More generally, Congress has failed to update its antifraud measures for Medicare, so that they too often harass honest providers rather than catch the real fraudsters. For instance, Medicare's antikickback law potentially criminalizes a vast array of practices that actually would be good for efficiency, like specialists in related areas partnering up. Such practitioners have to jump through all kinds of hoops to ensure that they do not get in trouble for referring patients to their partners.[51]

––––––––––––––––

Why is Medicare so inept at ferreting out improper payments? The answer is simple: the providers are politically potent. So potent, in fact, that the government practically allows them to redraft the PPS and RBRVS.[52]

Congress updates the PPS reimbursement system annually, and hospitals, which count on Medicare to provide about 30 percent of their revenue, lobby every year to make sure those updates work to their interests.[53] This has had an enormous influence on the program, which was originally supposed to promote uniform rates across the country. Yet Congress has given in to a series of ad hoc adjustments to the PPS. Most notably, it has allowed hospitals to reclassify themselves into different geographical areas to receive higher reimbursement rates. In fiscal year 2011, nearly 400 hospitals successfully lobbied Congress to reclassify them, increasing their reimbursement rates by an average of 10 percent.[54]

The politicization of the RBRVS has been worse than the PPS, for the AMA seems to have gained near-total control over the program. Updating the schedules is an enormous task, one that the CMS simply lacks the institutional capacity to do. Thus, it relies heavily upon the AMA's Relative Value Scale Update Committee (RUC). Closed to the public, the RUC is enormously powerful in determining where rates go every year; the CMS has just a handful of employees review the RUC recommendations, and accepts more than 90 percent of them.[55]

In more than 80 percent of the cases, the RUC recommends increases in reimbursement rates, in no small part because when the RUC polls practitioners to ask how much they charge, it tells them that their answers will be used to influence pricing for next year. The RUC also tends to overestimate the time practitioners must spend on procedures. In a few extreme cases, RUC estimates imply that some doctors spend so much time on procedures that they must be occupied by them twenty-four hours a day, seven days a week![56]

The RUC reflects an internal political battle within the doctor community between specialists and primary care physicians. The former outnumber the latter on the RUC by a large margin, and so specialty care is privileged by the RUC, despite the fact that aforementioned research shows that primary care is more valuable to health outcomes in Medicare.[57] Kerry Weems, the former acting administrator of the CMS, has stated, "I think there is a general consensus that the RUC has contributed to the poor state of primary care in the United States."[58]

What does this mean, when it is all said and done? It is simply this: Medicare might not be the open checkbook that it once was in the 1960s and 1970s, but it is pretty close. While the government took a step forward by instituting prospective fee schedules in Medicare, it failed to follow through. It leaves the providers essentially unregulated, and therefore free to exploit loopholes in the system that create socially perverse effects. It never beefed up its antifraud capacity, which costs the government billions of dollars every year. It even allows the providers to undermine the PPS and RBRVS by influencing the fee schedules.

The government has done this because the provider community is enormously powerful in Washington. In the 2011–2012 election cycle, the health service industry contributed more than $265 million to political campaigns, and spent nearly $1 billion on lobbying. While providers' interests are varied, they generally share a common goal: hands off Medicare. The providers grudgingly accept prospective pricing (that they themselves are integral in setting), but they will truck no substantial oversight. Washington has dutifully followed their restrictions, gravely undermining the original mission of Medicare to provide efficient and necessary care to America's elderly.

To appreciate more fully the power of these groups, it is worth looking at how they managed to unwind the hard-won reforms to the Medicare program in the mid-1990s. Spurred on by yet another financing crisis in

Medicare Part A, Democratic President Bill Clinton and congressional Republicans feuded bitterly over how to curb costs in Medicare during the 104th Congress of 1995–1996. Yet after the 1996 election, when the country reelected both sides to the same positions they had occupied, the two parties came together to pass the Balanced Budget Act of 1997 (BBA), which imposed some real limits on how much the government would be responsible for Medicare. In particular, the BBA enacted the Sustainable Growth Rate (SGR) to restrain future spending via a formula that takes into account real growth in the broader economy. The hope was that this would limit the seemingly unlimited obligation the feds have for senior care.[59]

It might have, if Congress had not unwound much of the BBA in later years due to pressure from the provider community. In fairness to the latter, the cuts imposed by the BBA had the same flaw as the PPS and RBRVS: they were top-down and did not empower the CMS to reward efficient providers and punish wasteful or corrupt ones. Still, Congress bowed to industry pressure again and again by simply restoring the cuts rather than finding a way to make the program work for less money. The give backs began in the late 1990s, when hospital margins started to turn negative and the industry lobbied heavily and successfully for relief.[60] More givebacks followed in 2000 and 2002 as industry pressure persisted.[61] Since 2003, Congress has also enacted a "doc fix" to shield doctors from SGR–mandated cuts to their reimbursement rates. This is now an annual ritual, which started because doctors revolted when the SGR called for a 4.7 percent rate cut in 2002. The cuts have only increased year after year, and for 2014 would have amounted to a 24 percent slash. The ten-year cost to Congress to restore these cuts permanently would be about $250 billion.[62]

Again, the key point here is not that the cuts inherent to the BBA were well-conceived; like the other top-down efforts to control Medicare costs, they were poorly designed. The point, rather, is that the provider community reacted vehemently and persuaded the Congress to walk away from the spirit of these reforms altogether. Congress could have revised the regulatory structure of Medicare to help the program meet these top-down spending targets; it simply chose not to, after immense industry pressure.

Medical service providers, as we have seen, are a powerful force on Capitol Hill. They have managed either to resist or substantially water down efforts to control Medicare spending, even when those costs to society are great indeed. But, powerful as they are, the providers cannot hold a candle to the senior lobby. The difference may be summed up thusly: Congress occasionally tries, and more or less fails, to curtail excessive spending by the providers; it almost never messes with senior citizens, and the handful of times it has gone against them, its efforts were totally, completely undone.

What is it that seniors want? Generally speaking, they oppose efforts to require them to contribute more to Medicare, and similarly refuse any alterations to the original (and, as we have seen, grossly inefficient) fee-for-service program. All told, Medicare is an extremely lucrative transfer of wealth from working-age adults to seniors. The net lifetime benefits per recipient (total benefits minus contributions from prior working years) range from about $100,000 to $250,000, depending on the income group, and are expected to grow over the next generation.[63] While its designers originally pitched Medicare as a social insurance program from which people received benefits that they paid for, it is in fact an enormous redistribution of wealth. And seniors have acted to ensure that the net benefits streaming to them are not decreased.

To facilitate that, they have sponsored entities like the American Association of Retired Persons (AARP), which combines a broad grassroots network with a sophisticated lobbying shop, to protect them.[64] As one Beltway insider commented, "It is hard to exaggerate the awe in which politicians hold the AARP. . . . It is by far the most powerful interest group on Capitol Hill."[65] A few examples from recent history demonstrate that it is always better to work with the AARP than against it. The AARP's lukewarm reception to Clinton's health care reform proposal, which would have reduced Medicare spending, contributed to its demise in 1994.[66] Similarly, the AARP opposed efforts by the GOP to pass a balanced budget amendment and trim Medicare in 1995 and 1996, contributing to an ultimate Clinton triumph at the ballot box in 1996.[67] Clinton and the congressional GOP learned this lesson well in 1997, as the BBA may have cut Medicare reimbursement rates for doctors, but it also permanently cut the percentage that seniors had to pay for Medicare Part B to 25 percent (down from 50 percent when originally enacted).[68] Similarly, the George W. Bush administration allowed the AARP to write key sections of the 2003 prescription drug benefit, which itself was a consequence of the decisive role the senior vote played in the 2000 presidential election.[69] When enacting the Affordable Care Act (a.k.a Obamacare), the Barack Obama administration cut Medicare Advantage as well as the Part A trust fund, but it smartly exempted Medigap policies from many of the regulations it imposed on other private plans. This was a boon to the AARP, whose revenues from endorsing Medigap plans now account for about half of its annual total. The senior lobby duly endorsed the reforms.[70]

Even without the AARP or similar organizations, no politician can cross seniors lightly. Put simply: they participate in politics, and their participation has only grown in the last half century. In 1952, the rate at which seniors voted in the presidential election was 72 percent; in 2000, it was up to 80 percent and was higher than any other age cohort. Seniors similarly vote more heavily in midterm elections, and they have shown a propensity to become more engaged, for instance by writing letters to congressmen, when their benefits are at stake.[71]

The potency of the senior vote was never more evident than in the backlash to the Medicare Catastrophic Coverage Act of 1988. The purpose of this act, which passed with bipartisan support and the blessing of the AARP, was to provide long-term care for seniors who could no longer take care of themselves. President Reagan and legislators were acutely concerned about the cost issue, so the program was to be funded by a $4 monthly premium assessed upon all seniors, with wealthier seniors (about 36 percent of the total) having to pay up to $800 more per year.[72] Meanwhile, the benefits would accrue primarily to low-income seniors; wealthier seniors were more likely to have Medigap insurance that indemnified them against costs that Medicare did not already cover, like catastrophic care. Still, seniors on balance would have benefited, so the AARP gave the program its blessing.

It grossly miscalculated. Wealthier seniors quickly organized in revolt against the extra premiums they had to pay, for little-to-no benefit, and began lobbying Congress to oppose the program. In this effort, they were joined by interest groups like the Association of Retired Federal Employees and Retired Officers Association, whose members were more likely to have coverage for this sort of care, as well as insurers who provided Medigap coverage.[73] Congressional supporters and the AARP were caught off guard by this opposition, especially when it gained traction among low-income groups. An October 1988 poll by the AARP found that support among low-income seniors was 70 percent; by the next summer, it had fallen to

47 percent. Support among high-income seniors declined from 63 percent to 38 percent.[74] Congress got the message and quickly did away with the program that year.

Nobody messes with the senior lobby anymore. The handful of negative experiences—in 1989, 1993–1994, and 1995–1996—has taught politicians that seniors and their pressure groups are not to be trifled with. It is much better to buy them off, as Clinton and the House GOP did in 1997, George W. Bush did in 2003, and Obama did in 2010.

From the perspective of the public good, the problem with this is that seniors are organized to defend an unsustainable program that has wasted countless billions of dollars. Moreover, as noted previously, they are receiving substantially more in benefit value than they paid in during their lifetime as workers. In fact, Medicare is now a transfer of wealth primarily to the country's wealthiest age cohort. In 1959, seniors were a truly pitiable group: an astonishing 35 percent of them were classified as poor. Today, however, the figure is just 9 percent—less than the rate for those under 18 (22 percent) or aged 18 to 64 (14 percent).[75] The public interest suggests that seniors, at least wealthier ones, should pay more, that the pretense of Medicare as something other than welfare be dispensed with once and for all. But, as the experience of the Catastrophic Coverage Act suggests, senior citizens collectively refuse to contribute more or have their benefits downgraded, and they have the political power to make sure that does not happen.

This book has told the story of a number of corrupt governmental policies; begun with the best of intentions, they are captured by factions who use them for their own benefit rather than the public interest. Importantly, as noted again and again, this need not be reducible to venality. Nowhere is that caveat more relevant than in this chapter. Seniors, doctors, hospitals, nurses, and all the other groups that have caused Medicare to spend substantially more than anybody once thought possible are all generally sympathetic, even laudable groups. Sure, there are some corrupt operators abusing the system; their numbers may even be substantial. But in the main, these groups do not intend to ruin the public's finances or make medical care less efficient.

But that really does not matter when it comes to corruption as it is understood in this book. As we have argued time and again, the government as constructed is not well suited to implementing programs like Medicare strictly for the public interest. The design of our system gives private interests the ability to transform policy, and that is exactly what seniors and providers have done. Sure, Medicare still serves the common good to a degree; it does indeed provide medical care to the elderly. However, the enormous problems in the program—that it does not provide care efficiently, that it too often provides unnecessary care, that it too often fails to provide necessary care, and that it provides it to people with the means to provide for themselves—means that it serves the public interest poorly. The private demands of seniors and providers too often come first.

What makes Medicare unique in our story is not so much the process that has created this corruption, but how much this corruption has cost the country. Assume, for the sake of argument, that 10 percent of this money has gone to purposes other than necessary and efficient care. (From what we have seen, the actual percentage is probably higher.) That amounts to nearly $800 billion that has been misspent in the first forty-five years of the program's existence.[76] As shocking as this figure is, the worst is still to come. If policies continue in the future as they have to date, the size of Medicare as a share of the nation's gross domestic product will double over the next forty years as the Baby Boomers retire.[77] That will have a disastrous effect on the public's finances, as well as on the broader economy.

Even so, why should we assume that the government has the competency to deal with this impending calamity? Medicare has been in crisis, off and on, since the early 1970s. These crises have been predictable yet unavoidable because they stem from a simple problem: Medicare provides benefits to factions within society that are extremely adept at ensuring those benefits continue, despite the obvious problems they pose to the public good. The government simply cannot say no to these interest groups, even at the cost of hundreds of billions of dollars. We should expect more of the same. Indeed, given the size and political potency of the Baby Boom generation, which is just now starting to receive Medicare benefits, the chances of fixing this broken program will probably decrease, if anything.

12

"A Robbery of the Great Majority"

The Politics of Corporate Taxation

PUBLIC SUPPORT of private business has a very august pedigree in our nation. No less an eminence than Alexander Hamilton laid out the original case for why the federal government in particular should worry about economic development. In the *Report on Manufactures* (1791) Hamilton frets about the reasons why private individuals would not engage in "the most useful and profitable employment" if left to their own devices. Americans were so used to agricultural pursuits that the "strong influence of habit" combined with the "fear of want of success in untried enterprises" would keep the country out of manufacturing. Moreover, they would have to contend with advanced (for the time) industrial economies that often actively supported their own industrialists.[1] How to compete?

Hamilton's answer is a comprehensive program to stimulate growth on the manufacturing front. He proposes tariffs on foreign goods that compete with American versions, prohibitions on exports of raw materials, exemptions of raw materials from importation duties, premiums and bounties to encourage development, and more.[2] All in all, Hamilton proposes lending public assistance to the search for private profit, in the belief that, over the long run, the benefits would accrue to society at large.

Today, both political parties essentially adhere to this view. Though the partisan rancor often generates a lot of heat, the main difference between them has more to do with emphases rather than first principles. Republicans prefer to expand programs like the Small Business Administration; Democrats like investments in green technology.

On paper, this often reads as noble and quite high-minded. Hamilton's prose in the *Report* is the literary embodiment of earnestness, and the quadrennial platforms of the Republican and Democratic parties brim with confidence about all the great ways they can develop the economy. However, in practice Hamiltonian economic stimulus lends itself to corruption. We encountered this reality in Chapters Two and Five on the nineteenth century: from the Tariff of Abominations to railroad cronyism to Gilded Age tariffs, we saw how our government can never quite live up to Hamilton's ideal. It is simply not capable of selecting economic winners in a socially responsible manner.

And yet Uncle Sam continues to try, blithely assuming that he can do something that in fact he cannot. Nowadays this means that government support of business creates a wide-ranging, patchwork, and occasionally bizarre system of corruption. After all, the contemporary economy is so immense, and the power of Washington effectively limitless, that the only real limits are what politicians imagine the government should do. So, government corruption can appear in surprising places.

Take an almost farcical example. Today, the National Football League enjoys expansive and lucrative antitrust exemptions that allow it to charge exorbitant fees for its broadcasts. Back in 1961, the NFL received such a bounty only for promising not to schedule games on Friday or Saturday in the fall, when high school and college football games are played. Moreover, at the behest of NFL lobbyists, Congress included the League in its definition of tax-exempt, nonprofit entities, despite the fact that its executives now clear seven-figure salaries every year.[3] How is it that one of the wealthiest, most powerful entertainment organizations in the world pays no taxes and squeezes broadcasters? The answer is simple: run the Hamiltonian ideal of nationalistic encouragement of socially useful businesses through our localistic, pluralistic system, and voilà! As far as the taxman is concerned, the NFL is no different than the Red Cross.

It all gets back to that fundamental disconnect between the policy aims of the government and the structure it must use to achieve them. The tension is aptly illustrated by how Hamilton directed his energies during the early days of the republic. He spent little time actually at the Constitutional Convention and presented a politically impractical quasi-monarchy that did not advance the debate a whit. And yet, he was, as Thomas Jefferson put it, a "host unto himself" when it came to policy innovation, or the ways that this new government could use its powers for the betterment of society. The grim, Calvinistic question that James Madison posed—what institutions should we build to constrain our inner devils?—was never his principal concern.

The Convention endorsed limited federal authority in 1787, but Hamilton's vision would win out over the long run. Madison was a major architect of the Convention's complicated system to force the government to behave responsibly, but his understanding of the schema assumed limits to what the government could do. Some of these were limits by which Hamilton simply could not abide, nor could subsequent generations. And so, absent proper institutional restraints, the government has often supported private business in a *corrupt* way. That is, under the guise of developing the economy in general, it has wasted untold billions of dollars funneling money to politically well-placed factions that offer a questionable return on the investment.

This is a story we began in Chapters One, Two, and Five when we examined nineteenth-century political economy. We also continued it in Chapter Nine when we looked at farm subsidies. This chapter concludes the story by looking more broadly at business-related corruption in the postwar era. As noted previously, there are many avenues by which this sort of corruption occurs, but we shall focus our efforts on two: the tariff and income tax codes. We do this for two reasons. First, this updates the story we told in Chapter Five; while the tariff regime was once the principal form of business payola, it has been replaced by the income tax. It is important to explain how and why that happened. Second, the tax code, through tax expenditures and leakage via aggressive tax sheltering, amounts to the largest kind of corporate payoff with the most far-reaching effects.

Of course, there are many other forms of business-related corruption we could discuss. For instance, corporate welfare vehicles like the Export-Import Bank, the Overseas Private Investment Corporation, and the Department of Energy's Loan Guarantee Program all have shown the same basic qualities that the corporate tax code exhibits.[4] While perhaps noble in their intentions, these programs misuse public resources in corrupt ways, showering benefits on the well-connected few at the expense of the public interest. So, this chapter in no way should be construed as an exclusive catalogue of this form of corruption; such a tale would probably take up an entire library shelf.

Rather, the story here is meant to provide a stark illustration of a general tendency. It will demonstrate clearly that, for all the changes over the last century in culture, economics, and even politics, government entanglement with business is still as rampant and fraught as ever. When the government tries to promote the private economy, the risk is always high that the result will be a violation of the public trust.

———————

As we saw in Chapter Five, the vast regime of protective tariffs—envisioned by giants like Hamilton and Henry Clay—had been perverted to benefit the giant industrial trusts and fund Republican political machines in states like New York, Rhode Island, and Pennsylvania. Today, of course, free trade is the dominant U.S. policy, and two of those three states have strong Democratic majorities (and a third is balanced between the two). So, what happened to the old political-economic system?

For one thing, Smoot-Hawley happened.

To be precise about it, the Tariff Act of 1930—named after its cosponsors, Senator Reed Smoot of Utah and Representative Willis Hawley of Oregon—happened. In the midst of the Great Depression, the Republican-dominated Congress in 1930 looked to boost the sinking economy with new, more robust tariff protections. Despite an utter lack of economic justification that extra protection would help the country, a massive logroll formed that basically roped in every interest that might like preferential tariff rates. In sum, Smoot-Hawley raised overall rates to levels not seen since the Tariff of Abominations in 1828. In doing so, it sparked an international trade war as other countries raised their rates in response.[5] The rate of economic decline quickened, and the Republicans were tossed from Congress in large numbers.

New Deal Democrats were much more disposed to free trade, following the historic preferences of their party, and they shifted trade policy accordingly. Yet in due course the Republican Party altered its views on trade as well, and not simply because Smoot-Hawley gave protectionism a bad name. Just as important was the evolution of the U.S. position in the world economy. Prior to World War II, the country's manufacturers had stiff foreign competition, especially from Great Britain. Afterward, the developed world was in ruins, except for the United States. This meant that American manufacturers suddenly had a decisive competitive edge. Big business wanted freer trade, and its many friends in Congress were responsive to this new preference. Facilitating this was a new internationalist sentiment that came to dominate both parties; free trade became a tool to advance foreign policy goals in the Cold War.

Importantly, Congress not only shifted its policy, it redesigned the policy process altogether. Much as it would do with military base closings,

Congress elected to tie its hands, for fear that it might not be able to resist parochial demands for exceptions to the free-trade rule.[6] Starting with the Reciprocal Trade Agreement Act of 1934, Congress gave the president the power to negotiate tariff reductions with foreign nations, even if that meant substantial cuts in rates.[7] The Trade Act of 1974 expanded the powers of the president to negotiate nontariff barriers (like voluntary export restraints) and created the fast track procedure that prevents Congress from amending or filibustering trade agreements negotiated by the executive branch.[8]

Protectionism, insofar as it happens today, occurs principally via two channels. The first is a nonpolitical, bureaucratic process, which was expanded by Congress in the Trade Act of 1974 due to concerns about stiffer foreign competition for key industries.[9] The second comes by relief directly from the president, which can take on a much more political tone. Importantly, the latter process gives Congress an opportunity to advocate protectionism for certain interest groups without creating a logroll that will ruin the entire regime. If enough members in Congress agitate strongly and persistently for a particular industry, they can force the president and foreign leaders to hammer out a new, more protectionist deal.[10] Of course, the president often does not need much encouragement. He is sensitive to industry-group pressure, too, as his reelection often depends on the support of Rust Belt states that house many struggling industries.[11]

The result over the last eighty years has been increasingly free trade, with an administrative relief process plus special exceptions for politically connected industries. Three examples of the latter are illustrative. The first, textiles, was once politically important because it linked cotton farmers in the South with manufacturers in New England, and it successfully exempted itself from much of the postwar free-trade system. Reviving Japan's economy was an integral part of the Dwight Eisenhower and John F. Kennedy administrations' policies, but the domestic textile industry was concerned about new competition.[12] By 1962, sustained pressure from Congress finally induced a substantial exception to the multilateral General Agreement on Tariffs and Trade.[13] But this did not settle the issue. By the time of the Richard Nixon administration, textile interests were again pushing for more relief, and persuaded House Ways and Means Chairman Wilbur Mills, normally a free trader, to back import quotas. Seeking to head off a protectionist logroll in Congress, the Nixon administration buckled under pressure. Later on, the Nixon-backed Trade Act of 1974 expanded the pathways of administrative relief for embattled industries like textiles.[14] To this day, the textile industry retains important protections, despite its greatly diminished importance in the domestic economy; the average consumer can pay 10 to 30 percent more for clothing because of protectionist duties.[15]

The steel industry has also enjoyed substantial exceptions to free trade, though the result of this favoritism has been mixed at best, especially for steelworkers in Pittsburgh and Birmingham. After World War II, the United States dominated the domestic and international steel market, and really had no competitors to speak of. But during the 1960s, the Japanese and Western Europeans developed their industrial capacity, in particular embracing new technologies. Additionally, the means to transport steel long distances became much more cost-effective, lowering barriers to competition. Meanwhile, the big domestic steel manufacturers largely rested on their oars, electing not to update their production techniques and instead offering ever-generous salaries and benefits to unionized workers.[16] By the end of the decade, the steelmakers were in trouble, and combined with the United Steelworkers union, began pressuring Congress for relief.[17] They consistently succeeded: Nixon, Ronald Reagan, and George H. W. Bush enacted or expanded voluntary export restrictions with competitor nations; Jimmy Carter delivered them de facto minimum prices by aggressively opposing unfair foreign practices; and George W. Bush imposed new tariffs of up to 30 percent on imported steel.[18]

Domestic automakers received similar protections, and unlike their fellow travelers in the steel industry have managed to hold on reasonably well. Again, like steel, the Big Three carmakers dominated the market through the 1960s. But a series of oil supply shocks sent gas prices soaring, and domestic consumers began preferring fuel-efficient Japanese cars to the gas guzzlers offered by Chrysler, Ford, and General Motors. Thus, the carmakers and the United Auto Workers began agitating in Congress, and finally induced President Reagan to secure an export reduction commitment from the Japanese, which was later expanded after more congressional pressure.[19] Domestic automakers and their union workers also received a massive government bailout in 2009. The funds had originally been earmarked for troubled financial institutions, but the Barack Obama administration repurposed the money to secure a key constituency in the must-win state of Michigan.[20]

All in all, what can we say about trade in the postwar era? At first blush, it suggests congressional responsibility, and thus runs contrary to our overarching thesis about corruption. Such a sudden onset of congressional responsibility is not unprecedented. As we saw in Chapter Ten, it happened before with military base closures. Unfortunately, in both instances legislative high-mindedness only followed extreme irresponsibility. Moreover, well-positioned industrial groups still can leverage their standing for protectionist carve-outs. Yet these are mere caveats to the general point that trade policy, more or less, now embodies a coherent, defensible, nationalistic idea. Whether one agrees or disagrees with this idea is beside the point, which is that the logroll is now gone and at least the policy makes some sense.

Still, we would be wise to hold off on popping the champagne corks. Just because Congress no longer uses the tariff to reward businesses at the expense of the public interest does not mean it has ceased and desisted altogether. Far from it. It simply means that Congress has discovered a new tool to aid its clients: the income tax code. As we shall see, while the tariff regime has indeed been cleaned up, Congress's overall approach to taxation remains extremely dirty. On balance, very little has changed.

———————

To understand the federal income tax properly, it is first necessary to realize that we are really talking about two different systems of taxation. The first is the system of graduated rates applied to corporations and individuals. This is usually the source of much partisan rancor, although Democrats and Republicans do not disagree as much as they think. Both sides are usually comfortable lowering rates (or keeping rates low) on middle-income earners. They even are of the opinion that the corporate tax rate could stand to be lowered. Where they usually disagree is on the issue of the top marginal individual tax rate; this is of great symbolic importance to both sides, but really only affects a portion of the income of a very small percentage of Americans.

The second is the much-less-discussed issue of tax expenditures, or the various preferences embedded in the tax code to favor particular taxpayers. It is this latter issue that shall be our primary focus, for corruption in the tax code is almost invariably found in the ways that these exceptions to rates are created. And on this issue we shall cast aspersions on both political parties. Both have proven themselves ready, willing, and able over the decades to exempt well-positioned business factions from paying their fair share.

Still, the two are closely related: to understand the one we have to have at least a nodding familiarity with the other. So let us begin with a brief look at the history of corporate and individual tax rates.

The income tax had its start during the Civil War as a temporary measure to raise revenue in the North, although it disappeared by 1872.[21] Twenty years later, it was revived after Democrats took complete control of the government. In their 1892 party platform, the Democrats railed against the old tariff system that we have discussed throughout this book:

> We denounce Republican protection as a fraud, a robbery of the great majority of the American people for the benefit of the few. We declare it to be a fundamental principle of the Democratic party that the Federal Government has no constitutional power to impose and collect tariff duties, except for the purpose of revenue only, and we demand that the collection of such taxes shall be limited to the necessities of the Government when honestly and economically administered.[22]

Once in charge of the government, however, it was not a simple matter of reducing tariffs. After all, they raised a lot of money, and as we saw in Chapter Five, the Republicans made sure that Civil War veterans received that money, in the form of a generous pension program established under the preceding Benjamin Harrison administration. Moreover, the economic recession following the Panic of 1893, plus the need to rebuild the navy, meant a new source of revenue had to be found.[23] Thus, the Wilson-Gorman Tariff Act of 1894 instituted a modest individual income tax.[24]

The Supreme Court struck it down as an unconstitutional direct tax (such devices must be levied upon states proportional to their population). Yet the progressive movement continued to push for it in the early twentieth century; for instance, Teddy Roosevelt was an early booster.[25] In a compromise with progressives in 1909, President William Howard Taft and Rhode Island senator Nelson Aldrich agreed to an excise tax on corporate profits (which was in truth a corporate income tax) and a proposed constitutional amendment to overturn the Court decision.[26] But the Republican old guard miscalculated when it figured that the amendment would never be ratified; in fact, a progressive tide was rising through the states and by 1913 the Sixteenth Amendment was the law of the land. The Underwood Tariff Act of that year would institute the first permanent income tax, which is with us to this day.

Until World War II, the individual income tax was a relatively modest source of federal revenue. Its top marginal rate was low—under 15 percent until the Great Depression—and a large personal exemption meant that only the wealthy paid. World War II changed that. Desperate for revenue, the government jacked up rates and reduced exemptions to make it a mass-based tax. Some 70 percent of all workers were paying income taxes during the war, and the number really never fell much in the decades to come. By 1975, about 45 percent of all tax revenue came from the income tax, whereas excise and customs duties fell to just 8.5 percent.[27]

High rates combined with a fast pace of economic growth for the first twenty-five years after World War II meant that Uncle Sam collected money hand over fist. Meanwhile, the taxpayer might have been paying more, but he was also making much more in real terms. Yet this regime began to fall apart in the 1970s. Productivity slowed, oil prices spiked, and the country was hit with stagflation, or high inflation plus weak economic growth. This was a problem for the average taxpayer because rates were not yet indexed for inflation. A tax revolt that began in California in the mid-1970s helped sweep Reagan into office, and the Economic Recovery Tax Act (ERTA) of 1981 basically set the parameters of the tax debate through the present day.[28] Both parties agree on low rates for low- and middle-income earners, and disagree hotly on the top marginal rate.[29]

The story of the corporate income tax rate is much the same. Raised to a high level during World War II, it remained there until the Tax Reform Act (TRA) of 1986, a bipartisan compromise that set the top marginal rate at 35 percent, where it remains to this day.[30]

And so, from 1913 to 1981, action on tax rates was relatively limited, with a few exceptions. Since 1981, the two sides have fought over the top rate and usually agreed to lower the rest of the rates. The most legislative activity has been on income and corporate tax expenditures, which are the deductions, exclusions, exemptions, and credits that Congress layers upon the basic rate structures.[31] In general, they are the ways that Congress narrows the tax base, which University of Chicago economist Henry Simons defines as the sum of the market value of consumption plus the change in value of total net worth.[32] Tax expenditures, unlike the basic rates, have long been a dynamic force within the code—indeed many of them require regular reauthorization—and their general trajectory has been up, up, and away.

The reason for this is that tax expenditures are really just spending in the tax code, and the government loves to spend money to favor factions of citizens. Rather than create a new program, a tax expenditure creates the effect of one by allowing beneficiaries to deduct the value of the new welfare from their tax payments.[33] Tax expenditures exist in both the income and corporate tax structures. Scholars generally identify several categories: need based (e.g., the deduction of medical expenses and the earned income tax credit), the promotion of tax equity (e.g., the deduction of state and local taxes), special group provisions (e.g., the exclusion of GI Bill benefits), general economic incentives (e.g., the preferential treatment of capital gains), and special economic incentives (e.g., special depletion allowances for mining, gas, and oil firms).[34]

As soon as Congress implemented the new income tax in the 1910s, it began creating exceptions to it. The early individual income tax excluded charitable donations, interest on state and local bonds, gifts and inheritances, life insurance, and more. In the first decade of the tax code's existence, a total of twenty-seven tax expenditures were created. Over the next sixty years, the government would add more than sixty new expenditures, an average of better than one per year.[35]

The TRA of 1986 stands out as a lone exception to the seemingly inexorable trend of more and more tax expenditures, but it arose almost by accident. Reagan's sweeping 1981 ERTA remains a point of controversy between liberals and conservatives, who are wont to bicker mostly over that top marginal rate. However, it was also stuffed with tax expenditures, particularly for businesses. So over-the-top was ERTA in its tax preference giveaways that the political class in Washington finally found the will (albeit temporarily) to clean up some of the mess that it had created over the prior sixty-five years.

ERTA presented a host of problems with tax expenditures, but one stands out above the rest. It expanded a Kennedy-era business tax credit for new investments with recovery periods of greater than three years; ERTA also sped up depreciation for structures, equipment, and light vehicles, and it allowed safe harbor leasing, which basically permitted businesses to purchase tax credits that others could not use. All of this combined to create a negative tax rate for businesses engaged in certain deficit-financed expansions. The result was a shocking increase in the number of tax shelters, and by 1986 tax expenditures amounted to 45 percent of federal budget outlays.[36] The political success of the income tax always rested upon a broad sense that it was fair, but by the middle of the 1980s major companies like Boeing, Dow, and General Electric were not only paying no taxes, but actually receiving net benefits through the tax code. Meanwhile, industries that did not rely heavily on capital expenditures, not to mention average taxpayers filing 1040s, claimed few or none of these sorts of benefits.[37]

Reagan had opposed closing tax loopholes during the 1980 campaign, arguing, not without merit, that these were in effect tax increases. Still, political pressure built during his first term and, fearing that his Democratic opponent would make hay out of the issue in 1984, he changed his position on loopholes.[38] The resulting TRA reduced individual tax rates across the board, cut corporate rates, and closed many of the most egregious loopholes. It worked, at least for a while.[39] By 1988, firms that had paid virtually nothing in the early years of the Reagan administration were now paying more than 20 percent.[40]

Unfortunately, while the TRA was a good reform, the government did not follow the spirit of the new law for very long. Here, a juxtaposition with the tariff regime is worthwhile. Congress, sensing a shift in the body politic toward free trade, transferred power away from itself, to bind the government to the new trade system. With income taxes, there was no such shift. While in theory everybody may want a simple, clean code, in practice hordes of interest groups and various factional representatives descend upon Washington every year to influence Congress—particularly the House Ways and Means Committee and the Senate Finance Committee—to carve out new exceptions. In short order, tax expenditures began to proliferate again.

And so, a quarter century after tax reform, it is desperately needed once more; today, there are more than 150 tax expenditure programs. The growth has largely been on the individual income tax side, as the two parties have combined to expand the breadth and depth of the American social welfare state. Conventionally, America is thought to have a relatively meager state compared to Western Europe, but when tax expenditures are factored in, net social welfare spending amounts to better than 25 percent of gross domestic product (GDP).[41]

Corporate tax expenditures, on the other hand, have been roughly constant, at least when measured as a share of GDP. In 1985, they were nearly 2 percent of GDP; they fell to 1 percent in 1988 and have more or less remained there ever since.[42] This is good news, but only in a modest sense. The 1986 TRA eliminated only the most politically vulnerable expenditures. Many still remain—more than eighty according to the Government Accountability Office, at a total annual cost of about $150 billion in foregone revenue—and many are of dubious social value.[43] A few of the minor expenditures are quite eye-popping for their absurdity:

- The "Apple Loophole" allows U.S. multinationals to defer taxes on certain passive incomes like royalties earned by foreign subsidiaries. By creating subsidiaries in Ireland, the Netherlands, Luxembourg, and the Virgin Islands, Apple has used this to reduce its tax burden substantially.[44]

- In 2004, Congress allowed a complete write-off of the purchase price of a professional sports team in just fifteen years. This prompted one wag to joke, "Does a sports franchise depreciate in value?" Of course not. It is merely a payoff to franchise owners.[45]

- NASCAR gets a special benefit as well. It is allowed to use accelerated depreciation to write down the cost of speedways in just seven years. This has saved International Speedway Corporation, owner of more than a dozen tracks, including the Daytona International Speedway, some $38 million.[46]

- Since 1918, the federal government has made allowances for mineral, gas, and oil deposits. This regularly works out to be a major tax benefit because it is hard to assess accurately how much of a deposit remains. Moreover the value of the deposit may be much greater than the amount invested in discovering and developing it.[47]

- The Historic Preservation Tax Credit offered $27 million for investors to fund a microbrewery at an old Coca-Cola plant in St. Louis.[48]

- Hollywood can deduct up to $15 million to produce television episodes where 75 percent of the compensation is for work done in the United States.[49]

- Logging companies can deduct up to $10,000 in reforestation expenses per unit of property. This may not sound like much, but its estimated ten-year cost is $4.8 billion.[50]

- Railroads enjoyed a tax credit for track maintenance from 2005 to 2007. This was retroactively extended to 2011 at a cost of $99 million.[51]

Tax breaks like this make for good headlines when one wants to write about the absurdity of the tax code, and indeed they have been included here for that very purpose. Still, they are not the main drivers of the corporate tax expenditure budget. Just a handful of provisions cost tens of billions of dollars per year, and they are worth looking at in depth. The most expensive, far and away, is accelerated depreciation. It accounts for more than 40 percent of all corporate tax expenditures. The 1986 TRA cut back on this to some extent, but did not eliminate it altogether. Businesses are allowed to deduct the cost of machinery, software, buildings, and more at a rate much faster than they actually lose their value. Thus, it amounts to a subsidy for businesses, particularly capital-intensive ones.[52] A review of extant scholarly studies conducted by the Congressional Research Service concludes that bonus depreciation "in general is a relatively ineffective tool for stimulating the economy."[53]

Accounting for about 20 percent of corporate tax expenditures is the foreign income exclusion. Foreign income is subject to U.S. income tax when it is repatriated through payment of dividends to the parent corporation, minus a credit for taxes paid overseas. In some sense, this is necessary to create a fair tax base—corporations should not have to be taxed twice (once by the United States, once by a foreign government)—but this has become the backbone for expansive schemes to avoid any and all taxation (more on this subsequently).[54]

Accounting for about 5 percent of total corporate tax expenditures is a research tax credit. In theory this may be a good idea, but research is an ambiguous concept in the tax code. Creative accountants have helped corporations take advantage of this, for instance by redesigning food wrappers and calling the effort research.[55]

Finally, accounting for 3 percent of corporate tax expenditures is the active financing loophole, often called the "GE Loophole." This allows corporations to defer taxes on some financial income that was really earned in the United States, but was shifted overseas. It is called the GE Loophole because GE's financing arm, GE Capital, makes such heavy use of it.[56]

In fact, the GE and Apple Loopholes point to a much bigger problem in the tax code, which the conventional understanding of tax expenditures only captures to a limited extent. That is, multinational firms can move profits around overseas to avoid paying federal taxes. In theory, corporations should not have to pay taxes on income earned overseas; they should pay it to the foreign government under which it was generated. Yet multinational companies use a whole host of artifices and tax shelters to shift domestic profits overseas. Meanwhile, it is virtually impossible for the federal government, with its existing tax laws and enforcement assets, at any rate, to assess how much is actually owed.

This problem is often called leakage, and it could cost up to another $150 billion in lost tax revenue per year.[57] By most accounts, it has gotten worse over the last twenty years.[58] In particular, there has been a marked increase in corporate tax sheltering practices.[59] Put simply, tax shelters are devices or investments created to take advantage of gaps in the tax law. Multinational corporations create shelters that span the globe, often housing money in countries like the Cayman Islands that are actively seeking tax refugees.[60] A recent study found that a handful of tiny countries book profits from U.S. subsidiaries that dwarf their GDP. Profits booked in Bermuda amounted to 1,643 percent of its GDP; in the Cayman Islands, 1,600 percent; in the Virgin Islands, 1,102 percent; in the Bahamas, 123 percent; in Luxembourg, 106 percent; and in Ireland, 42 percent. There is simply no way foreign companies are making so much profit in these countries; rather, they are finding novel ways to hide profits from the American taxman.[61] Moreover, a 2011 investigation by the Senate Committee on Homeland Security and Governmental Affairs found that much of this money is not really sitting in these foreign shelters; it is just listed there for tax purposes. According to Senate investigators, roughly half of the more than $500 billion in corporate earnings housed overseas was in fact invested in domestic financial institutions.

Many of the largest companies are now combining these aggressive tax avoidance schemes with generous tax expenditures to avoid paying any taxes. This was exactly the problem that induced the 1986 TRA. Reforms dealt with it, but only briefly; it is now back with a vengeance. A recent study looks at the companies on the Fortune 500 that were consistently profitable between 2008 and 2012, and found that their average tax rate was just 19.4 percent. Certain industries paid much more than others: utilities, industrial machinery, and telecommunications paid less than 10 percent on average; restaurants and grocery stores, publishers, retailers and wholesalers, and health care providers paid more than 25 percent. On top of this, many companies on net received enormous tax rebates during this period. Among the most well-known recipients were GE, claiming $3 billion in rebates; PG&E, $1.2 billion; Verizon, $535 million; and Boeing, $202 million.[62]

When we combine the generous corporate tax expenditures that the TRA did not eliminate with the ever-aggressive use of tax shelters, we find a striking result. Overall, corporate tax payments were 42 percent of total corporate profit in 1960, but had declined to 28 percent by 1980. By closing various loopholes, the TRA increased that number to 36 percent in 1990. However, the figure fell to 24 percent in 2005, and just 21 percent in 2010.[63] Some of this, naturally, is due to the increasingly globalized economy. But that can only explain a portion of the story. The rest has to do with a government that, when it is not actively creating new exemptions, looks the other way as multinational corporations shelter tens of billions of dollars in profits. Indeed, experts believe that the structure of the tax code encourages corporations to shuffle money overseas to hide from the U.S. taxman.[64]

How well does this spending in the tax code stand up under careful scrutiny? Is it justifiable according to a reasonable definition of the public interest? Some of it is; some of it isn't. So, we need to frame our questions with specificity.

A portion of these tax expenditures are really about keeping the code from creating perverse incentives. For instance, the government calculates the exemption on net imputed rent as an individual tax expenditure, at an annual "cost" of $75 billion. Net imputed rent is the difference between the fair market value of a home and what the owner actually pays to live there; he is both landlord and tenant, and in effect is paying himself a rent. If he were renting to a different person, he would have to report this as income on his taxes. However, there is an exclusion here because no money is actually changing hands. It is hard to raise an objection to this. Additionally, as noted previously, the decline of corporate taxes as a share of corporate profit is not altogether unjustifiable. As corporations make more money overseas, they naturally owe that to foreign governments, not the United States.

Moreover, the debate over individual tax expenditures is really a different matter than corporate tax expenditures. The former are usually about providing some sort of social welfare. Typically, reformers criticize them for being unfair and inefficient tools of public policy. For instance, the deductibility of employer-provided health insurance premiums helps defray the cost of health care, which is a socially desirable goal; however, it favors high-income earners who have more generous insurance policies. Additionally, the deduction makes taxpayers somewhat insensitive to price increases, so has probably contributed to health care inflation. In general, the debate over individual tax expenditures is an important one, but is beyond our scope here.

On the corporate side of the ledger, one study from the Tax Foundation concludes that of the estimated $150 billion spent on corporate expenditures in 2014, about $45 billion was properly corporate welfare, or subsidies to corporations. The rest was spent to make the code more neutral toward different types of income. Similarly, a portion of the untaxed overseas income is due to forces like globalization, but another portion is due to tax sheltering that the government could correct with tax reform.

When we drill it down, we are really looking to evaluate federal sponsorship of business via corporate welfare and tax shelters. Does *this* withstand scrutiny? Is it justifiable per the public interest?

The answer is simple: no. Tax experts have been complaining about this kind of spending for nearly a century. As early as the 1920s, they were warning about various forms of leakage in the tax code. Hopeful that the rise of conservative Republicans in the 1920s would rationalize the code, many were disappointed that it did not really happen (although rates were cut).[65] There were similar complaints in the 1940s, '50s, '60s, and '70s, with various, unsuccessful attempts to reform the code.[66] Today, just a quarter century after tax reform, experts are saying once again that the tax code needs to be rationalized.

Why is it that experts so consistently oppose these sorts of tax subsidies? On the whole, the consensus is that the social costs outweigh the benefits they provide. In particular, they violate, in one way or another, the major principles of sensible taxation. Let's look in particular at how corporate payoffs in the tax code are inefficient and inequitable.[67]

When it comes to efficiency, there are two major problems. The first is needless complexity. When first enacted, the income tax code was a mere eight pages. Today, it is volumes upon volumes (upon volumes upon volumes!). This creates huge compliance costs, not just for the taxpayer but also for the Internal Revenue Service. The average Fortune 500 company spends about $4.6 million every year just figuring out how to pay its taxes (or in the case of a favored firm like GE, how to maximize its rebate). Society-wide, the total cost is estimated at about $135 billion. The main driver of all this is not the rates, but rather the complicated deductions, credits, exemptions, and other exclusions that Congress creates year after year; between 2001 and 2010, Congress made nearly 450 changes per year.[68]

The second efficiency problem involves the misallocation of scarce resources. As the Reagan Department of the Treasury states in a report on tax reform:

> Over the years, the tax system has come to exert a pervasive influence on the behavior of private decision-makers. The resulting tax-induced distortions in the use of labor and capital and in consumer choices have severe costs in terms of lower productivity, lost production, and reduced consumer satisfaction.[69]

This is the main problem with tax shelters. They would not exist were it not for the tax laws, and the money invested in them would instead travel to more socially useful investments.[70]

An example can help illustrate just how distorting these effects can be. Normally, historians think of the explosion in the number of shopping malls in the early postwar era as a consequence of white flight from the cities, the expanded use of the automobile, increasing disposable income, etc. But Thomas Hanchett of the University of North Carolina identifies another source: tax sheltering. In 1954, the government initiated an accelerated depreciation program that was intended to help manufacturers. Yet it also allowed developers to write off construction expenses quite rapidly, and to claim these "losses" as offsets against other incomes. This created an enormous incentive to build shopping malls. In 1955, just five were erected nationwide; in 1956, twenty-five; in 1960, thirty-nine; and in 1965, forty-one. Many of these malls would have been built anyway, of course, but insofar as they were created because of tax incentives, the money was wasted from a society-wide perspective.[71]

The problem of equity is also of two types: horizontal equity and vertical equity. Tax expenditures and tax sheltering violate both. Horizontal equity is the principle that similarly situated groups are treated similarly for taxing purposes. Our corporate code does not do that. As noted previously, certain industries, like industrial machining and utilities, are taxed at a much more favorable rate than others, like wholesalers and health care providers. Much of this has to do with the politics of the tax code. Congress has long favored instruments like accelerated depreciation, which privilege capital-intensive industries; moreover, firms that operate overseas have substantially greater opportunities for tax arbitrage. There is no sound economic justification for these advantages. They are rather a result of politics.[72]

Vertical equity is embodied in the concept of tax progressivity. There is broad consensus in society that wealthier people or corporations should pay more money to the taxman via a higher rate of taxation. In theory, progressivity is embodied in the corporate code by the fact that the introductory rate is 15 percent, and it scales up to a maximum rate of 35 percent. In practice, tax expenditures and aggressive sheltering totally undermine this, as more profitable corporations have more resources to spend avoiding taxes. For instance, Jeff Gerth of ProPublica reports on one trick used by GE to reduce its tax burden:

"An important rule to live by," a senior GE tax lawyer, Rick D'Avino, told a conference in 2007, "is to ensure that the tax team has as many former government tax experts as possible" to "help see both sides of an issue more effectively." D'Avino, a GE vice president, mentioned the [Internal Revenue Service], Capitol Hill and Treasury as places to look when building a team and talked about how a former IRS lawyer working for GE helped the company build a "cooperative relationship" with the service.

The next year, GE hired the senior IRS official who was overseeing the service's transfer pricing program, under which large multinational companies like GE negotiate with the [Internal Revenue Service] about how to price products and services among subsidiaries. The subject is controversial because it can allow companies to shift profits to lower-tax countries.[73]

Ultimately, this gets back to the complexity of the code. Just a handful of specialists are able to understand today's tax laws, and only the wealthiest companies are able to hire them to reduce their tax burden. This is an advantage that small corporations simply do not have.

Take all of this together, and we wind up with two problems. The first is that, by deviating substantially from a simple and straightforward graduated corporate income tax, the government is in effect transferring wealth to tax-preferred companies from tax-disadvantaged companies, individual income taxpayers, and society at large. Those who can game the rules are subsidized by those who cannot. Importantly, these transfers often lack compelling economic or social justifications. The second problem relates to a concept introduced in Chapter Nine, in our discussion of farm subsidies: deadweight loss. When one factors in compliance costs, the money spent lobbying the government, the shift in resources to less-productive purposes, and so on, it is very possible that the gains to the tax-preferred entities are less than the harms incurred by society at large. This is a notoriously difficult concept to measure with precision, but when we consider the fact that society-wide compliance costs alone almost equal the total of corporate tax expenditures, we can appreciate that deadweight loss could be substantial. And that does not even begin to figure in the lost social and economic gains from investments that never happened because money was redirected into tax shelters.

So, if the tax code is an unfair, inefficient, and socially harmful mess that almost every disinterested expert has despised for nearly a century, why has it not been substantially reformed? It surely could be, if the government wanted to do it. In the case of tax expenditures, Uncle Sam could eliminate many of them simply by doing nothing; many of the corporate expenditures possess sunset provisions that require regular reauthorization by Congress. As for cutting down on aggressive tax sheltering, this problem is more difficult, as it is not obvious what income is genuinely earned overseas and what is being sheltered. Still, it could be done. Where there's a will, there's a way.

So why is there no will to do this, especially in light of the enormous budget deficits the government has run for so long? The answer is the same reason so many of the policies that we have studied persist: political corruption. In fact, tax expenditures today are a lot like the old tariff schedules of the Gilded Age, which we discussed in Chapter Five. They are a way to tinker with the tax code to favor factions in society: the government sets broad-based rates that it largely leaves unchanged over the decades, then sets up exceptions for well-placed interest groups. This is more important to our government than creating a fair, efficient tax code.

The principal culprit here is Congress. The legislature can choose to delegate responsibility to the bureaucracy, and has often done so on other matters, but it has retained primary authority over the income tax code because it is so politically useful. It is a noticeable and direct way to funnel money to preferred interest groups, which realize immediately that they have received a bounty and can easily credit Congress for securing it.[74] And when it comes to taxes, Congress has an institutional advantage over the president. Large tax laws contain many hundreds of provisions, and the president is ultimately left to choose between vetoing a massive new law, that perhaps, on balance, does a lot of social good, or accepting it with its corrupt carveouts.

Moreover, the balance of pressures placed upon Congress is uniquely tilted toward favoritism. In the field of industrial regulation, for example, there is often a battle between environmental groups and industry groups. This, as we argued in Chapter Eight, is far from a guarantee that the public interest will prevail, but the competition is at least helpful for that purpose. There is really no such competition over taxes. When Congress elects to give an industry a special tax break, who really loses? The public at large, but in such an indirect and imperceptible way that nobody really notices, which means there are no interest groups that emerge to oppose the payoff. There are public-spirited groups that fight for tax reform—think tanks like the Heritage Foundation on the right and Citizens for Tax Justice on the left—but they are seriously out-matched by entities like GE and Boeing, which have a financial stake in ensuring profitable outcomes.

Compounding this problem further is the narrow distribution of the taxing power in Congress. When the House of Representatives wants to spend money, the decision usually passes through several committees: the Budget Committee, which sets broad spending targets; the relevant authorizing committee, which decides what the money will be spent on particularly; and the Appropriations Committee, which decides how much money will be spent. A similar process exists in the Senate. The taxing power, in contrast, is disproportionately concentrated in the House Ways and Means Committee, which has priority over the Senate Finance Committee because of the constitutional mandate that all taxing legislation originate in the House. So, while Congress in general has a problem with parochialism, this dilemma is notably more serious when it comes to the taxing power.[75]

And again, following the overarching hypothesis of the book, there need be no malevolence at play for the tax code to be corrupted. Instead, corruption can flow from what former House Ways and Means ranking minority member Barber Conable calls "The ABC Syndrome":

> Suppose that someone—a business person, a wage earner, or a retired person approaches his or her representative in Congress and says, in effect: "What you have done in the tax system is fundamentally all right, but I have a very unusual situation, you see, and it is not fair for me to have to be taxed this way just because my neighbor thinks it is all right." Suppose further that the member of Congress looks at the matter and agrees with the taxpayer, called "A." The member takes the case to the Committee on Ways and Means, and the committee also finds that "A" is, indeed, in a different situation and should be treated differently, i.e., more fairly. So, "A" gets an exception in the tax code—an exception that fits all the other "A's" who are similarly situated. A year or so passes and along comes taxpayer "B," who tells Congress: "What you did for 'A' was good. It is an appropriate exception. But I am situated a little differently and what you did for 'A' is having an adverse effect on me. Please take a look and see if you don't agree." Of course, Congress does agree, and provides an exception to the exception in order to take care of "B." Then, about a year later, taxpayer "C" approaches Congress, and you know what happens. An exception to the exception to the exception for "C."[76]

In other words, we do not need to posit the existence of bad guys to explain a tax code that showers expenditures upon powerful corporations and looks the other way as they aggressively exploit tax shelters. All we need do is account for members with narrow perspectives: they see a constituent, a donor, a friend, or a political ally who needs some help; they have the power to help; so they help. Meanwhile, given our system's institutional design, there is really no agent in government with the power or the cosmopolitan perspective to counter congressional parochialism. Repeat this process hundreds of times a year, and we get the sort of code that we have. This is also how we wound up with the protective tariff regime discussed in Chapter Five.

Things turn a tad shadier when we account for the fact that members of Ways and Means are thoroughly lobbied and showered with generous campaign cash. As of July 20, 2014, in the 2013–2014 election cycle, for instance, the average Ways and Means Committee member had already received $1.3 million in contributions from political action committees and individuals, more than any other average member on the other committees. The average member of the Financial Services Committee, which oversees Wall Street, banked $1.1 million; the average member of the Energy and Commerce Committee, which has broad authority over the domestic economy, $1 million; the average member of the Agriculture Committee, $970,000; and the average member of the Budget Committee, $930,000.[77] Meanwhile, the big corporate players spend plenty to lobby. As noted previously, GE, Boeing, and Verizon have all received enormously favorable tax treatment in recent years; each of them shelled out an average of $16.4 million on lobbying from 2011 to 2013.

This money does not go to waste. A team of researchers led by Matthew D. Hill of the University of Mississippi recently took a look at the influence of lobbying on corporate tax bills. They find "corporate tax lobbyers exhibit lower effective tax rates and greater book-tax differences."[78] In other words, these corporations are not wasting their money. In the case of a megafirm like GE, it may spend upward of $20 million every year, but their federal tax rebate is measured in the billions—a huge return on its investment.

To see how influence peddling works in practice let's return to the fight over taxes in the 1980s, starting with ERTA of 1981. When Reagan ran for president in 1980, he allied himself with supply-siders in the Republican Party. They advocated lower income tax rates for all payers, believing that this would help producers create more and investors better direct capital to productive ends. Business-specific corporate tax expenditures were not at the top of his list; however they were a major priority for corporate America. It organized aggressively during this period to expand the investment tax credit created during the Kennedy years and also to speed up (already accelerated) depreciation. The famed Carlton Group formed in 1978; this informal collection of lobbyists included the heaviest of heavy hitters—

the Business Roundtable, the National Association of Manufacturers, the Chamber of Commerce, the National Federation of Independent Businesses, and so on. It met every Tuesday morning at the Sheraton-Carlton Hotel in Washington, to plot strategy on how to enact its 10-5-3 proposal, which would reduce the timeframe of depreciation to ten years for buildings, five years for equipment, and three years for vehicles.[79]

Again, Reagan himself did not prioritize such policies; his main focus was on tax rates. Still, he quickly found himself embracing new corporate tax expenditures. The reason was that congressional Democrats, led by House Ways and Means Committee Chairman Dan Rostenkowski, were drafting an alternative tax plan that did not reduce rates as much as Reagan wanted; rather, it was extremely favorable to businesses with its tax expenditure policies. Reagan had no choice but to counter the offers made by House Democrats, and soon both sides were locked in a bidding war for industry support. Eventually, congressional Democrats, belying their claims of populism against Reagan's elitism, actually offered full expensing for business equipment. In the end, Reagan won out due largely to his mastery of the bully pulpit. As Boston University political scientist Cathie Martin puts it: "Corporate tax benefits thus became the medium of exchange for buying legislative support. Because of the symbolic significance of the act, the near desperation of the political players, and the choice of corporate taxation as the unit of bargaining, special interests played an extremely prominent role and more concessions were made than usual."

Corporate interests would be highly influential five years later, when Congress and President Reagan hammered out the TRA of 1986, whose purpose was in part to fix the mess created by the logroll of 1981. Traditionally, the TRA is seen as a win for the public interest over the special interests, but that is only part of the story. In fact, ERTA helped some businesses more than others; large, capital-intensive concerns like GE made off like bandits, but small businesses, which are less likely to file under the corporate code, did not benefit as much. This coalition of "losers" (in quotes because of course they generally did quite well under ERTA, too!) worked with Reagan and congressional Democrats to shift the tax burden away from them and back toward the capital-heavy corporations. So, for instance, the Kennedy-era tax credit on new purchases was eliminated, accelerated depreciation was reduced somewhat, and overall corporate and individual rates were lowered. This helped some businesses at the expense of others, and those who were helped were integral to the bill's passage.[80]

Moreover, the TRA was itself chock full of special-interest giveaways. An investigation for the *Philadelphia Inquirer* by Donald Barlett and James Steele finds "at least 650 exemptions—preferences, really, for the rich and powerful—through the legislation, most written in cryptic legal and tax jargon that conceals the identity of the beneficiaries."[81] Little wonder, then, that the 1986 TRA is famous for how it drew lobbyists out of the woodwork. As journalists Jeffrey Birnbaum and Alan Murray report in *Showdown at Gucci Gulch*:

> The amount of time, money, and effort expended on tax lobbying throughout 1985 and 1986 was enough to overwhelm even the most cynical congressional observer. With billions of dollars of tax breaks on the line, major corporations, trade associations, and pressure groups hired the biggest names in Washington to protect themselves. . . . Some wags began to refer to the bill as the "Lobbyists' Relief Act of 1986" . . .
>
> Many of the lobbyists were former members of Congress and former aides, whose stock-in-trade was their expertise in the system and their access to old colleagues and bosses. The lucrative allure of tax reform caused ever more of these people to join the lobbyists' ranks. Congressional and administration officials were transformed, almost overnight, from being the people sought out for tax favors to the people who were doing the seeking.[82]

Little has changed since 1986, of course. In 2014, House Ways and Means Committee Chairman Dave Camp released a tax reform proposal that was not expected to go anywhere during the 113th Congress, and yet it drew heavy attention from tax lobbyists.[83] Similarly, a battle in 2014 to extend various business tax expenditures (like the GE Loophole) drew what one think tank calls an "army" of lobbyists. On the extender bill alone, 1,359 lobbyists attempted to contact members of Congress or their staff 12,378 times; 58 percent of these lobbyists had previously worked somewhere in the government.[84]

Shocking? Perhaps, although at this point, dear reader, we cannot help but wonder if you, like we, are now past the point of shock. Novel? Of course not. Very little has changed in the last twenty-five years, or for that matter in the last ninety years since the income tax was initiated. Corruption ultimately traces back to the simple argument of this book: our system lacks institutional mechanisms to keep politicians from exercising their expansive powers irresponsibly. In the case of the income tax, members of Congress have tools in their toolbox that they wish to use to help the people they meet, quite often the wealthiest and best-connected interest groups with the resources to ensure such an introduction. Meanwhile, no institutional actor is in much of a position to protect the public interest. So, year after year, the corporate tax code is littered with new expenditures and opportunities for sheltering that reduce efficiency and equity. Every disinterested observer hates it; nobody can stop it.

The second half of our study of corruption has looked at individual policies, rather than trace its development chronologically. And there is a subtle order extant here: as we progress through the post–New Deal era, each corrupt policy we examine is more wasteful than the one that preceded it. Agricultural subsidies are absurd, of course, but they probably do not waste as much as the pork barrel, which does not waste as much as Medicare, which does not waste as much as corporate tax expenditures and sheltering. At this point, we have reached some extremely large figures, approaching $100 billion per year. The next chapter will examine the regulatory breakdowns that preceded the 2008 economic collapse, which cost the American economy hundreds of billions of dollars.

Before we move on, however, there is a final point to make. It is one made before, but our story of taxation really underscores it: reforms do not last in our system unless they alter the underlying institutional arrangements that produced the initial corruption. This, of course, is why the 1986 TRA failed to clean the tax code once and for all. In the end, it was akin to a root canal. Painful and momentous, sure; but, unless one stops overindulging in sweets, it is something that will be needed again, sooner or later. Similarly, the TRA may have cleaned out some of the mess that past Congresses had left behind, but it did not dissuade future Congresses from the same bad habits.

Yet there is a larger, more ominous way that our story of taxes indicates the limits of reform. Return to the 1892 Democratic Party platform, which fulminated against "Republican protection" as a "fraud, a robbery of the great majority of the American people for the benefit of the few." This claim, while hyperbolic, had a great deal of merit. The tax regime by the end of the nineteenth century had become a massive logroll, often for the benefit of the wealthiest industrialists at the expense of the poorest farmers. Twenty years later, in 1913, the same progressive forces that were beginning to stir in 1892 finally had an opportunity to create an alternative to the tariff law. The income tax was supposed to be an efficient and equitable way to raise funds.

And here we are, some hundred years later, and damned if the income tax isn't worse than the tariff ever was. Just like the tariff of yore, it showers its benefits upon the giant firms, which use enormous political influence to leverage the parochialism of our system to their advantage. The tariff benefited the American Sugar Refining Company and Standard Oil at everybody else's expense; the corporate income tax benefits Verizon and GE at everybody else's expense. But the income tax is worse in the sense that average taxpayers are burdened with substantial compliance costs that never accompanied the tariff regime. As if that is not enough, the personal nature of the tax code has enabled politicians over the years to use it as a political tool. Franklin Delano Roosevelt's taxmen egregiously went after Andrew Mellon, but did not pursue a key FDR loyalist who may have cheated on his taxes, a young Texas congressman by the name of Lyndon Johnson; congressional Democrats assailed the Nixon administration for trying to misuse the IRS; and most recently high-ranking IRS officials gave conservative groups an overly-rigorous scrutiny that leftwing groups did not have to endure.

The reason why we often end up in the same place (or worse) is that, even at the height of our reformist zeal, we never look at the institutions that write the corrupt laws. These are the real problems; the policies themselves are merely the symptoms. Tomorrow, Congress could abolish the income tax and institute a value-added tax to generate revenue, and in a generation or two there would be a whole new set of corrupt arrangements to outrage and dispirit the citizenry.

The essential problem is that Hamilton, for all his foresight, did not perceive the limits of the institutions he sought to direct. In theory, it may be wonderful for a government to use the tax code, or other supportive fiscal policies, to favor particular businesses with an eye to the country's economic health. However, our government is not up to the task. It is a power it was never really designed to exercise, and when it wields the power anyway, it often ends up favoring private interests over the common good. Business-oriented corruption has dogged our history because every generation since Hamilton has more or less adhered to his views and has made the same mistakes. It is bound to continue unless and until we the people appreciate the limits of our system and either narrow our ambitions or redesign our government.

13

"The Pretorian Band"

Fannie Mae, Freddie Mac, and the Politics of Regulatory Capture

R EGULATORY POLICY has been a key aspect of American political economy since the Interstate Commerce Act of 1887, a law designed to
oversee the railroads. In the intervening years, the country has reached a
broad consensus—consisting of Republicans and Democrats, liberals and
conservatives—that limiting economic activity for the sake of goals like
consumer protection or environmental safety, is a worthwhile goal. More
often than not, public debates about regulation have to do with different
emphases; it is not a matter of whether economic activity should be re-
stricted, but to what extent.

Largely ignored in these debates is a peculiar feature of American regulatory policy: it was basically retrofitted atop a government whose central
purpose was never meant for it. Granted, the Framers of the Constitution
included in the founding document the Commerce Clause, and there was
little disagreement about its merits during the contentious ratification
phase. Even so, the meaning of that Clause in 1787 was quite different than
what it has since become. After all, the Constitution was conceived prior
to the Industrial Revolution, the great economic and social upheaval that
changed virtually everything. Most Americans in 1787 were independent
farmers; those who did not farm tended to be artisans or independent
craftsmen. Capital was scarce; industry scarcer still. There was no reason,
then, to worry about wealthy industrialists pursuing profit at the expense
of worker safety or air quality. Indeed, the greatest interstate commerce

controversy of the era had to do with a waterway dispute between Maryland and Virginia.[1]

When the problems of industrialization finally became too much for politicians to ignore, they amplified the Commerce Clause to deal with the new threats. As a legal matter, this expansion of federal authority was much more straightforward than, say, the acrobatics required to justify a federal chartering authority, which the Constitutional Convention originally denied for the new government. Still, we again confront the essential thesis of this book: expanding the powers of the government, regardless of legality, should have precipitated a reconceptualization of the structures of the institutions tasked with exercising those powers; it did not, and corruption was bound to follow.

We saw something like this in Chapter Seven, which reviewed the National Industrial Recovery Act (NIRA) of 1933. There, the government created poorly conceived, ad hoc institutions meant to wield the new regulatory powers, only to witness the liberal dream of the NIRA come crashing into a corporatist nightmare that probably slowed the economic recovery. Of course, a night-watchman state, where industry was totally unregulated, was unacceptable; moreover, the country was not prepared to design new institutions to handle this new regulatory authority. So, few lessons were learned from the NIRA debacle, and the nation's political leaders went right on regulating. And regulatory bodies went right on being captured by the very industries they were supposed to regulate.

Ultimately, the problem is that regulations are different from prohibitions. When the government prohibits something from happening altogether, it is implying that there is no net social value to be had from the outlawed activity. On the other hand, regulation merely restricts activity, which suggests that the activity does serve some social purpose, or at the least it cannot be outlawed without abridging core liberties. Either way, regulation involves a clash of socially acceptable values. Consider the case of environmental regulation that restricts pollution from a steel mill. On the one hand, there is the value of clean air. On the other hand, there is the value that comes from the mill's activity, which produces jobs for local workers and profits for the owners that can then be invested in other, socially useful activities. Ideally, society would like to maximize both goals, but in practice that is not possible, so the government, acting on society's behalf, must find a balance between those values.[2] Or consider speed limit laws. If the government wanted nobody to die in an auto accident, it would outlaw driving altogether, but that would destroy the economy. Thus, the speed limit is a regulation that attempts to balance two values that are at times at odds with one another: facilitating transportation and preserving life.

Complicating the government's delicate task in such matters is the fact that its institutions were never built to handle the regulatory questions that emerge in a modern, industrialized nation, and are therefore susceptible to factional meddling. While the public good certainly can and does win out sometimes, in many cases what is decisive is the particular array of interest groups who are lined up in the battle. Who has more money to rain upon legislators? Whose political supporters are more loyal to the cause? Whose supporters are more vocal? Whose supporters are better distributed across the political spectrum?

This is how regulatory capture happens. Regulators who are situated in the bureaucracy may seem free from politics—and indeed that was the original hope of progressives who wanted the government to expand its regulatory activities—but this independence is often illusory. At the very least, Congress ultimately has authority over whether an agency is independent in the first place, which means nobody in government is actually free from politics. More often than not, Congress can make sure regulators conform to political reality if it really wants to press its case. Moreover, the same forces that influence members of Congress can often work directly upon regulators, in a process that social scientists label cultural capture.

A recent, and calamitous, example of the costs of regulatory capture happened not that long ago, during the financial crisis of 2008. The financial services industry effectively captured its governmental regulators, who actually had the tools to prevent the crisis but did not use them. This shall be the focus of our chapter here, in particular the two government-sponsored enterprises (GSEs) at the center of the housing boom and bust: the Federal National Mortgage Association (Fannie Mae) and the Federal Home Loan Mortgage Corporation (Freddie Mac).

The GSEs are an extreme example of regulatory capture, which is why they are of interest. The scholarly literature on capture is so broad, it is literally impossible to review competently the breadth and depth of the problem. The best approach is to take an example that puts the problem in stark relief, and that is precisely what the GSEs do. As we shall see, Fannie Mae in particular was one of the largest and most powerful interests in American politics; while some interest groups' clout lasted much longer—organized labor, for instance—no interest wielded as much power as Fannie Mae did during its glory years. Put simply, virtually nobody dared to speak ill of it. Indeed, Peter Wallison, a scholar at the American Enterprise Institute who was a lonely critic of the GSEs during their heyday, was once jokingly warned by a friend that he better have somebody start his car in the morning if he decided to go after Fannie.[3] Anybody in a position to harm Fannie Mae's interests was either bought off or intimidated into backing down, even as the GSE was perfecting the sort of accounting shenanigans that brought down Enron and WorldCom, and later on as it was loading up its balance sheet with the subprime mortgages that eviscerated the economy in 2008.

Of course, discussing Fannie and Freddie is a fraught endeavor, for it gets to the heart of a partisan political question: who is to blame for the economic collapse? Liberals tend to blame deregulation, and thus prefer to point the finger at the George W. Bush administration (and factions within the Bill Clinton administration), but in fact it was conservatives who had called for stricter regulations of Fannie and Freddie, which complicates the meme. And so it was that *New York Times* financial columnist Joe Nocera invoked Hitlerism to attack the arguments of conservative skeptics like Wallison and Edward Pinto, saying that blaming Fannie and Freddie for the mortgage meltdown was propagating "The Big Lie."[4]

Nocera's hyperventilation is merely an effort to mobilize bias, to exclude a priori certain views that conflict with his own. Even so, this chapter shall avoid the thorny issue of the extent to which Fannie and Freddie's irresponsibility induced the economic collapse. Serious people have different views. Some think that, in the end, the two followed the private traders; others suggest that they were so large and influential that their decision to jump into the subprime market necessarily made them the leaders of it.[5] Our contention here will be more modest: Fannie and Freddie contributed in some way to the subprime mortgage crisis of 2008, and the inability of its captured regulators to control them therefore contributed as well. Maybe the crisis would have happened; maybe it would not have. Either way, the inability of the government to keep a watchful eye on the GSEs contributed to its depth and breadth. We thus can set aside this heated partisan debate about the importance of Fannie and Freddie; for our purposes, they were important enough.

To begin, we need a good definition of regulatory capture. The best available comes from two scholars, Daniel Carpenter and David Moss, who recently edited an important volume on the subject. According to them, capture is "the result or process by which regulation, in law or application, is consistently or repeatedly directed away from the public interest and toward the interests of the regulated industry, by the intent and action of the industry itself."[6]

This is a process that has been extant since the earliest efforts to regulate private industry. In 1892, Richard Olney, soon to be the attorney general for Grover Cleveland, advised a railroad executive:

> The [Interstate] Commerce Commission (ICC), as its functions have now been limited by the courts, is, or can be made, of great use to the railroads. It satisfies the popular clamor for a government supervision of the railroads, at the same time that that supervision is almost entirely nominal. Further, the older such a Commission gets to be, the more inclined it will be found to take the business and railroad view of things. It thus becomes a sort of barrier between the railroad corporations and the people and a sort of protection against hasty and crude legislation hostile to railroad interests. . . . The part of wisdom is not to destroy the Commission, but to utilize it.[7]

This view of the ICC, later vindicated in a careful study by political scientist Samuel Huntington, serves as a great summary of the value of capture. Having a captured regulator is better for a business than having no regulator at all, for the captured entity can quell public anxiety and make sure that the government actually supports the "regulated" business.[8]

As we saw in Chapter Six, Woodrow Wilson and his allies in the progressive movement thought the way around this would be to separate the bureaucrats from politics entirely. The idea was for the political process to settle upon broad goals, then let the trained experts in the bureaucracy use scientific principles to achieve them.[9] This philosophy carried into the New Deal, which created a vast array of independent regulatory bodies like the Civil Aeronautics Board, the Securities and Exchange Commission (SEC), and the Federal Communications Commission.

But by the 1950s, political scientists and economists were becoming aware of how capture occurred despite these protections. In 1955, economist Marvin Bernstein posited a life cycle of regulation, which ultimately ends with the agency becoming a servant of its industry: "the working agreement that a commission reaches with the regulated interests becomes so fixed that the agency has no creative force left to mobilize against the regulated groups. Its primary mission is the maintenance of the status quo in the regulated industry and its own position as a recognized protector of the industry."[10] This view of capture was so prevalent that, by the time of the Great Society, liberal reformers began to eschew the idea of independent regulators with broad mandates, and instead took to outlining more detailed instructions for them in the initial legislation. Yet that did not do much good, either. Political scientists in turn noticed that this merely placed the political battle over capture a further step out of public view, as the major fights happened over regulatory design.[11]

Recent scholars are not nearly as pessimistic as earlier generations. The old view was essentially that iron triangles—connections between regulators, interest groups, and congressional fiefdoms—invariably dominate public policy. In recent years, scholars have come to understand that a vast array of pressure groups can influence regulatory policy. Not only that, few areas of congressional oversight are cordoned off; instead, congressional committees and subcommittees can often compete for influence. Throw in the president and his advisors, the courts, academics, and even celebrities, and there are many interests that compete to direct regulatory policy, meaning that the old theory of Bernstein, while certainly insightful, is not sufficiently nuanced.

Moreover, different types of policy are more prone to capture than others.[12] For instance, policies that benefit society at large and whose costs are widely distributed (like Social Security) are not prime grounds for capture. On the other hand, policies whose benefits are narrow but whose costs are widely distributed can be captured, as select interest groups vie for the benefits while society at large barely notices the costs.[13]

In general, what this means is that sometimes regulatory policy can benefit the regulated, sometimes the nonregulated, sometimes both, and sometimes neither.[14] And so, to quote Moss and Carpenter, "regulatory capture is not an all or nothing affair."[15] It is, rather, a complex issue of degree, varying agency by agency. This is not to say that it does not happen, or that it is not a real problem for the public interest, just that the absolutist notions from the 1950s made it appear to be black and white, when it is really shades of gray.

One reason why regulatory capture is so difficult to generalize about is that there are a variety of mechanisms by which it can occur. In the first instance, it can happen when the agency itself is created, as political scientist Terry Moe details. In an extreme situation, an omnipotent interest group would want a regulatory agency that comes to independent decisions that help the group's bottom line, which means it would want it to hew to predictable, professional standards that the group itself influences. But, in case the winds of fortune shift, it would also want structural protections against an agency that goes rogue, like detailed legislative instructions to limit agency discretion or continued political oversight of some sort. In the same vein, it would demand it be housed in a safe cabinet department that lacks the institutional capacity to support a strong regulator. Practically speaking, few interest groups are so powerful, but this goal sets up the political game of designing regulatory agencies: interest groups battle one another to influence Congress to design regulators that they can capture.[16]

After the design phase, the methods of capture are numerous. For instance, every regulator is above all answerable to Congress, in one way or another, which gives pressure groups a point of access. Campaign contributions to well-positioned members of Congress can serve a number of functions for interest groups that want to influence regulators. They can indicate that the firm has resources to spend battling regulators in court. They can also signal that the firm has politicians willing to go to bat for it and potentially use their investigative power to put pressure on the regulators themselves. No agency wants to waste time and money fending off congressional inquiries, and every agency worries about Congress swooping in to seize some of its independence. Often, poking around the affairs of a well-connected firm or interest is simply not worth this kind of risk.[17]

Beyond influencing the legislature, interest groups can also capture an agency through cultural mechanisms, by which the regulators—independent of political pressure—come to adopt the ideology of those whom they regulate. There are a variety of ways this can happen, although they often elude the kind of quantitative methods used to track the influence of money. One way is through frequent and regular interactions, which enable the interest group to influence subtly the thinking of the regulators, so that the latter come to equate the interests of the former with the public good. This is often amplified by the so-called revolving door by which regulators travel into and out of the field that they are regulating. From a budgetary perspective, this practice is cost-effective for the taxpayers, as it effectively lets the industry subsidize the costs of training its own regulators, who take mediocre pay during their years in government service knowing they will reap a huge windfall when they exit; however, in practice it facilitates a homogenous worldview.[18]

Another way is through informational overload. In the twenty-first–

century economy, the task of regulation is often so technical and complicated that it requires frequent input from the regulated industry. This offers the industry an opportunity to inundate an agency with reams of information, which the agency is obliged to pour through. Slowly but surely, this steady stream of data can alter worldviews and lead to capture.[19]

If all this isn't enough, there is also good, old-fashioned peer pressure. Regulators are human beings, after all, and they are thus prone to the same nonrational thought processes that all humans are susceptible to. They are wont to adopt positions advanced by those whom they see as being in their peer group, by those in high social status, or by those in their social networks. Ironic, but true: Wilson's aspiration for independent regulators is often undermined by the childish desire to impress the cool kids.[20]

While theories about the financial crisis of 2008 vary dramatically, there seems to be a general consensus that regulators came to adopt the ideology of the financial services industry. They were captured, coming to believe, erroneously, that what was good for thrifts like Washington Mutual, investment firms like Goldman Sachs, and insurance companies like AIG was good for the country at large.[21]

For students of the history of banking, the preferred rejoinder might be "told you so!" Regulation of the finance industry has been, to borrow a phrase from scholars Charles Calomiris and Stephen Haber, "politics all the way down," virtually since the Founding. As we saw in Chapters One and Two, politics heavily influenced the design, operation, and fall of the First and Second Banks of the United States. Afterward, financial regulation in this country was dominated by a coalition of unit bankers, rural farmers, and populists who insured that, in essence, the country lacked anything approaching a national banking system. This system more or less held in place, despite its obvious limitations, until the savings and loan crisis of the 1980s.[22] Following that, a new political coalition came to dominate the banking industry, a strange alliance between the large banks—newly created after deregulation in the early 1990s made it easier to start branch banking—and urban activist groups. The two joined forces, such that the big banks promised to promote lending and credit extension to poor, minority areas, and the urban groups promised to vouch to federal regulators that these were good corporate citizens.[23]

The fact that the big banks had to ask permission from federal regulators to expand suggests a controversial, but nevertheless accurate, point: legislative deregulation was not the proximate cause of the financial crisis. For starters, deregulation, insofar as it cleaned out the vestiges of the old alliance, was a good thing from a prudential perspective (i.e., ensuring the safety and soundness of financial institutions). It enabled financial institutions to spread financial risk and improved access to good interest rates.[24] Additionally, prudential regulation actually increased during the period in question, thanks to the passage of the Sarbanes-Oxley Act of 2002, which put the onus on accounting firms and publicly traded corporations to keep honest books.

Indeed, financial services regulators had all the tools in their toolbox they might have needed to stop the subprime lending meltdown before it hit a critical level. They just chose not to utilize them because, in the words of author James Kwak, the industry had achieved "the practical equivalent of capture, with federal regulatory agencies adopting its favored positions."[25] Several failures stand out:

- The Federal Reserve and the SEC allowed banks to use credit default swaps to reduce equity cushions. These were overcomplicated hedges to cut down on the risk of other investment vehicles, but they turned out not to work when the panic came. Both regulators could have tamped down on the use of these over-the-counter derivatives if they wanted to. Instead, they elected not to.
- The SEC weakened its internal capacity to assess the risk of the largest banks and did not inspect a single one in the eighteen months prior to the collapse.
- All regulatory agencies took a laissez-faire approach to the credit ratings agencies, assuming that they could police themselves. Instead, perverse incentives induced the agencies to issue bad ratings that vastly overestimated the safety of the investments in question.
- The main prudential regulator of the GSEs, the Office of Federal Housing Enterprise Oversight (OFHEO), was an inept and lax regulator.
- The Office of Thrift Supervision (OTS) was not only lax, but actually encouraged poorly run financial entities to register as thrifts so that OTS could acquire the fees that came through regulation.[26]

If regulatory capture goes a long way to explaining these failures, then how did that capture occur in the first place? As it turns out, financial services regulators are uniquely susceptible to capture, facing the same problems other regulators must deal with as well as ones unique to themselves.

When it comes to uniqueness, consider again the inherent ambiguity behind regulation: these are activities that society deems valuable, just not to the level that would occur absent the regulation, whose purpose is to secure some other value in tandem. With financial services regulation, the purpose is ultimately to prevent a financial collapse akin to what happened in 2008. That is the harm. But unlike the harm of dirty air from too much industrial activity, there is a very real possibility that this harm will never be realized. Dirty air is a certainty; financial collapse is merely a risk. That makes it harder for regulators to defend their aggressive actions. For instance, in 2003, just as the economy was returning back to life from the dual shocks of recession and terrorist attack, would it really have been feasible for a regulator to bring the hammer down on Wall Street? That seems unlikely, given that the upside to the activity (economic growth) was very real and the downside (an economic collapse) was only a possibility.[27]

There are other unique factors as well. Who is it the regulators are supposed to protect? The Environmental Protection Agency (EPA) regulates polluters for the sake of the people who live nearby. The Occupational Safety and Health Administration (OSHA) sets forth regulations that manage workplace environments for the sake of workers. Financial regulators restrict the actions of banks, brokers, and insurers for the sake of . . . banks, brokers, and insurers! In other words, with the EPA and OSHA, the target of regulations and the beneficiaries of regulations are different, but with financial regulation the targets and beneficiaries are essentially the same. Prudential regulation, of course, is meant to protect the country at large from an economic collapse, but the way that it does that is by keeping the regulated firms from going under first.[28] That puts the financial regulators in a uniquely vulnerable position, as they are also, in a sense, servants of the firms they are supposed to monitor.

Moreover, financial institutions had special leverage over their regulators because they could revise their charters to fall under different regulators. Plus, financial regulatory law is soft, which means that it requires frequent interactions with regulated institutions, creating greater potential for cultural capture. That is enhanced by the increasingly technical nature of finance.[29] Forty years ago, it was centered almost entirely around stocks and bonds; today, brokers trade highly complicated instruments that are difficult to understand. That makes regulators especially dependent upon the industry for information.[30]

What's more, the financial services industry has the money and expertise needed for high level political access. The George W. Bush administration was decidedly cozy with the financial community; for instance,

Bush's final treasury secretary, Henry Paulson, had previously worked for Goldman Sachs. The Barack Obama administration also has a close relationship with the large financial institutions.[31] Despite the president's strong rhetoric against it, his policies—embodied primarily by the Wall Street Reform and Consumer Protection Act (a.k.a. Dodd-Frank), an early version of which seems to have been written by a law firm representing major financial corporations, and the Public Private Investment Program—were great boons for the industry.[32] A lot of this can be chalked up to the people that the president filled the government with; advisors like Rahm Emanuel and Larry Summers had close connections to Wall Street, as did Secretary of the Treasury Timothy Geithner.[33] Indeed, the latter refused to act on a presidential request to develop a plan to unwind Citi.[34] Not that any of this is a surprise coming from an administration helmed by Obama, whose 2004 senatorial campaign received hefty donations from the financial services industry, and who in 2008 outraised his Republican opponent John McCain by about 4:1 from Goldman Sachs.[35]

Financial institutions also have influence outside the White House, including at the Fed, which is tasked with regulating bank and financial holding companies as well as state banks in the Federal Reserve System.[36] The Fed is one of the most independent agencies in the entire government. Its board members have lengthy terms and do not serve at the pleasure of the president, its budget does not depend on Congress, its employment protocols do not stem from the Office of Personnel Management, and its staff is uniquely well educated.[37] Even so, the Fed remains a creature of politics. Indeed, it has been that way since its beginning, as a compromise between rural Democrats and northeastern financiers during the Wilson administration.[38] In general, there is a scholarly consensus today that the Fed is partially dependent upon the political agents of the government, especially the president. Several times over the years, Congress has tried to alter the Fed's charter because it was unhappy with its monetary policy. What this has usually meant is that the Fed never strays very far from the preferences of the commander in chief, who can protect it with his veto pen.[39]

The Fed also has strong ties to the big financial firms. Some of this is mediated by the political process, for the industry lobbies the White House aggressively on appointments. Some of it is cultural, whereby the institution's close geographical and social proximity to Wall Street means that the former often internalizes the views of the latter.[40]

The SEC is not so much concerned with prudential regulations, but ensuring that investors are protected from fraud.[41] Even so, the SEC played a significant role in the crisis because it had the capacity to rein in the hedge funds and other traders who were profiting off too-risky investment vehicles, and it elected not to.[42] Instead, at certain points, it relaxed capital requirements for these firms.[43] Politics was certainly at play here. Scholars find that well-placed political donations to legislators can scare off the SEC from pursuing enforcement actions against some and into levying smaller penalties on others.[44] But cultural issues influenced the agency as well. Scholars also find that SEC employees seem to have profited from insider information on upcoming regulatory actions.[45] In general, the close connection between the SEC and its regulated firms induced mistakes that one group of scholars attributes to "overconfidence, the confirmation bias, framing effects, and groupthink."[46]

Perhaps the worst regulator of the bunch was the OTS, which performed so poorly in the lead up to the financial crisis that the Dodd-Frank Law actually did away with it altogether. Its purpose was to monitor federal savings and loan associations; to give it some independence, the government decided that its budget would come not via the appropriations process but rather through fees it collected from regulated firms.[47] But in the late 1990s and early 2000s, the OTS went trolling for financial institutions, asking them to re-register as thrifts so that the OTS could collect the fees. In exchange, the agency promised a more lax regulatory environment. Little wonder that some of the worst offenders in the subprime crisis— now-defunct institutions like Washington Mutual and Countrywide—were overseen by the OTS. Indeed, at the peak of the crisis, it was actually lowering capital requirements and impeding the efforts of other agencies to draft new rules to make sure people could pay back the loans they were being given.[48]

Actually, the only reason that the OTS might be considered the worst regulator of the bunch is because the agency charged with watching over Fannie Mae and Freddie Mac, the OFHEO, was so inept that to call it a "regulator" stretches the definition of the word to meaningless proportions. This is exactly how Fannie Mae wanted it. It had such sway with Congress that it basically wrote the law empowering the OFHEO back in 1992, and Fannie Mae designed it exactly along the lines that Terry Moe's theory predicts: an agency that it could easily capture. As Nobel Prize–winning economist Gary Becker argues, the failure of the OFHEO to watch over Fannie and

Freddie was an "economically disastrous example of the capture theory . . . before and leading up to the financial crisis."[49]

To understand Becker's point, we have to ask ourselves a couple of questions. What exactly were Fannie and Freddie supposed to do in the first place? How were these GSEs organized internally, and how did that organization produce an interest that would eventually put the economy at risk? What resources could the GSEs bring to bear against would-be political opponents? Finally, how did the process of capture play itself out between 1992 and 2008?

Essentially a vestige of the mercantilist system, the GSEs were quite similar to the First and Second Banks of the United States: private entities granted exclusive privileges by the federal government to accomplish public purposes in addition to their profit-seeking endeavors. They are therefore not agents of the government, but rather instrumentalities of the government. They are not subject to the management laws that other departments, commissions, and bureaus have, nor do they have to rely on Congress for funding. However, their charters originate from the federal government, and they outline the privileges and expectations for the GSEs.[50]

In the broadest of terms, the purpose of Fannie Mae and Freddie Mac is to facilitate liquidity in the mortgage market. They do this not by originating mortgages, but by purchasing them from banks via revenue generated from bond sales. They often bundle and resell mortgage-backed securities, with a government guarantee that the principal will be repaid (though the investor takes on any interest risk). They make a profit in several ways. First, they can reap a reward based on the spread in interest rates; their borrowing costs are lower than purely private institutions, opening up unique arbitrage opportunities when playing on the spread between short- and long-term rates. They charge fees to banks for taking on the mortgages. And they hold some mortgage-backed securities as investment vehicles in their own portfolios.[51]

Fannie and Freddie's role evolved slowly over time. In 1934, the New Deal created the Federal Housing Administration (FHA) to offer mortgage insurance to lenders on qualified mortgages, and in 1938 it created Fannie Mae to purchase these FHA–insured loans; in later years, Fannie was allowed to purchase loans stemming from the Veterans Administration (VA). In an effort to reduce the budget deficit, the Lyndon Johnson administration decided to spin Fannie Mae off into a private corporation, thus removing from the federal ledger all of its outstanding obligations. The government also created the Government National Mortgage Association (Ginnie Mae) to securitize FHA and VA loans, freeing Fannie to focus on the private market. In the name of competition, the Richard Nixon administration and the Democratic-controlled Congress chartered Freddie Mac in 1970.[52]

Tasking them with injecting liquidity into the mortgage market, the federal government also granted them an extensive array of benefits to help them in their quest. Fannie and Freddie possessed a contingency line of credit at the Treasury Department, valued in the billions of dollars. Their securities were considered government securities for the purpose of the Securities and Exchange Act of 1934. They were exempt from registration under the Securities Act of 1933. The Fed was the fiscal agent of their securities, which were eligible as collateral for Fed discount loans and unlimited investment by national banks and state bank members of the Fed. Written between the lines of these formal benefits was perhaps their greatest asset: the belief that Fannie and Freddie enjoyed government backing.[53] Though their bond issues had to disclaim it explicitly, investors believed that, if push came to shove, the government would guarantee Fannie and Freddie. And indeed, the GSEs were bailed out after the financial crisis, just as investors predicted. Implicit federal backing enabled them to borrow money at a much lower rate than any of their prospective competitors.[54]

All in all, the Congressional Budget Office (CBO) valued this federal subsidy at $6.9 billion in 1996, $13.6 billion in 2001, and $23 billion in 2005.[55] Little wonder that their activity increased at a rapid rate after they were privatized; they had an edge over any and all competitors, valued in the billions of dollars. In 1970, their obligations amounted to $15.2 billion; in 1980, they had risen to $76.6 billion; they ballooned to $768 billion in 1990; and they were $2.4 trillion by 2000.[56] By the time of the financial crisis in 2008, over half of the nation's mortgage debt passed through either Fannie or Freddie.[57]

One might think that, given their federal charters and valuable stream of governmental largesse, Uncle Sam would have been dutiful in watching over his public-private creations. But, in fact, the opposite was the case, which is why Fannie and Freddie serve as such a perfect illustration of the dangers of regulatory capture. To appreciate this, we have to understand the push and pull of various forces within the GSEs, for that will help illustrate how and why they had such influence in Washington.

The appropriate way to think of the politics behind Fannie and Freddie is akin to a triangle, with each point or node representing a distinct interest in how the business should be conducted: first, and most obviously, were the shareholders and senior management, who were interested in maximizing profit; second were their potential regulators, like at the Treasury Department, who were most concerned about safety and soundness; finally, there were those most interested in the programmatic potential of the GSEs, namely their ability to extend home loans to poor and underserviced communities.

A sensible outcome would have required legislators and politicians to weigh carefully the competing interests of all three groups and design a system that maximizes the potential for profit and program without undermining prudential concerns. But our system is too often incapable of such rationality. Instead, and quite predictably, the relationship between the government and the GSEs was the result of a power struggle between the interests along the three nodes, and in particular an alliance that formed in the early 1990s between the profit node and the programmatic node. As a consequence, prudential concerns were tossed aside, and not really revisited by the government until the summer of 2008, by which point it was too late.[58]

The alliance between the profit and programmatic nodes was hammered out during the long negotiations accompanying the Federal Housing Enterprises Financial Safety and Soundness Act (FHEFSSA) of 1992, passed in the wake of the savings and loan crisis. That law set in motion an effort by the Department of Housing and Urban Development (HUD) to set progressively higher goals for low- to moderate-income borrowers: from 30 percent of the GSEs' total book in 1993, to 42 percent in 1997, and rising to 56 percent in 2008.[59] Meanwhile, the government looked the other way as Fannie and Freddie consistently lowered their lending standards. In fact, the government facilitated this irresponsibility at several crucial junctures, deciding, for instance, that the GSEs could get affordable housing credits under HUD for accepting subprime loans.[60] By 1997, the GSEs were offering 97 percent loan-to-value, unheard of just a few years prior. By 1999, they began pilot programs to get into the subprime market.[61] By 2001, they would accept loans with no down payment at all.[62]

As Fannie Mae declared in its 2006 10-K submission to the SEC:

We have made, and continue to make, significant adjustments to our mortgage loan sourcing and purchase strategies in an effort to meet HUD's increased housing goals and new subgoals. These strategies include entering into some purchase and securitization transactions with lower expected economic returns than our typical transactions. We have also relaxed some of our underwriting criteria to obtain goals-qualifying mortgage loans and increased our investments in higher-risk mortgage loan products that are more likely to serve the borrowers targeted by HUD's goals and subgoals, which could increase our credit losses.[63]

That the SEC accepted this filing without hesitation speaks to the political deal that was struck. The profit node of the GSE interest triangle would align with the programmatic node, at the expense of the prudential node. In other words, Fannie and Freddie would throw caution to the wind in the dual quests to maximize profit and provide funds for affordable housing, and the government would not raise a stink over the risks it was incurring.

This would be the way of the world for Fannie and Freddie for nearly twenty years, from the 1992 passage of the FHEFSSA until the financial crisis in 2008. How could this state of affairs have been so durable? Again, it was not a product of careful deliberation, but an implicit deal struck between the GSEs' stockholders, their senior management, and advocates of affordable housing in key stations within the government (HUD, congressional committees, etc.). But there were dissidents. Clearly, this was irresponsible, not just in historical retrospect but evident at the time, and there were interests out there concerned about good prudential regulation. How were they left on the outside looking in for so long?

The answer: an aggressive, often unprecedented effort at influence peddling by the profit node, which relentlessly used every resource available to keep the government from sniffing around the GSEs' books. As leftwing consumer advocate Ralph Nader writes:

[Fannie and Freddie] have [an] influence machine that is oiled by revolving doors, the care and feeding of key politicians across the nation, a quick-strike take-no-prisoners public relations operation, and targeted contributions to advocacy organizations—activities financed by slush funds created by generous forms of corporate welfare.[64]

The resources to fund this operation, ironically enough, can be traced back to the federal government itself. In 2001, the CBO found that, for every

$3 of its multibillion dollar subsidy, Fannie Mae and Freddie Mac kept approximately $1. That left billions of dollars to go back to the shareholders, senior management, and the GSEs' extensive political operations.[65]

The first weapon in the arsenal was, of course, campaign money. Given the limitations of campaign finance laws, it is not sufficient for buying influence; nevertheless, it is a necessary down payment. In 2002, Fannie distributed over $2 million to reelection funds, with the members of the Senate Banking Committee and House Financial Services Committee receiving the most cash.[66] Members of Congress are also tightly connected to their states and districts, which gave the GSEs another edge because they securitized mortgages in every state and congressional district in the country. To amplify the connection to local communities, they started opening district offices, which could also be used to hire the family and friends of important political officials.[67]

In addition to money and district attention, there was the GSEs' impressive lobbying operation. Fannie alone spent almost $8 million on lobbying in 2002, but there was much more to it than that.[68] The Fannie Mae Foundation offered extensive grants, nearly $35 million in 2001, often to well-placed charitable organizations, particularly those in the affordable housing sector. This solidified the alliance between the profit and programmatic nodes, ensuring that charity groups would join the fray whenever Fannie's preeminence was challenged.[69] To the same end, the GSEs cultivated an extensive alliance with related interest groups, like mortgage originators, realtors, and homebuilders. More often than not, a law or regulation that affected the GSEs affected the rest of them, so they had an incentive to team up with Fannie and Freddie. So extensive was Fannie and Freddie's influence within the industry that, when rival companies started a watchdog group called FM Watch, dedicated to checking their influence, Fannie allegedly leaned hard on higher-ups from Wells Fargo, GE Capital, and AIG to quit the group, or else lose their underwriting business.[70]

Fannie and Freddie also had the advantage of doing something that both sides of the political aisle supported. As University of Chicago economist Raghuram Rajan notes, economic inequality was growing rapidly during this period, yet budget constraints remained severe. Fannie Mae and Freddie Mac were a politically useful way to promote greater equality at no apparent cost to Uncle Sam because the subsidy was off the federal books. As long as the two GSEs hewed closely to the affordable housing goals, they were bound to avoid serious oversight. The GSEs, of course, were aware of this, and they worked aggressively to manage their public image as responsible stewards of the public good. Fannie even bankrolled two academic journals, *Housing Policy Debate* and the *Journal of Housing Research*, that predictably extolled the virtues of the GSEs. It also sponsored the Fannie Mae Papers, in which high-profile scholars like Joseph Stiglitz, a winner of the Nobel Prize in economics, and Peter Orszag, future Office of Management and Budget (OMB) director under Obama, declared that the GSEs did not pose a threat to the taxpayer.[71]

When push came to shove, probably nothing helped Fannie and Freddie more than their extensive networks of friends and allies. They took the concept of the revolving door to new heights. For nearly twenty years, Fannie Mae was led by two men whose primary background was in politics. Jim Johnson, former aide to Walter Mondale, ran Fannie Mae from 1990 until 2001 and led it during the fight over the FHEHSSA as well as its ramp-up into subprime lending. As journalists Gretchen Morgenson and Joshua Rosner argue:

> Johnson was the financial industry's leader in buying off Congress, manipulating regulators, and neutralizing critics, former colleagues say. His strategy of promoting Fannie Mae and protecting its lucrative government association, largely through intense lobbying, immense campaign contributions, and other assistance given to members of Congress, would be mimicked years later by companies such as Countrywide Financial, an aggressive subprime mortgage lender, Goldman Sachs, Citigroup, and others.[72]

Johnson was followed at Fannie by Franklin Raines, who had previously served as the director of Clinton's OMB. He continued Johnson's tradition of placing a heavy emphasis on politics, and was eventually forced out by Fannie Mae's board after accounting irregularities came to light in 2004.

Johnson and Raines were far from the only former political operatives brought into the GSEs. For instance, Newt Gingrich, who had played a vital role in squashing some reform efforts in the 1990s, received $1.6 million from Freddie Mac after he left Congress.[73] Other prominent pols with ties to Fannie or Freddie include former secretary of commerce, William Daley, former senator Steve Syms, and former congressman Vin Weber.[74] The GSEs were also careful to hire lesser-known but well-placed political people. For instance, Fannie Mae hired Herb Moses, the partner of Congressman Barney Frank, a Massachusetts Democrat who occupied a vital position on the House Financial Services Committee. It also hired the son of Senator Bob Bennett, a Republican of Utah, to work in a district office.[75] It even hired the former chief of staff of Congressman Richard Baker, Republican of Louisiana, who by far was the most ardent critic of the GSEs during the late 1990s and early 2000s.[76] It made him vice president of governmental affairs, but his job presumably had a lot to do with neutralizing his former boss.

Fannie and Freddie were able to attract such high-profile talent because they could pay for it. Ditto the campaign cash, the lobbying expenses, the charitable contributions, and the interest group network. It all cost money, which the GSEs were rolling in, thanks to that federal subsidy. Sure, they turned most of it over to homeowners, but they split the remainder between the shareholders, upper management, and an extensive operation to grease the political skids. Raines put it well in 1999: "We manage our political risk with the same intensity that we manage our credit and interest rate risks."[77]

Again, all of this was dedicated to preserving the alliance between the profit and program nodes at the expense of the prudential node. Fannie and Freddie committed themselves to ever higher profit and ever more affordable housing, and let the risks be damned. The purpose of this whole political operation was to protect it from politicians who might have thought this was a bad way to go. All in all, James Madison's warning about the Bank of the United States is an apt description for Fannie and Freddie; the GSEs were the "the pretorian band of the Government, at once its tool & its tyrant."[78]

Having understood what the GSEs were looking to do, and the resources they had to make that happen, it is now time to look at how the drama played out. We shall see how, in practice, Fannie and Freddie captured its regulators in the bureaucracy and its supervisors in Congress, largely along the terms outlined by Carpenter and Moss. The difference is that, whereas Carpenter and Moss rightly point out that capture is usually a shade of gray, it was black and white with Fannie Mae and Freddie Mac. For nearly two decades, they drove public policy for the benefit of the profit and programmatic nodes at the expense of the prudential node.[79]

To begin, Fannie utilized its already extensive resources to influence the FHEHSSA, the regulatory legislation enacted in 1992.[80] Thanks to pressure from Fannie on that bill, Congress created a weak regulator to watch over it.[81] The OFHEO was not placed in the Department of the Treasury, the Fed, or the SEC, where it might have been stronger. Instead, it was placed in HUD, a scandal-plagued agency with virtually no regulatory know-how.[82] Moreover, while other regulators like the OTS, the Fed, and the SEC did not have to go to Congress every year to request funds, the OFHEO did. This gave the GSEs an additional point of control over it, after they won over key appropriators through their largesse.[83] In this effort, the profit node was assisted by the programmatic node; neither wanted a strong regulator interfering with the GSEs' activities. As one deputy HUD secretary said, "They want to make us a regulator in name only."[84] And that is exactly what they did.

Fannie also heavily influenced the writing of the capital standards for the GSEs after the FHEHSSA became law, ensuring that they would be very weak. Following Moe's prediction about how an interest would want to build its own regulator, Fannie's ideal preference was for the rules to be written directly by the legislature, rather than leaving it up to regulatory discretion. It did not get its first choice—the job of writing the capital standards was handed to the OFHEO but Fannie still leaned upon Congress to set up a byzantine set of procedures to govern how the agency could craft them. Little wonder that it took the OFHEO six years to finally submit its capital standards for approval.[85]

Between the time of the chartering of the OFHEO and the financial collapse in 2008, Fannie and Freddie used their political capital expertly to ward off periodic assaults from various forces in the government. For instance, in 1996 the CBO produced a report saying that the GSEs kept about a third of a multibillion dollar subsidy, a bombshell claim because it directly challenged Fannie and Freddie's image as selfless promoters of American homeownership. As CBO Director June O'Neill later said, "They were outraged by this report or so they said. They said it was unfair, untrue, and could they come and see me? So Frank Raines and (Executive Vice President of Fannie Mae) Bob Zoellick came and met with me and the people from the CBO. All of us had the same feeling—that we were being visited by the mafia."[86]

Relatedly, in 2000 Gary Gensler, undersecretary of the treasury, testified before Congress and mildly suggested that it might be time to rein the GSEs in. Fannie responded with hardball tactics, releasing a statement saying that Gensler's comments had cost over two hundred thousand Americans a chance to buy a home because they diminished market confidence in the GSEs.[87]

Local politicians were also strong-armed. One of Fannie and Freddie's advantages was that they did not have to pay local taxes, which amounted to hundreds of millions of dollars in lost revenue for the nation's capital. When Washington Councilman Bill Lightfoot floated an idea in 1994 to repeal Fannie's exemption, he was overwhelmed with complaints from well-connected politicians, lobbyists, and charities who received assistance from the Fannie Mae Foundation. The next year, California Democrat Pete Stark tried to schedule a hearing on the District's budget problems. He had put together a proposal that would allow Washington to tax the GSEs, but he could not find any witnesses to testify on its behalf. As committee staffer Broderick Johnson recounted, "Many of them frankly told us that they could not do it because of philanthropic relationships they have with Fannie Mae."[88]

Even ostensible friends were not spared when they stepped out of line. In 1999, the Clinton OMB suggested that Fannie and Freddie pay registration fees for their securities. The Fannie Mae Foundation leaned on grant recipients to pressure the Clinton administration, as well as two dozen members of Congress and big city mayors. The entire proposal was killed in about fifty hours.[89]

The handful of congressional opponents were similarly no match for Fannie and Freddie. As mentioned previously, Gingrich worked behind the scenes to kill some legislation to make them pay governmental fees. And when Baker worked on a proposal to improve GSE regulation in the early 2000s, he could not even get a markup scheduled, due to a lack of interest among his colleagues.

In general, the GSEs were so powerful in Washington that they were free to be as imperious as they liked. For instance, to deflect from prying congressional investigators, Fannie Mae once created a phony "Coalition for Homeownership" to flood legislators with mail. When a handful of Republican congressmen looked into who actually sent the mail, they found out that many of the "members" of the Coalition in fact had no idea that Fannie Mae was using their names at all.[90] Naturally, nothing at all came of this absurd and egregious stunt. This was Fannie Mae. It could do what it wanted.

Of course, using such extensive political capital, perhaps the greatest reservoir ever collected since the height of the labor movement, to beat back penny-ante attacks from undersecretaries of the treasury or unhappy southern Republicans is like bringing Mickey Mantle to a tee-ball game. There was no challenge to it, and thus no real demonstration of the GSEs' true political power. That came later, after they became mired in an accounting scandal that nevertheless produced no meaningful reforms.

The story broke entirely by accident. After the Enron scandal came to light early in the George W. Bush administration, accounting firm Arthur Andersen was fingered as an accomplice. Because Freddie Mac used the firm as its accountant, it hired an outside evaluator to double-check its books. That was when all hell broke loose. Freddie Mac, and as it turned out Fannie Mae, had manipulated their financial statements to give a false sense of earnings, ensuring maximum bonuses for their top executives. Basically, both of the GSEs bet on interest rates, and supposedly had hedges in place in case the bets went bad, but their accounting for the hedges was done in a way to amortize their gains, smoothing out the various bumps on the road to maximize the bonuses for top managers.[91]

Not that the OFHEO had noticed any of this. In June 2003, this dutiful servant of the GSEs it was supposed to regulate reported the following to Congress:

> The Enterprises have remained safe and sound through another year of exceptional growth in the housing sector of our economy. In a year when more and more Americans have become homeowners, the public can take comfort in knowing that OFHEO is on the job, doing its part to ensure the strength and vitality of the nation's housing finance system.[92]

It was only after Freddie Mac conceded that its books were bad that the OFHEO caught the scent. Just six months after this glowing report, it was forced to admit of Freddie Mac:

> The company employed a variety of techniques ranging from improper reserve accounts to complex derivative transactions to push earnings into future periods and meet earnings expectations. Freddie Mac cast aside accounting rules, internal controls, disclosure standards, and the public trust in the pursuit of steady earnings growth. The conduct and intentions of the Enterprise were hidden and were revealed only by a chain of events that began when Freddie Mac changed auditors in 2002.[93]

By 2004, it had discovered that Fannie Mae was misbehaving as well.[94] The OFHEO slapped a $125 million civil suit on Freddie Mac, and the SEC upped it by $50 million later on. Fannie Mae was also fined, and reformers in Congress suddenly had some ammunition.[95]

But, amazingly, the GSEs prevailed over the reformers. They basically walked away scot-free, agreeing only to register voluntarily with the SEC. It was at this point that their many friends scattered all throughout the government proved so useful. Senator Bennett, for instance, watered down a receivership proposal in the Senate, and the rest of the GSEs' allies undercut a George W. Bush administration effort to take oversight from HUD and give it to the Treasury Department.[96] Talk about an amazing return on their investment; the GSEs were able to deflect potentially crippling reforms merely for offering a senator's son a job in a local office.

As startling as this was, it does not compare at all to what came next: Fannie and Freddie *still* kept bad books after the accounting scandal. Even with all this scrutiny, hardly anybody noticed that Fannie and Freddie began investing heavily in the subprime market around 2004, and doing so with borrowed money. With interest rates on the rise, mortgage originators could no longer make a profit by refinancing loans, so they started drifting farther into subprime territory, a place where the GSEs' lending standards normally did not take them. Losing market share, Fannie and Freddie decided to loosen their standards to compete with private mortgage-backed security instruments. They hid this from their regulators by not using the common definition of whether a loan was subprime. Instead of evaluating loans on their merits, they labeled as subprime only those loans that were purchased from subprime originators. By the time of the financial crisis, Fannie and Freddie claimed that only about 25 percent of their loans were subprime, but in fact the true number was upward of 40 percent. All in all, there were about twenty-seven million high-risk mortgages nationwide, and the GSEs backed about twelve million of them, with a total exposure of over one trillion dollars.[97]

Congress did not finally act until it was too late. In July 2008, it enacted the Housing and Economic Recovery Act, which did away with the OFHEO and empowered a new, independent agency, the Federal Housing Finance Agency, which had real authority over the GSEs' capital levels and internal controls. It also gave the government some tough receivership powers. Just two months later, with the economic crisis coming into full bloom, Fannie and Freddie went into voluntary conservatorship.[98]

In the final analysis, the only thing that brought down the GSEs was the financial crisis. They had even managed to survive the Enron fallout, so strong was their hold over the political process. If it was not for the subprime bubble finally popping, there is little reason to believe that Fannie Mae and Freddie Mac would not still be using their extensive political clout to mislead their regulators and stockholders, pad their management's bonuses, and take billions from the federal government.

The argument in this chapter is not antiregulation, just as the thesis of this book does not advocate a night-watchman state. The point, rather, is that our system of government often does a very poor job of making sure regulation serves the public interest. That is clearly what we saw here with the financial services industry in general, and Fannie Mae and Freddie Mac in particular. They are all a great example of the problem of regulatory capture, which occurs because the Wilsonian ideal of disinterested bureaucrats is often unachievable in our system. Separating regulators from the political process is very difficult, so the appearance of separation is often worse than useless. As we saw with Fannie Mae and Freddie Mac, and as Olney suggested to his railroad crony about the ICC, they were better off having a toothless regulator vouching for them than having none at all.

Having reached the end of our substantive case, it is important to make a final observation: we have come full circle. The argument of this book started by discussing the corruption inherent to the first two GSEs, the First and Second Banks of the United States. The experience with the Banks, the Second in particular, is eerily similar to the experience with Fannie Mae and Freddie Mac. The government created and sponsored entities that it simply lacked the capacity to control. Politicized and self-interested bank managers abused the public good out of ignorance, vanity, and venality. All the while, the government could practically do nothing about it until it was too late. As a consequence, the economy as a whole was harmed. Some 175 years later, the country let it happen all over again.

The inescapable conclusion from this observation is that we the people have done a very poor job of thinking through our innovations to the original grant of power in the Constitution. How else could we have made the same mistake that our forefathers made, except through ignorance—ignorance of the consequences of such novel institutions, ignorance of the unfortunate experiences of the past, ignorance of the foundations of Madisonian thought. Franklin Delano Roosevelt was not aware of this history when he created Fannie Mae; he just wanted to jump-start the housing market. Johnson was certainly ignorant of this history when he privatized Fannie Mae; he just wanted its obligations off the federal books because the Vietnam War and the Great Society were ballooning the deficit. Similarly, Nixon had no knowledge of history's lessons when he created Freddie Mac as competitor to Fannie Mae. In this way, the leaders were simply following the American people's demand to solve pressing problems without fussing over abstract concerns like whether our system could actually keep these entities in line.

That has been a sad but recurring theme throughout this work. For a country founded by men who were obsessed with how institutions could ensure a truly republican result, the citizenry has been decidedly disinterested in such questions for some two hundred years. The country hardly considers its past institutional mistakes when designing new structures; it hardly revisits core assumptions even when those institutions seem to be functioning poorly; it almost unquestionably accepts ad hoc structures whose provenance is decidedly political; and it is too quick to blame personalities rather than institutions when bad policy is produced.

Put bluntly, it has been decidedly *un*-Madisonian. And it has paid the price again and again, most recently from the damage caused by Fannie Mae and Freddie Mac.

CONCLUSION

A Republic No More

Having now completed our look at the history of corruption, let us return to the theory we outlined in the Introduction. Following Madisonian principles, we have argued that republican government ultimately depends on a proper constitutional design, rather than the virtue of the citizenry. Corruption happens when the government favors a faction or interest at the expense of the public good, and a well-designed government will provide checks and balances to prevent that from happening. However, our country—while gifted a reasonably well-balanced system in 1787—has subsequently unbalanced that regime.

In particular, we have argued that three expansions in governmental power have disrupted the Madisonian balance in four distinct ways. These distortions have produced political corruption, or the practice of advancing factional interests rather than the public good.

The first expansion was a new government power to develop the domestic economy. This was an idea hardly discussed at the Constitutional Convention, and indeed the delegates there voted down a power to charter corporations, but it was a priority for Alexander Hamilton, as exhibited in *Federalist* #11. There, Hamilton talks of a grand "American system" built on commerce, a phrase that inspired a generation of politicians. Since then, both sides of the political aisle have consistently advanced policies that, they claim, would help the nation's economy develop. We saw this in Chapters One and Two, which detailed the First and Second Banks of the United States; in Chapter Five, which looked at Republican efforts in the Gilded Age to spur development; in Chapter Seven, with the New Deal policies to jumpstart the economy; and finally in Chapters Ten and Twelve, as politicians have continued in this tradition to the present day.

Second, we noted that the government seeks to regulate the economy for noneconomic goals. This was a consequence of the social disruption produced by the Industrial Revolution, and with the rise of the progressive movement, regulation became a central theme of federal policy. The Constitution, of course, grants Congress the power to regulate interstate commerce, so the accretion of power here was different than with the First and Second Banks. Even so, the Framers never foresaw the Industrial Revolution and did not build governmental institutions to use a power as vast as the Commerce Clause now justifies. We examined federal regulatory policy in Chapter Seven, with the National Industrial Recovery Act, and in Chapter Thirteen, with financial regulation prior to the 2008 economic collapse.

Third, the government has acquired the power to supply social welfare to the citizenry, either from Washington itself (e.g., Social Security) or via third parties (e.g., the minimum wage). Again, this was a power wholly unanticipated at the Founding. For one thing, the country simply did not have resources to redistribute in such a way. One estimate of gross domestic product in 1789 pegs it at less than $6 billion (in 2014 dollars), or $1,500 per capita.[1] As we saw in Chapter Eleven, Medicare wastes more than that every year through fraudulent or erroneous billing claims. It was only after the fantastic wealth created by the Industrial Revolution that redistribution was possible. Moreover, such an endeavor requires a technical and advanced understanding of bureaucracy; the government of 1789 was really just a handful of clerks, and the science of public administration was nearly one hundred years away. Even so, the government has committed itself to such a program since the New Deal, as we saw in Chapter Seven, with the minimum wage and Social Security; in Chapter Nine, with farm subsidies; and in Chapter Eleven, with Medicare.

These expansions in power have created or exacerbated four weaknesses in our constitutional system. And it is through these four weak spots in the structure that corruption has seeped into the body politic.

First, these powers are too much for Congress to bear. Political scientist Morris Fiorina of Stanford University calls Congress "the keystone of the Washington establishment," an apt phrase.[2] Congress sits atop the governmental edifice and connects everything else together. The public usually thinks of the president occupying this position, but the Framers did not view matters this way, and instead imbued Congress with the sole authority to write the law.

Perhaps if the design of the legislature had been similar to what Hamilton proposed at the Constitutional Convention, or even what James Madison endorsed in the Virginia Plan, Congress would be capable of exercising the enhanced powers we have given it over the years. However, a two-part deal was struck in Philadelphia in 1787: Congress would retain a distinctly parochial flavor, and only be granted a discrete and limited set of powers. This was out of political necessity; popular support at the time for centralization was limited at best, and the Constitution even with this compromise barely won ratification in Virginia, where a defeat would have probably sunk it in New York, and doomed the whole endeavor.

But the politics began to change soon after ratification, as leaders decided that the government had to take on the nationalistic bent that proved so unpopular in 1787. George Washington's administration began the process of adding powers to the government, and thus primarily to Congress. As we have seen, this was a process that did not stop until the original intention was inverted: whereas Congress could once only do what the Constitution expressly allows, it is now essentially free to do whatever the Constitution does not expressly forbid.

And yet, for this expansive view of the institution's power, its structure was hardly altered. It remains, more or less, the same creature it has always been. Sure, the Seventeenth Amendment mandated that senators be popularly elected, but that only tweaked the basic compromise originally hammered out in Philadelphia. The legislature remains rooted in local communities, meaning that for all the powers that Congress possesses to shape the nation as a whole, there is not a single member of the body who can claim the entire populace as his constituency. Therefore, Congress is persistently inclined to address national problems by striking deals to satisfy a critical mass of local factions that have influence over well-placed members.

Per Woodrow Wilson, this tendency is only enhanced by the committee system in Congress, which parcels critical policy decisions out to a handful of members. That incentivizes high demanders—those with a particular interest in ensuring that policies represent a certain worldview—to migrate to the committees that oversee those policies.[3] Moreover, it offers those interest groups that might not be rooted in local communities an easy opportunity to influence public policy. Why bother lobbying 535 members of Congress and contributing to their campaigns when instead you can focus on the dozen or so critically important members on the right committees?

This organization might have been fine for the powers granted Congress in 1787, but it limits the institution's ability to carry out the nationalistic expectations we have for it today. Too often, Congress is inclined to use its nationalistic powers for factional purposes. We have seen this again and again, starting with Thomas Jefferson worrying to Washington about members of Congress being bought off by the Bank of the United States. We also saw it with the logroll that produced the Tariff of Abominations, with the control that Senate bosses had over patronage policy, with tariff policy in the Gilded Age, with New Deal development projects as well as the suspension of civil service laws, with the illiberal deals that cut out poor farmers from the benefits of Social Security and the Fair Labor Standards Act, with abominable farm bill carve-outs, with contemporary pork barrel spending under the guise of economic development, with huge grants of federal money and influence to medical service providers under Medicare, with corporate taxes, and with the ease that Fannie Mae and Freddie Mac purchased legislators. Indeed, if there is one point that this work has demonstrated thoroughly, it is that Congress simply cannot handle these extra powers. Time and again, it has proven itself irresponsible.

Second, the expansion of government power has denuded the force of the republican principle, which basically boils down to the idea that the majority shall rule. Of course, Madison did not think this principle was sufficient to safeguard a republic in the first place, for a majority of people are often quite fractious and, moreover, their representatives often go without rebuke at the ballot box for misbehavior. Thus, Madison was committed to a variety of additional safeguards, which we reviewed at length in the Introduction.

Wilson, as we saw in Chapter Six, was no fan of these ancillary protections, or at least thought many had outlived their usefulness. One of the problems Wilson identified was that our system of checks and balances inhibits the ability of the people to determine who is responsible for bad policies. The organization of Congress into a committee system, which was not embedded in the Constitution but quickly developed in the legislature, further undermines the determination of responsibility. This is a fair criticism, but only if we admit the context, which is that the powers and policy domain of the national government had increased enormously between the development of the original schema and Wilson's day. The Madisonian system would have made it difficult but not impossible for the people to determine responsibility for lousy policy in 1790, but often prohibitively difficult by 1890. The government simply has so much power over so many minute aspects of life for the people to know exactly who is responsible for any of the myriad policies it produces.

Without such knowledge, the relief that the republican principle can supply is limited indeed. If voters operate under such severe conditions of uncertainty that they cannot possibly tell who did what, then how will legislators be deterred from corruption? In some instances, a random development may serve to highlight corruption or gross inefficiency; the Watergate scandal comes to mind. But as a general rule, if the people simply lack the means to keep their representatives honest, the latter will possess great leeway to do as they please.

Some of this problem is due to the evolving complexity of society itself. In other words, if government had stayed within the boundaries originally intended by the Framers, we would still face a version of this problem. Take, for instance, the postal service, which the Constitution explicitly authorizes. The internal development of the country has enormously influenced the Post Office, whose organizational structure had to become much more complex. That makes it harder for the layperson to understand, and thus to keep Congress accountable for its management.

Yet it is undeniable that government activism has exacerbated this tendency. Indeed, we have confronted this fact again and again. Consider Nelson Aldrich's manipulation of the sugar tariff. Consider also the development of a congressional logroll during the New Deal to solidify the political position of the Democratic Party under the guise of combating unemployment, the generous rents provided to large farmers through the farm bill, the provision of inefficient and inequitable corporate tax expenditures, the granting to the American Medical Association the ability to write the reimbursement rates for Medicare Part B, the perfidious connection between earmarks, and the financial interests of legislators. This sort of gamesmanship all arose because of expansions in the scope of governmental authority, and it persists in part because the public simply lacks the requisite knowledge to isolate the culprits and throw them out of office. Indeed, more often than not the public did not even know that these particular corrupt acts occurred at all.

Of course, the Framers were not naïve about the potential problems that Congress might create, nor about the limits of the republican principle. Quite the contrary, they believed that legislatures were the most dangerous institutions for good republican governance, even if they might also be the most necessary for it, and that the public could at best provide an uncertain check against them. This is part of the reason why they empowered a president, who was supposed to be somewhat free from the political bric-à-brac, to keep Congress in line with his veto pen. Unfortunately, this check has been undermined by the democratization of the presidency, which leads to our third weak spot. This was not a consequence of the newly expansive powers of the government, but rather a separate institutional change that interacted with these new powers to produce corruption.

Granted, the idea of a democratic president being a problem sounds, at best, a little tone deaf to the modern ear. We democratized the institution in the 1820s and have never looked back because in this country we celebrate the rule of the people. Fair enough, but consider the ripple effects that this has had. Two issues in particular stand out. For starters, democratizing the presidency has meant thrusting the occupant into the political battle, where he must form an electoral coalition to win and retain his office. There is nothing to say that this coalition must reflect the national interest, even if it may amount to a numerical majority. Thus, whereas the Constitution envisions the president as separated from politics and (hopefully) free to look out for the public good, the actual occupant of the White House instead has an electoral incentive to place factional interests above the collective interest.

Moreover, a democratized president gave rise to permanent, national political parties. Acquiring the top office requires a coordinated effort across all regions and states to capture the White House, something that state-based or regional factions were simply incapable of doing. So, national parties formed to unite local politicos in pursuit of the White House. What this has further done is cement an alliance between the president and his partisan allies in Congress, something that runs contrary to the original vision sketched out by the Framers. In the initial schema, the president and the Congress were supposed to be rivals, locked in a battle that, so the hope went, would ultimately produce public-spirited policy. Yet a president who owes his election to a party effort, and more importantly whose reelection will require a similar effort, can ill afford to check his partisan friends in the legislature in such a way. This provides leverage for the factional forces that dominate Congress. They can say to a president: push too hard against us, and the full party effort might not be forthcoming.

Thus, democratizing the presidency has often had the opposite purpose that its advocates have long and loudly proclaimed. Andrew Jackson was the first to assert that the president spoke for the people at large, but altering the incentive structures inherent to the office now means that, quite often, he speaks for fractious interests that want to advance themselves at the expense of the public good.

This makes the presidency a breeding ground for corruption, which we saw with Jackson himself. Convinced he was the avatar of the national will, he nevertheless frequently bent the policy needle in ways that undermined the public good, as in his Bank War, or assaulted the rule of law, as with his removal of the Native Americans to the west. Subsequent eighteenth century presidents may not have misbehaved as spectacularly as Old Hickory, but their continuation and extension of his patronage system meant that they all disobeyed their oaths of office. The laws of the United States were not faithfully executed; instead, under the patronage regime, public administration suffered so that the partisan allies of the president, especially those in the Senate, could profit.

In recent years, the problem with the presidency is not so much what the occupant of the office has done as what he has not done. In a few instances, as with the New Dealers' use of patronage to rebuild the Democratic Party, the president has been a direct party to the corruption we have examined. More often than not, however, it is the Congress that behaves corruptly with the tacit support of the president. After all, the vast fortune wasted on farm subsidies and tax expenditures, the naked payouts to doctors and hospitals under Medicare's payment schedule updates, and the obscenely wasteful sums spent on pork barrel development projects could be stopped by a presidential veto that never seems to come. Instead, we have seen presidents try at times to bring rationality to these decidedly irrational programs—Dwight Eisenhower with the farm bill; George W. Bush with Fannie Mae and Freddie Mac—but usually give up upon discovering the strength of congressional resistance, deciding instead that it is not in the political interests of the president to pick a fight with his allies in Congress.

The fourth and final weak spot created by the growth of government is the array of constitutionally ad hoc institutions that have arisen. There are two types of such institutions, and their challenges are different, so let's take each in turn.

On the one hand, there are institutions created with public and private purposes. In this study, the First and Second Banks of the United States, Fannie Mae, and Freddie Mac fit this description. The government gave these institutions special protections, exemptions, and benefits, but did not assume direct control of them, instead preferring to oversee them. The problem with these institutions, as we saw, was that the private interests that controlled them used a portion of their federal spoils to persuade the government not to execute its oversight duties diligently. Jefferson, as we saw, fretted over favorable deals given to members of Congress by the Bank. With the Second Bank, Nicholas Biddle was not afraid to use the bounty generated in part from the federal subsidy to lobby important people like Daniel Webster and Henry Clay. Fannie and Freddie, as Franklin Raines put it, managed their political risk "with the same intensity" that they managed their economic risks. In all of these cases, what occurred was, per Madison, the development of a "pretorian band of the Government, at once its tool & its tyrant." The beneficence of the federal government was used to induce members of Congress and the executive to look the other way as these institutions put their private interests ahead of the public purposes they were chartered to fulfill. Fortunately, the Bank of the United States was reasonably well run, thanks to the excellence of Hamilton and later Albert Gallatin, but the same cannot always be said of the Second Bank, or Fannie and Freddie, all of which created economic hardship of some sort of another.

On the other hand, there is the massive federal bureaucracy, possessing only a public purpose and tasked with implementing the laws written by Congress and approved by the president. Of course, the bureaucracy has always existed in some form or another. Yet when the government first began it was just a couple dozen clerks; today, it numbers in the millions. This is not simply a numerical difference; it is a qualitative one as well. The bureaucracy is nominally part of the executive branch, but its operations are so massive and far flung that it is in essence now a fourth branch of the government, with its own unique relationship to the other branches.

Wilson, most prominent among progressive thinkers, thought that this would be a good thing. Let the president and Congress hammer out the broad strokes of public policy, he argued, but then empower an independent bureaucracy to employ a science of administration to ensure that the laws are implemented effectively and impartially. In fairness, this ideal is often realized in our system today, at least in areas where interest groups do not see much of an opportunity for private gain. However, where such incentives do exist, we have seen how the bureaucracy can fall prey to factionalism and corruption. The mechanisms have varied over the years, but the result is the same: interest groups can and do capture bureaucracies, transforming them from public-spirited enterprises into agents of private gain. This happened with the first such regulatory agency, the Interstate Commerce Commission. It happened with the National Recovery Administration, as well as with various regulatory commissions created by the New Deal. Most recently, it happened with the vast array of bodies tasked with overseeing Wall Street.

Both the government-sponsored enterprises and the bureaucracy are ad hoc because there was not a great deal of thought given to how these entities would fit into the constitutional schema. Instead, each was built with an eye to solving whatever problem was pressing at the time of its creation. This makes them quite susceptible to becoming the tools of private interests; short-sighted institutional designs create weaknesses that such forces can and do exploit. Again, this certainly does not happen all the time. Much of the bureaucracy is "boring" precisely because it does what it is supposed to do, and many of the government-sponsored enterprises, like the Federal Agricultural Mortgage Corporation (Farmer Mac), behave reasonably well. Still, as we have seen, the potential for corruption is certainly present, and it has been realized in many instances, with often disastrous consequences for the public good.

So, to take all of this together, what do we have? Put simply, we have the thesis of this book: the growth of governmental power beyond its initial boundaries, without corresponding shifts in its institutions, has altered the original design of the constitutional system; it has disrupted the Madisonian schema of checks and balances in ways that empower factions to achieve their preferred policies at the expense of the people at large. In other words, it creates the opportunity for corruption.

Critical histories such as this must inevitably confront a simple question: so what? If one is going to criticize the practices of government, there must be some kind of net harm that this behavior creates. And, in the case of political corruption, it is fair to wonder if maybe this is all just the necessary cost of doing business.

That was basically Hamilton's point to Jefferson and John Adams during the dinner conversation mentioned in Chapter One. He said of the British Constitution: "purge it of it's corruption, and give to it's popular branch equality of representation, & it would become an impracticable government: as it stands at present, with all it's supposed defects, it is the most perfect government which ever existed." Hamilton had in mind the use of corruption as a tool for great leaders to induce the self-interested to act on behalf of the public good, but maybe there is a larger point implicit in the background: this is just the way things work. If we want a government that does bold, important things, we must suffer a little corruption.

One also could argue further that, on balance, life has dramatically improved in the United States even as corruption has persisted. To begin, the economy has grown by leaps and bounds since the earliest days of the country; the Industrial Revolution changed everything, raising standards of living for everybody, in due course. So, why should we be so upset about corruption? It does not seem to have inhibited our prosperity; maybe it is in fact a good feature of government. The wheels need to be greased to make things better, under this line of thinking. Furthermore, the country has become much more liberal than the earliest days of the Founding. The Framers talked a boastful game about freedom and equality, but it was only subsequent, "corrupt" generations that ended slavery, granted women the right to vote, put an end to Jim Crow, and finally guaranteed civil and voting rights to African Americans. Why should we celebrate a republican vision that would systematically exclude such a large percentage of the country? And how bad can corruption be with all these groups now welcomed into the body politic?

Take all this together, and one might say that corruption is a problem—in the third world. Here, it is at most a nuisance. The United States is prosperous and open. Corruption has not impeded this, and indeed maybe it has helped.

This rejoinder may at first glance appear persuasive, but it has some serious problems. For starters, economic growth could have happened just as easily with a more republican form of government, and it probably would have been more equitable. As we have noted at many points, our objection is not with these governmental powers per se, but rather with the aggrandizement of power without a revision of the structure. So, the real debate is not whether we should have wanted the government to promote industrial development, for instance, but how it should have gone about doing that. And it did not do it terribly well. Recall our discussion of Gilded Age economic policies in Chapter Five; yes, the economy was developing on the whole, but there were widespread regional disparities that governmental policy exacerbated. A truly republican form of government would have implemented an updated version of Clay's American System, something that facilitated growth while also creating a balance between regions and interests.

A similar argument applies to contemporary political economy. While we gladly admit that the country is extremely wealthy, it still suffers from resource constraints. There are a multitude of public problems that go unaddressed or underaddressed because there simply is not the money to do anything about them. Meanwhile, how much does the government waste every year on Medicare or farm subsidies? How many worthwhile development projects were shunted aside so politicians could use earmarks to provide kickbacks to their wealthy supporters? How much did their indulgence of Fannie Mae and Freddie Mac contribute to the economic collapse in 2008? How wasteful is the politically inspired design of the tax code? Corruption too often engenders gross inefficiency in public expenditures, and as long as the country faces resource constraints, it is indeed a problem, regardless of the size of the gross domestic product.

As for the liberalization of the body politic, there is no doubt that this has been a positive development. And indeed, a truly republican government depends foremost upon the republican principle, which cannot be realized without the full and open participation of all interests in society. So, excluding women and minorities diminished the quality of republican governance for generations. Even in its ideal form, the republic outlined by Jefferson and Madison would have thus been sorely lacking because so many citizens would have been on the outside looking in.

Still, return to Madison's take on the republican principle, which we reviewed in the Introduction. He thought it a necessary, but insufficient condition of true republicanism. The state governments of the 1780s were some of the most democratized and liberal that the world had ever seen up until that point, and yet they were hotbeds of corruption. Madison understood that good political institutions were necessary to channel public opinion in the appropriate directions. Without them, the body politic was susceptible to corrupt rule by a fractious majority, even if the franchise was as liberal as it had ever been.

These insights have relevance today. Yes, the right to vote has been offered to every nonfelonious citizen eighteen and over. Yes, civil rights are protected today. Yes, society is more open than ever. But has this made the common good easier to achieve? Based on our analysis in the second half of this work, it is hard to argue that politicians now steer the government with an eye toward an enhanced and comprehensive vision of the public interest. Instead, it looks more and more like the massive policy logroll has simply been expanded to ensnare more factions. Everybody can vote, sure; everybody can organize, yes; but the end result is not so much an opportunity to inform the public good, but rather a chance to lobby for your own slice of the pie. Indeed, former Michigan governor George Romney may have put it best when he said:

> What did we have originally when the Constitution was written? They asked (Benjamin) Franklin, "What have you given us?" He said, "We've given you a republic, if you can keep it." Now, we didn't keep it. . . . We've

got a special interest democracy—a political process that is dominated by the special interests.[4]

That is a very apt phrase: "special interest democracy." The political process may be more open than ever before, but the payoff to the new invitees is an opportunity to mobilize into interest groups to get a piece of the action. A true republic, on the other hand, would bring all viewpoints into the body politic, and from these diverse views find the policies that benefit the citizenry as a whole. Our system does not do that.

And this is not what the people want; for all of the openness of our system of government today, confidence in it is at an all-time low. Consider the following public opinion data from the American National Elections Study (ANES). For decades, the ANES has asked respondents whether they trust the federal government to do what is right. In 1958, 73 percent answered "most of the time" or "just about always," whereas only 23 percent said "some of the time" or "never." By 1980, the numbers had shifted dramatically: only 25 percent said they trusted it most of the time or just about always. In 2012, just 12 percent of the public expressed such confidence.[5] The Gallup poll finds an even more disturbing trend. In 1972, 70 percent of respondents said they trusted the government to solve domestic problems either a "great deal" or a "fair amount." By 2013, those numbers had fallen to just 43 percent. Per Gallup, Congress's reputation has suffered the most: in 1972, 71 percent trusted it a great deal or a fair amount, but by 2013, just 34 percent did.[6]

More often than not, people are wont to blame particular politicians in office for the nation's troubles, but this decline in public consent of the government has occurred across generations. That suggests a systemic, rather than a personal problem. What could that be? Why is it that, with so much democracy, the people think the government still does not serve the interests of the governed? The answers are surely many and varied, but it seems indubitable that this is, at least in part, a public acknowledgment of the problem of corruption.

And so we return to one of the earliest metaphors we used to define corruption: it is like cancer or wood rot. It does not stay in one place in the government; it spreads throughout the system. When a faction succeeds in getting what it wants at the expense of the public good, it is only encouraged to push its advantage. By the same token, politicians who aid them and reap rewards for it have an incentive to do it some more, and to improve their methods to maximize their payoffs. Moreover, these successes inspire other politicians and factions to try their hands at raiding the treasury to see if they can do it, too. Thus, a vicious cycle is created that erodes public faith in government, which further contributes to the cycle. When people stop believing that anything can be done to keep the government in line, they stop paying attention carefully or maybe cease participating altogether. Ultimately, the public is supposed to be the steward of the government, but how well can it perform that task when it no longer believes doing so is worth its while? How does a democratic government prosper over the long term if the citizenry does not trust the government to represent its interests? How will that not result in anything but the triumph of factionalism over the common good?

The Declaration of Independence opens with this bold statement:

> We hold these truths to be self-evident, that all men are created equal, that they are endowed by their Creator with certain inalienable Rights, that among these are Life, Liberty, and the pursuit of Happiness.—That to secure these rights, Governments are instituted among Men, deriving their just powers from the consent of the governed.

This idea infuses the Constitution itself, which eschews the concept of mixed estates. The legitimacy of our government is supposed to derive from the people, and the people alone, who consent to the government because, they believe, it represents their interests. In its ultimate form, corruption eviscerates that sacred notion. The people stop believing that the government represents their interests, and the government in turn begins to operate based upon something other than consent.

Put simply, corruption strikes at the heart of our most cherished beliefs and assumptions about republican government. That makes it extremely dangerous to the body politic, regardless of what the Bureau of Economic Analysis says about the rate of GDP growth.

This brings us to the final question, which all true republicans—liberal or conservative, Democrat or Republican—must surely be asking themselves: *what in the world do we do about this mess?* A comprehensive answer is outside our purview here, as this work has been dedicated to detailing the nature of the problem. Still, we can make some cursory suggestions about how to reform our system of government.

To begin, we must note that several forms of corruption have been dealt with successfully. The patronage regime fell to pieces after the murder of James Garfield; it made a brief recovery during the Franklin Delano Roosevelt administration, but malfeasance in managing the Works Progress Administration prompted congressional outrage and led to the Hatch Acts. Similarly, the old tariff regime collapsed after World War II. The combination of the Smoot-Hawley disaster, the economic gains from trade to be realized after the war, and an internationalist, bipartisan consensus on foreign policy led to a largely free trade regime that holds to this day. Sure, trade-related favoritism and kickbacks still happen these days, but by and large tariffs are no way for politicians to reward interest groups. Even congressional recalcitrance to close military bases has been dealt with via the Base Realignment and Closure (BRAC) Commission. Importantly, in these three cases the changes were vouchsafed by substantial reforms of governing structures, consistent with Madisonian thinking that it is not ethics but rules that secure good government.

The problem, however, is that reform is often like trying to stop water from rolling downhill. Block one pathway from developing, you all but guarantee another will form. The tariff regime—an inefficient, crooked, and overcomplicated mess—was replaced by the income tax—which today is an inefficient, crooked, and overcomplicated mess. The patronage regime may be no more, and politicians no longer have the capacity to leverage government employment for reelection purposes, but the interest group society that has sprung up since the New Deal, and has since been embedded in our campaign finance laws, is easily as pernicious, if not more so, as it gives legislative conflicts of interests a legal protection. Politicians can now raise campaign cash hand over fist from factions they regulate, and hardly anybody looks askance. For a politician seeking reelection, that is infinitely more useful in the modern age than controlling who gets employed in a local road work crew. And what of the BRAC Commission? As we noted in Chapter Ten, it still protects important incumbents. Moreover, it is probably no coincidence that the practice of military earmarking really took off after members lost control over protecting local bases.

And so it goes down the line. Corruption will eventually manifest itself in other ways, just as happened when we ditched the tariff and embraced the income tax. And it all gets back to that essential disconnect between our expectations of this government and its capacity to meet those expectations. Absent either a tempering of the citizenry's expectations of governmental capacity, or a substantial reform of the structures of government, corruption will undoubtedly reappear.

Unfortunately, a proper rebalancing of the Madisonian scales seems highly improbable. This country has not had a serious conversation about the right mixture of government authority and institutions since the Founding, and it is very likely that—whereas a tenuous coalition barely existed then—nothing of the sort exists today. Indeed, the main political divide that separates right from left has much to do with these sorts of questions. Conservatives want smaller government without adjusting institutions; liberals prefer the inverse. Political polarization is easily the greatest it has been since World War II, so a broad-based reimagining of the constitutional balance seems fanciful in the extreme.

So, is the only option pessimism? Is the book in your hands in fact an obituary for the American republic? We think not. While we may not have a Madisonian moment within our grasp, we may yet be capable of a Mugwump moment.

Recall from Chapter Four that the Mugwumps grew out of the Liberal Republican movement that opposed Ulysses S. Grant, and ultimately aligned with ethically above-board Democrats like Grover Cleveland. Their goal was not to reinvent the American system of government but rather to curb the worst excesses of the regime.

Perhaps that is possible for America today. We the people may not be able to realign the Madisonian system, redesigning it so that it well and truly breaks "the violence of faction." But we might be able, for a time, to pass some sensible reforms that harass the factions, disrupt their pathways of corruption, and buy the nation a respite from the rampant graft that afflicts it. Yes, absent enduring structural reforms, pressure groups will find new ways to misuse government power; but perhaps we can throw them off their game for a little while.

Perhaps the model is not so much the Constitutional Convention of 1787, but rather the Pendleton Civil Service Act of 1883 or the Tax Reform Act of 1986. Neither solved any problems permanently, but both forced interest groups on their heels for a time.

What keeps such a coalition from forming? The answer is the ideological character of today's politics, in particular the two-party system.

Since the beginning of democratic politics, Americans may be sorted into three groups: the uninterested, the interested, and the disinterested. The uninterested constitute the vast majority of the citizenry; most of them vote, at least for president, but they do not pay a lot of attention. They either support a party in a knee-jerk fashion, or vote based on the ebb and flow of the business cycle. Above all, they need to be led by somebody else. The interested are those who are actively involved in politics for the private benefits they derive. Numerically, they amount to a tiny share of the country, but they plow enormous resources into politics to ensure that their favored policies are promoted. The disinterested have been the real fount of all reform movements. These are the people who take seriously the duties of republican citizenship, even though they derive no private gains from it.

The great reform movements of the eighty years between the Civil War and the Great Depression—the Mugwumps, the Populists, and the Progressives—all endeavored to unite disinterested citizens across the political spectrum against the interested. The problem today is that the disinterested citizens are hotly divided against one another—conservatives are the staunchest Republicans, liberals the staunchest Democrats. They are more inclined to blame one another for the nation's problems than to point the finger at the rampant corruption that the interested perpetuate today.

Yet for all their divisions on the ideological issues that are so salient, do they not all share a desire for government to be administered disinterestedly? Review again the issues discussed in the second half of this book—farm subsidies, the pork barrel, waste in Medicare, corporate tax fraud, and regulatory capture. Are not conservatives and liberals equally offended by the outrages we have catalogued here?

We think the answer is yes.

The problem, however, is that the disinterested have been set against one another via the two-party system. It is often said these days that ideologues have captured the two parties, and that this is a bad thing. Maybe so, but in our opinion it is worse that the two parties have captured the ideologues. What this has done is muted the influence of the disinterested to an enormous extent. They are set against one another—rather than allying around shared goals—and, moreover, they now co-mingle with interested pressure groups in either party. Thus, their ability to fight corruption is effectively nullified.

We end up with a perverse result: conservatives complain about corruption that favors the Democratic Party; liberals about corruption that favors the Republican Party; and neither side seems able to see that they are in fact complaining about the same things!

This is where the Mugwump movement can teach us important lessons. For how intensely the partisan battles burn today, they cannot hold a candle to the divisions of the 1870s and 1880s, when terrible memories of the Civil War remained embedded in the public mind. And yet the Mugwumps represented an alliance between one-time partisan foes who had the courage to break from the corrupt elements of both parties. Republican reformers broke from James G. Blaine's Half-Breeds and Grant's Stalwarts; Democratic reformers rejected the criminality of Tammany Hall. Together, they twice elected a genuinely decent president—Cleveland—and were instrumental in breaking apart the old patronage regime.

Why could that not happen today? Could not disinterested liberals and conservatives put aside temporarily their eternal war, for instance, on the top marginal tax rate to focus on cleaning out the corruption in the corporate tax code? How about suspending temporarily their disagreements about food stamps, and in general the interminable debate about social welfare for the poor, to cut flagrant corporate welfare from the farm bill? Similarly, they may disagree about the proper scope of military spending, but surely none of them prefers tax dollars be wasted on strategically useless but politically salient defense projects. They may also diverge on the extent to which the government should regulate financial markets, but none wants the financial services industry to capture regulators.

A full-blown reform agenda is beyond the scope of these concluding remarks, but in general it seems that there could be widespread agreement between disinterested conservatives and liberals in the following way: reduce the extent to which government favors the wealthy and well-connected. Government would grow smaller (a priority for conservatives) and would also stop facilitating social and economic inequality (a priority for liberals). To reappropriate that old phrase from Herbert Croly, perhaps this would merely be employing Jeffersonian means for Jeffersonian ends.

It would require strong leadership from certain quarters of both sides. Political inertia is powerful, and there is a generation-long sense of enmity that exists between conservatives and liberals. But, again, it compares not at all to the mutual animosities among Democrats and Republicans in the Gilded Age. If the disinterested on both sides could come together then around a sensible reform agenda, why can't we?

Acknowledgments

.

THIS BOOK would not have been possible without the assistance of many people, to whom I owe a debt of gratitude.

First, thanks to my wife, Lindsay. The love of my life, she has been my rock for more than a decade of marriage, and another decade before that. Without her love and support, this book would never have happened.

Next, thanks to my parents, John and Lyn, for their never-ending encouragement. They also graciously babysat our two young children—often at the last minute!—to help me meet my deadlines. Thanks also to my brother Eric, a fellow night owl who was often around during the wee hours when I needed to work through a difficult issue in the book.

Thanks to my mother-in-law, Kaye McKenzie, who likewise has a fount of support (and babysitting!) during the writing of this book.

Thanks to Roger Kimball, Katherine Wong, and all the folks at Encounter Books for their able assistance in making this idea become a reality. Similar thanks to Chris Crochetière and Heidi Grauel for their thoughtful edits. Thanks as well to Jonathan Last for putting in a good word for me with Encounter at the beginning, and for providing me encouragement whenever my spirits flagged.

Several very smart people were gracious enough to examine carefully an early manuscript of this project, and provide feedback. Many thanks for that to Jeffrey Anderson, Matt Continetti, Matthew Mitchell, Mike Needham, and Jean Yarbrough. Additionally, I am in debt to Gerry Daly, Sean Davis, Brandon Finnigan, Josh Jordan, Dan McLaughlin, Neil Stevens, Sean Trende, and Dan Wilson for providing helpful suggestions at critical junctures in this book's production.

Thanks to Bill Kristol, for whom I have had the privilege of working for four years. Gracious and forbearing as I took on this side project, he has also provided me with a wonderful forum to work through ideas that ultimately made it into this book.

Thanks to Yuval Levin and Meghan Clyne for letting me develop an early version of the Medicare chapter in the pages of *National Affairs*.

Thanks to Robert George, Brad Wilson, and Ch'nel Duke of the James Madison Program at Princeton University. They graciously invited me to give a talk last year, which formed the basis of the Introduction.

Thanks to Adam Bellow and Byrd Leavell, who helped me work through an early version of what this book ultimately became.

Finally, a note on the dedication. Lindsay's father, Dan McKenzie, passed away during the production of this book. He was my father-in-law and my friend. Always a source of insight and encouragement, he still was very excited about this project even as his health failed him, and never hesitated to offer a kind word. He is dearly missed.

Notes

Chapter One

1. Montesquieu, *The Spirit of the Laws*, ed. Anne M. Cohler, Basia C. Miller, and Harold S. Stone. (Cambridge: Cambridge University Press, 2010), 156–166.

2. Carl J. Richard, *The Founders and the Classics: Greece, Rome, and the American Enlightenment* (Cambridge, MA: Harvard University Press, 1994), 122.

3. Thomas Jefferson, *Jefferson: Autobiography, Notes on the State of Virginia, Public and Private Papers, Addresses, Letters*, ed. Merrill D. Peterson (New York: The Library of America, 1984), 19.

4. Joseph J. Ellis, *His Excellency, George Washington* (New York: Vintage Books, 2004), 141–143.

5. Samuel Eliot Morison, Henry Steele Commager, and William E. Leuchtenburg, *The Growth of the American Republic*, Volume 1, 7th edition (New York: Oxford University Press, 1980), 227–239.

6. Morison, Commager, and Leuchtenburg, *The Growth of the American Republic*, 229. For a good overview of Madison's early political career, see Richard Brookheiser, *Alexander Hamilton: American* (New York: Free Press, 2000), 22–50.

7. See Gordon S. Wood, *The Creation of the American Republic, 1776–1787* (Chapel Hill, NC: The University of North Carolina Press, 1998), 472.

8. James Madison, *Writings*, ed. Jack N. Rakove (New York: The Library of America, 1999), 161.

9. Madison, *Writings*, 69–80.

10. Madison, *Writings*, 79.

11. See Brookheiser, *Alexander Hamilton*, 13–50.

12. Thomas Jefferson, "Anas," in *The Works of Thomas Jefferson*, Federal edition, ed. Paul Leicester Ford (New York: G.P. Putnam's Sons, 1904–1905), http://oll.libertyfund.org/index.php?option=com_staticxt&staticfile=show.php&title=1734.

13. See Edward J. Larson and Michael P. Winship, *The Constitutional Convention: A Narrative History from the Notes of James Madison* (New York: The Modern Library, 2005), 47–51.

14. Iseult Honohan, *Civic Republicanism* (London: Routledge, 2002), 29.

15. Herbert J. Storing, *What the Anti-Federalists Were For: The Political Thought of the Opponents of the Constitution* (Chicago: University of Chicago Press, 1981), 17–28, 121–124. See also Jackson Turner Main, *The Anti-Federalists: Critics of the Constitution, 1781–1788* (New York: W. W. Norton & Company, 1961), 121–130.

16. See Garrett Ward Sheldon, *The Political Philosophy of James Madison* (Baltimore, MD: The Johns Hopkins University Press, 2001), 37–38.

17. Wood, *Creation of the American Republic*, 501–502.

18. Madison, *Writings*, 78–79. See also Honohan, *Civic Republicanism*, 103–104.

19. See Wood, *Creation of the American Republic*, 494–511.

20. Madison, *Writings*, 297.

21. Madison, *Writings*, 160, 161.

22. See Honohan, *Civic Republicanism*, 39. See also J. G. A. Pocock, *The Machiavellian Moment: Florentine Political Thought and the Atlantic Republican Tradition* (Princeton: Princeton University Press, 1975), 522.

23. See Wood, *Creation of the American Republic*, 606–610. See also David F. Epstein, *The Political Philosophy of the Federalist* (Chicago: The University of Chicago Press, 1984), 4.

24. Gordon Wood calls this the "end of classical politics." See Wood, *Creation of the American* Republic, 606–610. See also Honohan, *Civic Republicanism*, 104–105.

25. Ray Nothstine, "Madison the Politician," *Action Institute Power Blog*, February 3, 2012, http://blog.acton.org/archives/29084-madison-the-politician.html.

26. Nicholas P. Trist, "Memoranda from Montpellier on September 27, 1834," in *The Records of the Federal Convention of 1787*, ed. Max Farrand (New Haven: Yale University Press, 1911), Volume 3, http://oll.libertyfund.org/?option=com_staticxt&staticfile=show.php%3Ftitle=1785&Itemid=27.

27. See Colleen A. Sheehan, *James Madison and the Spirit of Republican Self-Government* (Cambridge: Cambridge University Press, 2009), 6–9. See also Lance Banning, *The Sacred Fire of Liberty: James Madison & the Founding of the Federal Republic* (Ithaca, NY: Cornell University Press, 1995), 295–296, 331–332, 371.

28. Alexander Hamilton, *Hamilton: Writings*, ed. Joanne B. Freeman (New York: The Library of America, 2001), 202.

29. Hamilton, *Writings*, 205.

30. Hamilton, *Writings*, 206–207.

31. Jefferson, "Anas," in *The Works*.

32. See Michael P. Federici, *The Political Philosophy of Alexander Hamilton* (Baltimore, MD: The Johns Hopkins University Press, 2012), 70.

33. See Sheehan, *James Madison*, 118–119; Pocock, *The Machiavellian Moment*, 522–531; and Lance Banning, *The Jeffersonian Persuasion: Evolution of a Party Ideology* (Ithaca, NY: Cornell University Press, 1978), 47–48. Madison argued that Montesquieu's system of government "can never be defended against the criticisms which it has encountered. (He) was in politics not a Newton or a Locke, who established immortal systems, the one in matter, the other in mind. He was in his particular science what Bacon was in universal science: He lifted the veil from the venerable errors which enslaved opinion, and pointed the way to those luminous truths of which he had but a glimpse himself." Madison, *Writings*, 510.

34. Banning, *Jeffersonian Persuasion*, 127.

35. The possible exception might be Edmund Randolph, named the nation's first attorney general. The governor of Virginia at the time of the Constitutional Convention, the Virginia Plan was submitted under his name. He was a strong nationalist but ultimately abstained from signing the document submitted to the states because he feared it lacked sufficient checks and balances. Nevertheless, he changed his mind as a delegate to the Virginia ratifying convention and ultimately supported the document,

for fear of leaving Virginia on the outside looking in. See Larson and Winship, *Constitutional Convention*, 175.

36. Hamilton, *Writings*, 208.

37. Murray N. Rothbard, *A History of Money and Banking in the United States: The Colonial Era to World War II* (Auburn, AL: Ludwig von Mises Institute, 2005), 47–62.

38. Morison, Commager, and Leuchtenburg, *The Growth of the American Republic*, 239.

39. Hamilton, *Writings*, 531, 532.

40. Hamilton's interest in having the national government assume the state debts had a civic element to it, in addition to the economic benefits. He argues, "If all the public creditors receive their dues from one source, distributed with an equal hand, their interest will be the same. And having the same interest, they will unite in the support of the fiscal arrangements of the government. . . . These circumstances combined one sure to the revenue laws a more ready and more satisfactory execution." Alexander Hamilton, *Alexander Hamilton: A Biography in His Own Words*, ed. Mary-Jo Kline (New York: Newsweek, 1973), 226. The issue of state assumption drew regional criticisms, especially from Virginia, which had paid off its debts. But the real sticking point turned out to be how to repay the debt. Hamilton wanted to pay the current holders of the debt, many of whom were speculators who had bought debt from soldiers, their widows, and poor farmers for pennies on the dollar. The Republicans (who by this point had not yet solidified their critique) reacted quite negatively to this, though they failed ultimately to offer a practical alternative. See Banning, *Jeffersonian Persuasion*, 143–144.

41. Hamilton, *Writings*, 535.

42. See Hamilton, *Writings*, 575–612.

43. See Hamilton, *Writings*, 647–734.

44. John P. Kaminski, ed., *The Founders on the Founders: Word Portraits from the American Revolutionary Era* (Charlottesville, VA: The University of Virginia Press, 2008), 199.

45. See Federici, *Political Philosophy*, 199–213; and John C. Miller, *Alexander Hamilton and the Growth of the New Nation* (Piscataway, NJ: Transaction Publishers, 2003), 253–254.

46. See Banning, *Jeffersonian Persuasion*, 129–140; and Ron Chernow, *Alexander Hamilton* (New York: Penguin Books, 2004), 295.

47. Chernow, *Alexander Hamilton*, 363.

48. See Banning, *Jeffersonian Persuasion*, 204.

49. In fact, Jefferson facilitated the process of passing the assumption plan through Congress; it was only later that Jefferson and Madison would grasp the implications of Hamilton's economic program, and Jefferson in particular would come to regret the part he played in getting an early item of it implemented. See the "Anas" in Jefferson, *The Works*.

50. See, for instance, Philip Freneau's not-so-subtly titled, "Rules for Changing a Limited Republican Government into an Unlimited Hereditary One." (Philip Freneau, "Rules for Changing a Limited Republican Government into an Unlimited Hereditary One," http://www.constitution.org/cmt/freneau/republic2monarchy.htm.) Even the normally sober and judicious Madison suspected a creeping monarchy. In an anonymous essay written for the *National Gazette* in December 1791, Madison worried that the centralization of power in the executive would pave the way for a hereditary government. See Madison, *Writings*, 498–500. The way Republicans connected otherwise disconnected items together to "perceive" a grand monarchical plot also looks somewhat

silly in historical retrospect. For instance, Pennsylvania senator William Maclay was convinced as early as July 1789 that there was a plot lurking, with Vice President John Adams at its head, to implement "high toned government" that centralized power in the presidency. A central piece of data? Adams's extravagant title for President Washington! See Banning, *Jeffersonian Persuasion*, 119–121.

51. See Pocock, *Machiavellian Moment*, 529–531. This was also a lesson they drew from the Roman republic, which they believed had become corrupted in the first century BC, resulting in the rise of the emperors. See Richard, *Founders and the Classics*, 87–88.

52. Madison suggested giving Congress the power "to grant charters of incorporation in cases where the public good may require them, and the authority of a single State may be incompetent" to the Convention on August 18, 1787. On September 14, it was voted down by the Convention. See Madison, *Writings*, Vol. 4.

53. See Banning, *Sacred Fire*, 331–332. See also Madison, *Writings*, 480–490; and Hamilton, *Writings*, 613–646.

54. See Jack N. Rakove, *James Madison and the Creation of the American Republic* (New York: Pearson Longman, 2007), 115.

55. See Chernow, *Alexander Hamilton*, 293–301.

56. See Chernow, *Alexander Hamilton*, 379; Richard Sylaa, Robert E. Wright, and David J. Cowen, "Alexander Hamilton, Central Banker: Crisis Management During the US Financial Panic of 1792," *Business History Review*, 83 (Spring 2009); David J. Cowan, "The US Panic of 1792: Financial Crisis Management and the Lender of Last Resort," *Journal of Economic History*, 60, no. 4 (December 2000).

57. *Founders Online*, "To Thomas Jefferson from James Madison, 10 July 1791," http://founders.archives.gov/documents/Jefferson/01-20-02-0266. See also Robert Allen Rutland, *James Madison: The Founding Father* (New York: Macmillan Publishing Company, 1987), 100–104.

58. *Founders Online*, "To Thomas Jefferson from James Madison, 8 August 1791," http://founders.archives.gov/documents/Jefferson/01-22-02-0017.

59. See Garrett Ward Sheldon, *The Political Philosophy of Thomas Jefferson* (Baltimore, MD: The Johns Hopkins University Press, 1991), 89–90.

60. Jefferson, "Anas," in *The Works*. In general, historian Jack Rakove labels such reports of congressional speculation "well founded." Rakove, *James Madison*, 113. See also Rutland, *James Madison*, 102. Chernow also reports that Hamilton had privately suggested to Duer in summer of 1791 what he thought an appropriate price for Bank scrip should be. See Chernow, *Alexander Hamilton*, 359.

61. Jefferson, *Writings*, 994.

62. *Founders Online*, "To Thomas Jefferson from James Madison, 8 August 1791," http://founders.archives.gov/documents/Jefferson/01-22-02-0017.

63. Madison, *Writings*, 163.

Chapter Two

1. See Samuel Eliot Morison, Henry Steele Commager, and William E. Leuchtenburg, *The Growth of the American Republic*, Volume 1, 7th edition (New York: Oxford University Press, 1980), 382–384.

2. The Republican share of the popular vote (such as it was) from 1804 to 1820 was 72.9 percent in 1804, 66.5 percent in 1808, 53.2 percent in 1812, 68.6 percent in 1816, and 100 percent in 1820. Its share of Congress increased from 72.5 percent in 1802 to

83.9 percent in 1820. See Kenneth C. Martis, *The Historical Atlas of Political Parties in the United States Congress, 1789–1989* (New York: MacMillan Publishing Company, 1989), 77–86; and Walter Dean Burnham, *Voting in American Elections: The Shaping of the American Political Universe Since 1788* (Bethesda, MD: Academica Press, 2010), 58–61.

3. The closest any faction has come is the GOP streak of presidential victories from 1860 to 1880, but the Democrats regularly controlled the Congress from 1874 onwards.

4. See Raymond Walters, Jr., *Albert Gallatin: Jeffersonian Financier and Diplomat* (Pittsburgh, PA: University of Pittsburgh Press, 1969), 171–172.

5. The principal exponent of this justification was Gallatin. See Walters, Jr., *Albert Gallatin*, 179.

6. Quoted in William Earl Weeks, *John Quincy Adams and American Global Empire* (Lexington, KY: The University Press of Kentucky, 1992), 182.

7. Forrest McDonald, *The Presidency of Thomas Jefferson* (Lawrence, KS: The University Press of Kansas, 1976), 139.

8. See McDonald, *Presidency of Thomas Jefferson*, 139–152.

9. That turn of phrase was used by Jefferson in a letter to Brigadier General George Rogers Clark in 1780: "In the event of peace on terms which have been contemplated by some powers we shall form to the American union a barrier against the dangerous extension of the British Province of Canada and add to the Empire of liberty an extensive and fertile country, thereby converting dangerous enemies into valuable Friends." Thomas Jefferson, *The Works of Thomas Jefferson*, Federal Edition, ed. Paul Leicester Ford (New York: G.P. Putnam's Sons, 1904–1905), http://oll.libertyfund.org/index.php?option=com_staticxt&staticfile=show.php&title=1734.

10. See Robert Allen Rutland, *The Presidency of James Monroe* (Lawrence, KS: The University Press of Kansas, 1990), 88–89.

11. See Ralph C. H. Catterall, *The Second Bank of the United States* (Chicago: University of Chicago Press, 1903), 2.

12. See Walters, Jr., *Albert Gallatin*, 254–255.

13. See William Graham Sumner, *Andrew Jackson* (New York: Chelsea House Publishers, 1980), 265; and George Rogers Taylor, "A Brief History of the Second Bank of the United States," in *Jackson vs. Biddle's Bank: The Struggle Over The Second Bank of the United States*, 2nd edition, ed. George Rogers Taylor (Lexington, MA: Heath and Company, 1972), 1.

14. See Thomas Jefferson, "First Annual Message," December 8, 1801. Online by Gerhard Peters and John T. Woolley, *The American Presidency Project*, http://www.presidency.ucsb.edu/ws/?pid=29443; and Andrew Burnstein and Nancy Isenberg, *Madison and Jefferson* (New York: Random House, 2010), 438–439.

15. See Morison, Commager, and Leuchtenburg, *Growth of the American Republic*, 365–380.

16. See Daniel Walker Howe, *What Hath God Wrought: The Transformation of America, 1815–1848* (Oxford: Oxford University Press, 2007), 72–73.

17. See Noble E. Cunningham, Jr., *The Presidency of James Monroe* (Lawrence, KS: University Press of Kansas, 1996), 167; George Dangerfield, *The Era of Good Feelings* (Chicago: Ivan R. Dee, 1989), 167; Michael F. Holt, *The Rise and Fall of the American Whig Party: Jacksonian Politics and the Onset of Civil War* (Oxford: Oxford University Press, 199), 4, 85–86; and Rutland, *Presidency of James Monroe*, 195–196. A lingering hesitation had to do with federal expenditures for internal improvements. Clay was a strong proponent of such endeavors, but Madison and Monroe balked, both vetoing

bills that invested in transportation projects. But even this scruple would eventually pass. Both Madison and Monroe occasionally signed transportation projects into law, and both of them spent substantially more than their predecessors on internal improvements. And John Quincy Adams—Monroe's successor and the last of the Republicans—had no such hesitation. Still, most governmental investments in transportation during this period occurred on the state level, as with the Erie Canal. See Cunningham, Jr., *Presidency of James Monroe*, 47–52; Howe, *What Hath God Wrought*, 86–92; James E. Lewis, Jr., *John Quincy Adams: Policymaker for the Union* (Wilmington, DE: Scholarly Resources, Inc., 2001), 108; and Rutland, *Presidency of James Monroe*, 165–166, 205.

18. Quoted in Henry Ammon, *James Monroe: The Quest for National Identity* (Charlottesville, VA: The University Press of Virginia, 1990), 345–346.

19. Historian Robert Remini, perhaps the greatest scholar on Andrew Jackson, has characterizes the so-called Era of Good Feelings of the Monroe tenure as the "Era of Corruption." In his three-volume biography of Jackson, he writes: "Government officials were indeed engaged in questionable, if not illegal, activities and many of these activities involve enormous sums of money. From the president of the United States down through several cabinet of officers into the Washington bureaucracy in reaching beyond to officials in the several states, a degree of malfeasance in the conduct of official business was beginning to come to light in an ever-increasing number of exposures." Robert V. Remini, *Andrew Jackson, Volume Two: The Course of American Freedom, 1822–1832* (Baltimore, MD: The Johns Hopkins University Press, 1981), 13.

20. Harry L. Watson, *Liberty and Power: The Politics of Jacksonian America* (New York: Hill and Wang, 2006), 80–81.

21. See Chester Collins Maxey, National Municipal Review; "A Little History of Pork" (Washington, DC: National Municipal League, 1919), 691–705.

22. See Howe, *What Hath God Wrought*, 254; and Lewis, Jr., *John Quincy Adams*, 113.

23. See Mary W. M. Hargreaves, *The Presidency of John Quincy Adams* (Lawrence, KS: University Press of Kansas, 1985), 194–196; and Howe, *What Hath God Wrought*, 274–275.

24. See Robert V. Remini, *Daniel Webster: The Man And His Time* (New York: W. W. Norton & Company, 1997), 352, 452–453, 466.

25. See Remini, *Jackson, Volume Two*, 16.

26. See Remini, *Jackson, Volume Two*, 398.

27. See Remini, *Jackson, Volume Two*, 21–24. Helming the Treasury Department during Monroe's administration was William Crawford of Georgia, an ambitious, powerful politician who was not above using his office to punish his enemies and reward his friends. For instance, he had allowed the Bank of Illinois to decide which notes it would accept from land office receivers, and the Bank ultimately accepted only notes from Crawford supporters. However, he did not allow that consideration to the Bank of Edwardsville, whose director was Illinois senator Ninian Edwards, a Crawford rival. It was only after Edwards resigned his position at the Bank that the blacklisting ended.

28. See Dangerfield, *The Era of Good Feelings*, 168.

29. See Catterall, *Second Bank*, 22; and Thomas Payne Govan, *Nicholas Biddle: Nationalist and Public Banker, 1786–1844* (Chicago: University of Chicago Press, 1959), 51.

30. See Edward K. Eckert, "William Jones: Mr. Madison's Secretary of the Navy," *The Pennsylvania Magazine of History and Biography* 96, no. 2 (April 1972): 177–178.

31. Robert V. Remini, *Andrew Jackson and the Bank War* (New York: W. W. Norton & Company, 1967), 27.

32. See Taylor, "A Brief History," 4.

33. See George Dangerfield, *The Awakening of American Nationalism, 1815–1828* (New York: Harmer & Row, 1965), 81.

34. See Catterall, *Second Bank*, 39–47.

35. See Dangerfield, *Awakening*, 82; and Taylor, "A Brief History," 4.

36. See Howe, *What Hath God Wrought*, 142–143; and Murray N. Rothbard, *The Panic of 1819: Reactions and Policies* (Auburn, AL: Ludwig von Mises Institute, 2007), 185–324.

37. See Dangerfield, *Awakening*, 78–79; and Dangerfield, *Era*, 168.

38. Catterall, *Second Bank*, 61–62.

39. Dangerfield, *Awakening*, 82.

40. See Rothbard, *Panic of 1819*, 324.

41. Dangerfield, *Era*, 187.

42. Quoted in Dangerfield, *Era*, 187.

43. Bray Hammond, "The Second Bank of the United States," *Transactions of the American Philosophical Society, New Series* 43, no. 1 (1953): 83.

44. See Ralph C. H. Catterall, "The Issues of the Second Bank of the United States," *The Journal of Political Economy* 5, no. 4 (September 1897): 432; Catterall, *Second Bank*, 112–113; Taylor, "A Brief History," 6–7.

45. See Hammond, "The Second Bank," 83; and Catterall, *Second Bank*.

46. See Bray Hammond, "Jackson, Biddle, and the Bank of the United States," *The Journal of Economic History* 7, no. 1 (May 1947): 3.

47. See H. W. Brands, *The Life and Times of Andrew Jackson* (New York: Random House, 2005), 459, 463; Remini, *Jackson, Volume Two*, 399; Robert V. Remini, *Henry Clay: Statesman for the Union* (New York: W. W. Norton & Company, 1991), 191; and Watson, *Liberty and Power*, 140–141.

48. A particularly damning example of this generosity to the molders of public opinion concerns a loan to the editors of the *New York Courier and Inquirer* in 1831, made with essentially no security. See Catterall, *Second Bank*, 256–260.

49. See Howard Bodenhorn, *A History of Banking in Antebellum America: Financial Markets and Economic Development in an Era of Nation-Building* (Cambridge: Cambridge University Press, 2000). The case of the "3 percents" is another example of the Bank's true priorities. In 1831, the secretary of the treasury informed Biddle that half of the 3 percents—stocks issued in 1792 for revolutionary war debt—were to be paid off. But Biddle was short on cash and sent his agent, Thomas Cadwalader, to Europe to negotiate a deal to buy the Bank some time. Cadwalader cut a deal with the House of Baring wherein it would buy up the 3 percents for the Bank, though the securities would not go into Bank hands. But the Bank was forbidden by its charter to purchase government debt, and Biddle was forced to repudiate Cadwalader's plan after public outcry. See Remini, *Bank War*, 120–121; and Sumner, *Andrew Jackson*, 309.

50. See Howe, *What Hath God Wrought*, 367. Remini argues that Jackson was "perverse, too. If told he must do one thing, the chances were extremely good that he would do exactly the opposite. In some ways what was most disturbing of all was his passion for revenge. Whenever someone crossed him, he would go to heroic lengths to even accounts." Remini, *Bank War*, 22. See also Bertram Wyatt-Brown, "Andrew Jackson's Honor," *Journal of the Early Republic* 17 (Spring 1997): 1–36.

51. See Cunningham, *Presidency of James Monroe*, 60–63; Howe, *What Hath God Wrought*, 70–76; and Anthony F. C. Wallace, *The Long, Bitter Trail: Andrew Jackson and the Indians* (New York: Hill and Wang, 1993), 50–51.

52. Andrew Jackson, "Veto Message," December 6, 1832. Online by Gerhard Peters

and John T. Woolley, *The American Presidency Project*, http://www.presidency.ucsb.edu/ws/?pid=6704.

53. Andrew Jackson, "Fourth Annual Message," December 4, 1832. Online by Gerhard Peters and John T. Woolley, *The American Presidency Project*, http://www.presidency.ucsb.edu/ws/?pid=29474.

54. See John Joseph Wallis and Barry R. Weingast, "Equilibirium Impotence: Why the States and not the American National Government Financed Economic Development in the Antebellum Era," NBER Working Paper #1139 (Cambridge, MA: National Bureau of Economic Research, 2005), http://www.nber.org/papers/w11397.

55. See Howe, *What Hath God Wrought*, 360–362.

56. Remini, *Jackson, Volume 2*, 236–237.

57. See Robert V. Remini, *Andrew Jackson & His Indian Wars* (New York: Viking, 2001), 81.

58. See Hargreaves, *Presidency of John Quincy Adams*, 199–208.

59. See Daniel Feller, *The Jacksonian Promise: America, 1815–1840* (Baltimore, MD: The Johns Hopkins University Press, 1995), 180–181; Howe, *What Hath God Wrought*, 353–355; Remini, *Indian Wars*, 243–244; and Wallace, 77.

60. This is a phrase coined by the Roman jurist Ulpian.

61. See Jean Alexander Wilburn, "The Supporters of the Bank," in *Jackson vs. Biddle's Bank: The Struggle Over The Second Bank of the United States*, 2nd edition, ed. George Rogers Taylor (Lexington, MA: Heath and Company, 1972), 180–207; and Jean Alexander Wilburn, *Biddle's Bank: The Crucial Years* (New York: Columbia University Press, 1967), 63–120.

62. See Howe, *What Hath God Wrought*, 375; and Remini, *Bank War*, 19–25.

63. See Catterall, *Second Bank*, 216–230; Holt, *American Whig Party*, 15–16; and Remini, *Bank War*, 74.

64. See Sumner, *Andrew Jackson*, 298–299.

65. Andrew Jackson, "Veto Message [Of The Re-authorization of Bank of the United States]," July 10, 1832. Online by Gerhard Peters and John T. Woolley, *The American Presidency Project*, http://www.presidency.ucsb.edu/ws/?pid=67043.

66. Quoted in Remini, *Bank War*, 98–99.

67. See Holt, *American Whig Party*, 24; Howe, *What Hath God Wrought*, 387; Robert V. Remini, *Andrew Jackson, Volume Three: The Course of American Democracy, 1833–1845* (Baltimore, MD: The Johns Hopkins University Press, 1984), 88–101.

68. See Holt, *American Whig Party*, 387–389.

69. See Frank Otto Gatell, "Spoils of the Bank War: Political Bias in the Selection of Pet Banks," *The American Historical Review* 70, no. 1 (October 1964): 35–58.

70. In particular, Biddle was concerned that Jackson was going farther than simply using the Bank to pay bills while placing new tax revenue into the pets. Taney had indeed given a few pets drafts against the Bank as a form of protection against retaliation from the latter. But the pets used these to expand their loans, and ultimately had to call them into the Bank, which naturally aroused the suspicions of Biddle that the government was looking to empty the Bank altogether. See Peter Temin, *The Jacksonian Economy* (New York: W. W. Norton & Company, 1967), 61–62.

71. See Holt, *American Whig Party*, 25; Howe, *What Hath God Wrought*, 391; Temin, *Jacksonian Economy*, 61; and Watson, *Liberty and Power*, 157.

72. Quoted in Bray Hammond, *Banks and Politics in America: From the Revolution to the Civil War* (Princeton, NJ: Princeton University Press, 1985), 418.

73. Remini, *Jackson, Volume 3*, 111.

74. See Jacob P. Meerman, "The Climax of the Bank War: Biddle's Contraction, 1833–34," *Journal of Political Economy* 71, no. 4 (August 1963): 379–386.

75. See Govan, *Nicholas Biddle*, 255–260.

Chapter Three

1. E. E. Schattschneider, *Party Government: American Government in Action* (New Brunswick, NJ: Transaction Publishers, 2008), 1.

2. See John H. Aldrich, *Why Parties? The Origin and Transformation of Party Politics in America* (Chicago: University of Chicago Press, 1995), 29–36, 45–48. For good discussions of the problem of collective action, see Russell Hardin, *Collective Action* (Baltimore, MD: The Johns Hopkins University Press, 1982); and Manur Olson, *The Logic of Collective Action: Public Goods and the Theory of Groups* (Cambridge, MA: Harvard University Press, 1971). For a relatively intuitive description of the (largely technical) problem of social choice, see Kenneth A. Shepsle and Mark S. Bonchek, *Analyzing Politics: Rationality, Behavior, and Institutions* (New York: W. W. Norton & Company, 1997) 39–136.

3. There has been a wealth of fantastic scholarly literature on political parties in the last twenty-five years. See, for instance, Gary W. Cox and Matthew D. McCubbins, *Legislative Leviathan: Party Government in the House* (Berkeley, CA: University of California Press, 1993); and Gary W. Cox and Matthew D. McCubbins, *Setting the Agenda: Responsible Party Government in the U.S. House of Representatives* (Cambridge: Cambridge University Press, 2005). For an interesting take that connects legislative parties of the present day to those in the 1790s, see William F. James Connelly, Jr., *Madison Rules America: The Constitutional Origins of Congressional Partisanship* (Lanham, MD: Rowman & Littlefield Publishers, 2011).

4. See Joseph A. Schlesinger, *Ambition and Politics: Political Careers in the United States* (New York: Rand McNally, 1966).

5. See Schattschneider, *Party Government*, 51; and E. E. Schattschneider, *The Semisovereign People: A Realist's View of Democracy in America* (Fort Worth, TX: Harcourt Brace Jovanovich College Publishers, 1975), 66–73.

6. For more on opposition to political parties in the eighteenth century, see Gerald Leonard, *The Invention of Party Politics: Federalism, Popular Sovereignty, and Constitutional Development in Jacksonian Illinois* (Chapel Hill, NC: The University of North Carolina Press, 2002), 1; and Richard Hofstadter, *The Idea of a Party System: The Rise of Legitimate Opposition in the United States, 1790–1840* (Berkeley, CA: University of California Press, 1970), 40–59. For more on this battle between the "Cosmopolitans" and the "Localists," see Jackson Turner Main, *Political Parties Before the Constitution* (Chapel Hill, NC: The University of North Carolina Press, 1973), 365–366.

7. James Madison, "Parties," in *Writings*, ed. Jack N. Rakove (New York: The Library of America, 1999), 161.

8. Madison's essay "Parties" for the *National Gazette* makes this thinking explicit:

In every political society, parties are unavoidable. A difference of interests, real or supposed, is the most natural and fruitful source of them. The great object should be to combat the evil: 1. By establishing a political equality among all; 2. By withholding unnecessary opportunities from a few to increase the inequality of property by an immoderate, and especially an unmerited, accumulation of riches; 3. By the silent operation of laws which, without violating the rights of property, reduce extreme wealth towards a state of mediocrity and raise extreme indigence towards a state of comfort; 4. By abstaining from measures which operate differently on different interests, and particularly such as favor one interest at the expense of another; 5. By making one party a check on the other so far as the existence of parties cannot be prevented nor their views accommodated. If this is not the language of reason, it is that of republicanism. (Madison, "Parties," 504)

9. See Leonard, *Invention of Party Politics*, 1–11; Hofstadter, *Idea of a Party System*, 127; and Major L. Wilson, *The Presidency of Martin Van Buren* (Lawrence, KS: The University Press of Kansas, 1984), 28.

10. See Noble E. Cunningham, Jr., *The Jeffersonian Republicans: The Formation of Party Organization, 1789–1801* (Chapel Hill, NC: The University of North Carolina Press, 1957), 147–178.

11. Thomas Jefferson, "Inaugural Address," March 4, 1801. Online by Gerhard Peters and John T. Woolley, *The American Presidency Project*, http://www.presidency.ucsb.edu/ws/?pid=25803 7-29-13.

12. See Leonard, *Invention of Party Politics*, 35–39; and Martin Van Buren, *The Autobiography of Martin Van Buren*, ed. John C. Fitzpatrick (Washington, DC: Government Printing Office, 1920), 124–125.

13. That line is taken from Martin Van Buren, "Letter to Thomas Ritchie," *American History Online, Inc.*, http://www.fofweb.com.

14. See Ted Widmer, *Martin Van Buren* (New York: Henry Holt and Company, 2005), 65.

15. See Donald B. Cole, *Vindicating Andrew Jackson: The 1828 Election and the Rise of the Two-Party System* (Lawrence, KS: University Press of Kansas, 2009), 88–89; Donald B. Cole, *Martin Van Buren and the American Political System* (Princeton, NJ: Princeton University Press, 1984), 65–87; and Richard P. McCormick, *The Second American Party System: Party Formation in the Jacksonian Era* (New York: W. W. Norton & Co., 1966), 104–121.

16. See Van Buren, "Letter to Thomas Ritchie"; Wilson, *Presidency of Martin Van Buren*, 26; and Cole, *Martin Van Buren and the American Political System*, 96–104.

17. See Carl Russell Fish, *The Civil Service and the Patronage* (New York: Longmans, Green & Co., 1905); and Leonard D. White, *The Federalists: A Study in Administrative History, 1789–1801* (New York: The Free Press, 1948), 257–271.

18. See White, *Federalists*, 179.

19. Adams allowed a few sons-in-law to receive government appointments. Nepotism was a factor in the hiring decisions of other prominent Federalists, including Secretary of State Timothy Pickering and Secretary of the Treasury Oliver Wolcott, Jr. In general, Governor James McHenry of New Hampshire summarized Washington and Adams's appointment policy best:

During the whole of the administration of general Washington, appointments to office, were invariably made, not with a view to the extension of executive influence or future elections, but upon the ground of the fitness and qualifications of the purpose for the offices to be filled, in a regard to inequitable distribution of them among the several states. The rule was not followed with the same punctilious observance by Mr. Adams. He thought it an essential part of the art of governing to apply the influence of her wards, through the medium of appointments offices, to future elections . . . I fear above all things, the operation of this principle upon the conduct of the needy man of talents, who believes in no religion, the ambitious rich man without virtue or honesty, and your political adventurers and office hunters of every description. (Quoted in White, *Federalists*, 277)

20. Quoted in White, *Federalists*, 273.

21. See Edward J. Larson, *A Magnificent Catastrophe: The Tumultuous Election of 1800, America's First Presidential Campaign* (New York: Free Press, 2007), 91–98.

22. See Larson, *Magnificent Catastrophe*, 266–268.

23. See Cunningham, *Formation*, 13–14.

24. Quoted in Leonard D. White, *The Jeffersonians: A Study in Administrative History, 1801–1829* (New York: The Macmillan Company, 1951), 348. See also Noble E. Cunningham, Jr., *The Jeffersonian Republicans: Party Operations, 1801–1809* (Chapel Hill, NC: The University of North Carolina Press, 1963), 15–33; Fish, *Civil Service*, 30–31; and White, *Jeffersonians*, 348–352.

25. Carl Russell Fish, "Removal of Officials by the Presidents of the United States," *Annual Report of the American Historical Association For The Year 1899*, Volume I (Washington, 1900), 84–85.

26. See Fish, "Removal," 84–85.

27. For a good discussion of these pressures, see Cunningham, *Party Operations*, 300–301, McCormick, *Second American Party System*, 343–353; Joel H. Silbey, *The American Political Nation, 1838–1893* (Stanford, CA: Stanford University Press, 1991), 41–60; and Leonard D. White, *The Jacksonians: A Study in Administrative History, 1829–1861* (New York: The Macmillan Company, 1954), 12.

28. For the influence of these men in administration personnel policy, see Cole, *Martin Van Buren*, 195; and Robert V. Remini, *Martin Van Buren and the Making of the Democratic Party* (New York: Columbia University Press, 1961), 197.

29. Andrew Jackson, "First Annual Message," December 8, 1829. Online by Gerhard Peters and John T. Woolley, *The American Presidency Project*, http://www.presidency .ucsb.edu/ws/?pid=29471.

30. Fish, "Removal," 84–85.

31. See Cole, *Martin Van Buren*, 195.

32. See White, *Jeffersonians*, 316–318.

33. Fish, "Removal," 84.

34. See Fish, *Civil Service*, 249–251.

35. Carl Russell Fish counts only eighty removals among the civilian workforce, "and an unusually large number were made for cause, the service having become exceedingly disordered under Jackson." Fish, "Removal," 75. See Elbert B. Smith, *The Presidencies of Zachary Taylor and Millard Fillmore* (Lawrence, KS: University Press of Kansas, 1988), 57.

36. See Wilson, *Presidency of Martin Van Buren*, 205.

37. See Fish, "Removal," 84.

38. See Gary May, *John Tyler* (New York: Henry Holt and Company, 2008), 100–101.

39. For considerations on Polk's use of patronage, see Paul H. Bergeron, *The Presidency of James K. Polk* (Lawrence, KS: The University Press of Kansas, 1987), 137–143; John Devoti, *The Patriotic Business of Seeking Office: James K. Polk and the Patronage* (Lanham, MD: University Press of America, 2006); Norman A. Graebner, "James K. Polk: A Study in Federal Patronage," *The Mississippi Valley Historical Review* 38, no. 4 (March 1852): 614–632; John Seigenthaler, *James K. Polk* (New York: Henry Holt and Company, 2003), 114–115, 132–133; and White, *Jacksonians*, 312. For more on Taylor and Fillmore, see Smith, *Taylor and Fillmore*, 57–58. For Pierce, see Larry Gara, *The Presidency of Franklin Pierce* (Lawrence, KS: The University Press of Kansas, 1991), 49–50; and Michael Holt, *Franklin Pierce* (New York: Henry Holt and Company, 2010), 67–71. For Buchanan, see David Meerse, "Buchanan's Patronage Policy: An Attempt to Achieve Political Strength," *Pennsylvania History* 40, no. 1 (January 1973): 39–48; Elbert B. Smith,

The Presidency of James Buchanan (Lawrence, KS: The University Press of Kansas, 1975), 21–22, 98–104, 121; and White, *Jacksonians*, 313, 341.

40. See White, *Jacksonians*, 12, 327–329.

41. See White, *Jacksonians*, 334–340.

42. See White, *Jacksonians*, 284–294.

43. See White, *Jeffersonians*, 303.

44. White, *Jacksonians*, 266–267.

45. White, *Jacksonians*, 175.

46. See Kim Long, *The Almanac of Political Corruption, Scandals and Dirty Politics* (New York: Delta Trade Paperbacks, 2007), 37.

47. See Fish, *Civil Service*, 136–137.

48. See Matthew A. Crenson, *The Federal Machine: Beginnings of Bureaucracy in Jacksonian America* (Baltimore, MD: The Johns Hopkins University Press, 1975), 84–86.

49. See Edward W. Chester, "The Impact of the Covode Congressional Investigation," *Western Pennsylvania Historical Magazine* 42 (December 1959): 349.

50. U.S. Congress. *House Select Committee on Alleged Corruptions in Government. The Covode Investigation: Report No. 648* (Washington, DC: 1860), 16; and Jean H. Baker, *James Buchanan* (New York: Henry Holt and Company, 2004), 113.

51. See U.S. Congress, *House Select Committee*, 4–29. The *New York Times*, a newspaper then in its infancy, wrote a scathing editorial blasting Buchanan over the Covode findings:

> Mr. Buchanan's fertility of resource, as set forth in this report, is even more remarkable than either his fortitude or his courage. We think the variety and ingeniousness of the devices to which he resorted, to bring about the passage of the Lecompton bill, must make everybody regret that the Constitution of the United States does not make the President's term of office four or five times as long. In the dangerous crisis in national affairs which we all foresee, the presence of so ready a gentleman at the head of affairs would be invaluable. It is not everybody who can turn all the resources of the Government to such good account for the accomplishment of a single object. We are not likely to have many Presidents who will be able to make the Custom House, the Post-Office, the Foreign Embassies and Consulships, the Navy, the Public Printing, the poor newspapers, and "Divine Providence," work in concert for the promotion of the passage of a nefarious bill by the House of Representatives. When the nation gets such a man into office, common prudence seems to dictate the propriety of keeping him there. (*New York Times*, "President Buchanan and the Report of the Covode Committee," June 20, 1860.)

52. See Mark Grossman, *Political Corruption in America: An Encyclopedia of Scandals, Power, and Greed* (Santa Barbara, CA: ABC-CLIO, Inc., 2003), 78.

Chapter Four

1. The phrase "Gilded Age" comes from a novel by Mark Twain and Charles Dudley Warner called *The Gilded Age: A Tale of Today.*

2. Henry Adams, *The Education of Henry Adams* (New York: Barnes & Noble, 2009), 254. For a contrary take, see Mark Wahlgren Summers, *The Era of Good Stealings* (New York: Oxford University Press, 1993), 10–22.

3. See Paul P. Van Riper, *History of the United States Civil Service* (Evanston, IL: Row, Peterson and Company, 1958), 60–61.

4. See Carl Russell Fish, *The Civil Service and the Patronage* (New York: Longmans, Green & Co., 1905), 173–174.

5. See Phillip Shaw Pauldan, *The Presidency of Abraham Lincoln* (Lawrence, KS: The University Press of Kansas, 1994), 35–36. Fish puts the number of Lincoln removals at 1,457 out of 1,639 total offices on the presidential level. See Fish, *Civil Service*, 170.

6. Carl Russell Fish, "Lincoln and the Patronage," *The American Historical Review* 8, no. 1 (October 1902): 56.

7. See Pauldan, *Presidency of Abraham Lincoln*, 36; and Harry J. Carman and Reinhard H. Luthin, *Lincoln and the Patronage* (New York: Columbia University Press, 1943), 9–10.

8. See Carman and Luthin, *Lincoln*, 285.

9. Fish, *Civil Service*, 170.

10. See Fish, "Lincoln," 66. Unfortunately for those members of Congress, Lincoln was killed before the positions were formally filled, and Andrew Johnson refused to honor the agreement.

11. See Albert Castel, *The Presidency of Andrew Johnson* (Lawrence, KS: The University Press of Kansas, 1979), 4, 49–51. Regarding Johnson's "intemperate" speech, Radical Republican Zachariah Chandler said, "The inauguration went off very well except that the Vice President Elect was too drunk to perform his duties & disgraced himself & the Senate by making a drunken foolish speech." See U.S. Senate, "Andrew Johnson, 16th Vice President (1865)," http://www.senate.gov/artandhistory/history/common/generic/VP_Andrew_Johnson.htm.

12. See Carl Russell Fish, "Removal Of Officials By the Presidents of the United States," *Annual Report of the American Historical Association For The Year 1899, Volume I* (Washington, 1900), 83; Fish, *Civil Service*, 188–189; and Hans L. Trefousse, *Andrew Johnson: A Biography* (New York: W.W. Norton & Company, 1989), 276.

13. See David O. Stewart, *Impeached: The Trial of Andrew Johnson and the Fight for Lincoln's Legacy* (New York: Simon and Schuster, 2009), 164, 181–192.

14. See Fish, *Civil Service*, 193; and TeachingAmericanHistory.org, "Tenure Of Office Act," http://teachingamericanhistory.org/library/document/tenure-of-office-act.

15. See Charles C. Thach, Jr., *The Creation of the Presidency, 1775–1789: A Study in Constitutional History* (Indianapolis, IN: Liberty Fund, 2007), 124–142. In 1926, the Supreme Court overturned the Tenure of Office Act, relying heavily upon the debates in the First Congress, especially Madison's argument. See *Myers v. United States*, 272 U.S. 52 (1926).

16. See Matthew Josephson, *The Politicos, 1865–1896* (New York: Harcourt, Brace & World, Inc., 1938), 79.

17. Adams, *Education*, 207.

18. See David M. Jordan, *Roscoe Conkling of New York: Voice in the Senate* (Ithaca, NY: Cornell University Press, 1971), 123–124. The compromise retained the act but allowed the president to appoint a temporary replacement for offices he suspended. Even so, the power of removal remained distributed between the president and the Senate. See Richard E. Welch, Jr., *The Presidencies of Grover Cleveland* (Lawrence, KS: The University Press of Kansas, 1988), 53–54.

19. See Jordan, *Roscoe Conkling*, 120; and Lewis L. Gould, *Grand Old Party: A History of the Republicans* (New York: Random House, 2003), 60.

20. Adams, *Education*, 212.

21. Quoted in Jordan, *Roscoe Conkling*, 192. It is worth pointing out that recent scholars have presented an alternative view of Grant, one markedly different from his reform-minded contemporaries as well as early scholars who saw him as a diffident chief executive. Much of this revision has to do with the mainstreaming of Grant's far-sighted views on civil rights. For examples of this view, see Josiah Bunting III, *Ulysses S. Grant*

(New York: Times Books, 2004), 107–116; Alvin Stephen Felzenberg, *The Leaders We Deserved (And A Few We Didn't): Rethinking the Presidential Rating Game* (New York: Basic Books, 2008), 278–286; Jean Edward Smith, *Grant* (New York: Simon and Schuster, 2001); and C-SPAN.org, "C-SPAN 2009 Historians Presidential Leadership Survey," http://legacy.c-span.org/PresidentialSurvey/Overall-Ranking.aspx. We are suspicious of this revision, wondering how these aspects of Grant's tenure can be disaggregated. After all, corruption offered the pro-South Democractic Party an easy wedge issue to pursue on the national level: the idea that the Republican Party had become indecent and no longer worthy of holding national political power. Democrats used this attack to great effect in 1874 and 1876, ultimately leveraging their political rebound to force an end to Reconstruction. So, it seems to us that Grant's lax administration undermined faith in Republican governance, led to a Democratic comeback (as the latter was the only alternative), and thus undermined the long-term goal of Reconstruction.

22. See Smith, *Grant*, 481–490; and Kenneth D. Ackerman, *The Gold Ring: Jim Fisk, Gould, and Black Friday, 1869* (New York: Dodd, Mead & Co., 1988).

23. See Gould, *Grand Old Party*, 71; Jordan, *Roscoe Conkling*, 223; and Smith, *Grant*, 593–595.

24. See Robert W. Cherny, *American Politics in the Gilded Age* (Wheeling, IL: Harlan Davidson, Inc., 1997), 55; Thomas C. Reeves, *Gentleman Boss: The Life of Chester A. Arthur* (New York: Alfred A. Knopf, 1975), 80; Smith, *Grant*, 590–592; and, Leonard D. White, *The Republican Era: 1869–1901: A Study In Administrative History* (New York: The MacMillan Company, 1963), 372–374.

25. See White, *The Republican Era*, 370–372.

26. See Justus D. Doenecke, *The Presidencies of James A. Garfield & Chester A. Arthur* (Lawrence, KS: University Press of Kansas, 1981), 46; Ari Hoogenboom, *Rutherford B. Hayes: Warrior & President* (Lawrence, KS: University Press of Kansas, 1995), 439–440, 469–470; Ari Hoogenboom, *The Presidency of Rutherford B. Hayes* (Lawrence, KS: University Press of Kansas, 1988), 206; and Mark Wahlgren Summers, *Rum, Romanism, & Rebellion: The Making of a President, 1884* (Chapel Hill, NC: The University of North Carolina Press, 2000), 71–72.

27. See Eric Foner, *Reconstruction: America's Unfinished Revolution, 1863–1877* (New York: Harper & Row, 1988), 347–349.

28. See Foner, *Reconstruction*, 384–389.

29. See Cherny, *American Politics*, 59; Michael F. Holt, *By One Vote: The Disputed Election of 1876* (Lawrence, KS: The University Press of Kansas, 2008), 175–203; and Hoogenboom, *Hayes*, 277–278.

30. *National Party Conventions, 1831–2004* (Washington, DC: CQ Press, 2005), 196. The pro-Grant forces would have carried the day had they won a previous dispute over the unit rule, which would have bound an entire state's delegates to the candidate who enjoyed the support of a majority of the delegation. If that had passed, Grant would have picked up enough spare delegates in New York, Pennsylvania, and the states of the old Confederacy to win.

31. See Josephson, *Politicos*, 85.

32. Adams, *Education*, 208.

33. Quoted in William Dudley Foulke, *The Life of Oliver P. Morton, Including His Important Speeches* (Indianapolis, IN: Bowen-Merrill Co., 1899), 257. See also Donald Barr Chidsey, *The Gentleman from New York: A Life of Roscoe Conkling* (New Haven: Yale University Press, 1935), 152; and Josephson, *Politicos*, 90–91. In Indiana, the Republicans and Democrats regularly employed money at campaign time to purchase "floaters," unaffiliated voters whose ballots were literally for sale to the highest bidder.

34. Josephson, *Politicos*, 91.

35. See Bunting, *Ulysses*, 82; Chidsey, *Gentleman from New York*, 151–152; Gary Ecelbarger, *Black Jack Logan: An Extraordinary Life in Peace and War* (Guilford, CT: The Lyons Press, 2005), 252–265; James Pickett Jones, *John A. Logan: Stalwart Republican from Illinois* (Carbondale, IL: Southern Illinois University Press, 2001), 37–82, 127; and James P. Jones, "Radical Reinforcement: John A. Logan Returns to Congress," *Journal of the Illinois State Historical Society* 68, no. 4 (September 1975): 324–336.

36. See Lee F. Crippen, *Simon Cameron, The Ante-Bellum Years* (Oxford, OH: The Mississippi Valley Press, 1942), xi.

37. See Crippen, *Simon Cameron*, 7–18.

38. See Crippen, *Simon Cameron*, 113.

39. See Crippen, *Simon Cameron*, 35–39. See also Stewart, John D. Stewart, "The Great Winnebago Chieftain: Simon Cameron's Rise to Power, 1860–1867," *Pennsylvania History* 39 (1972): 25.

40. See Stewart, "Great Winnebago," 22.

41. See Crippen, *Simon Cameron*, 162.

42. See Erwin Stanley Bradley, *The Triumph of Militant Republicanism: A Study of Pennsylvania and Presidential Politics, 1860–1872* (Philadelphia: University of Pennsylvania Press, 1964).

43. Ernest B. Furgurson, *Freedom Rising: Washington in the Civil War* (New York: Knopf, 2004), 110.

44. Quoted at Carman and Luthin, *Lincoln*, 149–150. See also Bradley, *Triumph of Militant Republicanism*, 183; and Mark R. Wilson, *The Business of Civil War: Military Mobilization and the State, 1861–1865* (Baltimore, MD: The Johns Hopkins University Press, 2006), 153. The House resolution of censure, which Cameron eventually had stricken from the record, read as follows:

> Resolved, that Simon Cameron, late Secretary of War, by investing Alexander Cummings with the control of large sums of the public money, and authority to purchase military supplies, without restriction, without requiring from him any guarantee for the faithful performance of his duties, when the services of competent public officers were available, and by involving the government in a vast number of contracts with persons not legitimately engaged in the business pertaining to the subject matter of such contracts, especially in the purchase of arms for future delivery, hesitant adopted a policy highly injurious to the public service, and deserves the censure of the house. (Abraham Lincoln, *Lincoln: His Writings and Speeches, 1859–1865* [New York: Library of America, 1989], 327.)

45. See Bradley, *Triumph of Militant Republicanism*, 179; and Carman and Luthin, *Lincoln*, 131.

46. See Bradley, *Triumph of Militant Republicanism*, 208–210, 250; and Milton Rugoff, *America's Gilded Age: Intimate Portraits from an Era of Extravagance and Change, 1850–1890* (New York: Henry Holt and Company, 1989), 26.

47. For details of Cameron's victory in 1867, see Brooks M. Kelly, "Simon Cameron and the Senatorial Nomination of 1867," *The Pennsylvania Magazine of History and Biography* 87, no. 4 (October 1963): 375–392; and also Stewart, "Great Winnebago," 34.

48. See Kin Long. *The Almanac of Political Corruption, Scandals & Dirty Politics* (Westminster, MD: Delta Trade Paperbacks, 2007), 37.

49. See Bradley, *Triumph of Militant Republicanism*, 409; and John M. Dobson, *Politics in the Gilded Age: A New Perspective on Reform* (New York: Praeger Publishers, 1972), 28–29.

50. See Bradley, *Triumph of Militant Republicanism*, 304–305.

51. See Bradley, *Triumph of Militant Republicanism*, 324.

52. See Dobson, *Politics*, 28; and Jordan, *Roscoe Conkling*, 224.

53. Quoted in Bradley, *Triumph of Militant Republicanism*, 422.

54. See Frank B. Evans, *Pennsylvania Politics, 1872–1877: A Study in Political Leadership* (Harrisburg, PA: The Pennsylvania Historical and Museum Commission, 1966), 13.

55. For more on Philadelphia, see Evans, *Pennsylvania Politics*, 15; Peter McCaffery, *When Bosses Ruled Philadelphia* (University Park, PA: The Pennsylvania State University Press, 1993), 112; and Lincoln Steffens, *The Shame of the Cities* (Mineola, NY: Dover Publications, 2004), 138–141. For more on Pittsburgh, see McCaffery, *When Bosses Ruled*, 17, 23, 70–75; and Steffens, *Shame*, 115–116.

56. See Evans, *Pennsylvania Politics*, 38–45.

57. See Stewart, *Impeached*, 295.

58. See Jordan, *Roscoe Conkling*, 95–96.

59. See Chidsey, *Gentleman*, 151; Jordan, *Roscoe Conkling*, 127; and Rugoff, *Gilded Age*, 26.

60. See Dorman B. Eaton, *The "Spoils" System and Civil Service Reform in the Custom-House and Post Office At New York* (New York: G.P. Putnam's Sons, 1881), 22–23; and Jordan, *Roscoe Conkling*, 133.

61. See Jordan, *Roscoe Conkling*, 133–134.

62. See Hoogenboom, *Presidency*, 132; and Reeves, *Gentleman Boss*, 62.

63. Hans L. Trefousse, *Rutherford B. Hayes* (New York: Times Books, 2002), 93.

64. See White, *The Republican Era*, 123–124.

65. See Hoogenboom, *Hayes*, 111; and Reeves, *Gentleman Boss*, 82–83.

66. See Sean Dennis Cashman, *America in the Gilded Age: From the Death of Lincoln to the Rise of Theodore Roosevelt* (New York: New York University Press, 1993), 248.

67. See Jordan, *Roscoe Conkling*, 210; and Reeves, *Gentleman Boss*, 83. In general, Arthur was a good collector for the purposes of the Conkling machine. He made sure that the machine was well taken care of, but he also had the respect of the business community. See Jordan, *Roscoe Conkling*, 209; and Zachary Karabell, *Chester Alan Arthur* (New York: Times Books, 2004), 29–30.

68. Quoted in W. B. Wedgwood, *Civil Service Reform: Illustration 1. The Plunder System; 2. The Spoils System; 3. The Competitive System; 4. The Educational and Prize System* (Portland, ME: Stephen Berry, 1888), 82–83.

69. See Eaton, "Spoils System," 23.

70. See Eaton, "Spoils System," 23–27; and White, *The Republican Era*, 118–120.

71. Quoted in Horace White, *The Life of Lyman Trumbull* (Boston: Houghton Mifflin Company, 1913), 341.

72. See Summers, *Rum, Romanism, & Rebellion*, 62. See also Cashman, *Gilded Age*, 249–252; Gould, *Grand Old Party*, 72; Neil Rolde, *Continental Liar From the State of Maine: James G. Blaine* (Gardiner, ME: Tilbury House Publishers, 2007), 177–183; and Rugoff, *Gilded Age*, 27.

73. Quoted in Holt, *By One Vote*, 123.

74. See Ari Hoogenboom, *Outlawing the Spoils: A History of the Civil Service Reform Movement* (Urbana, IL: University of Illinois Press, 1968), 141–154.

75. Trefousse, *Hayes*, 95.

76. See Hoogenboom, *Presidency*, 131.

77. See Hoogenboom, *Hayes*, 135.

78. Hoogenboom, *Presidency*, 143; and Hoogenboom, *Outlawing the Spoils*, 155–187.

79. See *National Party Conventions*, 69–71, 194.

80. See *National Party Conventions*, 69–71; and Kenneth D. Ackerman, *Dark Horse: The Surprise Election and Political Murder of President James A. Garfield* (New York: Carroll & Graf Publishers, 2003), 119–156.

81. See Ackerman, *Dark Horse*, 235–207; and Doenecke, *Presidencies*, 42–43.

82. Quoted in H. H. Alexander, *The Life of Guiteau* (Philadelphia: National Publishing Company, 1882), 49.

83. See Cashman, *Gilded Age*, 255–258; and Homer E. Socolofsky and Allan B. Spetter, *The Presidency of Benjamin Harrison* (Lawrence KS: University Press of Kansas, 1987), 10, 38–39.

Chapter Five

1. See Nathaniel Wright Stephenson, *Nelson W. Aldrich: A Leader in American Politics* (Port Washington, NY: Kennikat Press, 1971), 120.

2. Sean Dennis Cashman, *America in the Gilded Age: From the Death of Lincoln to the Rise of Theodore Roosevelt*, 3rd edition (New York: New York University Press, 1993), 11.

3. Samuel Eliot Morison, Henry Steele Commager, and William E. Leuchtenburg, *The Growth of the American Republic*, Volume Two, 7th edition (New York: Oxford University Press, 1980), 33–34; John F. Stover, *American Railroads* (Chicago: University of Chicago Press, 1970), 45; and Albro Martin, *Railroads Triumphant: The Growth, Rejection & Rebirth of a Vital American Force* (New York: Oxford University Press, 1992), 25.

4. See John A. Garraty, *The New Commonwealth, 1877–1890* (New York: Harper Torchbooks, 1968), 9; Morrison, Commager, and Leuchtenberg, *Growth*, 38–39; and Stover, *American Railroads*, 67, 89–90.

5. Quoted in Ray Ginger, *Age of Excess: The United States from 1877–1914* (New York: MacMillan Publishing Company, 1975), 104–105.

6. See Mark Wahlgren Summers, *Rum, Romanism, & Rebellion: The Making of a President, 1884* (Chapel Hill, NC: The University of North Carolina Press, 2000), 62. See also Cashman, *Gilded Age*, 249–252; Lewis Gould, *The Presidency of William McKinley* (Lawrence, KS: The University Press of Kansas, 1890), 72; Neil Rolde, *Continental Liar From the State of Maine: James G. Blaine*, (Gardiner, ME: Tilbury House Publishers, 2007), 177–183; and Milton Rugoff, *America's Gilded Age: Intimate Portraits from an Era of Extravagance and Change, 1850–1890* (New York: Henry Holt and Company, 1989), 27.

7. See Robert W. Cherney, *American Politics in the Gilded Age* (Wheeling, IL: Harlan Davidson, Inc., 1997), 54; Donald Barr Chidsey, *The Gentleman from New York: A Life of Roscoe Conkling* (New Haven: Yale University Press, 1935), 178; David M. Jordan, *Roscoe Conkling of New York: Voice in the Senate* (Ithaca, NY: Cornell University Press, 1971), 187; Leland L. Sage, *William Boyd Allison: A Study in Practical Politics* (Iowa City, IA: State Historical Society of Iowa, 1956), 124–125; and Jean Edward Smith, *Grant* (New York: Simon and Schuster, 2001), 552–553.

8. See John Steele Gordon, *An Empire of Wealth: The Epic History of American Economic Power* (New York: Harper Collins Publishers, 2004), 219–220; and Maury Klein, *Union Pacific: Birth of a Railroad, 1862–1893* (Garden City, NY: Doubleday, 1987), 291.

9. For a thorough and even handed analysis, see Klein, *Union Pacific*, 295–302.

10. See Eric Foner, *Reconstruction: America's Unfinished Revolution, 1863–1877* (New York: Harper & Row, 1988), 384–389.

11. See Gordon, *Empire of Wealth*, 212–216; Scott B. MacDonald and Jane E. Hughes, *Separating Fools From Their Money: A History of American Financial Scandals* (New Brunswick, NJ: Transaction Publishers, 2010), 46–48; and Stover, *American Railroads*, 110–113.

12. See Matthew Josephson, *The Robber Barons* (New York: Harcourt Brace Jovanvoich, 1962); Morrison, Commager, and Leuchtenberg, *Growth*, 43; David J. Rothman, *Politics and Power: The United States Senate, 1869–1901* (Cambridge, MA: Harvard University Press, 1966), 195–201; and Stover, *American Railroads*, 123.

13. Quoted in Josephson, *Robber Barons*, 354.

14. See Lawrence Goodwyn, *Democratic Promise: The Populist Movement in America* (New York: Oxford University Press, 1976), 117; Albro Martin, *Enterprise Denied: Origins of the Decline of American Railroads, 1897–1917* (New York: Columbia University Press, 1971), 17; Morrison, Commager, and Leuchtenberg, *Growth*, 41–42, and Stover, *American Railroads*, 127. By the end of the nineteenth century, railroads were in a squeeze. Revenues grew during the latter half of the nineteenth century, but mileage grew even further. On top of that, bad management and rate wars had driven many into bankruptcy, and many more to the brink. That led to a massive consolidation of the railroads, so that by 1906 two-thirds of the roads were controlled by just seven companies. See Martin, *Enterprise*, 36; and Stover, *American Railroads*, 135.

15. See Glenn Porter, *The Rise of Big Business, 1860–1920* (Wheeling, IL: Harlan Davidson, 2006), 10–30.

16. See Richard Franklin Bensel, *The Political Economy of American Industrialization, 1877–1900* (Cambridge: Cambridge University Press, 2000), 285–286.

17. It is this demand that often creates the misimpression that this was a period of laissez-faire, but the phrase fails to capture just how essential government policy was to business success. Yes, business wanted an absence of regulation, but they demanded tariff protection and the active maintenance of the gold standard.

18. See Bensel, *Political Economy*, 321–349; Gordon, *Empire of Wealth*, 237–238; Alfred H. Kelly, Winfred A. Harbison, and Herman Belz, *The American Constitution: It's Origins and Development*, 6th edition (New York: W.W. Norton & Company, 1983), 397–412; Robert G. McCloskey, *The American Supreme Court*, 4th edition (Chicago: University of Chicago Press, 2005), 79–101; Morrison, Commager, and Leuchtenberg, *Growth*, 44; and Stover, *American Railroads*, 134.

19. See Bensel, *Political Economy*, 321–349.

20. See Bensel, *Political Economy*, 453.

21. See Ron Chernow, *The House of Morgan: An American Banking Dynasty and the Rise of Modern Finance* (New York: Atlantic Monthly Press, 1990), 73–78.

22. See Bensel, *Political Economy*, 366, 370–381, 392–395.

23. This in turn meant that the various silver purchase acts were, in effect, nothing more than corporate welfare for the owners of silver mines of the Mountain West.

24. See Bensel, *Political Economy*, 417–418.

25. See Bensel, *Political Economy*, 457–509; Gordon, *Empire of Wealth*, 272; Stuart McConnell, *Glorious Contentment: The Grand Army of the Republic, 1865–1900* (Chapel Hill, NC: The University of North Carolina Press, 1992), 143–153; and Theda Skocpol, *Protecting Soldiers and Mothers: The Political Origins of Social Policy in the United States* (Cambridge, MA: The Belknap Press of Harvard University Press, 1992), 109–137.

26. See Matthew Josephson, *The Politicos, 1865–1896* (New York: Harcourt, Brace & World, Inc., 1938), 458–459, 638; David Graham Phillips, *The Treason of the Senate* (Chicago: Quadrangle Books, 1964), 89.

27. See Rothman, *Politics and Power*, 160.

28. See Josephson, *Robber Barons*, 347; and Josephson, *Politicos*, 445.

29. See Rothman, *Politics and Power*, 186–187.

30. Louis Overacker, *Money in Elections* (New York: The MacMillan Company, 1932),

133. See also Joanne Reitano, *The Tariff Question in the Gilded Age: The Great Debate of 1888* (University Park, PA: The Pennsylvania State University Press, 1994), 112–113.

31. Other Standard Oil Letters implicated senators Mark Hanna of Ohio, Boies Penrose and Matthew Quay of Pennsylvania, John McLaurin of South Carolina, Joseph Bailey of Texas, and Nathan Scott and Stephen Elkins of West Virginia. Representative Joseph Sibley of Pennsylvania was also revealed to be a crucial contact of Standard Oil in the Congress. Bailey was implicated as being tied to Standard Oil by pulling strings to get its dummy corporation invited back into Texas, and in return was alleged to have received assistance in purchasing a ranch. See William A. Cocke, *The Bailey Controversy* (San Antonio, TX: The Cocke Company, 1908).

32. William Randolph Hearst, "The History of the Standard Oil Letters," *Hearst's Magazine* 21, no. 11 (May 1912): 2210.

33. Quay's only real policy interest in government was the tariff, and this can be credited to the fact that it was the main concern of the industrial and commercial elements that contributed so generously to his machine. See James A. Kehl, *Boss Rule in the Gilded Age: Matt Quay of Pennsylvania* (Pittsburgh, PA: University of Pittsburgh Press, 1981), 129.

34. See William Alan Blair, "A Practical Politician: The Boss Tactics of Matthew Stanley Quay," *Pennsylvania History* 56, no. 2 (April 1989): 85; and Kehl, *Boss Rule*, 63.

35. Kehl, *Boss Rule*, 27. See Homer E. Socolofsky and Allan B. Spetter, *The Presidency of Benjamin Harrison* (Lawrence, KS: The University Press of Kansas, 1987), 10.

36. See Kehl, *Boss Rule*, 59–62.

37. William Randolph Hearst, "New Standard Oil Letters and Their Lessons," *Hearst's Magazine* 21, no. 12 (June 1912): 48b.

38. The Standard Oil Letters also show Archbold interacting with local politicians in Pennsylvania to influence state judicial nominations. None of that could have occurred with at least Quay's tacit approval. See William Randolph Hearst, "Standard Oil and the Judiciary: The Citadel of Trust Defence is in the State and Federal Courts," *Hearst's Magazine* XII, no. 3 (September 1912).

39. Quoted in John Lukacs, *Philadelphia Patricians & Philistines, 1900–1950* (Philadelphia: ISHI Publications, 1981), 69.

40. See Blair, "Practical Politician," 80; Walter Davenport, *Power and Glory: The Life of Boies Penrose* (New York: G.P. Putnam's Sons, 1935), 55; Josepheson, *Politicos*, 408–409; Kehl, *Boss Rule*, 64–65; and Philip S. Klein and Ari Hoogenboom, *A History of Pennsylvania* (New York: McGraw-Hill Book Company, 1973), 322.

41. See Davenport, *Power and Glory*, 152–154.

42. See Charles W. Calhoun, *Minority Victory: Gilded Age Politics and the Front Porch Campaign* (Lawrence, KS: The University Press of Kansas, 2008), 126–129; Kehl, *Boss Rule*, 93–114; and Socolofsky and Spetter, *Presidency*, 11.

43. Penrose's lifelong ambition was to become mayor of Philadelphia, but it was never to be. He came close to the nomination in 1894, but an anti-Penrose faction stopped him by hinting they possessed a photograph of him exiting a house of prostitution. See Lukacs, *Philadelphia*, 65.

44. Quoted in Davenport, *Power and Glory*, 126. Unsurprisingly, Penrose was also caught up in the Standard Oil Letters scandal. See William Randolph Hearst, "Some Startling Revelations that Hitherto Unpublished Standard Oil Letters Contain," *Hearst's Magazine* XXII, no. 2 (August 1812).

45. See Phillips, *Treason*, 79–80; Lincoln Steffens, *The Struggle for Self-Government* (New York: McClure, Phillips & Co., 1906), 126; and Stephenson, *Nelson W. Aldrich*, 63.

46. See Horace Samuel Merrill and Marion Galbraith Merrill, *The Republican Command, 1897–1913* (Lexington, KY: The University Press of Kentucky, 1971), 21.

47. See Merrill and Merrill, *Republican Command*, 17; Stephenson, *Nelson W. Aldrich*, 134; and Phillips, *Treason*, 79.

48. See Joanne Reitano, *The Tariff Question in the Gilded Age: The Great Debate of 1888* (University Park, PA: The Pennsylvania State University Press, 1994), 3–4.

49. Quoted in Morison, Commager, and Leuchtenburg, *Growth of the American Republic*, 232.

50. Phillips, *Treason*, 83.

51. Steffens, *Struggle*, 121. See also Merrill and Merrill, *Republican Command*, 25; Jerome L. Sternstein, "Corruption in the Gilded Age Senate: Nelson W. Aldrich and the Sugar Trust," *Capitol Studies* 6, no. 1 (Spring 1978); and Clarence A. Stern, *Republican Heyday: Republicanism Through the McKinley Years* (Ann Arbor, MI: Edwards Brothers, 1962), 22.

52. See Merrill and Merrill, *Republican Command*, 21–22; and Stephenson, *Nelson W. Aldrich*, 93.

53. See Phillips, *Treason*, 81; Steffens, *Struggle*, 142–143; Stephenson, *Nelson W. Aldrich*, 97–98; and Sternstein, "Corruption."

54. Quoted in Bensel, *Political Economy*, 464.

55. Quoted in Lukacs, *Philadelphia*, 72.

Chapter Six

1. For the links between the progressive movement and the Liberal Republican and Mugwump movements, see Nancy Cohen, *The Reconstruction of American Liberalism, 1865–1914* (Chapel Hill, NC: The University of North Carolina Press, 2002).

2. See George E. Mowry, *The Progressive Movement 1900–1920: Recent Ideas and New Literature* (Washington, DC: The American Historical Association, 1958), 1. The important role of the South has often been overlooked, but southern Democrats were integral to the passage of much progressive legislation during this period, as the Republican Party was still dominated by northeastern conservatives. For an excellent study of this, see David Sarasohn, *The Party of Reform: Democrats in the Progressive Era* (Jackson, MS: University Press of Mississippi, 1989).

3. See James Chace, *1912: Wilson, Roosevelt, Taft & Debs - The Election That Changed The Country* (New York: Simon & Schuster, 2004), 191–198; John Allen Gable, *The Bull Moose Years: Theodore Roosevelt and the Progressive Party* (Port Washington, NY: Kennikat Press, 1978), 87; and Sidney M. Milkis, *Theodore Roosevelt, The Progressive Party, and the Transformation of American Democracy* (Lawrence, KS: The University Press of Kansas, 2009), 202–217.

4. Quoted at Michael McGerr, *A Fierce Discontent: The Rise and Fall of the Progressive Movement in America* (Oxford: Oxford University Press, 2003), 74. See also Richard Hofstadter, *The Age of Reform* (New York: Vintage Books, 1955), 129–173.

5. See Gable, *Bull Moose*, 88; and Mowry, *Progressive Movement*, 2.

6. See John Milton Cooper, Jr., *Woodrow Wilson: A Biography* (New York: Alfred A. Knopf, 2009), 415; Harry Bruinius, *Better for All the World: The Secret History of Forced Sterilization and America's Quest for Racial Purity* (New York: Vintage, 2007); and *Buck v. Bell* 274 U.S. 200 (1927).

7. Quoted in Steven L. Piott, *American Reformers, 1870–1920: Progressives in Word and Deed* (Lanham, MD: Rowman & Littlefield Publishers, 2006), 25.

8. For an overview of the progressive movement's influence on public policy, see Jay Cost, *Spoiled Rotten* (New York: Broadside Books, 2012), 26–43.

9. See Lewis L. Gould, *The Presidency of Theodore Roosevelt* (Lawrence, KS: The University Press of Kansas, 1991), 40–51.

10. See Gould, *Theodore Roosevelt*, 106, 159–164.

11. See Lewis L. Gould, *The Presidency of William Howard Taft* (Lawrence, KS: The University Press of Kansas, 2009), 101.

12. See Cooper, *Woodrow Wilson*, 232–235; H. W. Brands, *Woodrow Wilson* (New York: Times Books, 2003), 82–83; Kendrick A. Clements, *The Presidency of Woodrow Wilson* (Lawrence, KS: The University Press of Kansas, 1992), 49–51; Arthur S. Link, *Woodrow Wilson and the Progressive Era, 1910–1917* (New York: Harper & Row, 1954), 71–75.

13. See Cooper, *Woodrow Wilson*, 229–231; Clements, *Presidency*, 48–50; Link, *Woodrow Wilson*, 67–73.

14. See Gould, *Theodore Roosevelt*, 158–164.

15. See Cooper, *Woodrow Wilson*, 222–254; Brands, *Woodrow Wilson*, 35–36; Clements, *Presidency*, 40–44; Link, *Woodrow Wilson*, 43–53.

16. See Cooper, *Woodrow Wilson*, 344–346; Clements, *Presidency*, 36–40; Link, *Woodrow Wilson*, 35–43.

17. See Cooper, *Woodrow Wilson*, 345–354; Clements, *Presidency*, 44, 81; Link, *Woodrow Wilson*, 235–239.

18. Croly offers a fair summary of Roosevelt's agenda in *Progressive Democracy*: "Roosevelt progressivism can fairly be charged with many ambiguities, but in one essential respect its meaning is unmistakable. Its advocates are committed to a drastic reorganization of the American political and economic system, to the substitution of a frank social policy for the individualism of the past, and to the realization of this policy, if necessary, by the use of efficient governmental instruments" (Croly, *Progressive Democracy*, 15).

19. Croly, *Progressive Democracy*, 15.

20. Herbert Croly, *The Promise of American Life* (New York: The Macmillan Company, 1914), 409.

21. See Ronald J. Pestritto and William J. Atto, "Introduction to American Progressivism," in *American Progressivism*, ed. Ronald J. Pestritto and William J. Atto (Lanham, MD: Lexington Books, 2008), 3. See John Dewey, *Liberalism and Social Action* (Amherst, NY: Prometheus Books, 2000), 53–54, for his take on the "crisis of liberalism." See William Allen White, "From The Old Order Changeth," in *The Gilded Age and Progressive Era, 1877–1920*, ed. John D. Buenker (Acton, MA: Copley Publishing Group, 2002), 604, for his call to live by the Declaration of Independence, rather than the Constitution. Here is Goodnow on the problem of "extreme individualism" of social contract theory in the United States:

> The result was the adoption in this country of a doctrine of unadulterated individualism. Every one had rights. Social duties were hardly recognized, or if recognized little emphasis was laid upon them. It was apparently thought that every one was able and willing to protect his rights, and that as a result of the struggle between men for their rights and of the compromise of what appeared to be conflicting rights would arise an effective social organization. . . . secured merely through stressing our rights. The emphasis is being laid more and more on social duties . . . man under modern conditions is primarily a member of society and that only as he recognizes his duties as a member of society can he secure the greatest opportunities as an individual." 63. "For it is only as individuals limit their conceptions of their rights by considerations of social justice and expediency, only as they come to recognize the existence and the imperative character of their

social duties, that we can hope for the development of that social efficiency which is necessary both for individual happiness and the public welfare. (Frank Johnson Goodnow, *The American Conception of Liberty and Government* [Providence, RI: Standard Printing Company, 1916], 12)

22. "Progressive Party Platform of 1912," November 5, 1912. Online by Gerhard Peters and John T. Woolley, *The American Presidency Project*, http://www.presidency.ucsb.edu/ws/?pid=29617.

23. Theodore Roosevelt, "Inaugural Address," March 4, 1905. Online by Gerhard Peters and John T. Woolley, *The American Presidency Project*, http://www.presidency.ucsb.edu/ws/?pid=25829 1904.

24. In the *Promise of American Life*, Croly frames the innovation as necessary to hold on to the "promise" that America has implicitly made to its citizens:

The Promise of American life is to be fulfilled—not merely by a maximum amount of economic freedom, but by a certain measure of discipline; not merely by the abundant satisfaction of individual desires, but by a large measure of individual subordination and self-denial. And this necessity of subordinating the satisfaction of individual desires to the fulfillment of a national purpose is attached particularly to the absorbing occupation of the American people, -- viz.: of accumulating wealth. The automatic fulfillment of the American national Promise is to be abandoned, if at all, precisely because the traditional American confidence in individual freedom has resulted in a morally and socially undesirable distribution of wealth. (Croly, *Promise*, 22)

In other words, to save something old, the progressives had to do something new.

25. Woodrow Wilson, *Congressional Government: A Study in American Politics* (Boston, MA: Houghton Mifflin Company, 1885), 332.

26. See Ronald J. Pestritto, *Woodrow Wilson and the Roots of Modern Liberalism* (Lanham, MD: Rowman & Littlefield Publishers, 2005), 14–47.

27. Woodrow Wilson, *A History of the American People*, Volume V (New York: Harper & Brothers, 1902), 198–199.

28. Woodrow Wilson, *Constitutional Government in the United States* (New York: The Columbia University Press, 1908), 46.

29. Woodrow Wilson, *The Study of Public Administration* (Washington, DC: Public Affairs Press, 1955), 16–17.

30. Woodrow Wilson, *Cabinet Government in the United States* (Stamford, CT: The Overbrook Press, 1947), 6–7.

31. Wilson, *Cabinet Government*, 16–17.

32. See Pestritto, *Woodrow Wilson*, 25; Daniel D. Stid, *The President as Statesman: Woodrow Wilson and the Constitution* (Lawrence, KS: University Press of Kansas, 1998), 38; and Jeffrey K. Tulis, *The Rhetorical Presidency* (Princeton, NJ: Princeton University Press, 1987), 118–119.

33. See Jean Yarbrough, *Theodore Roosevelt and the American Political Tradition* (Lawrence, KS: The University Press of Kansas, 2012), 138–193.

34. Wilson, *Constitutional Government*, 59–60.

35. See Stid, *President as Statesman*, 74–75.

36. See Stid, *President as Statesman*, 168.

37. See Richard E. Neustadt, *Presidential Power and the Modern Presidents: The Politics of Leadership from Roosevelt to Reagan* (New York: The Free Press, 1990).

38. See Gene Healy, *The Cult of the Presidency: America's Danger Devotion to Executive*

Power (Washington, DC: The Cato Institute, 2008), 2–7; Clinton Rossiter, *The American Presidency* (New York: Harcourt, Brace & World, 1956), 4–25; and Theodore J. Lowi, *The Personal President: Power Invested, Promise Unfulfilled* (Ithaca, NY: Cornell University Press, 1985), 6–8.

39. Neustadt, *Presidential Power*, 150.

40. See Samuel Kernell, *Going Public: New Strategies in Presidential Leadership* (Washington, DC: CQ Press, 1993), 2–3.

41. Quoted in Stid, *President as Statesman*, 1.

42. See Tulis, *Rhetorical Presidency*, 147–161.

43. See Charles I. Jones, *Separate But Equal Branches: Congress and the Presidency* (New York: Chatham House Publishers, 1999), vii–viii; and James L. Sundquist, "The New Era of Coalition Government in the United States," *Political Science Quarterly* 103 (1988–89): 629.

44. See Stephen Skowronek, *The Politics Presidents Make: Leadership from John Adams to Bill Clinton* (Cambridge, MA: The Belknap Press of Harvard University Press, 1998).

45. See Matthew N. Beckman, *Pushing the Agenda: Presidential Leadership in U.S. Lawmaking, 1953–2004* (Cambridge: Cambridge University Press, 2010), 4–13.

46. Lowi, *Personal President*, 11. See also George C. Edwards, III, *The Strategic President: Persuasion & Opportunity in Presidential Leadership* (Princeton, NJ: Princeton University Press, 2009), x–xi, 9–12, 59–60, 152–153.

47. Quoted in Beckman, *Pushing the Agenda*, 3.

48. See Pestritto, *Woodrow Wilson*, 127–128; and Pestritto and Atto, "Introduction," 18–19.

49. Woodrow Wilson, *The Study of Public Administration* (Washington, DC: Public Affairs Press, 1955), 13.

50. David Epstein and Sharyn O'Halloran, *Delegating Powers: A Transaction Cost Politics Approach to Policy Making Under Separate Powers* (Cambridge: Cambridge University Press, 1999), 8–9.

Chapter Seven

1. See John W. Dean, *Warren G. Harding* (New York: Times Books, 2004), 155–160; and David J. Goldberg, *Discontented America: The United States in the 1920s* (Baltimore, MD: The Johns Hopkins University Press, 1999), 59–61.

2. See Paul K. Conkin, *The New Deal* (Wheeling, IL: Harlan Davidson, 1992), 11.

3. See Paul P. Van Riper, *History of The United States Civil Service* (Evanston, IL: Row, Peterson and Company, 1958), 320.

4. See Van Riper, *History*, 340. See also Morris P. Fiorina, "The Decline of Collective Responsibility in American Politics," *Daedalus* 109, no. 3 (Summer, 1980): 45.

5. Quoted in Van Riper, *History*, 318.

6. See Daniel Mark Scroop, *Mr. Democrat: Jim Farley, the New Deal and the Making of Modern American Politics* (Ann Arbor, MI: University of Michigan Press, 2009), 103.

7. Quoted in Sean J. Savage, *Roosevelt: The Party Leader, 1932–1945* (Lexington, KY: University Press of Kentucky, 1991), 21.

8. See James T. Patterson, *The New Deal and the States: Federalism in Transition* (Princeton, NJ: Princeton University Press, 1969), 170; and Savage, *Roosevelt*, 22.

9. See Patterson, *New Deal*, 172.

10. See Gavin Wright, "The Political Economy of New Deal Spending: An Econometric Analysis," *The Review of Economics and Statistics* 56, no. 1 (February 1974), 35. Future Republican presidential nominee Thomas Dewey of New York complained about this

timing, arguing that it was a factor in his loss of the governorship in 1938. See Searle F. Charles, *Minister of Relief: Harry Hopkins and the Depression* (Syracuse, NY: Syracuse University Press, 1963), 167.

11. See Jim F. Couch and William F. Shughart, *The Political Economy of the New Deal* (Fairfax, VA: The Locke Institute, 1998); John Joseph Wallis, "Employment, Politics, and Economic Recovery during the Great Depression," *The Review of Economics and Statistics* 69, no. 3 (August 1987): 519; Wright, "The Political Economy," 35; Gary M. Anderson and Robert D. Tollison, "Congressional Influence and Patterns of New Deal Spending, 1933–1939," *Journal of Law and Economics* 34, no. 1 (April 1991): 161–175; Don C. Reading, "New Deal Activity and the States, 1933 to 1939," *The Journal of Economic History* 33, no. 4 (December 1973): 792–810; and Robert K. Fleck, "Electoral Incentives, Public Policy, and the New Deal Realignment," *Southern Economic Journal* 65, no. 3 (January 1999): 377–404.

12. See John Joseph Wallis, Price Fishback, and Shawn Kantor, "Politics, Relief, and Reform: The Transformation of America's Social Welfare System During the New Deal," Working Paper 11080 (Cambridge, MA: National Bureau of Economic Research, January 2005), http://www.nber.org/papers/w11080; and Priscilla Ferguson Clement, "The Works Progress Administration in Pennsylvania, 1935 to 1940," *The Pennsylvania Magazine of History and Biography* 95, no. 2 (April 1971): 245.

13. Quoted in Katie Louchhem, ed., *The Making of the New Deal: The Insiders Speak* (Cambridge, MA: Harvard University Press, 1983), 191–192. See also Paul A. Kurzman, *Harry Hopkins and the New Deal* (Fair Lawn, NJ: R. E. Burdick, Inc., 1974), 137–138.

14. Stanley High, another Hopkins colleague, made essentially the same point. See Charles, *Minister of Relief*, 174.

15. In a generally sympathetic account, a key biographer notes that while Hopkins was far from the worst offender in Washington in terms of mixing relief and patronage, he used some of his power to serve both the Democrats and his benefactor, Franklin D. Roosevelt. Charles, *Minister of Relief*, 205.

16. See Charles, *Minister of Relief*, 142–143, 162–163; Savage, *Roosevelt*, 19–20.

17. Quoted in Clement, "Works Progress Administration," 247. Politicians in Chicago behaved similarly, forming a Works Progress Administration "social club" that they used to pressure relief workers into voting Democratic. See Jason Scott Smith, *Building New Deal Liberalism: The Political Economy of Public Works, 1933–1956* (Cambridge: Cambridge University Press, 2006), 150–154.

18. See Savage, *Roosevelt*, 136; and Van Riper, *History*, 340.

19. See Smith, *Building*, 177–178.

20. Quoted in Thomas L. Stokes, *Chip Off My Shoulder* (Princeton, NJ: Princeton University Press, 1940), 537.

21. Quoted in Nick Taylor, *American-Made: The Enduring Legacy of the WPA: When FDR Put the Nation To Work* (New York: Bantam Books, 2008), 389.

22. See Susan Dunn, *Roosevelt's Purge: How FDR Fought to Change the Democratic Party* (Cambridge, MA: The Belknap Press of Harvard University Press, 2010), 128.

23. Quoted in Dunn, *Roosevelt's Purge*, 115. The *Cedar Rapids Gazette* accused Hopkins of using the Works Progress Administration as a "political whip."

24. Stokes, *Chip Off*, 535.

25. Stokes, *Chip Off*, 537.

26. Quoted in Smith, *Building*, 172.

27. See Smith, *Building*, 174.

28. Van Riper, *History*, 340–341.

29. Franklin Delano Roosevelt similarly used his connections with political machines in Chicago and Kansas City to pressure senators William Dieterich of Illinois and Harry Truman of Missouri to vote for Alben Barkley in his bid to become Senate Majority Leader in 1937. In the case of Chicago, boss Ed Kelly told Dieterich that Illinois might lose Works Progress Administration funds if Barkley did not succeed. See Savage, *Roosevelt*, 37.

30. See Stephen P. Erie, *Rainbow's End: Irish-Americans and the Dilemma of Urban Machine Politics, 1840–1945* (Berkeley, CA: University of California Press, 1988), 128–139.

31. See Savage, *Roosevelt*, 49.

32. See Oliver E. Allen, *The Tiger: The Rise and Fall of Tammany Hall* (Cambridge, MA: Da Cap Press, 1993), 232–254; Conkin, *New Deal*, 16–17; Charles LaCerra, *Franklin Delano Roosevelt and Tammany Hall of New York* (Lanham, MD: University Press of America, 1997), 43–52; and Jean Edward Smith, FDR (New York: Random House, 2008), 70–76, 117–118.

33. See Lyle W. Dorsett, *Franklin D. Roosevelt and the City Bosses* (Port Washington, NY: Kennikat Press, 1977), 57–59; LaCerra, *Franklin Delano Roosevelt*, 88–89; and Mason B. Williams, *City of Ambition: FDR, La Guardia, and the Making of Modern New York* (New York: W. W. Norton & Co., 2013), 126.

34. See Williams, *City of Ambition*, 191.

35. On Philadelphia, see Irwin F. Greenberg, "Philadelphia Democrats Get a New Deal: The Election of 1933," *The Pennsylvania Magazine of History and Biography* 97, no. 2 (April 1973): 210–232; Stefano Luconi, "Bringing out the Italian-American Vote in Philadelphia," *The Pennsylvania Magazine of History and Biography* 117, no. 4 (October 1993): 251–285; Stefano Luconi, "Machine Politics and the Consolidation of the Roosevelt Majority: The Case of Italian Americans in Pittsburgh and Philadelphia," *Journal of American Ethnic History* 15, no. 2 (Winter 1996): 32–59; and Stefano Luconi, "The New Deal Realignment and the Italian-American Community of Philadelphia," *Journal of American Studies* 28, no. 3 (December 1994): 403–422. On Pittsburgh, see Bruch M. Stave, *The New Deal and the Last Hurrah: Pittsburgh Machine Politics* (Pittsburgh, PA: University of Pittsburgh Press, 1970).

36. See Savage, *Roosevelt*, 56–68; and Gene Delon Jones, "The Origin of the Alliance between the New Deal and the Chicago Machine," *Journal of the Illinois State Historical Society (1908–1984)* 67, no. 3 (June 1974): 253–274.

37. See Savage, *Roosevelt*, 52–56.

38. As Lyon et al. put it: "We have no formal official version of the economic doctrines underlying the NRA. There is instead an accumulation of public statements emanating from different government officials and varying widely in emphasis and completeness." (Leverett S. Lyon, et al. *The National Recovery Administration: An Analysis and Appraisal* [Washington, DC: The Brookings Institution, 1935], 756).

39. See Donald R. Brand, *Corporatism and the Rule of Law: A Study of the National Recovery Administration* (Ithaca, NY: Cornell University Press, 1988), 82–83; G. William Domhoff and Michael J. Webber, *Class and Power in the New Deal: Corporate Moderates, Southern Democrats, and the Liberal-Labor Coalition* (Stanford, CA: Stanford University Press, 2011), 1–7; Ellis W. Hawley, "A Partnership Formed, Dissolved, and in Renegotiation: Business and Government in the Franklin D. Roosevelt Era," in *Survival of Corporatism During the New Deal Era, 1933–1945*, ed. Robert F. Himmelberg (New York: Garland Publishing, Inc., 1994), 97–101; Robert F. Himmelberg, "The Triumph of the Revisionists: The N.I.R.A.," in *Survival of Corporatism During the New Deal Era, 1933–1945*, ed. Robert F. Himmelberg (New York: Garland Publishing, Inc., 1994), 129–130; William E. Leucht-

enburg, *Franklin D. Roosevelt and the New Deal, 1932–1940* (New York: Harper Perennial, 2009), 56; Arthur M. Schlesinger, Jr., *The Age of Roosevelt, Volume II, 1933–1935: The Coming of the New Deal* (Boston, MA: Mariner Books, 2003), 92; Amity Shlaes, *The Forgotten Man: A New History of the Great Depression* (New York: Harper Collins, 2007), 150–152.

40. Gerald D. Nash, "Experiments in Industrial Mobilization: WIB and NRA," in *Survival of Corporatism During the New Deal Era, 1933–1945*, ed. Robert F. Himmelberg (New York: Garland Publishing, Inc., 1994), 328; and see Robert D. Cuff, *The War Industries Board: Business-Government Relations During World War I* (Baltimore, MD: The Johns Hopkins University Press, 1973), 1.

41. Quoted in Ellis W. Hawley, *The New Deal and the Problem of Monopoly: A Study in Economic Ambivalence* (New York: Fordham University Press, 1996), 17.

42. Leuchtenburg, *Franklin D. Roosevelt*, 57–58.

43. See David Traxel, *Crusader Nation: The United States in Peace and the Great War, 1898–1920* (New York: Alfred A. Knopf, 2006), 176–177.

44. See Cuff, *War Industries Board*, 1–4; Robert H. Ferrell, *Woodrow Wilson & World War I, 1917–1921* (New York: Harper & Row, 1985), 104–107; and Ronald Schaffer, *America in the Great War: The Rise of the War Welfare State* (New York: Oxford University Press, 1991), 40–54.

45. Rhonda F. Levine, *Class Struggle and the New Deal: Industrial Labor, Industrial Capital, and the State* (Lawrence, KS: University Press of Kansas, 1988), 78.

46. See Schlesinger, *Coming*, 108–109.

47. See Bernard Bellush, *The Failure of the* NRA (New York: W. W. Norton & Company, 1975), 38–39; Hawley, *New Deal*, 56; Himmelberg, "Triumph of the Revisionists," 159; Peter H. Irons, *The New Deal Lawyers* (Princeton, NJ: Princeton University Press, 1982), 32–33; Leuchtenberg, *Franklin D. Roosevelt*, 109.

48. See Himmelburg, "Triumph of the Revisionists," 159.

49. Levine, *Class Struggle*, 80.

50. Quoted in Levine, *Class Struggle*, 95. This was a general complaint heard from many western politicians in the populist tradition, like William Borah and Burton K. Wheeler. See Bellush, *Failure*, 18–22; Leuchtenburg, *Franklin D. Roosevelt*, 67; and Schlesinger, *Coming*, 101. Franklin Delano Roosevelt enlisted a special panel, headed by famed attorney Clarence Darrow, to investigate it. When Darrow came out with a report roundly criticizing the National Industrial Recovery Act for unfairness to small business, Johnson attacked him vehemently. Since then, historians have noted that the Darrow Committee drew conclusions that were not merited in many respects, but in other respects its inferences remain valid. See Bellush, *Failure*, 142–145; Michael Hannon, "Clarence Darrow and the National Recovery Review Board," *University of Minnesota Law Library*, http://darrow.law.umn.edu/trialpdfs/National_Recovery_Review_Board.pdf; and Clarence Darrow, "Statement of Clarence Darrow," in *Investigation of the National Recovery Administration: Hearings before the Committee On Finance, United States Senate, Seventy-Fourth Congress, First Session* (Washington, DC: United States Printing Office, 1935).

51. See Shlaes, *The Forgotten Man*, 217–225.

52. See Jonah Goldberg, *Liberal Fascism: The Secret History of the American Left from Mussolini to the Politics of Meaning* (New York: Doubleday, 2007), 155; and George F. Will, "Trifle with the Government? Just Ask Jacob Maged," *The Washington Post*, Thursday, September 16, 2010. African Americans complained bitterly about the National Recovery Administration, some dubbing it the "Negro Removal Act," for how restrictions in hours and employment always seemed to hit them the hardest. See Goldberg, *Liberal*

Fascism, 156; and John B. Kirby, *Black Americans in the Roosevelt Era: Liberalism and Race* (Knoxville, TN: The University of Tennessee Press, 1980), 41–42.

53. See William L. Anderson, "Risk and the National Industrial Recovery Act: An Empirical Evaluation," *Public Choice* 103, no. 1/2 (April 2000): 139–161.

54. Lyon et al., *National Recovery Administration*, 771.

55. Lee J. Alston and Joseph P. Ferrie, *Southern Paternalism and the American Welfare State: Economics, Politics, and Institutions in the South, 1865–1965* (Cambridge: Cambridge University Press, 1999), 152.

56. Alston and Ferrie, *Southern Paternalism*, 8.

57. Quoted in Gavin Wright, *Old South, New South: Revolutions in the Southern Economy Since the Civil War* (Baton Rouge, LA: The Louisiana State University Press, 1986), 222.

58. See Robert K. Fleck, "Democratic Opposition to the Fair Labor Standards Act of 1938," *The Journal of Economic History* 62, no. 1 (March 2002): 49–50; Leuchtenburg, *Franklin D. Roosevelt*, 261; Andrew J. Seltzer, "The Political Economy of the Fair Labor Standards Act of 1938," *The Journal of Political Economy* 103, no. 6 (December 1995): 1307–1308; and Wright, *Old South*, 219–220.

Chapter Eight

1. Louise Overacker, "Labor's Political Contributions," *Political Science Quarterly* 54, no. 1 (March 1939): 56. See also Bryant Putney, *Labor in Politics* (Washington, DC: Editorial Research Reports, 1940), 9.

2. Quoted in Melvyn Dubofsky and Foster Rhea Dulles, *Labor in America: A History*, 6th edition (Wheeling, IL: Harlan-Davidson, 1999), 295. Hillman had a similar viewpoint. See Charles A. Madison, "Sidney Hillman: Leader of the Amalgamated," *The American Scholar* 18, no. 4 (Autumn 1949): 465.

3. See Melvyn Dubofsky, *John L. Lewis: A Biography* (Urbana, IL: University of Illinois Press, 1986), 181–204; Madison, "Sidney Hillman," 465; Louise Overacker, "Campaign Funds in the Presidential Election of 1936," *The American Political Science Review* 31, no. 3 (June 1937): 485.

4. See Putney, *Labor in Politics*, 15.

5. Madison, "Sidney Hillman," 465. That year, labor accounted for 16 percent of Democratic National Committee contributions that were at least one thousand dollars. Louise Overacker, "Campaign Finance in the Presidential Election of 1940," *The American Political Science Review* 35, no. 4 (August 1941): 723.

6. J. David Greenstone, *Labor in American Politics* (Chicago: University of Chicago Press, 1977), 41.

7. See Herbert B. Asher, et al., *American Labor Unions in the Electoral Arena* (Lanham, MD: Rowman & Littlefield, 2001), 11; Anthony Corrado, et al., *The New Campaign Finance Sourcebook* (Washington, DC: The Brookings Institution, 2005), 17–18; and Raymond La Raja, *Small Change: Money, Political Parties, and Campaign Finance Reform* (Ann Arbor, MI: The University of Michigan Press, 2011), 65.

8. See James C. Foster, *The Union Politic: The CIO Political Action Committee* (Columbia, MO: University of Missouri Press, 1975); and Louise Overacker, "American Government and Politics: Presidential Campaign Funds, 1944," *The American Political Science Review* 39, no. 5 (October 1945): 902.

9. See Steve Fraser, *Labor Will Rule: Sidney Hillman and the Rise of American Labor* (New York: The Free Press, 1991), 495, 538. For a contemporary take from a strong labor advocate, see Joseph Gaer, *The First Round: The Story of the CIO Political Action Committee* (New York: Duell, Sloan and Pearce, 1944), 171–173.

10. See Asher, *American Labor Unions*, 4; and Taylor E. Dark, *The Unions and the Democrats: An Enduring Alliance* (Ithaca, NY: Cornell University Press, 1999), 49–50.

11. See Dark, *Unions*, 55; and Robert H. Zieger and Gilbert J. Gall, *American Workers, American Unions*, 3rd edition (Baltimore, MD: The Johns Hopkins University Press, 2002), 230–233.

12. Archie Robinson, *George Meany and His Times: A Biography* (New York: Simon and Schuster, 1981), 243–244. Money, of course, remained central to labor's power. It gave $1.8 million to Democrats in 1958, $3.8 million in 1964, and $7.6 million in 1968, when it almost singlehandedly propped up the Democratic campaign. Labor also chipped in 118 million leaflets, 638 phone banks, a staff of nearly 25,000 to man the phone banks, and 72,000 canvassers. Yet even for all its efforts, it still never had a majority to break through the conservative coalition's opposition; even Johnson and Meany, for all their power, could not repeal the reviled Taft-Hartley Act. See Graham K. Wilson, *Unions in American National Politics* (New York: St. Martin's Press, 1979), 18, 63.

13. For examples of this, see Jay Cost, *Spoiled Rotten* (New York: Harper Collins, 2011), 138–154, 202–274.

14. James H. Rowe, "Oral History Interview with James H. Rowe," *Harry S. Truman Library and Museum*, http://www.trumanlibrary.org/oralhist/rowejhap.htm.

15. Suzanne Farkas, *Urban Lobbying: Mayors in the Federal Arena* (New York: New York University Press, 1971), 44.

16. Edwin M. Epstein, *The Corporation in American Politics* (Englewood Cliffs, NJ: Prentice-Hall, 1969), 38–61.

17. Louis F. Powell, Jr., *Attack on American Free Enterprise System*, The Powell Archives (Lexington, VA: Washington and Lee University), http://law.wlu.edu/deptimages/ Powell%20Archives/PowellMemorandumTypescript.pdf, 25–26.

18. See Gary Andres, *Lobbying Reconsidered: Politics Under The Influence* (New York: Pearson, 2009), 42; Jeffrey M. Berry and Clyde Wilcox, *The Interest Group Society*, 4th edition (New York: Pearson, 2007), 28; and Benjamin C. Waterhouse, *Lobbying America: The Politics of Business from Nixon to NAFTA* (Princeton, NJ: Princeton University Press, 2014), 58–66. This was a message that resonated not just with the Chamber, which represented mostly smaller businesses. In 1973, the Business Roundtable formed to represent larger corporations. Its executive committee included executives from Campbell's Soup, GE, AT&T, General Motors, Alcoa, Exxon, DuPont, Hewlett-Packard, International Paper, and others. See Sar A. Levitan and Martha R. Cooper, *Business Lobbies: The Public Good and the Bottom Line* (Baltimore, MD: The Johns Hopkins University Press, 1984), 34–40.

19. See Jeffrey M. Berry, *The New Liberalism: The Rising Power of Citizen Groups* (Washington, DC: The Brookings Institution, 1999).

20. See Mark J. Rozell, Clyde Wilcox, and David Madland, *Interest Groups in American Campaigns: The New Face of Electioneering* (Washington, DC: CQ Press, 2006), 73–74.

21. See Corrado et al., *New Campaign*, 20–25; La Raja, *Small Change*, 78–79. The 1974 amendments to the Federal Elections Campaign Act also limited the maximum amount of money that could be spent on a campaign, including from a candidate's own funds. However, the Supreme Court eventually struck that down. The Federal Elections Campaign Act also allowed businesses and corporations to spend unlimited "soft money" on party building activities not directly related to federal campaigns; this provision was outlawed by the 2003 Bipartisan Campaign Reform Act (commonly called McCain-Feingold).

22. Rozell, Wilcox, and Madland, *Interest Groups*, 81, 83.

23. See John R. Wright, *Interest Groups and Congress: Lobbying, Contributions, and Influence* (New York: Pearson, 2003), 130. Another strategy around campaign finance limits is the coordination of political action committee contributions by joining with other like-minded committees or soliciting direct contributions for preferred candidates. See Paul S. Herrnson, "Interest Groups, PACs, and Campaigns," in *The Interest Group Connection: Electioneering, Lobbying, and Policymaking in Washington*, ed. Paul S. Hernson, Ronald G. Shaiko, and Clyde Wilcox (Chatham, NJ: Chatham House Publishers, 1998), 39.

24. Hermson, "Interest Groups," 38.

25. See William T. Gormley, Jr., "Interest Group Interventions in the Administrative Process: Conspirators and Co-Conspirators," in *The Interest Group Connection: Electioneering, Lobbying, and Policymaking in Washington*, ed. Paul S. Hernson, Ronald G. Shaiko, and Clyde Wilcox (Chatham, NJ: Chatham House Publishers, 1998), 213–223; Anthony J. Nownes, *Total Lobbying: What Lobbyists Want (and How They Try To Get It)* (Cambridge: Cambridge University Press, 2006), 62; Wright, *Interest Groups and Congress*, 2–4, 39–72, 82–88.

26. See Andres, *Lobbying*, 2, 63.

27. See Berry and Wilcox, *Interest Group Society*, 72; Hugh A. Bone, "Political Parties and Pressure Group Politics," *Annals of the American Academy of Political and Social Science* 319 (September 1958): 73; Mark A. Peterson and Jack L. Walter, "Interest Group Response to Partisan Change: The Impact of the Reagan Administration upon the National Interest Group System," in *Interest Group Politics*, 2nd edition, ed. Allan J. Cigler and Burdett A. Loomis (Washington, DC: Congressional Quarterly, 1986), 162; and Rozell, Wilcox, and Madland, *Interest Groups*, 36–37.

28. In general, political scientists see a shift toward interest groups working not alone, but rather in broad networks. Sometimes they are predominantly partisan; sometimes they are not. This is a notable change from an earlier scholarly literature that viewed interest groups operating in relative isolation of one another in what were called "iron triangles" or "subgovernments" that gave virtually exclusive authority in any given policy domain to select interest groups, congressmen on key subcommittees, and bureaucrats. For more on "iron triangles," see J. Leiper Freeman, *The Political Process: Executive Bureau-Legislative Relations*, rev. ed. (New York: Random House, 1965); Ernest Griffith, *Impasse of Democracy* (New York: Harrison-Hilton Books, 1939); and George J. Stigler, "The Theory of Economic Regulation," *Bell Journal of Economics and Management Science 2*, no. 1 (Spring 1971): 15–43. For the new revisionist take, see R. Douglas Arnold, *Congress and the Bureaucracy* (New Haven, CT: Yale University Press, 1979); Berry and Wilcox, *Interest Group Society*, 148–169; Colton C. Campbell and Roger H. Davidson, "Coalition Building in Congress: The Consequences of Partisan Change," in *The Interest Group Connection: Electioneering, Lobbying, and Policymaking in Washington*, ed. Paul S. Hernson, Ronald G. Shaiko, and Clyde Wilcox (Chatham, NJ: Chatham House Publishers, 1998), 117–118; Hugh Heclo, "Issue Networks and the Executive Establishment," in *The New American Political System*, ed. Anthony King (Washington, DC: The American Enterprise Institute, 1978); and Kevin W. Hula, *Lobbying Together: Interest Group Coalitions in Legislative Politics* (Washington, DC: Georgetown University Press, 1999).

29. In a recent survey of lobbyists, researchers find that they spend most of their time trying to build relationships. See Rogan Kersh, "The Well-Informed Lobbyist: Information and Interest Group Lobbying" in *Interest Group Politics, 6th edition*, eds. Allan J. Cigler and Burdett A. Loomis (Washington, DC: CQ Press, 2002), 225–248. See also Dan Clawson, Alan Neustadtl, and Denise Scott, *Money Talks: Corporate PACs and*

Political Influence (New York: Basic Books, 1992), 106–107, on the importance of building relationships.

30. See, for instance, Henry W. Chappell, Jr., "Campaign Contributions and Congressional Voting: A Simultaneous Probit-Tobit Model," Review of Economics and Statistics 64 (1982): 77–83; and Janet M. Grenzke, "PACs and the Congressional Supermarket: The Currency is Complex," American Journal of Political Science 33 (1989): 1–24. For a time, the best—and perhaps only—decent accounts of the influence of lobbying came from journalists who had spent a career in Washington. See, for instance, Jackson's profile of political action committee maestro Tony Coelho. Brooks Jackson, Honest Graft: Big Money and the American Political Process (Washington, DC: Farragut Publishing Company, 1990).

31. R. Kenneth Goodwin and Barry J. Seldon, "What Corporations Really Want from the Government: The Public Provision of Private Goods," in Interest Group Politics, 7th edition, ed. Allan J. Cigler and Burdett A. Loomis (Washington, DC: CQ Press, 2002), 206.

32. See Jonathan C. Brooks, A. Colin Cameron, and Colin A. Carter, "Political Action Committee Contributions and U.S. Congressional Voting on Sugar Legislation," American Journal of Agricultural Economics 80 (1998): 441–454; Maria M. Correia, "Political Connections, SEC Enforcement and Accounting Quality," http://papers.ssrn.com/sol3/papers.cfm?abstract_id=1458478; Louay M. Constant, "When Money Matters: Campaign Contributions, Roll Call Votes, and School Choice in Florida," State Politics & Policy Quarterly 6, no. 2 (Summer 2006): 195–219; Andrew Eggers and Jens Hainmueller, "Political Investing: The Common Stock Investments of Members of Congress, 2004–2008," http://www.yale.edu/leitner/resources/papers/Eggmueller_PoliticalInvesting.pdf; Diana Evans, "Before the Roll Call: Interest Group Lobbying and Public Policy Outcomes in House Committees," Political Research Quarterly 49, no. 2 (June 1996): 287–304; Roger Faith, Donald R. Leavens, and Robert D. Tollison, "Antitrust Pork Barrel," Journal of Law and Economics 25, no. 2 (October 1982): 329–342; Matthew C. Fellowes and Patrick J. Wolf, "Funding Mechanisms and Policy Instruments: How Business Campaign Contributions Influence Congressional Votes," Political Research Quarterly 57, no. 2 (June 2004): 315–324; Meng Gao and Jiekun Huang, "Capitalizing on Capitol Hill: Informed Trading By Hedge Fund Managers," http://papers.ssrn.com/sol3/papers.cfm?abstract_id=1707181; Sanford C. Gordon and Catherine Hafer, "Flexing Muscle: Corporate Political Expenditures as Signals to the Bureaucracy," The American Political Science Review 99, no. 2 (May 2005), 245–261; Richard L. Hall and Kristina C. Miler, "What Happens After the Alarm? Interest Group Subsidies to Legislative Overseers," The Journal of Politics 70, no. 4 (October 2008): 990–1005; Richard L. Hall and Frank W. Wayman, "Buying Time: Moneyed Interests and the Mobilization of Bias in Congressional Committees," The American Political Science Review 84, no. 3 (September 1990): 797–820; William J. Hunter and Michael A. Nelson, "Tax Enforcement: A Public Choice Perspective," Public Choice 82, no. 1/2 (1995): 53–67; James B. Kau, Donald Keenan, and Paul H. Rubin, "A General Equilibrium Model of Congressional Voting," Quarterly Journal of Economics 97 (1982): 271–293; Laura I. Langbein and Mark A. Lotwis, "The Political Efficacy of Lobbying and Money: Gun Control in the U.S. House, 1986," Legislative Studies Quarterly 15, no. 3 (August 1990): 413–440; Joseph P. McGarrity and Daniel Sutter, "A Test of the Structure of PAC Contracts: An Analysis of House Gun Control Votes in the 1980s," Southern Economic Journal 67 (2000): 41–63; Franklin G. Mixon, Jr., "Public Choice and the EPA: Empirical Evi-

dence on Carbon Emissions Violants," *Public Choice* 83, no. 1/2 (April 1995): 127–137; Brian Kelleher Richter, Krislert Samphantharak, and Jeffrey F. Timmons, "Lobbying and Taxes," *American Journal of Political Science* 53, no. 4 (October 2009): 893–909; Peter Schweizer, *Throw Them All Out* (Boston, MA: Houghton Mifflin Harcourt, 2011), xiii–xxvii; Ahmed Tahoun and Laurence van Lent, "The Personal Wealth Interests of Politicians and Government Intervention in the Economy," http://papers. ssrn.com/sol3/papers.cfm?abstract_id=1570219; Christopher Witko, "PACs, Issue Context, and Congressional Decisionmaking," *Political Research Quarterly* 59, no. 2 (June 2006): 283–295; Marily Young, Michael Reksulak, and William F. Shughart II, "The Political Economy of the IRS," *Economics and Politics* 13, no. 2 (July 2001): 201–218; and Alan J. Ziobrowski, et al., "Abnormal Returns from the Common Stock Investments of the U.S. Senate," *Journal of Financial and Quantitative Analysis* 39, no. 4 (December 2004): 661–676.

33. See Robert A. Dahl, *Who Governs?: Democracy and Power in an American City*, 2nd ed. (New Haven, CT: Yale University Press, 2005) for the best take on the modern pluralist argument.

34. Theodore J. Lowi, *The End of Liberalism: Ideology, Policy, and the Crisis of Public Authority* (New York: W. W. Norton & Company, 1969), 70.

35. Lowi, *End of Liberalism*, 70–71.

36. Lowi, *End of Liberalism*, 86–90.

Chapter Nine

1. See R. Douglas Hurt, *American Agriculture: A Brief History*, revised edition (West Lafayette, IN: Purdue University Press, 2002), 221.

2. See Murray R. Benedict, *Farm Policies of the United States, 1790–1950: A Study of Their Origins and Development* (New York: The Twentieth Century Fund, 1953), 147; Bruce L. Gardner, *American Agriculture in the Twentieth Century: How It Flourished and What It Cost* (Cambridge, MA: Harvard University Press, 2002), 176–201; and Hurt, *American Agriculture*, 266.

3. Federal Reserve Bank of St. Louis, "Index of Farm Prices of Crops for United States," http://research.stlouisfed.org/fred2/series/M04059USM323NNBR.

4. See John Mar Hansen, *Gaining Access: Congress and the Farm Lobby, 1919–1981* (Chicago: University of Chicago Press, 1991), 27–28; and Hurt, *American Agriculture*, 266.

5. See Gardner, *American Agriculture*, 215–216; and E. C. Pasour, Jr. and Randal R. Rucker, *Plowshares and Pork Barrels: The Political Economy of Agriculture* (Oakland, CA: The Independent Institute, 2005), 85–86.

6. John Steinbeck, *The Grapes of Wrath*, revised edition (New York: Penguin Classics, 2006), 233.

7. See Roger Biles, *The South and the New Deal* (Lexington, KY: The University Press of Kentucky, 1994), 39.

8. See Christiana McFadyen Campbell, *The Farm Bureau: A Study of the Making of National Farm Policy, 1933–1940* (Urbana, IL: University of Illinois Press, 1962), 53–56; Hansen, *Gaining Access*, 79–86.

9. Arthur M. Schlesinger, Jr., *The Age of Roosevelt, Volume II, 1933–1935: The Coming of the New Deal* (Boston, MA: Mariner Books, 2003), 72–73.

10. See G. William Domhoff and Michael J. Webber, *Class and Power in the New Deal: Corporate Moderates, Southern Democrats, and the Liberal-Labor Coalition* (Stanford, CA: Stanford University Press, 2011), 90–113; Wayne D. Rasmussen, "The New Deal Farm Programs: What They Were and Why They Survived," *American Journal of Agricultural*

Economics 65, no. 5 (December 1983): 1158–1162; and George Brown Tindall, *The Emergence of the New South, 1913–1945* (Baton Rouge, LA: Louisiana State University Press, 1967), 393.

11. See Edwin Griswold Nourse, *Three Years of the Agricultural Adjustment Administration* (Washington, DC: The Brookings Institution, 1937), 342; and Gavin Wright, *Old South, New South: Revolutions in the Southern Economy Since the Civil War* (Baton Rouge, LA: The Louisiana State University Press, 1986), 226.

12. See Campbell, *Farm Bureau*, 53–58, 85–102.

13. See Biles, *South*, 44–50; Gunnar Myrdal, *An American Dilemma: The Negro Problem and Modern Democracy, Volume I* (New Brunswick, NJ: Transaction Publishers, 2002), 258; and Gunnar Myrdal, *An American Dilemma: The Negro Problem and Modern Democracy, Volume II* (New Brunswick, NJ: Transaction Publishers, 2002), 1247; and Schlesinger, *Age of Roosevelt*, 73.

14. See Biles, *South*, 43; Nourse, *Three Years*, 343; Myrdal, *American Dilemma, Vol. I*, 257; Wright, *Old South*, 228.

15. Quoted in Tindall, *Emergence*, 413. See also William E. Leuchtenburg, *Franklin D. Roosevelt and the New Deal, 1932–1940* (New York: Harper Perennial, 2009), 135; and Nourse, *Three Years*, 347.

16. See Biles, *South*, 56; Warren C. Whatley, "Labor for the Picking: The New Deal in the South," *Journal of Economic History* 43, no. 4 (December 1983): 905–929; Myrdal, *American Dilemma, Vol. I*, 260; and Wright, *Old South*, 228–235.

17. See Tindall, *Emergence*, 544.

18. Myrdal, *American Dilemma, Vol. I*, 253–254.

19. Myrdal, *American Dilemma, Vol. I*, 260.

20. Price V. Fishback, William C. Horrace, and Shawn Kantor, "Did New Deal Grant Programs Stimulate Local Economies? A Study of Federal Grants and Retail Sales during the Great Depression," *The Journal of Economic History* 65, no. 1 (March 2005): 61–62.

21. See Biles, *South*, 46; Leuchtenburg, *Franklin D. Roosevelt*, 138; Edward L. Schapsmeier and Frederick H. Schapsmeier, *Henry A. Wallace of Iowa: The Agrarian Years, 1910–1940* (Ames, IA: Iowa State University Press, 1968), 200–204; Schlesinger, *Age of Roosevelt*, 78–81.

22. See Willard W. Cochrane and C. Ford Runge, *Reforming Farm Policy: Toward a National Agenda* (Ames, IA: Iowa State University Press, 1992), 41; and Andrew Schmitz, Hartley Furtan, and Katherine Baylis, *Agricultural Policy, Agribusiness, and Rent-Seeking Behavior* (Toronto: University of Toronto Press, 2002), 221.

23. See Benedict, *Farm Policies*, 431–432.

24. See Hurt, *American Agriculture*, 320–321.

25. See Tom Arrandale, et al., *Farm Policies: The Politics of Soil, Surpluses, and Subsidies* (Washington, DC: Congressional Quarterly, Inc., 1984), 110; and Pasour and Rucker, *Plowshares*, 117.

26. For data on farm prices, government payments, and the ongoing surplus, see David Orden, Robert Paarlberg, and Terry Roe, *Policy Reform in American Agriculture: Analysis and Prognosis* (Chicago: University of Chicago Press, 1999), 25, 59, 62.

27. See Clifton B. Luttrell, *The High Cost of Farm Subsidies* (Washington, DC: The Cato Institute, 1989), 15; Schmitz, Furtan, and Baylis, *Agricultural Policy*, 224; and Gardner, *American Agriculture*, 218.

28. See Willard W. Cochrane and Mary E. Ryan, *American Farm Policy, 1948–1973* (Minneapolis, MN: University of Minnesota Press, 1976), 300.

29. See Cochrane and Runge, *Reforming*, 43; Virgil W. Dean, *An Opportunity Lost: The*

Truman Administration and the Farm Policy Debate (Columbia, MO: The University of Missouri Press, 2006), 49–77; Hurt, *American Agriculture*, 321; Luther Tweeten, *Foundations of Farm Policy*, 2nd edition, revised (Lincoln, NE: University of Nebraska Press, 1979), 432.

30. See Dean, *Opportunity Lost*, 78–109.

31. See Cochrane and Runge, *Reforming*, 44; Virgil W. Dean, "Why Not The Brannan Plan?" *Agricultural History* 70, no. 2 (Spring 1996): 268–282; Dean, *Opportunity Lost*, 148.

32. See Reo M. Christenson, *The Brannan Plan: Farm Politics and Policy* (Westport, CT: Greenwood Press, 1959), 34; Cochrane and Runge, *Reforming*, 44; Tweeten, *Foundations*, 464.

33. See Dean, *Opportunity Lost*, 171; and Hansen, *Gaining Access*, 212.

34. See Stephen Wagner, *Eisenhower Republicanism: Pursuing the Middle Way* (DeKalb, IL: Northern Illinois University Press, 2006), 44–59.

35. See Cochrane and Ryan, *American Farm Policy*, 32–33.

36. See Wagner, *Eisenhower*, 53–57; Tweeten, *Foundations*, 464–465; Cochrane and Ryan, *American Farm Policy*, 33; Gardner, *American Agriculture*, 217; Hugh Ulrich, *Losing Ground: Agricultural Policy and the Decline of the American Farm* (Chicago: Chicago Review Press, 1989), 106.

37. See Cochrane and Runge, *Reforming*, 46–48; Tweeten, *Foundations*, 469. Kennedy also tried unsuccessfully to centralize power on this issue in the executive. He proposed having the president submit finished legislation to Congress that the latter could vote on, but not amend. Congress never seriously considered this alternative, as its ability to curry favor with the farm bloc was essential to the political well-being of so many of its members. See Cochrane and Ryan, *American Farm Policy*, 41.

38. See Cochrane and Ryan, *American Farm Policy*, 300.

39. See Ulrich, *Losing Ground*, 119; Ken A. Ingersent and A. J. Rayner, *Agricultural Policy in Western Europe and the United States* (Cheltenham, UK: Edward Elgar, 1999), 203–205, 274, 297.

40. See Ingersent and Rayner, *Agricultural Policy*, 270; Arrandale et al., *Farm Policies*, 135; Cochrane and Ryan, *American Farm Policy*, 303; Tweeten, *Foundations*, 472.

41. See Ulrich, *Losing Ground*, 139–145; Ingersent and Rayner, *Agricultural Policy*, 203, 291.

42. See Cochrane and Runge, *Reforming*, 51. On Reagan's failed efforts to cut the farm program, see Hurt, *American Agriculture*, 356. Once again, conservatives from the Farm Belt undermined a Republican president's effort to bring the costs under control.

43. See Daniel Imhoff, *Food Fight: The Citizen's Guide to the Next Food and Farm Bill* (Healdsburg, CA: Watershed Media, 2012), 65; Brian M. Riedel, "The Cost of America's Farm Subsidy Binge: An Average of $1 Million Per Farm," *Heritage Foundation Backgrounder* no. 1510 (December 10, 2001); Schmitz, Furtan, and Baylis, *Agricultural Policy*, 236.

44. See Veronique de Rugy, "Updated: The History of Farm Bill Spending," *Mercatus Institute*. January 21, 2014. www.mercatus.org; Daren Bakst and Diane Katz, "A Farm Bill Primer: 10 Things You Should Know About the Farm Bill," *Heritage Foundation Backgrounder* no. 2797 (May 14, 2013); Matt Mitchell, "Farm Bill Replaces Conspicuous Subsidies with Inconspicuous Subsidies," *Mercatus Institute* (February 4, 2014), http://neighborhoodeffects.mercatus.org; Matt Mitchell, "9 Reasons the Farm Bill is Bad for America," *The Federalist* (February 4, 2014), http://www.thefederalist.com; Brad Plumer, "The $956 farm bill, in one," *Washington Post* (January 28, 2014), http://www.washingtonpost.com; Brad Plumer, "The Farm Bill is up for a Final Vote Soon. Here's

Why So Many People Hate It," *Washington Post* (February 3, 2014), http://www
.washingtonpost.com; Douglas Elmendorf, "Letter to the Honorable Frank D. Lucas,"
Congressional Budget Office (January 28, 2014), http://www.cbo.gov.

45. Luther Tweeten, "Farm Commodity Programs: Essential Safety Net or Corporate
Welfare?" in *Agricultural Policy for the 21st Century*, ed. Luther Tweeten and Stanley R.
Thompson (Ames, IA: Iowa State Press, 2002), 1; and de Rugy, "Updated."

46. See Jean Yavis Jones, Charles E. Hanrahan, and Jasper Womach, "What is a Farm
Bill?" *Congressional Research Service* RL30956 (May 5, 2001), 1.

47. See Matt Mitchell, "Why do Almost All Economists Oppose U.S. Farm Policy?"
Mercatus Institute (July 9, 2013), http://neighborhoodeffects.mercatus.org.

48. See Tweetwen, "Farm Commodity," 2–4.

49. See Bruce L. Gardner, *The Governing of Agriculture* (Lawrence, KS: The Regents
Press of Kansas, 1981), 82; and Tweeten, "Farm Commodity," 28.

50. See Luther Tweeten, "The Twelve Best Reasons for Commodity Programs: Why
None Stands Scrutiny," *Choices* (Second Quarter 1995): 5. Tweeten, "Farm Commodity,"
18.

51. See D. Gale Johnson, *Trade and Agriculture: A Study of Inconsistent Policies* (New
York: John Wiley & Sons, Inc., 1950), 89–90.

52. See Ken G. Glozer, *Corn Ethanol: Who Pays? Who Benefits?* (Stanford, CA: Hoover
Institution Press, 2011), 158–159; and Christopher P. Knittel, "Corn Belt Moonshine:
The Costs and Benefits of US Ethanol Subsidies," *American Enterprise Institute*, http://
www.aei.org/AmericanBoondoggle.

53. See Jayson Lusk and Jody Campiche, "State and National Effects of Selected Farm
and Food Policies" (Arlington, VA: Mercatus Research, Mercatus Center at George Mason University, forthcoming).

54. See Mitchell, "Why Do Almost All Economists"; D. Gale Johnson, *Farm Commodity Programs: An Opportunity for Change* (Washington, DC: American Enterprise Institute for Public Policy Research, 1973), 2; Gardner, *American Agriculture*, 239; Tweeten,
"Twelve Best," 4.

55. See Michael K. Wohlgenant, "Sweets for the Sweet: The Costly Benefits of the
U.S. Sugar Program," *American Enterprise Institute*, http://www.aei.org/American
Boondoggle.

56. See Vincent Smith, "Premium Payments: Why Crop Insurance Costs Too Much,"
American Enterprise Institute, http://www.aei.org/AmericanBoondoggle; and Brian M.
Riedel, "How Farm Subsidies Became America's Largest Corporate Welfare Program,"
Heritage Foundation Backgrounder no. 1520 (February 25, 2002).

57. There have long been limits to how much any given farmer can collect from
Uncle Sam, but there are plenty of loopholes to exploit. See Pasour and Rucker, *Plowshares*, 183; and Luttrell, *High Cost*, 117. Moreover, insurance subsidies, which are featured heavily in the 2014 farm bill, are not subject to means tests or payment ceilings.
See Romina Boccia, "Farm Bill Should End Secrecy in Crop Insurance Subsidies," Heritage Foundation Issue Brief No. 3675 (Washington, DC: Heritage Foundation, July 23,
2012).

58. See Imhoff, *Food Fight*, 87; Johnson, *Trade*, 89–90; Brian M. Reidel, "Another Year
at the Federal Trough: Farm Subsidies for the Rich, Famous, and Elected Jumped Again
in 2002," *Heritage Foundation Backgrounder* no. 1763 (May 24, 2004).

59. See Gardner, *American Agriculture*, 78; Mitchell, "9 Reasons."

60. See Johnson, *Farm Commodity*, 54–61; Gardner, *Governing*, 75–77; E. C. Pasour,
Jr., "The High Cost of Farm Subsidies," *Heritage Foundation Backgrounder* no. 388 (October 22, 1984).

61. See Cochrane and Ryan, *American Farm Policy*, 13; and Carolyn Dimitri, Anne Effland, and Neilson Conklin, "The 20th Century Transformation of U.S. Agriculture," Economic Information Bulletin Number 3 (Washington, DC: U.S. Department of Agriculture, Economic Research Service, June 2005). www.ers.usda.gov.

62. See Hansen, *Gaining Access*, 167. A big reason for the collapse in farm representation had to do with the Supreme Court mandate of "one man, one vote" in legislative districts. That had the effect of shifting representation from rural areas into urban ones. See Bill Winders, *The Politics of Food Supply: U.S. Agricultural Policy in the World Economy* (New Haven, CT: Yale University Press, 2009), 101.

63. See Hansen, *Gaining Access*, 94, 126–147. Why did the Farm Bureau back the Grand Old Party's emphasis on flexible price supports? The reason was that much of the output in the Corn Belt was used to feed livestock, especially hogs. So, they had an incentive to keep prices low. Moreover, Corn Belt farmers did not want southern cotton farmers to begin to diversify their crops and become competitors, which they feared would happen with price supports. See Winders, *Politics*, 90–92.

64. See Ulrich, *Losing Ground*, 101.

65. See Kenneth A. Shepsle and Barry R. Weingast, "The Institutional Foundations of Committee Power," *The American Political Science Review* 81, no. 1 (March 1987): 85–104.

66. See Harold D. Guither, *The Food Lobbyists: Behind the Scenes of Food and Agri-Politics* (Lexington, MA: Lexington Books, 1980), 1–16.

67. See William P. Browne, *Private Interests, Public Policy, and American Agriculture* (Lawrence, KS: University Press of Kansas, 1988), 91–109.

68. Quoted in Matt Mitchell, "Watering the Seeds of Farm Programs and Farm Income Growth," *Mercatus Institute* (January 23, 2014), http://mercatus.org.

69. William P. Browne, *Cultivating Congress: Constituents, Issues, and Interests in Agricultural Policymaking* (Lawrence, KS: University Press of Kansas, 1995), 28.

70. See John Ferejohn, "Logrolling in an Institutional Context: A Case Study of Food Stamp Legislation," in *Congress and Policy Change*, ed. Gerald C. Wright, Jr., Leroy N. Rieselbach, and Lawrence C. Dodd (New York: Agathon Press, Inc., 1986), 223–256; Hansen, *Gaining Access*, 201–211.

71. As Bullock and Coggins put it:

> To a very large degree after the first generation, government payouts are used to pay farm mortgages. Should those government payments be taken away, many people would be unable to afford their mortgage payments, and would go bankrupt. Because land values would drop, rural banks would be forced to take large losses on their now-"bad" loans, and many of them would go out of business as well. It is not difficult to imagine the resultant serious financial crisis in rural areas, and how such a crisis might upset large parts of the wide economy.
>
> . . . If capitalization is fairly complete, perhaps there is some truth to the view that the billions of dollars of payments doled out under the various agricultural programs since the Great Depression have done nothing more than fulfill an obligation to the farmers of that original generation. According to this view, the benefits paid to farmers during the early years of the programs are sunk costs, and since that time farmers have enjoyed very little real benefits. (David S. Bullock and Jay S. Coggins, "Do Farmers Receive Huge Rents for Small Lobbying Efforts?" in *Agricultural Policy for the 21st Century*, ed. Luther Tweeten and Stanley R. Thompson [Ames, IA: Iowa State Press, 2002], 154–155)

Chapter Ten

1. Chester Collins Maxey, "A Little History of Pork," *National Municipal Review* (1919): 693.

2. See John A. Ferejohn, *Pork Barrel Politics: Rivers and Harbors Legislation, 1947–1968* (Stanford, CA: Stanford University Press, 1974), 4–5.

3. See Theodore J. Lowi, "Four Systems of Policy, Politics, and Choice," *Public Administration Review* 32, no. 4 (July–August 1972): 299; and James Q. Wilson, "The Politics of Regulation," in *The Politics of Regulation*, ed. James Q. Wilson (New York: Basic Books, 1980), 366.

4. See R. Douglas. Arnold, *Congress and the Bureaucracy: A Theory of Influence* (New Haven, CT: Yale University Press, 1979), 123–124.

5. See R. Douglas Arnold, "Legislators, Bureaucrats, and Locational Decisions," *Public Choice* 37, no. 1 (1981): 107–132; Ferejohn, *Pork Barrel*, 58; John A. Hird, "The Political Economy of Pork: Project Selection at the U.S. Army Corps of Engineers," *The American Political Science Review* 85, no. 2 (June 1991): 429–456; and Kenneth A. Shepsle and Barry R. Weingast, "Political Preferences for the Pork Barrel: A Generalization," *American Journal of Political Science* 25 (1981): 96–111.

6. See Citizens Against Government Waste, "Congressional Pig Book, 1991," http://cagw.org/Content/pig-book-1991; Citizens Against Government Waste, "Congressional Pig Book, 1994," http://cagw.org/Content/pig-book-1994; and Whitehouse.gov, "Table 1.1—Summary of Receipts, Outlays, and Surpluses or Deficits (–): 1789–2019," http://www.whitehouse.gov/sites/default/files/omb/budget/fy2015/assets/hist01z1.xls. Diana Evans argues in her book *Greasing the Wheels* that the pork barrel is potentially useful for more nationalistic purposes. Leaders can use it to "build the majority coalitions necessary to pass broad-based, general interest legislation. Leaders do so by tacking a set of targeted district benefits onto such bills, using the benefits as a sort of currency to purchase legislators' such bills, using the benefits as a sort of currency to purchase legislators' votes for the leaders' policy preferences, much as political action committees make campaign contributions in the hope of swaying members' votes" (Diana Evans, *Greasing the Wheels: Using Pork Barrel Projects to Build Majority Coalitions in Congress* [Cambridge: Cambridge University Press, 2004], 2). Still, as she admits, this is a problematic process if replicated over time. The highway bill is a good example. In 1987, legislators used pork barrel demonstration projects to secure legislator support. Four years later, at the time to reauthorize the program, the costs of the pork barrel ballooned. More and more legislators figured out what the highway bill sponsors had done five years earlier and strategically positioned themselves to receive some highway pork!

7. See David R. Mayhew, *Congress: The Electoral Connection* (New Haven, CT: Yale University Press, 1974), 13–16.

8. See Ferejohn, *Pork Barrel*, 49.

9. Randall Fitzgerald and Gerald Lipson, *Pork Barrel: The Unexpurgated Grace Commission Story of Congressional Profligacy* (Washington, DC: Cato Institute, 1984), xviii.

10. See Richard Munson, *The Cardinals of Capitol Hill: The Men and Women Who Control Government Spending* (New York: Grove Press, 1993), 33.

11. See Ferejohn, *Pork Barrel*, 6–7; Barry R. Weingast and William J. Marshall, "The Industrial Organization of Congress; or, Why Legislatures, Like Firms, Are Not Organized as Markets," *Journal of Political Economy* 96 (February 1988): 132–168; Kenneth A. Shepsle and Barry R. Weingast, "Positive Theories of Congressional Institutions," *Legislative Studies Quarterly* 19, no. 2 (May 1994): 149–179; Kenneth A. Shepsle and Barry R. Weingast, "Legislative Politics and Budget Outcomes," in *Federal Budget Policy in the*

1980s, ed. Gregory B. Mills and John L. Palmer (Washington, DC: The Urban Institute Press, 1984); and Scott A. Frisch, *The Politics of Pork: A Study of Congressional Appropriation Earmarks* (New York: Routledge, 1998).

12. Barry R. Weingast and William J. Marshall, "The industrial organization of Congress; or, Why legislatures, like firms, are not organized as markets," *Journal of Political Economy* 96 (February 1998): 132–168.

13. Fitzgerald and Lipson, *Pork Barrel*, xiv–xv.

14. See Arnold, *Congress and the Bureaucracy*, 65–68.

15. See Arnold, *Congress and the Bureaucracy*, 165–206.

16. Keith Krehbiel, *Information and Legislative Organization* (Ann Arbor, MI: University of Michigan Press, 1992), 5.

17. See John H. Aldrich, *Why Parties? The Origin and Transformation of Political Parties in America* (Chicago: University of Chicago Press, 1995); David W. Rohde, *Parties and Leaders in the Postreform House* (Chicago: University of Chicago Press, 1991); D. Roderick Kiewiet and Matthew D. McCubbins, *The Logic of Delegation: Congressional Parties and the Appropriations Process* (Chicago: University of Chicago Press, 1991); Steven S. Smith, *Party Influence in Congress* (Cambridge: Cambridge University Press, 2007); Gary W. Cox and Matthew D. McCubbins, *Setting the Agenda: Responsible Party Government in the U.S. House of Representatives* (Cambridge: Cambridge University Press, 2005); Gary W. Cox and Matthew D. McCubbins, *Legislative Leviathan: Party Government in the House* (Berkeley, CA: University of California Press, 1993).

18. See Theodore Anagnoson, "Federal Grant Agencies and Congressional Election Campaigns," *American Journal of Political Science* 26 (1982): 547–561; Bruce Ray, "Congressional Losers in the U.S. Federal Spending Process," *Legislative Studies Quarterly* 3 (1980): 359–372; Barry Rundquist and David Griffith, "An Interrupted Time-Series Test of the Distributive Theory of Military Policy-Making," *Western Political Quarterly* 24 (1976): 620–626; Carol Goss, "Military Committee Membership and Defense Related Benefits," *Western Political Quarterly* 25 (1972): 216–233; John R. Gist and R. Carter Hill, "Political and Economic Influences on the Bureaucratic Allocation of Federal Funds: The Case of Urban Development Action Grants," *Journal of Urban Economics* 16 (1984): 158–172; H. A. Chernick, "An Economic Model of the Distribution of Project Grants," in *Fiscal Federalism and Grants-in-Aid*, ed. P. Mieszkowski and W. H. Oakland (Washington, DC: Urban Institute, 1979); Gary Zuk and Nancy R. Woodbury, "U.S. Defense Spending, Electora Cycles, and Soviet-American Relations," *The Journal of Conflict Resolution* 3, no. 3 (September 1986): 445–468; but that is contradicted by Miroslav Nincic and Thomas R. Cusack, "The Political Economy of U.S. Military Spending," *Journal of Peace Research* 16, no. 2 (1979): 101–115.

19. See Eric Schickler, *Disjointed Pluralism: Institutional Innovation and the Development of the U.S. Congress* (Princeton, NJ: Princeton University Press, 2001), 4; and Richard L. Hall and Bernard Grofman, "The Committee Assignment Process and the Conditional Nature of Committee Bias," *The American Political Science Review* 84, no. 4 (December 1990): 1163.

20. See Robert M. Stein and Kenneth N. Bickers, *Perpetuating the Pork Barrel: Policy Subsystems and American Democracy* (Cambridge: Cambridge University Press, 1995), 135–136.

21. See Robert M. Stein and Kenneth N. Bickers, "Congressional Elections and the Pork Barrel," *The Journal of Politics* 56, no. 2 (May 1994): 377–399. See also R. Michael Alvarez and Jason L. Saving, "Deficits, Democrats, and Distributive Benefits: Congressional Elections and the Pork Barrel in the 1980s," *Political Research Quarterly* 50, no. 4

(December 1997): 809–831; R. Michael Alvarez and Jason L. Saving, "Congressional Committees and the Political Economy of Federal Outlays," *Public Choice* 92, no. 1/2 (July 1997): 55–73; Michael J. Rich, "Distributive Politics and the Allocation of Federal Grants," *The American Political Science Review* 83, no. 1 (March 1989): 193–213; Robert C. Lowry and Matthew Potoski, "Organized Interest and the Politics of Federal Discretionary Grants," *The Journal of Politics* 66, no. 2 (May 2004): 513–533; and Paul A. C. Koistinen, *State of War: The Political Economy of American Warfare, 1945–2011* (Lawrence, KS: The University Press of Kansas, 2012), 63–64.

22. William D. Hartung, "The Shrinking Military Pork Barrel: The Changing Distribution of Pentagon Spending, 1986–1996," in *The Changing Dynamics of U.S. Defense Spending*, ed. Levon V. Sigal (Westport, CT: Praeger, 1999), 29.

23. See Cato Institute, *Cato Handbook for Policymakers, 1997* (Washington, DC: The Cato Institute, 1997), 120.

24. Tom A. Coburn, *The Department of Everything*, November 2012, http://www
.coburn.senate.gov/public/index.cfm?a=Files.Serve&File_id=00783b5a-f0fe-4f80-90d6-
019695e52d2d, 4.

25. Morton H. Halperin and Kristen Lomansey, "Playing the Add-on Game In Congress: The Increasing Importance of Constituent Interests and Budget Constraints in Determining Defense Policy," in *The Changing Dynamics of U.S. Defense Spending*, ed. Levon V. Sigal (Westport, CT: Praeger, 1999), 100.

26. James Madison, "Notes on the Debates in the Federal Convention. June 29th, 1787," Yale University Law School, http://avalon.law.yale.edu/18th_century/debates_
629.asp,

27. See Rebecca U. Thorpe, *The American Warfare State: The Domestic Politics of Military Spending* (Chicago: The University of Chicago Press, 2014), 9–10.

28. See Michael O'Hanlon, "The U.S. Defense Spending Context," in in *The Changing Dynamics of U.S. Defense Spending*, ed. Levon V. Sigal (Westport, CT: Praeger, 1999), 9; and Thorpe, *American Warfare State*, 9–10.

29. Bruce J. Schulman, *From Cotton Belt to Sun Belt: Federal Policy, Economic Development, & The Transformation of the South, 1938–1980* (Durham, NC: Duke University Press, 2007), 136.

30. Fitzgerald and Lipson, *Pork Barrel*, 15.

31. See Halperin and Lomansey, "Playing the Add-on Game."

32. As Rundquist and Carsey put it, the equilibrium "is a distributive politics based largely on the majority party using the committee system to structure policy making. We see historical instances during which this equilibrium is disrupted, but the general pattern in the rolling average analysis is that after such a disruption takes place, the effects return to the overall pattern of relationships" (Barry Rundquist and Thomas M. Carsey, *Congress and Defense Spending: The Distributive Politics of Military Procurement* [Norman, OK: University of Oklahoma Press, 2002], 140). See also Rundquist and Griffith, "Interrupted"; Barry Rundquist, Jungho Rhee, S. Fox, and Jeong-Hwa Lee, "Modeling State Representation on Defense Committees in Congress: 1959–1989," *American Politics Quarterly* 25 (1997): 35–55; Barry, Runquist, Jeong-Hwa Lee, and Jungho Rhee, "The Distributive Politics of Cold War Defense Spending: Some State Level Evidence," *Legislative Studies Quarterly* 21, no. 2 (May 1996): 265–281.

33. See Thorpe, *American Warfare State*, 93.

34. S. V. Date, "Why Are We Hauling Pennsylvania Coal All the Way to Germany?" NPR, http://www.npr.org/blogs/itsallpolitics/2014/03/14/290238727/long-dead-
congressmans-earmark-lives-on-in-europe.

35. Hartung, "Shrinking Military Pork Barrel," 29; and Cato Institute, Cato Handbook, 118.

36. Halperin and Lomansey, "Playing the Add-on Game," 85–96.

37. See Fitzgerald and Lipson, *Pork Barrel*, 16.

38. Koistinen, *State of War*, 64. See also Michael S. Rocca, "Military Base Closures and the 1996 Congressional Elections," *Legislative Studies Quarterly* 28, no. 4 (November 2003): 529–550.

39. Fitzgerald and Lipson, *Pork Barrel*, 13.

40. Kenneth R. Mayer, "Closing Military Bases (Finally): Solving Collective Dilemmas Through Delegation," *Legislative Studies Quarterly* 20, no. 3 (August 1995): 393. See also Koistinen, *State of War*, 64.

41. See Hartung, "Shrinking Military Pork Barrel," 43.

42. See Marcia Lynn Whicker and Nicholas A. Giannatasio, "The Politics of Military Base Closure: A New Theory of Influence," *Public Administration Quarterly* 21, no. 2 (Summer 1997): 176–208.

43. William Safire, *Safire's New Political Dictionary* (New York: Random House, 1993), 596. See also Frisch, *Politics of Pork*, 51, 65.

44. Rick K. Wilson, "An Empirical Test of Preferences for the Political Pork Barrel: District Level Appropriations for River and Harbor Legislation, 1889–1913," *American Journal of Political Science* 30, no. 4 (November 1986): 725.

45. See Ferejohn, *Pork Barrel Politics*, 1–8.

46. See Ferejohn, *Pork Barrel Politics*, 133–183.

47. See Arnold, *Congress and the Bureaucracy*, 139–155.

48. See Alison F. Del Rossi, "The Politics and Economics of Pork Barrel Spending: The Case of Federal Financing of Water Resource Development," *Public Choice* 85, no. 3/4 (1995): 299.

49. See Hird, "Political Economy," 447. See also James T. Murphy, "Political Parties and the Porkbarrel: Party Conflict and Cooperation in House Public Works Committee Decision Making," *The American Political Science Review* 68, no. 1 (March 1974): 169–185.

50. See Fitzgerald and Lipson, *Pork Barrel*, 3.

51. See James M. Ridenour, *The National Parks Compromised: Pork Barrel Politics and America's Treasures* (Merrillville, IN: ICS Books, 1994), 17, 81.

52. See Citizens Against Government Waste, "Congressional Pig Book, 2004," http://cagw.org/Content/pig-book-2004.

53. See Ridenour, *National Parks Compromised*, 96. See also Frisch, *Politics of Pork*, 43–44.

54. Citizens Against Government Waste, "Pig Book, 2004."

55. Costas Panagopoulos and Joshua Schank, *All Roads Lead to Congress: The $300 Billion Fight Over Highway Funding* (Washington, DC: CQ Press, 2008), xiii.

56. See Frisch, *Politics of Pork*, 41–42.

57. See Panagopolous and Schank, *All Roads Lead*, 173.

58. See Jay Cost, *Spoiled Rotten* (New York: Harper Collins, 2012), 254.

59. Andrew T. Young and Russell S. Sobel, "Recovery and Reinvestment Act Spending at the State Level: Keynsian Stimulus or Distributive Politics?" *Public Choice* 155 (2013): 456–461.

60. See Michael Leo Owens and Amy Yuen, "The Distributive Politics of 'Compassion in Action': Federal Funding, Faith-Based Organizations, and Electoral Advantage," *Political Research Quarterly* 65, no. 2 (June 2012): 422–442.

61. David P. Baron, "Distributive Politics and the Persistence of Amtrak," *The Journal of Politics* 52, no. 3 (August 1990): 912.

62. Linda R. Cohen and Roger G. Noll, *The Technology Pork Barrel* (Washington, DC: The Brookings Institute, 1991), 53.

63. Cohen and Noll, *Technology Pork Barrel*, 74–78.

64. Cohen and Noll, *Technology Pork Barrel*, 378.

65. See James D. Savage, *Funding Science in America: Congress, Universities, and the Politics of the Academic Pork Barrel* (Cambridge: Cambridge University Press, 1999), 3.

66. See Citizens Against Government Waste, "Pig Book, 2004."

67. Rob Porter and Sam Walsh, "Earmarks in the Federal Budget Process," Harvard Law School Federal, Budget Policy Seminar, Briefing Paper No. 16, http://www.law.harvard.edu/faculty/hjackson/Earmarks_16.pdf, 2–10.

68. See Frisch, *Politics of Pork*, 83–106; and Jeffrey Lazarus, "Giving the People What They Want? The Distribution of Earmarks in the U.S. House of Representatives," *American Journal of Political Science* 54, no. 2 (April 2010): 343; and Jeffrey Lazarus, "Party, Electoral Vulnerability, and Earmarks in the U.S. House of Representatives," *The Journal of Politics* 71, no. 3 (July 2009): 1050.

69. Frances E. Lee, "Geographic Politics in the U.S. House of Representatives: Coalition Building and Distribution of Benefits," *American Journal of Political Science* 47, no. 4 (October 2003): 714.

70. See Michael S. Rocca and Stacy B. Gordon, "Earmarks as a Means and an End: The Link Between Earmarks and Campaign Contributions in the U.S. House of Representatives," *The Journal of Politics* 75, no. 1 (January 2013): 251.

71. Frisch, *Politics of Pork*, 16; Porter and Walsh, "Earmarks," 9.

72. Daniel P. Franklin, *Making Ends Meet: Congressional Budgeting in the Age of Deficits,* (Washington, DC: CQ Press, 1993), 163.

73. Congressional Research Service, *Earmarks in Appropriation Acts: FY 1994, FY 1996, FY 1998, FY 2000, FY 2002, FY 2004, FY 2005* (Washington, DC: Congressional Research Service, 2006).

74. Charles R. Babcock, "Earmarks Became Contractor's Business," *WP Politics*, http://www.washingtonpost.com/wp-dyn/content/article/2006/02/20/AR200602 2001154.html.

75. See Porter and Walsh, "Earmarks"; and Richard Doyle, "Real Reform or Change for Chumps: Earmark Policy Developments, 2006–2010," *Public Administration Review* (January/February 2011).

76. Citizens Against Government Waste, "Congressional Pig Book, 2013," http://cagw.org/Content/pig-book-2013.

77. Peter Schweizer, *Throw Them All Out: How Politicians and Their Friends Get Rich Off Insider Stock Tips, Land Deals, and Cronyism that Would Send the Rest of Us To Prison* (Boston: Houghton Mifflin Harcourt, 2011), 51.

78. Schweizer, *Throw Them All Out*, 52–54.

79. Schweizer, *Throw Them All Out*, 55–56.

80. *Washington Post*, "Capitol Assets: A Close-Up Look at Congressional Wealth," http://www.washingtonpost.com/blogs/gallery/capitol-assets/.

81. Ibid.

82. Ibid.

83. Ibid.

84. Ibid.

Chapter Eleven

1. Portions of this chapter originally appeared in Jay Cost, "Madison's Medicare Problem," *National Affairs* no. 17 (Fall 2013): 83–96. Reprinted with permission from *National Affairs*.

2. See Charles A. Reich, "The New Property," *The Yale Law Journal* 73, no. 5 (April 1964): 733–787, in particular 734–736 and 768–769.

3. See Kimberly J. Morgan and Andrea Louise Campbell, *The Delegated Welfare State: Medicare, Markets, and the Governance of Social Policy* (Oxford: Oxford University Press, 2011), 6–8.

4. See Edward F. Lawlor, *Redesigning the Medicare Contract: Politics, Markets, and Agency* (Chicago, IL: The University of Chicago Press, 2003), 65–71.

5. See Harry S. Truman, "Special Message to the Congress on Health and Disability," May 19, 1947, *The American Presidency Project*, presidency.ucsb.edu/ws/?pid=128992.

6. Ronald J. Vogel, *Medicare: Issues in Political Economy* (Ann Arbor, MI: University of Michigan Press, 1999), 22.

7. See Jonathan Oberlander, *The Political Life of Medicare* (Chicago: The University of Chicago Press, 2003), 21–22; and Monte M. Poen, *Harry S. Truman Versus the Medical Lobby: The Genesis of Medicare* (Columbia, MO: University of Missouri Press, 1979), 55.

8. See Theodore R. Marmor, *The Politics of Medicare*, 2nd edition (New York: Aldine De Gruyter, 2000), 15, 77; and Oberlander, *Political Life*, 23–25.

9. See Paul J. Feldstein, *The Politics of Health Legislation: An Economic Perspective*, 3rd edition (Chicago: Health Administration Press, 2006), 273–275.

10. See Frank D. Campion, *The AMA and U.S. Health Policy Since 1940* (Chicago: Chicago Review Press, 1984), 259.

11. See Campion, *AMA and U.S.*, 273.

12. Oberlander, *Political Life*, 31.

13. See Avik Roy, *How Medicaid Fails the Poor* (New York: Encounter Books, 2013).

14. Quoted in National Academy of Social Insurance, *Reflections on Implementing Medicare*, ed. M. G. Gluck and V. Reno (Washington, DC: National Academy of Social Insurance, January, 2001), 2–3. For a good general description of the various parts of the Medicare program, see Marilyn Moon, *Medicare: A Policy Primer* (Washington, DC: The Urban Institute Press, 2006), 181–199.

15. Social Security Act 1801. [42 U.S.C. 1395].

16. See Nicholas Bagley, "Bedside Bureaucrats: Why Medicare Reform Hasn't Worked," Public Law and Legal Theory Research Paper No. 325 (Michigan: University of Michigan Law School, March 2013): 526–527; Feldstein, *Politics of Health*, 278–279; Rick Mayes, "The Origins, Development, and Passage of Medicare's Revolutionary Prospective Payment System," *Journal of the History of Medicine and Allied Sciences* 62, no. 3 (January 2007): 21–55; Jonathan Oberlander, "Medicare: The Great Transformation," in *Health Politics and Policy*, 4th edition, ed. James A. Morone, Theodor J. Litman, and Leonard S. Robins (Clifton Park, NY: Delmar Cengage Learning, 2008), 314; Mark Schlesinger and Terrie Wetle, "Medicare's Coverage of Health Services," in *Renewing the Promise: Medicare and Its Reform*, ed. David Blumenthal, Mark Schlesinger, and Pamela Brown Drumheller (Oxford: Oxford University Press, 1988), 59–60; Paul Starr, *The Social Transformation of American Medicine* (New York: Basic Books, 1982), 375. Claims processing in traditional Medicare is still handled by nongovernmental organizations like BlueCross BlueShield, as well as private insurers. See Beaufort B. Longest, Jr., *Health Policymaking in the United States*, 4th edition (Chicago: Health Administration Press, 2006), 364–365. Interestingly, the law also provided capital reim-

bursements to hospitals, which, as one scholar puts it, gave them a "license to spend." The payment structure of Medicare in fact was an important contributor in the shift in the business model of hospitals, encouraging even the nonprofits to be more "capitalistic." See Starr, *Social Transformation*, 376; and Rosemary Stevens, *In Sickness and in Wealth: American Hospitals in the Twentieth Century* (New York: Basic Books, 1989), 284, 293–305.

17. See David Blumenthal, "Medicare: The Record To Date," in *Renewing the Promise: Medicare and Its Reform*, ed. David Blumenthal, Mark Schlesinger, and Pamela Brown Drumheller (Oxford: Oxford University Press, 1988), 26–27; Michael F. Cannon and Michael D. Tanner, *Healthy Competition: What's Holding Back Health Care and How To Free It* (Washington, DC: Cato Institute, 2007), 85; Feldstein, *Politics of Health*, 278–279; Oberlander, *Political Life*, 31.

18. Incidental Economist, "Careful What You Wish For," *The Incidental Economist* (August 21, 2009), http://theincidentaleconomist.com/wordpress/careful-what-you-wish-for/.

19. Blumenthal, "Medicare," 25.

20. This conclusion is drawn from an analysis of data provided by the Centers for Medicare & Medicaid Services: http://www.cms.gov/Research-Statistics-Data-and-Systems/Statistics-Trends-and-Reports/NationalHealthExpendData/NationalHealth AccountsHistorical.html. See also Sue A. Blevins, *Medicare's Midlife Crisis* (Washington, DC: Cato Institute, 2001), 55; David Blumenthal and William Hsiao, "Payment of Physicians Under Medicare," in *Renewing the Promise: Medicare and Its Reform*, ed. David Blumenthal, Mark Schlesinger, and Pamela Brown Drumheller (Oxford: Oxford University Press, 1988), 119–120; Philip J. Funigiello, *Chronic Politics: Health Care Security from FDR to George W. Bush* (Lawrence, KS: University Press of Kansas, 2005), 162–163, Oberlander, *Political Life*, 131; and Vogel, *Medicare*, 15.

21. See Eric R. Kingson and Edward D. Berkowitz, *Social Security and Medicare: A Policy Primer* (Westport, CT: Auburn House, 1993), 23–25; Christopher J. Conover, *The American Health Economy Illustrated* (Washington, DC: AEI Press, 2012), 274; and Oberlander, *Political Life*, 88.

22. See Bagley, "Bedside Bureaucrats," 539; Judith Bentkover, et al., "Medicare's Payment of Hospitals," in *Renewing the Promise: Medicare and Its Reform*, ed. David Blumenthal, Mark Schlesinger, and Pamela Brown Drumheller (Oxford: Oxford University Press, 1988), 92; Campion, *AMA and U.S.*, 328; Longest, *Health Policymaking*, 393; and Oberlander, "Transformation," 315.

23. Howard Wolinsky and Tom Brune, *The Serpent on the Staff: The Unhealthy Politics of the American Medical Association* (New York: G.P. Putnam's Sons, 1995), 75.

24. See Nicholas Laham, *A Lost Cause: Bill Clinton's Campaign for National Health Insurance* (Westport, CT: Praeger, 1996), 67; and Mayes, "Origins."

25. For a general overview, see David G. Smith, *Paying for Medicare: The Politics of Reform* (New York: Aldine De Gruyter, 1992), 23–126.

26. See Benktover et al., "Medicare's Payment," 94.

27. See Rick Mayes and Robert A. Berenson, *Medicare Prospective Payment and the Shaping of U.S. Health Care* (Baltimore, MD: The Johns Hopkins University Press, 2006), 65.

28. See Marilyn Moon, *Medicare Now and in the Future*, 2nd edition (Washington, DC: The Urban Institute Press, 1996); and Smith, *Paying for Medicare*, 127–230.

29. See Blumenthal and Hsiao, "Payment of Physicians," 120–121.

30. See Blevins, *Midlife Crisis*, 60; Oberlander, "Transformation," 318; Moon, *Medi-*

care Now and in the Future, 57–58; Chapin White, "Why Did Medicare Spending Growth Slow Down?" *Health Affairs* 27, no. 3 (2008): 793–802; Bruce C. Vladeck, "Medicare's Prospective Payment System at Age Eight: Mature Success or Midlife Crisis?" *University of Puget Sound Law Review* 14, no. 3 (Spring 1991): 454.

31. See Bagley, "Bedside Bureaucrats," 519–520.

32. See Bagley, "Bedside Bureaucrats," 528–529; Federal Trade Commission and the Department of Justice, "Improving Health Care: A Dose of Competition," *Journal of Health Politics, Policy, and Law* 31, no. 6 (June 2006): 437–472; David A. Hyman, *Medicare Meets Mephistopheles* (Washington, DC: Cato Institute, 2006), 21–22; and Canon and Tanner, *Healthy Compeition*, 87.

33. See Uwe E. Reinhardt, "The Medicare World from Both Sides: A Conversation with Tom Scully," *Health Affairs* 22, no. 6 (2003): 168. See also Mayes and Berenson, *Medicare Prospective Payment*, 146.

34. See Charles Ornstein, "Even After Doctors Are Sanctioned or Arrested, Medicare Keeps Paying," *ProPublica* (April 16, 2014), http://www.propublica.org/article/even-after-doctors-are-sanctioned-or-arrested-medicare-keeps-paying.

35. See Bagley, "Bedside Bureaucrats," 543; Canon and Tanner, *Healthy Compeition*, 82; Mayes and Berenson, *Medicare Prospective Payment*, 148; and Daniel P. Kessler, "Real Medicare Reform," *National Affairs* 13 (Fall 2012), http://www.nationalaffairs.com/publications/detail/real-medicare-reform.

36. See John C. Scott and Daniel P. Gitterman, "Lobbyists, Groups, and the New-New Politics of Medicare," Paper presented at the Annual Meeting of the American Political Science Association (Washington, DC: September 3, 2010), 8.

37. See Henry J. Aaron and Jeanne M. Lambrew, *Reforming Medicare: Options, Tradeoffs, and Opportunities* (Washington, DC: The Brookings Institution Press, 2008), 146; Bentkover, et al., "Medicare's Payment," 94–95; and Moon, *Medicare Now and in the Future*, 60–62.

38. See Bagley, "Bedside Bureaucrats," 542; Oberlander, "Transformation," 317; and Vladeck, "Medicare's Prospective," 466.

39. See Aaron and Lambrew, *Reforming Medicare*, 146; and Federal Trade Commission and the Department of Justice, "Improving Health Care."

40. See Peter Whoriskey and Dan Keating, "Medicare Pricing Drives High Healthcare Costs," *The Washington Post* (December 31, 2013); Peter Whoriskey and Dan Keating, "Spinal Fusions Serve as Case Study for Debate Over When Certain Surgeries are Necessary," *The Washington Post* (October 27, 2013); and Peter Whoriskey and Dan Keating, "Hospice Firms Draining Billions from Medicare," *The Washington Post* (December 26, 2013).

41. See Peter Whoriskey and Dan Deating, "An Effective Eye Drug is Available for $50. But Many Doctors Choose a $2,000 Alternative," *The Washington Post* (December 7, 2013).

42. Jonathan Skinner, Elliott S. Fisher, and John E. Wennberg, "The Efficiency of Medicare," in *Analyses in the Economics of Aging*, ed. David A. Wise (Chicago: University of Chicago Press, 2005).

43. See Daniel Feenberg and Jonathan Skinner, "Federal Medicare Transfers Across States: Winners and Losers," *National Tax Journal* 53, no. 3 (September 2000): 713–732; Elliott S. Fisher, et al., "The Implications of Regional Variations in Medicare Spending, Part 2: Health Outcomes and Satisfaction with Care," *Annals of Internal Medicine* 138, no. 4 (February 2003): 288–322; and Katherine Baicker and Amitabh Chandra, "Medicare Spending, the Physician Workforce, and Beneficiaries' Quality of Care," *Health*

Affairs (April 2004), http://content.healthaffairs.org/content/early/2004/04/07/hlthaff
.w4.184/suppl/DC1.

44. See Moon, *Medicare Now and in the Future*, 58.

45. See Elaine Silverman and Jonathan Skinner, "Medicare Upcoding and Hospital Ownership," *Journal of Health Economics* 23, no. 2 (March 2004): 369–389.

46. See Fred Schulte and David Donald, "Cracking the Codes: How Doctors and Hospitals Have Collected Billions in Questionable Medicare Fees," *The Center for Public Integrity* (September 15, 2012), http://www.publicintegrity.org/2012/09/15/10810/
how-doctors-and-hospitals-have-collected-billions-questionable-medicare-fees.

47. See Aaron and Lambrew, *Reforming Medicare*, 146–147.

48. Centers for Medicare and Medicaid Services, "Medicare Fee-for-Service 2012 Improper Payments Report," http://www.cms.gov/Research-Statistics-Data-and-Systems/
Monitoring-Programs/CERT/Downloads/MedicareFeeforService2012Improper
PaymentsReport.pdf, 13.

49. See Jeffrey Young, "Tenet Healthcare 'Proud' To Settle Medicare Fraud Charges for $43 Million," *Huffington Post* (April 11, 2012), http://www.huffingtonpost.com/
2012/04/11/tenet-healthcare-settlement_n_1417742.html; and Reinhardt, "Medicare World."

50. Leslie Paige, "Medicare Fraud: All Talk, No Action," *Citizens Against Government Waste* (April 2014), http://cagw.org/media/wastewatcher/
medicare-fraud-all-talk-no-action.

51. See David A. Hyman, "Health Care Fraud and Abuse: Market Change, Social Norms, and the Trust 'Resposed in the Workmen,'" *Journal of Legal Studies* XXX, no. S2 (June 2001): 549, 565–566; and Hyman, *Medicare Meets Mephistopheles*, 36–39.

52. See Longest, *Health Policymaking*, 260–261.

53. See Phoebe Lindsay Barton, *Understanding the U.S. Health Services System*, 3rd edition (Chicago: Health Administration Press, 2007), 271.

54. See Moon, *Medicare Now and in the Future*, 58; Daniel P. Kessler, "Real Medicare Reform," 81; Uwe E. Reinhardt, "The Pricing of U.S. Hospital Services: Chaos Behind a Veil of Secrecy," *Health Affairs* 25, no. 1 (2006): 60; and Vladeck, "Medicare's Prospective," 470–471.

55. See Joe Eaton, "Little-Known AMA Group Has Big Influence on Medicare Payments," *Center for Public Integrity* (October 27, 2010), http://www.publicintegrity
.org/2010/11/07/2333/little-known-ama-group-has-outsized-influence-medicare-pay
ments; and Brian Klepper, "How the RUC Escaped a Challenge to Our Deeply-Flawed Reimbursement System," *The Health Care Blog* (February 6, 2013), http://thehealthcare
blog.com/blog/2013/02/06/the-untouchables/.

56. See Robert Centor, "The RUC is a Symptom. RBRVS is the Disease," *The Health Care Blog* (February 12, 2013), http://thehealthcareblog.com/blog/2013/02/12/the-ruc-is-
a-symptom-rbrvs-is-the-disease/; Peter Whoriskey and Dan Keating, "How a Secretive Panel Uses Data That Distort Doctors' Pay," *The Washington Post* (July 20, 2013).

57. See Roy M. Poses, "US Senate Subcommittee Asks What the RUC is About," *Health Care Reneal Blog* (January 31, 2013), http://hcrenewal.blogspot.com/2013/01/
us-senate-subcommittee-asks-what-ruc-is.html.

58. Quoted in Roy M. Poses, "The RUCkus Continues: Former Medicare Administrator Calls the 'RUC Process' 'Incredibly Flawed,' and the AMA Chair Says He's Inaccurate," *Health Care Renewal Blog* (June 25, 2009), http://hcrenewal.blogspot
.com/2009/06/ruckus-continues-former-medicare.html.

59. See Aaron and Lambrew, *Reforming Medicare*, 18–19, 142–143; Mayes and Berenson, *Medicare Prospective Payment*, 142.

60. See Conover, *American Health Economy*, 114; and Joseph P. Newhouse, "Medicare Policy in the 1990s," Working Paper 8531 (Cambridge, MA: National Bureau of Economic Research, October 2001), 36.

61. Barton, *Understanding*, 202.

62. See Mary Agnes Carey, "FAQ on Medicare Doctor Pay: Why is it so Hard to Fix?" *Kaiser Health News* (February 27, 2013), http://www.kaiserhealthnews.org/stories/2011/december/15/faq-doc-fix.aspx; Stuart Guterman, "The 'Doc Fix'—Another Missed Opportunity," *The New England Journal of Medicine* (April 30, 2014), http://www.nejm.org/doi/full/10.1056/NEJMp1401460; and Paige, "Medicare Fraud," 17.

63. See Conover, *American Health Economy*, 47, 73.

64. See Henry J. Pratt, "Old Age Associations in National Politics," *Annals of the American Academy of Political and Social Science* 415 (September 1974): 106.

65. Quoted in Vogel, *Medicare*, 128.

66. See Jacob S. Hacker, *The Road to Nowhere: The Genesis of President Clinton's Plan for Health Security* (Princeton, NJ: Princeton University Press, 1997), 133.

67. See Charles R. Morris, *The AARP: America's Most Powerful Lobby and the Clash of Generations* (New York: Times Books, 1996), 53–55; and Vogel, *Medicare*, 129.

68. See Hyman, *Medicare Meets Mephistopheles*, 16.

69. See Funigiello, *Chronic Politics*, 293–294; and Carol S. Weissert and William G. Weissert, *Governing Health: The Politics of Health Policy*, 3rd edition (Baltimore, MD: The Johns Hopkins University Press, 2006), 130–131.

70. Avik Roy, "How the AARP Made $2.8 Billion By Supporting Obamacare's Cuts to Medicare," *Forbes Online* (September 22, 2012), http://www.forbes.com/sites/aroy/2012/09/22/the-aarps-2-8-billion-reasons-for-supporting-obamacares-cuts-to-medicare/; and Kessler, "Real Medicare Reform," 90–91.

71. See Andrew Louise Campbell, *How Policies Makes Citizens: Senior Political Activism and the American Welfare State* (Princeton, NJ: Princeton University Press, 2003), 2, 29.

72. See Hyman, *Medicare Meets Mephistopheles*, 42–43; and Richard Himelfarb, *Catastrophic Politics: The Rise and Fall of the Medicare Catastrophic Coverage Act of 1988* (University Park, PA: The Pennsylvania State University Press, 1995), 61.

73. See Himelfarb, *Catastrophic Politics*, 76; Daniel Béland and Alex Waddan, *The Politics of Policy Change: Welfare, Medicare, and Social Security Reform in the United States* (Washington, DC: Georgetown University Press, 2012), 89–94; Julie Rovner, "Congress 'Catastrophic' Attempt to Fix Medicare," in *Intensive Care: How Congress Shapes Health Policy* (Washington, DC: The American Enterprise Institute and the Brookings Institute, 1995), 169–170.

74. Himelfarb, *Catastrophic Politics*, 63.

75. See Vogel, *Medicare*, 76; and Assistant Secretary for Planning and Evaluation, Human Services Policy Staff, "Information on Poverty and Income Statistics: A Summary of 2013 Current Population Survey Data," *Department of Health and Human Services* (September 2013), http://aspe.hhs.gov/hsp/13/PovertyAndIncomeEst/ib_poverty2013.cfm.

76. That figure is not adjusted for inflation, doing so would suggest more than one trillion dollars in current dollars has been wasted.

77. John D. Shatto and M. Kent Clemens, "Projected Medicare Expenditures under Illustrative Scenarios with Alternative Payment Updates to Medicare Providers," *Centers for Medicare & Medicaid Services* (May 31, 2013), http://www.cms.gov/Research-Statistics-Data-and-Systems/Statistics-Trends-and-Reports/ReportsTrustFunds/Downloads/2013TRAlternativeScenario.pdf, 19. See also James Antos, "Preparing for the Retirement of the Baby Boomers," in *Medicare: Preparing for the Challenges of the 21st Century*, ed. Robert D. Reischauer, Stuart Butler, and Judith R. Lave (Washington,

DC: Brookings Institution Press, 1998), 48. For a good take on the political impact of the Boomer generation, see Frederick R. Lynch, *One Nation Under AARP: The Fight Over Medicare, Social Security, and America's Future* (Berkeley, CA: University of California Press, 2011).

Chapter Twelve

1. Alexander Hamilton, *Hamilton: Writings*, ed. Joanne B. Freeman (New York: The Library of America, 2001), 670.

2. Hamilton, *Hamilton: Writings*, 697–707.

3. Gregg Easterbrook, "How the NFL Fleeces Taxpayers," *The Atlantic* (October 2013), http://www.theatlantic.com/magazine/archive/2013/10/how-the-nfl-fleeces-taxpayers/309448/.

4. For a general look at corporate welfare outside the tax code, see Timothy P. Carney, *The Big Ripoff: How Big Business and Big Government Steal Your Money* (New York: Wiley, 2006), 53; Stephen Slivinski, "The Corporate Welfare Budget Bigger Than Ever," Cato Policy Analysis No. 415 (October 10, 2001), http://www.cato.org/sites/cato.org/files/pubs/pdf/pa415.pdf, 2; Tad DeHaven, "Corporate Welfare in the Federal Budget," Cato Policy Analysis No. 703 (July 25, 2012), http://www.cato.org/sites/cato.org/files/pubs/pdf/PA703.pdf, 2; Stephen Slivinski, "The Corporate Welfare State: How the Federal Government Subsidies U.S. Businesses," Cato Policy Analysis No. 592 (May 14, 2007), http://www.cato.org/sites/cato.org/files/pubs/pdf/pa592.pdf. For the Export-Import Bank, see Keith Hennessey, "Kill Export Subsidies. Kill the Ex-Im Bank," *Keith-Hennessey.com* (July 1, 2014), http://keithhennessey.com/2014/07/01/kill-ex-im/; Ralph Nader, *Unstoppable: The Emerging Left-Right Alliance to Dismantle the Corporate State* (New York: Nation Books, 2014), 44; Carney, *Big Ripoff*, 78–82; William H. Becker and William M. McClenahan, Jr., *The Market, the State, and the Export-Import Bank of the United States, 1934–2000* (Cambridge: Cambridge University Press, 2003); Diane Katz, "The Export-Import Bank: A Government Outfit Mired in Mismanagement," Heritage Foundation Issue Brief #4208 (April 29, 2014), http://www.heritage.org/research/reports/2014/04/the-exportimport-bank-a-government-outfit-mired-in-mismanagement; Veronique de Rugy, "Testimony on the US Export-Import Bank," *Mercatus Center* (June 25, 2014), http://mercatus.org/sites/default/files/deRugy-exim-testimony-062314.pdf; Sallie James, "Times To X Out the Ex-Im Bank," Cato Trade Policy Analysis No. 47 (July 6, 2011), http://www.cato.org/publications/trade-policy-analysis/time-x-out-exim-bank; Diane Katz, "U.S. Export-Import Bank: Corporate Welfare on the Backs of Taxpayers," Heritage Foundation Issue Brief No. 4198 (April 11, 2014); Slivinski "Corporate Welfare Budget"; Veronique de Rugy, "Ex-Im Funds Flow To Few States, But All Bear the Risk," *Mercatus Center at George Mason University* (July 30, 2014), http://mercatus.org/sites/default/files/derugy-exim-assistance-by-state-final.pdf; Peter Schweizer, *Throw Them All Out: How Politicians and their Friends Get Rich Off Insider Stock Tips, Land Deals, and Cronyism That Would Send the Rest of Us to Prison* (New York: Houghton Mifflin Harcourt, 2011), xxii–xxiii. For the Overseas Private Investment Corporation, see Carney, *Big Ripoff*, 67–73. For the Loan Guarantee Program, see Citizens Against Government Waste, "CAGW Names Energy Sec. Steven Chu 2011 Porker of the Year," (February 14, 2012), http://cagw.org/content/cagw-names-energy-sec-steven-chu-2011-porker-year-0; Schweizer, *Throw Them All Out*, 78–85; Government Accountability Office, "Department of Energy: Further Actions Are Needed to Improve DOE's Ability to Evaluate and Implement the Loan Guarantee Program" (July 2010), http://www.gao.gov/assets/310/306983.pdf.

5. See Stephen D. Cohen, Robert A. Blecker, and Peter D. Whitney, *Fundamentals of U.S. Foreign Trade Policy: Economics, Politics, Laws, and Issues*, 2nd edition (Boulder, CO: Westview Press, 2003), 32–33.

6. See Judith Goldstein, *Ideas, Interests, and American Trade Policy* (Ithaca, NY: Cornell University Press, 1993), 147; Gary Mucciaroni, *Reversals of Fortune: Public Policy and Private Interests* (Washington, DC: The Brookings Institution, 1995), 75; and Nitsan Chorev, *Remaking U.S. Trade Policy: From Protectionism to Globalization* (Ithaca, NY: Cornell University Press, 2007), 58.

7. See Goldstein, *Ideas*, 138; and Mucciaroni, *Reversals of Fortune*, 76.

8. See John M. Rothgeb, Jr., *U.S. Trade Policy: Balancing Economic Dreams and Political Realities* (Washington, DC: CQ Press, 2001), 130–131. See Cohen, Blecker, and Whitney, *Fundamentals*, 121.

9. See Mucciaroni, *Reversals of Fortune*, 76–77, 91.

10. See Mucciaroni, *Reversals of Fortune*, 68–69.

11. See Chorev, *Remaking*, 62.

12. See Rothgeb, *U.S. Trade Policy*, 104–105.

13. See I. M. Destler, *American Trade Politics*, 4th edition (Washington, DC: Institute for International Economics, 2005), 25–27.

14. See Chorev, *Remaking*, 77–81; Mucciaroni, *Reversals of Fortune*, 86; Destler, *American Trade Politics*, 29; and Cohen, Blecker, and Whitney, *Fundamentals*, 38–39.

15. See Lydia DePillis, "America's Strange Trade Policy Makes Your Jeans More Expensive than They Should Be," *The Washington Post* (October 9, 2013), http://www.washingtonpost.com/blogs/wonkblog/wp/2013/10/09/americas-strange-trade-policy-makes-your-jeans-more-expensive-than-they-should-be/. Similar protections exist for sugar as well. See Bryan Riley, "U.S. Trade Policy Gouges American Sugar Consumers," Heritage Foundation Backgrounder #2914 (June 5, 2014), http://www.heritage.org/research/reports/2014/06/us-trade-policy-gouges-american-sugar-consumers. For an account of how political contributions influence agricultural tariff support in Congress, see Kishore Gawande and Bernard Hoekman, "Lobbying and Agricultural Trade Policy in the United States," (Washington, DC: World Bank), https://openknowledge.worldbank.org/bitstream/handle/10986/8802/wps3819.pdf?sequence=1.

16. See Cohen, Blecker, and Whitney, *Fundamentals*, 159; Goldstein, *Ideas*, 223.

17. See Chorev, *Remaking*, 119–120.

18. See Cohen, Blecker, and Whitney, *Fundamentals*, 158–159.

19. See Destler, *American Trade Politics*, 77–79; and Goldstein, *Ideas*, 230–233.

20. Tariff laws also remain a locus for penny ante corruption, as long as it does not threaten the overall free trade regime. For instance, as a U.S. senator, Barack Obama was responsible for loosening restrictions on hazardous materials that benefitted Nufarm, an Australian chemical company, and Astellas Pharma, a Japanese drug manufacturer, at a total cost of $12 million in foregone revenue to the government. Both of these firms have offices in Obama's home state of Illinois. See Justin Rood, "Despite Rhetoric, Obama Pushed Lobbyists' Interests," ABC News, http://abcnews.go.com/blogs/headlines/2007/07/despite-rhetori/; and Jay Starkman, *The Sex of a Hippopotamus: A Unique History of Taxes and Accounting* (Atlanta, GA: Twinset, Inc., 2008), 147.

21. See Joel Slemrod and Jon Bakija, *Taxing Ourselves*, 4th edition (Cambridge, MA: The MIT Press, 2008), 21–22.

22. Democratic Party Platforms, "Democratic Party Platform of 1892" (June 21, 1892). Online by Gerhard Peters and John T. Woolley, *The American Presidency Project*, http://www.presidency.ucsb.edu/ws/?pid=29585.   .

23. See W. Elliot Brownlee, *Federal Taxation in America* (Cambridge: Cambridge University Press, 2004), 46–47; Bennet D. Baack and Edward John Ray, "Special Interests and the Adoption of the Income Tax in the United States," *Journal of Economic History* 45 (September 1985): 613–614.

24. Integral in its passage through the House was William Jennings Bryan, the future nominee of the Democratic party. See Steven R. Weisman, *The Great Tax Wars: Lincoln—Teddy Roosevelt—Wilson—How the Income Tax Transformed America* (New York: Simon & Schuster Paperbacks, 2002), 131–172. In an ironic twist, Nelson Aldrich in the Senate managed to work his magic to keep tariff rates from being substantially lowered (this despite him being in the minority party). So, the income tax was implemented *without* substantial reductions in rates.

25. See Weisman, *Great Tax Wars*, 201.

26. See Starkman, *Sex of a Hippopotamus*, 159–160.

27. See Slemrod and Bakija, *Taxing Ourselves*, 23; Joseph A. Pechman, *Federal Tax Policy*, 5th edition (Washington, DC: The Brookings Institution, 1987), 63; John F. Witte, *The Politics and Development of the Federal Income Tax* (Madison, WI: University of Wisconsin Press, 1985), 126; and Richard Goode, *The Individual Income Tax*, revised edition (Washington, DC: The Brookings Institution, 1976), 302.

28. See Pechman, *Federal Tax Policy*, 115; C. Eugene Steuerle, *The Tax Decade: How Taxes Came to Dominate the Public Agenda* (Washington, DC: The Urban Institute Press, 1992), 25; and Brownlee, *Federal Taxation*, 150–151.

29. See Brownlee, *Federal Taxation*, 150–151.

30. See Slemrod and Bakija, *Taxing Ourselves*, 23.

31. See Shai Akabas, Brian Collins, and Alex Gold, "Tax Expenditures: How Do They Work?" *Bipartisan Policy Center* (July 9, 2014), http://bipartisanpolicy.org/blog/economy/2014/07/09/how-do-tax-expenditures-work; and Pechman, *Federal Tax Policy*, 79. The term "tax expenditures" is met with a bit of controversy, as some conservatives do not appreciate the term's implied inversion of who actually *owns* the money in the first place. A more neutral phrase might be "tax preferences," although this chapter will stick with "tax expenditures" because it is how a large preponderance of scholars and experts understand the concept.

32. See Daniel Shaviro, "Beyond Public Choice and Public Interest: A Study of the Legislative Process as Illustrated by Tax Legislation in the 1980s," *University of Pennsylvania Law Review* 139, no. 1 (November 1990): 13.

33. See C. Eugene Steuerle, *Contemporary U.S. Tax Policy*, 2nd edition (Washington, DC: The Urban Institute Press, 2008), 293; and Department of the Treasury, "Tax Reform for Fairness, Simplicity, and Economic Growth" (November 27, 1984), http://www.treasury.gov/resource-center/tax-policy/Documents/tres84v1All.pdf, 1.

34. See Witte, *Politics and Development*, 272.

35. See Starkman, *Sex of a Hippopotamus*, 260–261; Witte, *Politics and Development*, 78, 289; Shaviro, "Beyond Public Choice," 12; and Joseph A. Pechman, "Erosion of the Individual Income Tax," *National Tax Journal* 10, no. 1 (March 1957): 2.

36. See Pechman, *Federal Tax Policy*, 130–131, 160–161; Brownlee, *Federal Taxation*, 142; Steuerle, *Contemporary*, 86–87; and Department of the Treasury, "Tax Reform," xv.

37. See Robert S. McIntyre and David Wilhelm. Corporate Taxpayers & Corporate Freeloaders: Four Years of Continuing, Legalized Tax Avoidance by America's Largest Corporations 1981–84. (Washington, DC: Citizens for Tax Justice, 1985), 4.

38. See Brownlee, *Federal Taxation*, 141–142.

39. See Brownlee, *Federal Taxation*, 174; and Steuerle, *Contemporary*, 123.

40. See Citizens for Tax Justice, "It's Working, but . . ." (October 1989), http://www.ctj.org/pdf/itsworkingbut.pdf, 1.

41. See Bruce Bartlett, *The Benefit and the Burden: Tax Reform, Why We Need It And What It Will Take* (New York: Simon and Schuster Paperbacks, 2012), 93; Christopher Howard, *The Welfare State Nobody Knows: Debunking Myths about U.S. Social Policy* (Princeton, NJ: Princeton University Press, 2007), 205; and Steuerle, *Contemporary*, 151.

42. See Allison Rogers and Eric Toder, "Trends in Tax Expenditures, 1985–2016," *Tax Policy Center* (September 16, 2011), http://www.taxpolicycenter.org/UploadedPDF/412404-Tax-Expenditure-Trends.pdf, 9.

43. See Government Accountability Office, "Corporate Tax Expenditures: Information on Estimate Revenue Losses and Related Federal Spending Programs" (March 2013), http://www.gao.gov/assets/660/653120.pdf; and Martin A. Sullivan, *Corporate Tax Reform: Taxing Profits in the 21st Century* (New York: APress, 2011).

44. Citizens for Tax Justice, "Why the Senate's Tax Extenders Bill is a Travesty, and How It Can Be Made Tolerable" (May 15, 2014), http://ctj.org/ctjreports/2014/05/why_the_senates_tax_extenders_bill_is_a_travesty_and_how_it_can_be_made_tolerable.php#.U-G54YBdXnohttp://ctj.org/pdf/taxextendersreport.pdf.

45. Quoted in Starkman, *Sex of a Hippopotamus*, 267.

46. See Starkman, *Sex of a Hippopotamus*, 267; and Tom Coburn, "Reforming Tax Expenditures & Ending Special Interest Giveaways" (June 2011), http://www.coburn.senate.gov/public/index.cfm?a=Files.Serve&File_id=90c095d7-12e7-4e29-af57-4b83e0ddcb74, 11

47. Pechman, *Federal Tax Policy*, 264–265.

48. Coburn, "Reforming," 10.

49. Coburn, "Reforming," 13.

50. Coburn, "Reforming," 16.

51. Coburn, "Reforming," 19.

52. See The Century Foundation, *Bad Breaks All Around: The Report of the Century Foundation Working Group on Tax Expenditures* (New York: The Century Foundation Press, 2002), 117–119; Citizens for Tax Justice, "Why the Senate's"; Jeremy Horpedahl and Brandon M. Pizzola, "A Trillion Little Subsidies," *Mercatus Center*, http://mercatus.org/sites/default/files/TaxExpenditures_Horpedahl_v1-0.pdf; Government Accountability Office, "Corporate Tax Expenditures," 11.

53. Gary Guenther, "Section 179 and Bonus Depreciation Expensing Allowances: Current Law, Legislation Proposals in the 112th Congress, and Economic Effects," CRS Report for Congress (Washington, DC: Congressional Research Service, August 14, 2012), i.

54. See Pechman, *Federal Tax Policy*, 171–172; and Government Accountability Office, "Corporate Tax Expenditures," 11.

55. See Citizens for Tax Justice, "Why the Senate's."

56. See Government Accountability Office, "Corporate Tax Expenditures," 11; Citizens for Tax Justice, "Why the Senate's"; and Americans for Tax Fairness, "Corporate Lobbying on Tax Extenders and the 'G.E. Loophole'" (March 2014), http://www.americansfortaxfairness.org/files/Corporate-Lobbying-on-Tax-Extenders-and-the-GE-Loophole-3.pdf.

57. See Century Foundation, *The Bad Breaks All Around: The Report of the Century Foundation Working Group on Tax Expenditures* (New York: The Century Foundation Press, 2002).

58. See Bartlett, *Benefit*, 152; and Eric M. Patashnik, *Reforms at Risk: What Happens*

After Major Policy Changes are Enacted (Princeton, NJ: Princeton University Press, 2008), 52. See Jia Lynn Yang, "Post Analysis of Dow 30 Firms Shows Declining Tax Burden as a Share of Profit," *The Washington Post* (March 26, 2013).

59. See Patashnik, *Reforms at Risk*, 52; and Tanina Rostain and Milton C. Regan, Jr., *Confidence Games: Lawyers, Accountants, and the Tax Shelter Industry* (Cambridge, MA: The MIT Press, 2014), 4. For details on some of these practices—like the "Double Irish" and the "Dutch Sandwich"—see Jane G. Gravelle, "Tax Havens: International Tax Avoidance and Evasion," CRS Report for Congress (Washington, DC: Congressional Research Service, January 23, 2013), 9–10; Jeff Gerth, "5 Ways GE Plays the Tax Game," *ProPublica* (April 4, 2011), http://www.propublica.org/article/5-ways-ge-plays-the-tax-game; Jesse Drucker, "Google 2.4% Rate Shows How $60 Billion is Lost to Tax Loopholes" (October 21, 2010), http://www.bloomberg.com/news/2010-10-21/google-2-4-rate-shows-how-60-billion-u-s-revenue-lost-to-tax-loopholes.html; and Nelson D. Schwartz and Charles Duhigg, "Apple's Web of Tax Shelters Saved it Billions, Panel Finds," *The New York Times* (May 20, 2013).

60. For a basic review of tax sheltering, see Joseph Bankman, "The Tax Shelter Problem," *National Tax Journal* LVII, no. 4 (December 2004): 925; Department of the Treasury, *The Problem of Corporate Tax Shelters: Discussion, Analysis and Legislative Proposals* (Washington, DC: Department of the Treasury, 1999), 9–10; and Steuerle, *Tax Decade*, 31.

61. Richard Phillips, Steve Wamhoff, and Dan Smith, "Offshore Shell Games, 2014: The Use of Offshore Tax Havens by Fortune 500 Companies," *Citizens for Tax Justice* (June 2014), http://ctj.org/pdf/offshoreshell2014.pdf, 14.

62. See Robert S. McIntyre, Matthew Gardner, and Richard Phillips, "The Sorry State of Corporate Taxes: What Fortune 500 Firms Pay (or Don't Pay) in the USA and What They Pay Abroad—2008 to 2012," *Citizens for Tax Justice* (February 2014), http://www.ctj.org/corporatetaxdodgers/sorrystateofcorptaxes.pdf.

63. See Federal Reserve Bank of St. Louis, Federal Reserve Economic Data (FRED), "Tax Receipts on Corporate Income, Corporate Profits Before Tax (Without IVA and CCAdj)," http://research.stlouisfed.org/fred2/graph/?g=OOi. A significant portion of this decline does indeed have to do with globalization, or the fact that more profits are simply being earned overseas and paid to foreign governments. Still, that cannot account for the entirety of the drop, especially since globalization has been occurring in one fashion or another over the last forty years, but much of the decline has happened just over the last decade or so.

64. See Yang, "Post Analysis."

65. See Witte, *Politics and Development*, 91–92.

66. See Shaviro, "Beyond Public Choice," 11–12; Witte, *Politics and Development*, 115; Brownlee, *Federal Taxation*, 171–175; and Roger A. Freeman, *Tax Loopholes: The Legend and the Reality* (Washington, DC: AEI-Hoover Policy Studies, 1973), 1.

67. See David G. Davies, *United States Taxes and Tax Policy* (Cambridge: Cambridge University Press, 1986). 17.

68. See Muccarioni, *Reversals of Fortune*, 37; The Century Foundation, *Bad Breaks*, 5; Slemrod and Bakija, *Taxing Ourselves*, 3; Pechman, *Federal Tax Policy*, 131; and Jason J. Fichtner and Jacob M. Feldman, "The Hidden Cost of Tax Compliance," *Mercatus Center*, http://mercatus.org/sites/default/files/Fichtner_TaxCompliance_v3.pdf, 5.

69. Department of the Treasury, "Tax Reform," 4.

70. See Steuerle, *Contemporary*, 59; and Steuerle, *Tax Decade*, 32.

71. See Thomas W. Hanchett, "U.S. Tax Policy and the Shopping-Center Boom of the 1950s and 1960s," *The American Historical Review* 101, no. 4 (October 1996): 1082–1110.

72. This problem exists on the individual side of the ledger as well. For instance, a homeowner pays a lower tax bill than a renter, all else being equal. See Slemrod and Bakija, *Taxing Ourselves*, 7.

73. Gerth, "5 Ways."

74. See David Epstein and Sharyn O'Halloran, *Delegating Powers: A Transaction Cost Politics Approach to Policy Making Under Separate Powers* (Cambridge: Cambridge University Press, 1999), 201–202.

75. See Stanley S. Surry, "The Congress and the Tax Lobbyist: How Special Tax Provisions Get Enacted, *Harvard Law Review* 70, no. 7 (May 1957): 1156–1166.

76. Barber Conable, *Congress and the Income Tax* (Norman, OK: Oklahoma University Press, 1989), 41.

77. Author's analysis of data from OpenSecrets.org (August 9, 2014).

78. See Matthew D. Hill, et al., "The Effectiveness and Valuation of Political Tax Minimization," http://papers.ssrn.com/sol3/papers.cfm?abstract_id=230393, 28; Dennis P. Quinn and Robert Y. Shapiro, "Business Political Power: The Case of Taxation," *American Political Science Review* 85, no. 3 (September 1991): 851–874; and Brian Kelleher Richter, Krislert Samphantharak, and Jeffrey F. Timmons, "Lobbying and Taxes," *American Journal of Political Science* 53, no. 4 (October 2009): 893–909.

79. See Benjamin C. Waterhouse, *Lobbying America: The Politics of Business from Nixon to NAFTA* (Princeton, NJ: Princeton University Press, 2014), 203–228; Cathie J. Martin, *Shifting the Burden: The Struggle Over Growth and Corporate Taxation* (Chicago: University of Chicago Press, 1991), 37–47, 115–117; and Cohen, Blecker, and Whitney, *Fundamentals.*

80. Martin, *Shifting*, 170; and Timothy J. Conlan, Margaret T. Wrightson, and David R. Beam, *Taxing Choices: The Politics of Tax Reform* (Washington, DC: CQ Press, 1989), 231–232.

81. See Donald L. Barlett and James B. Steele, "The Great Tax Giveaway: How the Influential Win Billions in Special Tax Breaks (Part 1)," *The Philadelphia Inquirer* (April 10, 1988), http://www.barlettandsteele.com/journalism/inq_tax_1.php.

82. Jeffrey H. Birnbaum and Alan S. Murray, *Showdown at Gucci Gulch: Lawmakers, Lobbyists, and the Unlikely Triumph of Tax Reform* (New York: Vintage Books, 1987), 177–178.

83. See Jerry Markon, "As Momentum Builds Toward Tax Reform, Lobbyists Prepare for a Fight," *The Washington Post* (March 9, 2013); and Richard Rubin and Julie Bykowicz, "Lobbying Fury Begins Over Tax Revamp Unlikely to Advance," *Bloomberg* (February 27, 2014), http://www.bloomberg.com/news/2014-02-27/lobbying-fury-begins-over-tax-revamp-unlikely-to-advance.html.

84. Americans for Tax Fairness, "Corporate Lobbying," 3–4.

Chapter Thirteen

1. Maryland State House, "The Mt. Vernon Compact & The Annapolis Convention," http://msa.maryland.gov/msa/mdstatehouse/html/compact_convention.html.

2. See Michael D. Reagan, *Regulation: The Politics of Policy* (Boston: Little, Brown and Company, 1987), 2.

3. Peter J. Wallison, *Bad History, Worse Policy: How a False Narrative about the Financial Crisis Led to the Dodd-Frank Act* (Washington, DC: The AEI Press, 2013), 25.

4. Joe Nocera, "The Big Lie," *The New York Times* (December 23, 2011), http://www.nytimes.com/2011/12/24/opinion/nocera-the-big-lie.html?_r=0.

5. See Russell Roberts, "Gambling with Other People's Money: How Perverted Incentives Caused the Financial Crisis," *Mercatus Center* (May 2010); and David G. Tarr, "'The

Political, Regulatory and Market Failures that Caused the U.S. Financial Crisis," http://papers.ssrn.com/sol3/papers.cfm?abstract_id=1322297, 7; Peter Schweizer, *Architects of Ruin: How Big Government Liberals Wrecked the Economy—and How They Will Do It Again If No One Stops Them* (New York: Harper, 2009), at page 174, agrees with Wallison that Fannie and Freddie, along with government support of low income housing via the Community Reinvestment Act, were the primary culprits. Meanwhile Robert Scheer, *The Great American Stickup: How Reagan Republicans and Clinton Democrats Enriched Wall Street While Mugging Main Street* (New York: Nation Books, 2010), at page 174, argues that this had nothing to do with it.

6. Daniel Carpenter and David A. Moss, "Introduction," in *Preventing Regulatory Capture: Special Interest Influence and How To Limit It* (Cambridge: Cambridge University Press, 2014), 13.

7. Quoted in Carpenter and Moss, "Introduction," 6.

8. See Samuel P. Huntingdon, "The Marasmus of the ICC: The Commission, the Railroads, and the Public Interest," *Yale Law Journal* 61 (April 1952).

9. See Reagan, *Regulation*, 5; and David Vogel, "The 'New' Social Regulation in Historical and Comparative Perspective," in *Regulation in Perspective*, ed. Thomas K. McCraw (Cambridge, MA: Harvard University Press, 1981), 155–185.

10. See Marver H. Bernstein, "The Life Cycle of Regulatory Commissions," in *The Politics of Regulation: A Reader*, ed. Samuel Krislov and Lloyd D. Musolf (Boston: Houghton Mifflin Company, 1964), 85–86; and Louis L. Jaffe, "Effective Limits of the Administrative Process," *Harvard Law Review* 67, no. 7 (May 1954): 1105–1135. For later, more explicitly economic analyses, see George J. Stigler, "The Theory of Economic Regulation," *The Bell Journal of Economics and Management Science* 2, no. 1 (Spring 1971): 3–21; and Sam Peltzman, "Toward a More General Theory of Regulation," NBER Working Paper No. 133 (Cambridge, MA; National Bureau of Economic Research, April 1976). For good summaries of this literature in general, see William J. Novak, "A Revisionist History of Regulatory Capture," in *Preventing Regulatory Capture: Special Interest Influence and How To Limit It* (Cambridge: Cambridge University Press, 2014), 25–48; and Richard A. Posner, "The Concept of Regulatory Capture: A Short, Inglorious History," in *Preventing Regulatory Capture: Special Interest Influence and How To Limit It* (Cambridge: Cambridge University Press, 2014), 49–56.

11. See Terry M. Moe, "The Politics of Bureaucratic Structure," in *Can the Government Govern?*, ed. John E. Chubb and Paul E. Peterson (Washington, DC: The Brookings Institution, 1989): 267–330, which studies the Consumer Products Safety Commission, the Occupational Health and Safety Administration, and the Environmental Protection Agency.

12. See Kenneth J. Meier, *Regulation: Politics, Bureaucracy, and Economics* (New York: St. Martin's Press, 1985); and Terry M. Moe, "Control and Feed Back in Economic Regulation: The Case of the NLRB," *The American Political Science Review* 79, no. 4 (December 1985): 1094–1116.

13. See James Q. Wilson, "The Politics of Regulation," in *The Politics of Regulation*, ed. James Q. Wilson (New York: Basic Books, 1980), 367–370; and Reagan, *Regulation*, 60.

14. See Paul Sabatier, "Policy-Making by Regulatory Agencies: Toward a Framework of Analysis," *National Resources Journal* 17 (July 1977): 415–460.

15. David A. Moss and Daniel Carpenter, "Conclusion: A Focus on Evidence and Prevention," in *Preventing Regulatory Capture: Special Interest Influence and How To Limit It* (Cambridge: Cambridge University Press, 2014), 452. As Wilson puts it, "when one examines matters closely, they appear to be a good deal more complicated than is assumed

by either liberal or conservative critics of clientelism" (James Q. Wilson, "Introduction," in *The Politics of Regulation*, ed. James Q. Wilson [New York: Basic Books, 1980], 3–41).

16. See Moe, "Politics of Bureaucratic." As a partial demonstration of this thesis, Strattmann demonstrates that financial services interest groups have the capacity to use campaign contributions to influence legislative votes on regulations of their industry. Thomas Strattmann, "Can Special Interests Buy Congressional Votes? Evidence from Financial Services Legislation," *Journal of Law and Economics* 45, no. 2 (October 2002): 347–373.

17. See Gene M. Grossman and Elhanan Helpman, "Protection for Sale," *The American Economic Review* 84, no. 4 (September 1994): 833–850; Sanford C. Gordon and Catherine Hafer, "Flexing Muscle: Corporate Political Contributions As Signals to the Bureaucracy," *American Political Science Review* 99, no. 02 (May 2005): 245–261; Ernesto Dal Bo and Rafael Di Tella, "Capture By Threat," http://papers.ssrn.com/sol3/papers.cfm?abstract_id=269117; and Matthew C. Fellowes and Patrick J. Wolf, "Funding Mechanisms and Policy Instruments: How Business Campaign Contributions Influence Congressional Votes," *Political Research Quarterly* 57, no. 2 (June 2004): 314–324. Atif Mian, Amir Sufi, and Francesco Trebbi, "The Political Economy of the US Mortgage Default Crisis," *The American Economic Review* 100, no. 5 (December 2010): 1967–1998 show that special interest donations induced votes for the Troubled Asset Relief Program in October 2008, although less so in conservatives.

18. See James Kwak, "Cultural Capture and the Financial Crisis," in *Preventing Regulatory Capture: Special Interest Influence and How to Limit It* (Cambridge: Cambridge University Press, 2014), 76–77; and Jon D. Hanson and David G. Yosifon, "The Situation: An Introduction to the Situation Character, Critical Realism, and Deep Capture," http://papers.ssrn.com/sol3/papers.cfm?abstract_id=938005.

19. See Nolan McCarty, "Complexity, Capacity, and Capture," in *Preventing Regulatory Capture: Special Interest Influence and How to Limit It* (Cambridge: Cambridge University Press, 2014), 99–123.

20. See Kwak, "Cultural Capture," 80.

21. See Simon Johnson and James Kwak, *13 Bankers: The Wall Street Takeover and the Next Financial Meltdown* (New York: Vintage Books, 2001), 118. Baxter calls this a "deep capture," operating on such a subtle level that it went largely unnoticed until it was too late. See Lawrence G. Baxter, "'Capture' In Financial Regulation: Can We Channel It Toward the Common Good?" *Cornell Journal of Law & Public Policy* 21 (2011): 181–182.

22. See Charles W. Calomiris and Stephen H. Haber, *Fragile By Design: The Political Origins of Banking Crises & Scarce Credit* (Princeton, NJ: Princeton University Press, 2014), 153–202; Thomas Romer and Barry R. Weingast, "Political Foundations of the Thrift Debacle," in *Politics and Economics in the Eighties*, ed. Albert Alesina and Geoffrey Carliner (Chicago: University of Chicago Press, 1991), 201; and Eugene Nelson White, "The Political Economy of Banking Regulation, 1864–1933," *The Journal of Economic History* 42, no. 1 (March 1982): 33–40.

23. See Calomiris and Haber, *Fragile By Design*, 203–255; and Howard Husock, "The Trillion-Dollar Bank Shakedown That Bodes Ill for Cities," *City Journal* (Winter 2000).

24. See Calomiris and Haber, *Fragile By Design*, 265–266.

25. Kwak, "Cultural Capture," 93. See also Caolimiris and Haber, *Fragile By Design*, 273.

26. See James R. Barth, Gerard Caprio, Jr., and Ross Levin, *Guardians of Finance: Making Regulators Work For Us* (Cambridge, MA: The MIT Press, 2012), 86; and Baxter, 181. Levitin's summary is apt: "federal regulators did not lack the tools necessary

to limit bank leverage and rein in the mortgage market. They lacked the motivation" (Adam J. Levitin, "The Politics of Financial Regulation and the Regulation of Financial Politics," http://papers.ssrn.com/sol3/papers.cfm?abstract_id=2401298, 59–60).

27. As we shall see, the GSEs treated its opponents quite peremptorily.

28. See Mark Jickling and Edward V. Murphy, "Who Regulates Whom? An Overview of U.S. Financial Supervision," *Congressional Research Service* (December 8, 2010): 108.

29. See Baxter, 187. For how this affects bailouts of big industries, see Gary H. Stern and Ron J. Feldman, *Too Big To Fail: The Hazards of Bank Bailouts* (Washington, DC: Brookings Institution Press, 2009), 2.

30. See Johnson and Kwak, *13 Bankers*, 94.

31. See David Skeel, *The New Financial Deal: Understanding The Dodd-Frank Act and Its (Unintended) Consequences* (New York: Wiley, 2011), 43; and Johnson and Kwak, *13 Bankers*, 188.

32. On the Public-Private Investment Program, see Timothy P. Carney, *Obamanomics: How Barack Obama is Bankrupting You and Enriching His Wall Street Friends, Corporate Lobbyists, and Union Bosses* (Washington, DC: Regnery, 2009), 160–161. On Dodd-Frank, see Charles Gasparino, *Bought and Paid For: The Unholy Alliance Between Barack Obama and Wall Street* (New York: Sentinel, 2010), 233; Ron Suskind, *Confidence Men: Wall Street, Washington, and the Education of a President* (New York: Harper, 2011), 4; and Johnson and Kwak, *13 Bankers*, 188. On the law firm that supposedly wrote Dodd-Frank, see Skeel, *New Financial Deal*, 49–50.

33. See Charles R. Geisst, *Wall Street: A History* (Oxford: Oxford University Press, 1997), 165; Suskind, *Confidence Men*, 242; and Carney, *Obamanomics*, 165.

34. See Suskind, *Confidence Men*, 218–220, 246–247, 458.

35. See Roger D. Hodge, *Mendacity of Hope: Barack Obama and the Betrayal of American Liberalism* (New York: Harper, 2010), 24; and Carney, *Obamanomics*, 165.

36. Jickling and Murphy, "Who Regulates," 33.

37. See Paul E. Peterson and Mark Rom, "Macroeconomic Policymaking: Who is in Control?" in *Can the Government Govern?*, ed. John E. Chubb and Paul E. Peterson (Washington, DC: The Brookings Institution, 1989), 156–157.

38. See Allan H. Meltzer, "Politics and the Fed," http://papers.ssrn.com/sol3/papers .cfm?abstract_id=1586534, 2.

39. See Irwin L. Morris, *Congress, the President, and the Federal Reserve* (Ann Arbor, MI: The University of Michigan Press, 2002), 33–45; Peterson and Rom, "Macroeconomic Policymaking," 155; Meltzer, "Politics," 14–19; and Henry W. Chappell, Jr., and Rob Roy McGregor, "Fed Chat: FOMC Transcripts and the Politics of Monetary Policymaking," http://papers.ssrn.com/sol3/papers.cfm?abstract_id=235882.

40. See Peterson and Rom, "Macroeconomic Policymaking," 153; Jean-Charles Rochet, *Why Are There So Many Banking Crises? The Politics and Policy of Bank Regulation* (Princeton: Princeton University Press, 2008); and Willem H. Buiter, "Central Banks and Financial Crises," Paper at the Federal Reserve Bank of Kansas City's symposium on "Maintaining Stability in a Changing Financial System," at Jackson Hole, Wyoming, August 21–23, 2008, http://online.wsj.com/public/resources/documents/Fed-Buiter081608 .pdf, 100–103.

41. See Jickling and Murphy, "Who Regulates," 18–19.

42. See Johnson and Kwak, *13 Bankers*, 140–141, 149–150.

43. See Baxter, 181; and Geisst, *Wall Street*, 407, 410–414.

44. See Maria M. Correia, "Political Connections, SEC Enforcement and Accounting Quality," http://wwrn.com/abstract=1458478.

45. See Shivaram Rajgopal and Roger M. White, "Stock PIcking Skills of SEC Employees," http://www.darden.virginia.edu/web/uploadedFiles/RajgopalSECtradingpaper.PDF.

46. See Stephen J. Choi and Adam C. Pritchard, "Behavioral Economics and the SEC," http://papers.ssrn.com/sol3/papers.cfm?abstract_id=500203.

47. See Jickling and Murphy, "Who Regulates."

48. See Kwak, *13 Bankers*; Baxter, 181; Johnson and Kwak, *13 Bankers*, 143; and Binyamin Applebaum and Ellen Nakashima, "Banking Regulator Played Advocate Over Enforcer / Agency Let Lenders Grow Out of Control, Then Fail," *The Washington Post* (November 23, 2009).

49. Gary Becker, "'Capture' of Regulators by Fannie Mae and Freddie Mac-Becker," http://www.becker-posner-blog.com/2011/06/capture-of-regulators-by-fannie-mae-and-freddie-mac-becker.html.

50. See Thomas H. Stanton, *Government-Sponsored Enterprises: Mercantilist Companies in the Modern World* (Washington, DC: The AEI Press, 2002), xiv; and Kevin R. Kosar, "Government-Sponsored Enterprises (GSEs): An Institutional Overview," *Congressional Research Service* (April 23, 2007), 3–6.

51. See Viral V. Acharya, Matthew Richards, Stijn van Nieuwerburgh, and Lawrence J. White, *Guaranteed to Fail: Fannie Mae, Freddie Mac, and the Debacle of Mortgage Finance,* (Princeton, NJ: Princeton University Press, 2011), 12–14; and N. Eric Weiss, "GSE's and the Government's Role in Housing Finance: Issues for the 113th Congress," *Congressional Research Service* (September 13, 2013), 1–5.

52. Acharya et al., 16; and Andrew J. Boyack, "Laudable Goals and Unintended Consequences: The Role and Control of Fannie Mae and Freddie Mac," http://digital commons.wcl.american.edu/cgi/viewcontent.cgi?article=1631&context=aulr, 1495–1502.

53. See Ross Guberman, "Balancing Act," *The Washingtonian* (August 2002); and Ralph Nader, "How Fannie and Freddie Influence the Political Process," in *Serving Two Masters Yet Out of Control*, ed. Peter J. Wallison (Washington, DC: The AEI Press, 2001), 112.

54. See Stanton, *Government-Sponsored*, xiv; David Reiss, "The Federal Government's Implied Guarantee of Fannie Mae and Freddie Mac's Obligations: Uncle Sam Will Pick Up The Tab," *Georgia Law Review* 42, no. 4 (Summer 2008): 1042; and Weiss, "GSE's and the Government's Role in Housing Finance," 5.

55. See Acharya et al.; and Dwight M. Jaffee, "Reforming the U.S. Mortgage Market Through Private Market Incentives," Paper prepared for presentation at "Past, Present, and Future of the Government-Sponsored Enterprises," Federal Reserve Bank of St. Louis (November 17, 2010), 9.

56. Stanton, *Government-Sponsored*, 4.

57. Boyack, "Laudable Goals," 1506.

58. See Jonathan G. S. Koppell, *The Politics of Quasi-Government: Hybrid Organizations and the Dynamics of Bureaucratic Control* (Cambridge: Cambridge University Press, 2003), 104; Wallison, *Bad History*, 98–100; and Peter J. Wallison, "Introduction," in *Serving Two Masters Yet Out of Control*, ed. Peter J. Wallison (Washington, DC: The AEI Press, 2001), 1.

59. Acharya et al., 34; and Carol D. Leonnig, "How HUD Mortgage Policy Fed the Crisis," *The Washington Post* (June 10, 2008).

60. See Mark Calabria, "Fannie, Freddie, and the Subprime Mortgage Market," Cato Institute Briefing Papers (March 7, 2011); and Wallison, *Bad History*, 108, 118–123.

61. See Steven A. Holmes, "Fannie Mae Eases Credit To Aid Mortgage Lending," *The New York Times* (September 30, 1999).

62. Wallison, *Bad History*, 125. See also Calabria, "Fannie, Freddie."

63. Quoted in Wallison, *Bad History*, 169.

64. Nader, "How Fannie and Freddie," 111. See also Koppell, *Politics of Quasi-Government*, 98–101.

65. See Guberman, *Balancing Act*; and Robert S. Seiler, Jr., "Estimating the Value and Allocation of Federal Subsidies," in *Serving Two Masters Yet Out of Control*, ed. Peter J. Wallison (Washington, DC: The AEI Press, 2001), 14.

66. Opensecrets.org, "Fannie Mae: House Totals," http://www.opensecrets.org/orgs/congcmtes.php?id=D000000205&cycle=2002.

67. See Nader, "How Fannie and Freddie," 117.

68. Opensecrets.org, "Fannie Mae," http://www.opensecrets.org/orgs/lobby.php?id=D000000205.

69. See Guberman, *Balancing Act*.

70. See Koppell, *Politics of Quasi-Government*, 99; Wallison, *Bad History*, 25; Gretchen Morgenson and Joshua Rosner, *Reckless Endangerment: How Outsized Ambition, Greed, and Corruption Created the Worst Financial Crisis of Our Time* (New York: St. Martin's Griffin, 2012), 29; and Guberman, *Balancing Act*.

71. See Morgenson and Rosner, *Reckless Endangerment*, 74–75. It is thus ironic—or perhaps convenient—that in his nontechnical book on economic collapse, Stiglitz pointed the finger at conservative scholars like Wallison for pointing the finger at Fannie Mae and Freddie Mac. See Joseph Stiglitz, *Freefall: America, Free Markets, and the Sinking of the World Economy* (New York: W. W. Norton & Company, 2010), 10–11.

72. Morgenson and Rosner, *Reckless Endangerment*, 10.

73. Eric Lichtblau, "Gingrich's Deep Ties to Fannie Mae and Freddie Mac," *The New York Times* (February 3, 2012).

74. See Owen Ullmann, "Crony Capitalism: American Style," *The International Economy* (July/August 1999).

75. Matt Canham, "Fannie, Freddie Donate Big to Utah Senator," *Salt Lake Tribune* (September 12, 2008).

76. See Morgenson and Rosner, *Reckless Endangerment*, 245.

77. Binyam Applebaum, Carol D. Leonnig, and David S. Hilzenrath, "How Washington Failed to Rein in Fannie, Freddie / As Profits Grew, Firms Used Their Power To Mask Peril," *The Washington Post* (September 14, 2006).

78. *Founders Online*, "To Thomas Jefferson From James Madison, 8 August 1791," http://founders.archives.gov/documents/Jefferson/01-22-02-0017.

79. See Stanton, *Government-Sponsored*, 44. As Fannie Mae's former chief executive officer wrote to Franklin Reines in 2002, "The old political reality was that we always won, we took no prisoners, and we faced little organized political opposition." He added: "We used to, by virtue of our peculiarity, be able to write, or have written, rules that worked for us. We now operate in a world where we will have to be 'normal.' The [Securities and Exchange Commission] is our standard for disclosure and our arbiter for the rules, not our own proofreaders." See James R. Hagerty, "Fannie Mae Ex-Officials May Face Legal Action Over Accounting," *Wall Street Journal* (May 24, 2006). Of course, as we shall see, Fannie Mae did not begin behaving "normally" at that point. Indeed, it continued to hide much of their subprime activity from the government, and the truth of their exposure did not become evident until after it had collapsed.

80. Freddie Mac played a much less significant role in this process. Freddie did not

get spun off from the Federal Home Loan Bank System until 1989, which meant that by 1992, when the Federal Housing Enterprises Financial Safety and Soundness Act was written, it was still behaving like a federal agency. It had slightly different interests than Fannie, and many fewer political contacts. So, Fannie's preferences carried more weight during this period. See Koppell *Politics of Quasi-Government*.

81. See Applebaum, Leonnig, and Hilzenrath, "How Washington Failed"; Koppell, *Politics of Quasi-Government*, 110–119; and Stephen Labaton, "Power of the Mortgage Twins," *The New York Times* (November 12, 1991).

82. See Acharya, et al., 32; and Tad DeHaven, "Three Decades of Politics and Failed Policies at HUD," Cato Institute Policy Analysis No. 655.

83. See Oonagh McDonald, *Fannie Mae & Freddie Mac: Turning the American Dream into a Nightmare* (London: Bloomsbury Academic, 2012), 61–68, 97–102, 266–269.

84. Labaton, "Power."

85. See Koppell, *Politics of Quasi-Government*, 111–114; McDonald, *Fannie Mae & Freddie Mac*, 155; and John C. Weicher, "Setting GSE Policy through Charters, Laws, and Regulations," in *Serving Two Masters Yet Out of Control*, ed. Peter J. Wallison (Washington, DC: The AEI Press, 2001), 121–122.

86. Morgenson and Rosner, *Reckless Endangerment*, 96.

87. See Applebaum, Leonnig, and Hilzenrath, "How Washington Failed"; and John D. Copeland, "Ethics Matters: Congressional Friends Stopped Reforms of Fannie, Freddie," *Springfield Business Journal* (November 8, 2008), http://sbj.net/main.asp?ArticleID=83712&SectionID=48&SubSectionID=&S=1.

88. See Guberman, *Balancing Act*; and Morgenson and Rosner, *Reckless Endangerment*, 67.

89. Nader, "How Fannie and Freddie," 117.

90. See Morgenson and Rosner, *Reckless Endangerment*, 167–171; and Wallison, *Bad History*, 49–50.

91. See Geisst, *Wall Street*, 393; Morgenson and Rosner, *Reckless Endangerment*, 154; Bethany McLean, "The Fall of Fannie Mae," *Fortune* (January 24, 2005); Wallison, *Bad History*, 10, 32; and Paula Dwyer, "Freddie Mac Attack," *Bloomberg Businessweek* (July 6, 2003).

92. See Office of Federal Housing Enterprise Oversight, "Report To Congress" (June 2003).

93. Office of Federal Housing Enterprise Oversight, "Report of the Special Examination of Freddie Mac" (December 2003).

94. See Office of Federal Housing Enterprise Oversight, "Report of Findings to Date Special Examination of Fannie Mae" (September 17, 2004); and Office of Federal Housing Enterprise Oversight, "Report of the Special Examination of Fannie May" (May 2006).

95. See Richard E. Mendales, "The Fall and Rise of Fannie and Freddie: Securitization After the Meltdown," http://papers.ssrn.com/sol3/papers.cfm?abstract_id=1489574, 24–26.

96. See Acharya et al., 41–42; Applebaum, Leonnig, and Hilzenrath, "How Washington Failed"; Canham, "Fannie, Freddie Donate"; Wallison, *Bad History*, 50–51.

97. See Calabria, "Fannie, Freddie"; Christopher L. Peterson, "Fannie Mae, Freddie Mac, and the Home Mortgage Foreclosure Crisis," http://papers.ssrn.com/sol3/papers .cfm?abstract_id=1489110, 162–163; Edward Pinto, "Triggers of the Financial Crisis," http://www.aei.org/files/2010/03/15/PintoFCICTriggers.pdf; Boyack, "Laudable Goals," 1511–1512; Wallison, *Bad History*, 6, 12–13; and Jaffee, "Reforming," 4–6.

98. N. Eric Weiss, "GSE's and the Government's Role in Housing Finance," 1; N. Eric Weiss, "Fannie Mae's and Feddie Mac's Financial Status: Frequently Asked Questions," *Congressional Research Service* (August 13, 2013), 22; Charles P. Kindleberger and Robert Z. Aliber, *Manias, Panics, and Crashes: A History of Financial Crises*, 6th edition (New York: Palgrave Macmillan, 2011), 87.

Conclusion

1. Louis Johnston and Samuel H. Williamson, "The Annual Real and Nominal GDP for the United States, 1789–Present," *Economic History Services* (March 2004). http://www.eh.net/hmit/gdp/.

2. Writes Fiorina, "Contrary to what is popularly believed, the bureaucrats are not the problem. Congressmen are. The Congress is the key to the Washington establishment. The Congress created the establishment, sustains it, and most likely will continue to sustain and even expand it" (Morris Fiorina, *Congress: The Keystone of the Washington Establishment* [New Haven, CT: Yale University Press, 1989], 4).

3. Bruce L. Benson, "Why are Congressional Committees Dominated by 'High-Demand' Legislators?: A Comment on Niskanen's View of Bureaucrats and Politicians," *Southern Economic Journal* 48, no. 1 (July 1981): 68–77.

4. "George W. Romney—A Republic No More," YouTube video, 3:24, posted by "LibertyPen," June 20, 2012, https://www.youtube.com/watch?v=p_LT9lKUtnk.

5. SDA: Survey Documentation and Analysis, http://sda.berkeley.edu/.

6. GALLUP, "Trust in Government," http://www.gallup.com/poll/5392/trust-government.aspx.

Index

Housing and Economic Recovery Act (2008), 300
Howe, Daniel Walker, 53
Hoyt, Jesse, 79
Huntington, Collis, 113, 115
Huntington, Samuel, 282

Ickes, Harold, 158, 162
Illinois, 91
immigrants, 85
Industrial Revolution, 125, 129, 304, 312
inefficiency, of tax code, 268–69
inflation, 32, 118, 240, 261
Inouye, Daniel, 218
insecticide, 200, 202
internal improvements, 9, 42, 155, 221–25;
    Clay's view of, 192; corruption involving, 61, 82; Jackson's spending on, 54, 213; Jefferson's spending on, 44; Republican embrace of, 47, 48. See also canals; railroads; roads
International Speedway Corporation, 264
Interstate Commerce Act (1887), 10, 117, 130, 136, 180, 278
Interstate Commerce Commission (ICC), 136–37, 282, 301, 310
Ireland, 264, 266
irrigation, 193
Issa, Darrell, 228

Jackson, Andrew, 76, 104; as military hero, 47; as national bank foe, 52–53, 55–59, 61; Native Americans persecuted by, 53, 55, 61, 309; patronage dispensed by, 14, 73–75, 82, 106, 173; personal rule of, 53, 54, 61; as presidential candidate, 68, 69, 73; reformist self-image of, 42, 53–54, 213; Southern backing of, 48–49
James II, king of England, 21
Japan, 257, 258
Jay, John (Federalist statesman), 27
Jay, John (grandson), 100
Jefferson, Thomas, 23, 27, 30, 46, 128, 149, 230; Britain viewed by, 31; Congressional allies of, 67; debt assumption brokered by, 34; foreign policy of, 44–45, 61; Hamilton viewed by, 24, 33; national bank viewed by, 20, 56, 111, 130, 180, 306; patronage dispensed by, 71–72; as presidential candidate, 42, 43
Jefferson, William, 230

Jeffersonian Republicans: Clinton allied with, 99; divisions among, 47, 53, 67–68, 69; electoral victory of, 41, 43, 45–46, 67; "Empire of Liberty" envisioned by, 42, 46, 48; Federalist principles adopted by, 13–14, 38, 42, 44, 60, 61, 67; Jackson censured by, 58; nonpartisan self-image of, 66–67; Second Bank and, 42, 49–50, 57; state banks and, 59; War of 1812 and, 55
Johnson, Andrew, 53, 85–87, 91, 93, 96, 99
Johnson, Broderick, 298
Johnson, Hiram, 134
Johnson, Hugh, 163
Johnson, Jim, 295
Johnson, Lyndon: Fannie Mae privatized by, 290–91, 301; farm subsidies and, 198, 201; Medicare created by, 236–37, 238; military bases closed by, 220; organized labor and, 178; poverty targeted by, 147; as strong executive, 144, 145; tax questions surrounding, 277
Jones, Charles O., 145–46
Jones, Edward, 157
Jones, William, 50–51
judicial independence, 5

Kansas-Nebraska Act, 76, 80
Kantor, Shawn, 197
Kelly, Edward, 161
Kendall, Amos, 58
Kennedy, John F., 146, 198, 201, 236, 257, 273, 274
Kennedy, Edward M., 57
Kentucky, 158–59
Kernan, Francis, 100, 105
Kernell, Samuel, 144
kickbacks, 49, 78, 246, 316
Know-Nothings, 85, 94
Koistinen, Paul C., 220
Krehbiel, Keith, 215
Krugman, Paul, 203
Kwak, James, 286

labor unions. See organized labor
LaFollette, Robert, 134, 160
La Guardia, Fiorello, 160
lame ducks, 146
land grant colleges, 193
land offices, 79–80
Landrum-Griffith Act, 178
Lawrence, David L., 161

Pennsylvania Railroad, 113

Penrose, Boies, xi, 96, 119, 122, 123–24, 125, 130, 229

pesticide, 200, 202

pharmaceutical industry, 185–86

Phelps, Dodge & Company, 101, 102

Philadelphia, 50, 51, 56, 80, 97, 124, 161, 176

Phillips, David Graham, 123, 126, 127

photovoltaics program, 224

Pickering, Thomas, 67

Pierce, Franklin, 76, 77, 78

Pinto, Edward, 281

Pittsburgh, 97, 161, 258

Platt, Orville, 119, 126

Platt, Thomas, 98, 99, 105, 119

Plunkitt, George Washington, xii, 228–29

political action committees (PACs), 177, 184–85

political parties, 12, 14, 62–64, 66, 150, 182, 215, 304, 308, 317–19

Polk, James K., 76, 87, 94

populists, 125, 127, 134, 193, 285, 317, 318

pork barrel spending, 15, 54, 210–30, 276, 306, 309, 318

Post Office, 70, 74, 75–76, 78–79, 84, 89, 307

Powell, Lewis, 183

Presidio, 222

principal-agent problem, 4, 233

printing contracts, 72, 78, 93, 225

progressive movement, 14–15, 131–50, 182, 193, 260, 304, 318

progressivity, of tax code, 269

prohibition, 135

Promise of American Life, The (Croly), 136, 151

prospective payment system (PPS), 241, 242–46, 248

Public Broadcasting Service (PBS), 65

public goods, 65, 81

Public Private Investment Program, 288

public works. See internal improvements

Public Works Administration, 155, 156

Pure Food and Drug Act (1906), 137

Quay, Matthew, xi, 93, 96, 110, 119, 122–25, 128, 178, 229

"Quids," 53, 68

Railroad Retirement Board, 206

railroads, 89, 93, 129, 193; corruption involving, 90, 113–15, 254; direct subsidies to, 9, 98, 112, 211, 223, 224, 264; regulation of, 10, 115, 136, 137, 278

Raines, Franklin, 295, 296, 297, 310

Rajan, Raghuram, 294

Ramspeck Act (1940), 159

Randolph, Edmund, 25, 31–32

Randolph, John, 68

rational choice theory, 4

Reagan, Ronald: budget deficits under, 241; efficiency in government sought by, 214, 216, 227; farm subsidies under, 202; Medicare policies of, 250; protectionist policies of, 258; as strong executive, 144, 145; tax policies of, 261, 262–63, 273, 274

Reciprocal Trade Agreement Act (1934), 257

Reconstruction, 86–87, 89–90, 91, 99, 107, 114

regulatory capture, 279–302, 310, 319

Reid, Harry, 225, 228, 230

Relative Value Scale Update Committee (RUC), 246–47

Remini, Robert, 50, 53

Report on Manufactures (Hamilton), 253–54

republican principle, 3, 11, 306, 307, 313

Republicans, 14, 60; Buchanan investigated by, 80; business allied with, 116, 120, 133, 253; civil service reform and, 104–5; during Great Depression, 152; Liberal, 90, 93, 98, 102, 134, 147, 318; Lincolnian, 34, 38, 84–85, 192–93; in New York, 98–99, 160; organized labor vs., 177; in Pennsylvania, 96, 97, 122, 125, 157; post–Civil War split among, 90–91; progressives opposed by, 134–35; Radical, 86–87; Whigs absorbed by, 85, 112; under Wilson, 145, 151

research and development, 224–25

research tax credit, 265

resource-based relative value scale (RBRVS), 241–46, 248

Retired Officers Association, 250

Rhetorical Presidency, The (Tulis), 144

Rhode Island, 22, 25, 125–26, 128

Richardson, William, 89

Richberg, Donald, 162

Ritchie, Thomas, 73

Rivers and Harbors Bill, 221–22

roads, 155, 203, 211

Robertson, William, 105

Rockefeller, John D., Jr., 120, 122, 136, 190

Vietnam War, 301
Views of the Political System of the United States (Madison), 3–4
Virginia, 67
Virginia Plan, 7, 24–25, 305
Virgin Islands, 264, 266
volunteer militias, 46

Wagner, Robert, 175
Wagner Act (National Labor Relations Act), 175–76, 177
Walker, Jimmy, 160
Wallace, Henry, 197
Wallison, Peter, 281
Walpole, Robert, 21
War Industries Board, 147, 162–63
War of 1812, 43, 46–47, 49, 55, 211, 213
Washburn, Elihu, 87–88
Washington, George, 37, 39, 44, 66, 180, 305, 306; appointments of, 70, 72; coup foiled by, 22; election to presidency of, 31–32; as nationalist, 7; public finance viewed by, 2; second presidential term of, 42
Washington Mutual, 285, 289
Watergate scandal, 307
Watson, Harry, 48
Wearin, Otha, 158
Weber, Vin, 295
Webster, Daniel, 49, 52, 76, 91, 310
Weed, Thurlow, 99
Weems, Kerry, 247
Weingast, Barry, 215
Wells Fargo, 294
Wendell, Cornelius, 80
Wheeler, Burton, 158
Whigs, 81, 94, 99, 116, 125; anti-Jacksonian origins of, 75; economic policies of, 34, 38, 133, 166; patronage attacked by, 79;

Republican absorption of, 85, 112; during slavery debates, 65, 76; Van Buren's view of, 68
Whiskey Ring, 88–89, 102
Whitaker and Baxter (public relations firm), 236
White, Leonard, 79
White, William Allen, 138
Wickard v. Filburn (1942), 10
Widener, Peter, 124
Williams, Aubrey, 158
Wilson, Henry, 114
Wilson, Woodrow, 152, 160, 166, 305–6; academic career of, 139–40; Constitutional change backed by, 134, 139; farm credit program of, 193; Federal Reserve formed under, 288; as governor, 143; Newtonian metaphor of, 6, 8–9, 13; Parliament viewed by, 141–42; as president, 143–46, 151; as progressive, 14, 131; Roosevelt vs., 135; scientific management idealized by, 133, 147, 215, 282, 285, 301, 310; separation of powers opposed by, 10–11, 132–33, 140–41, 306
Wilson-Gorman Tariff Act (1894), 260
Workers Alliance, 158
workmen's compensation, 143
Works Progress Administration (WPA), 156–58, 159, 160–61, 169, 213, 316
WorldCom, 281
World War I, 147, 151, 162, 193
Wright, Silas, 49

Yarbrough, Jean, 143
yellow dog contracts, 177
Young, Bill, 228

Zoellick, Robert, 297